Canada

Coast to Coast in Canada's
Great Cities, Mountains, Parks, and Attractions

ECONOGUIDE.COM | 2002

Corey Sandler

Contemporary Books

Chicago   New York   San Francisco   Lisbon   London   Madrid   Mexico City
Milan   New Delhi   San Juan   Seoul   Singapore   Sydney   Toronto

Contemporary Books

A Division of The **McGraw-Hill** *Companies*

1 2 3 4 5 6 7 8 9 0   LBM/LBM   0 9 8 7 6 5 4 3 2 1

ISBN 0-8092-2623-5
ISSN 1532-057X

This book was set in Stone Serif by Word Association, Inc.
Printed and bound by Lake Book Manufacturing

Cover photograph copyright © PhotoDisc

Econoguide is a registered trademark of Word Association, Inc.

This book is printed on acid-free paper.

To Arlene, Herb, Sonya, and Dan: Our Founders

Contents

Acknowledgments   vii

PART I   INTRODUCTION TO CANADA   1
1. Oh, Canada   1
2. Canada's Climate   13
3. Getting Around Canada   19
4. A Very Brief History of Canada   23
5. Traveling for Less   29

PART II   BRITISH COLUMBIA   39
6. British Columbia   39
7. Vancouver   53
8. Victoria and Vancouver Island   63
9. Coastal Mountains and Interior British Columbia   81

PART III   ALBERTA   91
10. Alberta   91
11. Calgary   97
12. Edmonton   115
13. Banff, Lake Louise, and Jasper   129

PART IV   SASKATCHEWAN AND MANITOBA   137
14. Saskatchewan   137
15. Regina   141
16. Saskatoon   145
17. Manitoba   149

PART V   ONTARIO   155
18. Ontario   155
19. Ottawa, Kingston, and the Thousand Islands   161
20. Toronto   171
21. Niagara Region   181
22. Southern Ontario   189
23. Northern Ontario   193

PART VI   QUÉBEC   201
24. Québec   201
25. Montréal   207
26. Outside of Montréal: Laval and the Laurentians   225
27. The Eastern Townships   231
28. Québec City   235
29. The South Shore   243
30. Lower Saint Lawrence to the Gaspé and the
    Magdalen Islands   245
31. The North Shore of the Saint Lawrence   249
32. Western Québec   253

PART VII   ATLANTIC CANADA   255
33. Atlantic Canada   255
34. Newfoundland and Labrador   257
35. Prince Edward Island   267
36. New Brunswick   275
37. Nova Scotia   283

PART VIII   THE GREAT NORTHWEST   297
38. Nunavut   297
39. Northwest Territories   303
40. Yukon Territory   315

Appendix: National Historic Sites in Canada   321
Discount Coupons   327
Quick-Find Index to Canada   339

Acknowledgments

As always, dozens of hard-working and creative people helped move my words from the keyboard to the book you hold in your hands.

Among the many to thank are Adam Miller and Julia Anderson of Contemporary Books.

Andrea Boucher edited the manuscript with high skill and good humor.

As always, thanks to Janice Keefe for running the office and the author so efficiently.

My appreciation extends to the visitors bureaus of Canada, they are some of the most professional public relations staffs I deal with for any of my books.

And, thanks to you for buying this book. We all hope you find it of value; please let us know how we can improve the book in future editions. (Enclose a stamped envelope if you'd like a reply; no phone calls.)

Corey Sandler
Econoguide Travel Books
P.O. Box 2779
Nantucket, MA 02584 USA

To send electronic mail, use the following address: **info@econoguide.com.**
You can also consult our Web page at: **www.econoguide.com.**

I hope you'll also consider the other books in the *Econoguide* series by Corey Sandler. You can find them at bookstores, or ask your bookseller to order them.

Econoguide Walt Disney World Resort, Universal Orlando
Econoguide Disneyland Resort, Universal Studios Hollywood
Econoguide Las Vegas
Econoguide Miami
Econoguide Washington, D.C., Williamsburg
Econoguide Pacific Northwest

Econoguide London
Econoguide Paris
Econoguide Cruises
Golf U.S.A.

About the Author

Corey Sandler is a former newsman and editor for the Associated Press, Gannett Newspapers, Ziff-Davis Publishing, and IDG. He has written more than 160 books on travel, video games, and computers; his titles have been translated into French, Spanish, German, Italian, Portuguese, Polish, Hebrew, and Chinese. When he's not traveling, he hides out with his wife and two children on Nantucket island, thirty miles off the coast of Massachusetts.

Part I
Introduction to Canada

Chapter 1
Oh, Canada

Oh, Canada.

The world's second largest country has the world's best collection of natural wonders. It is book-ended on each coast by some of the most interesting, cosmopolitan big cities anywhere. In the vast middle and north are thousands of square miles of magnificent wilderness.

Even better: Canada is relatively undiscovered by outsiders, and in recent years it is a first-class travel bargain.

What's the best thing about Canada?

Is it the spectacular electric-blue glaciers of Alberta?

Is it the company of a pod of whales as you cruise the Inside Passage between the incredibly green Vancouver Island to the west and the snow-capped Coastal Mountains on the mainland?

Or perhaps it's a thundering herd of Peary Caribou or a solo Peregrine Falcon on remote Baffin Island in Nunavut?

Is it the oh-so-familiar but oh-so-impressive rush of water over Niagara Falls?

Is it cosmopolitan Montréal, one of the most stylish cities on earth? Or the mix of Asia and Europe and Canada in the handsome port city of Vancouver?

Do you hanker for a big white cowboy hat from the Calgary Stampede? Or a Saguenay tourtière for dinner?

Is your idea of nature's perfection the view from the top of mile-high Blackcomb Mountain? Or the extraordinary flowerpot rocks at sea level in the Bay of Fundy?

Do you enjoy historical restorations where you can step back into time and learn about the people, trades, and events of times past? Canada has more such preserved forts, towns, and places than anywhere else I know.

And so I'll tell you the best thing about Canada: It's the fact that you can find all of this and more in one friendly place.

About This Book

How do you cover a huge country such as Canada within the covers of a book of 350 or so pages?

1

For that matter, how could you give Canada justice in a book of 600 pages or even 1,200 pages?

My goal in *Econoguide Canada* is not to describe everything in Canada. Instead I'll concentrate on just the best in every province and territory.

At the heart of the idea behind *Econoguide* travel books is this goal: to show how to get the most out of your time and money in travel.

If you're looking for an encyclopedia, bring a truck to the bookstore and pick up one of the heavyweights that promises to tell you about every roadside attraction, every little museum, and every town, no matter how insignificant or unworthy of your time or money.

As much as I love Canada, I can't recommend every inch to every reader. What you'll find here is an eclectic selection of the best and most interesting.

About Canada

Canada is second in size only to the Russian Federation, which spreads across eastern Europe and northern Asia.

The nearly four million square miles of Canada include the world's longest coastline, with shores on three oceans: the Atlantic, Pacific, and the Arctic. Canada has the world's longest unfortified border, stretching from Maine to the state of Washington. The United States is its only contiguous neighbor; in the far north the narrow Nares Strait separates Ellesmere Island from Greenland.

Canada has ten provinces and three territories: Alberta (with its capital in Edmonton); British Columbia (Victoria); Prince Edward Island (Charlotte-town); Manitoba (Winnipeg); New Brunswick (Fredericton); Nova Scotia (Halifax); Ontario (Toronto); Quebec (Quebec City); Saskatchewan (Regina); Newfoundland and Labrador (Saint John's); Northwest Territories (Yellowknife); Yukon Territory (Whitehorse); and Nunavut (Iqaluit).

Nunavut Territory, created out of a portion of the giant Northwest Territories, is the largest political entity of Canada. The largest province is Québec.

Here are the sizes and estimated populations:

	Square Miles	Population	Population Density
Canada	3,849,674	30,000,000	7.8 per square mile
Nunavut Territory	740,000	34,000	1 per 22 square miles
Quebec	594,705	7,139,000	12 per square mile
Northwest Territories	550,000	30,000	1 per 18 square miles
Ontario	412,490	10,754,000	26 per square mile
British Columbia	366,275	3,725,000	10.2 per square mile
Alberta	255,220	2,697,000	10.6 per square mile
Saskatchewan	251,635	990,000	4 per square mile
Manitoba	250,935	1,114,000	4.4 per square mile
Yukon Territory	86,611	31,500	1 per 6 square miles
Newfoundland and Labrador	156,144	552,000	3.5 per square mile
New Brunswick	28,346	738,000	26 per square mile
Nova Scotia	21,419	909,000	42.4 per square mile
Prince Edward Island	2,184	135,000	61.8 per square mile

World Champions. The world's five largest countries in area are:

	Square Miles	Population
1. Russian Federation	6,592,800	148,000,000
2. Canada	3,849,674	29,000,000
3. China	3,696,100	1,200,000,000
4. United States	3,675,031	249,000,000
5. Brazil	3,300,171	165,000,000

For comparison's sake, Alaska, the largest American state, is 656,424 square miles in size, with a total population of more than 627,000 and a population density of just under one person per square mile. For all the United States the population density is about 77 per square mile, or ten times more people in a given area, on average, than in Canada.

One reason for Canada's low population density is this: there's a whole bunch of empty up north. About 90 percent of the country's entire population live within a one-hundred-mile-long band between the Atlantic and Pacific oceans along the border with the United States. Because of the harsh northern climate, only 12 percent of the land is suitable for agriculture.

There's a lot to see north of the population centers; it's just that there aren't a whole bunch of towns, people, and roads to get there. You'll have to travel by small airplane or boat, but the rewards are well worth the effort.

Canada's southernmost point is Pelee Island south of Detroit at latitude 41 degrees, on a line with Providence, Rhode Island; Cheyenne, Wyoming; and Ogden, Utah in the United States. To the north it extends above the Arctic Circle to latitude 83 degrees, within five hundred miles of the North Pole. From coast to coast it extends from longitude 54 degrees to 141 degrees west.

The terrain varies from thousands of miles of coastline to some eighty-three peaks that are greater than ten thousand feet in height.

The Regions of Canada

Geologists divide Canada into six physical regions:
- **Canadian Shield.** Central and northern Québec and Ontario and eastern Manitoba
- **Appalachian Mountains.** Newfoundland, Nova Scotia, New Brunswick, Prince Edward Island, and southeastern Québec
- **Great Lakes–Saint Lawrence Lowlands.** Lower Québec and Ontario
- **Interior Plains.** Manitoba, Saskatchewan, and eastern Alberta
- **Western Cordillera.** Western Alberta, British Columbia, and The Yukon Territory
- **The Arctic.** The Northwest Territories and Nunavut

The huge inland sea of Hudson Bay extends into the heart of Canada; wrapped around the bay is a rocky region known as the **Canadian Shield**. Canada's largest geographical feature, covering about half the country, it begins to the north of the Saint Lawrence River, stretching east to Labrador, south to Kingston on Lake Ontario, and northwest as far as the Arctic Ocean.

CANADA

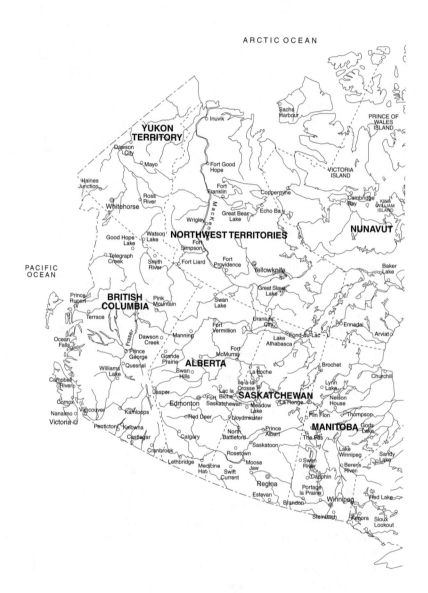

ARCTIC OCEAN

PRINCE OF
WALES
ISLAND

Sachs
Harbour

Inuvik

**YUKON
TERRITORY**

Dawson
City

Mayo

Fort Good
Hope

VICTORIA
ISLAND

Haines
Junction

Fort
Franklin

Coppermine

Cambridge
Bay

KING
WILLIAM
ISLAND

Ross
River

Great Bear
Lake

Echo Bay

Whitehorse

Wrigley

NORTHWEST TERRITORIES

NUNAVUT

Good Hope
Lake

Watson
Lake

Fort
Simpson

Telegraph
Creek

Smith
River

Fort Liard

Fort
Providence

Yellowknife

Baker
Lake

PACIFIC
OCEAN

Great Slave
Lake

Prince
Rupert

Pink
Mountain

Swan
Lake

**BRITISH
COLUMBIA**

Terrace

Fort
Vermillion

Uranium
City

Ennadai

Fort
McMurray

Fond-du-Lac

Arviat

Ocean
Falls

Dawson
Creek

Manning

Lake
Athabasca

Prince
George

Grande
Prairie

ALBERTA

Brochet

Williams
Lake

Quesnel

Swan
Hills

La Loche

Lynn
Lake

Churchill

Campbell
River

Ile-à-la-
Crosse

Jasper

Lac la
Biche

Fort
Saskatchewan

SASKATCHEWAN

La Ronge

Nelson
House

Comox

Edmonton

Meadow
Lake

Flin Flon

Thompson

Nanaimo

Vancouver

Kamloops

Red Deer

Lloydminster

MANITOBA

Gods
Lake

Victoria

Penticton

Kelowna

North
Battleford

Prince
Albert

The Pas

Castlegar

Calgary

Saskatoon

Lake
Winnipeg

Sandy
Lake

Cranbrook

Rosetown

Berens
River

Lethbridge

Medicine
Hat

Moose
Jaw

Swan
River

Dauphin

Swift
Current

Portage
la Prairie

Red Lake

Regina

Estevan

Brandon

Winnipeg

Steinbach

Kenora

Sioux
Lookout

The very hard rock surface is from the Precambrian era, among the oldest rocks on the planet. The gneiss and granite rocks of the shield are 3.5 billion years old, about three quarters the age of the Earth. Scraped by the advance and retreat of glaciers, the shield has only a thin layer of soil that supports a boreal forest of spruce, fir, tamarack, and pine.

The Canadian Shield includes highland plateaus dotted with thousands of lakes and rivers; almost 25 percent of the world's fresh water is located here.

A treasure trove of minerals are found in the region, including gold, silver, zinc, copper, and uranium. Most of Canada's great mining towns are located there, including Sudbury and Timmins in Ontario, Val d'Or in Quebec, and Flin Flon and Thompson in Manitoba.

To the east are the upper **Appalachian Mountains**, covering Newfoundland, Nova Scotia, New Brunswick, Prince Edward Island, and part of Québec. The ancient mountains have been eroded by glaciers, wind, and water during the course of 300 million years. The highest elevation, less than 4,200 feet, is in the Shickshock Mountains on the Gaspé Peninsula. The coastline in the region is very complex with deep indentations caused by glaciers and erosions.

The area was the first settled by Europeans; archeologists have discovered a thousand-year-old Norse settlement at l'Anse aux Meadows in Newfoundland.

About 250 miles off the coast of Newfoundland the shallow continental shelf allows mixing of ocean currents and nutrients, creating the Grand Banks. It is one of the richest fishing grounds in the world, but overfishing during the last half of this century has damaged the stock. The area has been at the center of contentious disputes among fleets from Canada and other nations, including the United States, Russia, and other European nations.

On land agriculture flourishes in the fertile valleys that include the Saint John River Valley, New Brunswick, and the Annapolis Valley, Nova Scotia.

From Québec City to Lake Huron, the **Great Lakes–Saint Lawrence Lowlands** is Canada's most productive agricultural area and is the industrial heartland of the country. Here you'll find Canada's two largest cities, Montreal and Toronto. Half the population of Canada live in this small region, and 70 percent of Canada's manufactured goods are produced here.

The large expanses of Lake Erie and Lake Ontario temper the climate in parts of the Niagara Peninsula, permitting the cultivation of grapes, peaches, pears, and other fruits.

The Saint Lawrence Seaway allows ocean vessels to travel deep into the continent, one of the world's longest inland waterways that stretches 2,300 miles from the Atlantic Ocean to the western end of Lake Superior. The entire Seaway is navigable about nine months of the year, and most winters Canadian Coast Guard icebreakers keep the Saint Lawrence River open year-round as far as Montréal.

The **Interior Plains**, or prairies, rise from Manitoba to Alberta and spread north through the Mackenzie River Valley to the Arctic Ocean.

The plains of Alberta, Saskatchewan, and Manitoba are among the richest grain-producing regions in the world with what seem like endless fields of wheat, canola, and other crops.

Alberta is Canada's leading producer of petroleum. The sedimentary rocks underlying the prairies have important deposits of oil, natural gas, and potash. In the Red Deer River valley eons of desert-like conditions have created strange shapes in the sandstone known as "hoodoos." The same forces of erosion have uncovered some of the largest concentrations of dinosaur fossils in the world.

The **Western Cordillera** is the rocky spine of mountains along the Pacific coastline, part of a fold of hills that reaches from South America to Alaska. Included in this region are some of the highest mountains in Canada in the Rocky Mountains on the border of Alberta and British Columbia. The geology here is relatively young; signs of geologically recent volcanic activity can be seen in Garibaldi Provincial Park in southern British Columbia and at Mount Edziza in the north.

But the highest peaks of Canada are not in the Rockies but in the Saint Elias Mountains, an extension of the Cordillera that stretches north into the Yukon and Alaska. The highest point in Canada, 19,850-foot-high Mount Logan, rises in a huge icefield in the southwest corner of the Yukon, the largest icecap south of the Arctic Circle.

In the interior of British Columbia the land varies from alpine snowfields to deep valleys where desert-like conditions prevail. On the leeward side of the mountains, for example, a rain-shadow effect is created, forcing farmers in the Okanagan Valley to irrigate their orchards and vineyards.

Finally, the **Arctic** region to the north consists of hundreds of islands covering an area of almost 2 million square miles that reaches to Canada's northern tip above the Arctic Circle.

North of the tree line is a place of harsh beauty. During the short summer daylight is nearly continuous; flowers bloom on the tundra, and temperatures can briefly move past 80 degrees. But the winters are long, bitterly cold, and dark.

There are almost no roads in the Northwest Territories and Nunavut; the Dempster Highway makes a lonely excursion to remote Inuvik above the Arctic Circle. Elsewhere in the Arctic, communities are visited by bush pilots and a handful of scheduled air services.

Where the mainland ends is a maze of islands in the Baffin Region. A complex route through the straits and sounds makes up the Northwest Passage, the fabled route to the Orient sought by many early explorers.

As the Inuit (formerly known as Eskimos) regain autonomy in places such as Nunavut, many names of settlements and geography are being changed into the Inuktitut language. For example the people of Frobisher Bay on Baffin Island decided to rename their community Iqaluit, which means "place of fish." Iqaluit is the new capital of Nunavut.

Canada On Sale

Let's get one of the most important things about Canada out of the way right up front: in recent years the international exchange rate for Canadian dollars has made for tremendous savings for visitors from the United States and some other nations that have strong economies.

As we go to press in mid-2001, the U.S. dollar is worth about $1.53 in Canadian currency; going the other way, a Canadian dollar was worth about 66 cents in U.S. funds. A hotel room or a piece of clothing priced at $153.49 Canadian cost American visitors about $100.

At the same time, a British pound was worth $2.15 in Canadian currency. A hotel room priced at $108.62 Canadian would cost about £50.

You can obtain the latest exchange rates from many major newspapers including *The Wall Street Journal* and from online sources. One of many currency conversion programs available on the web is offered by Expedia at ▣ www.expedia.com.

All of this doesn't mean that everything is 35 percent off for Americans in Canada. Items that are imported into Canada from elsewhere in the world are likely to be marked up to reflect the exchange rate. But products of Canada— including food, hotel rooms, museum, and attraction admission prices—are usually a great bargain.

I've criss-crossed Canada many times to research this book, and in recent years it is an enjoyable exercise to reduce the effective cost of everything you buy by about a third. In fact it was more than a bit painful to return home and realize that the awful $10 soup and sandwich at Boston's Logan Airport really cost $10 instead of an almost-acceptable $6.60.

Whenever you convert from one country's currency to another, a percentage of the exchange is pocketed by the bank or company that is making the swap. You'll get the best deal by going directly to a bank and the worst deal by spending money with a merchant who keeps some of the difference as gain and then takes your money to a bank that will reduce the value of your transaction by extracting its own profit on the deal.

The best way to make your purchases in Canada is with a credit card, which converts currency at the most favorable inter-bank rate, usually adding a percentage point or two as a service charge. Be sure to check with your credit company to determine their policies and use the card with the best rate.

Almost every store, restaurant, and attraction will accept Visa, MasterCard, or American Express cards; the receipt you sign will be denominated in Canadian dollars but converted by your credit card on the statement you receive at home.

A second option is to use an ATM card from your home bank to obtain Canadian cash from a teller machine. Again, you should receive a good rate on the currency exchange, although your bank may apply a service charge for use of the card in a foreign country.

You can also obtain travelers checks denominated in Canadian dollars before you travel. The exchange rate is usually good, but you may have to pay a service charge for the travelers checks, and you may end up with some leftover checks at the end of your trip that will have to be converted to U.S. dollars—with a cost for that service.

You'll receive the least bang for your bucks by using American currency or travelers checks at stores.

Finally, there is no guarantee the disparity in exchange rates between the United States and Canada will continue, although the American economy has been outperforming that of Canada, on a relative basis, for many years.

Crossing the Border

U.S. citizens or permanent residents of the United States can enter Canada without a passport or visa.

Most crossings, especially by private car, are simple and routine. A Customs agent will ask your place of birth and purpose of entry; they may enter your vehicle's driver's license into a computer database to verify some of your answers.

You may be pressed a bit harder if you are entering by bus or train or in a rented vehicle. And it has been my experience that some arrivals by airline can be much more formalized than arrival by car.

In any case, you should carry with you some evidence of citizenship, such as a passport if you have one, a birth or baptismal certificate, voter registration card, or a certificate of citizenship or naturalization. Combine these with a driver's license or other form of identification that has a photo.

Permanent residents of the United States who are not citizens should carry a Resident Alien Card with them into Canada.

Single parents traveling with children must provide proof of citizenship for the child as well as a letter of consent from the absent parent.

If you are not a U.S. citizen or permanent resident, you must have a valid passport; check with the Canadian consulate before travel to see if additional papers are required for entry to Canada or re-entry to your home country.

Personal Possessions

Clothing and goods for personal use by the visitor during their stay in Canada are admitted free of duty.

You may bring a limited amount of tobacco and alcohol products for personal use without paying duty; the drinking age is eighteen in Alberta, Manitoba, and Québec and nineteen in other provinces.

If you are entering with valuable items such as jewelry, cameras, tape recorders, computers, or sporting equipment, you should consider whether to register them with the customs service in your home country before you depart or carry proof of purchase to prove they were bought outside of Canada.

Gifts other than tobacco and alcoholic beverages brought into or mailed to Canada by non-residents are allowed free entry if the value of gifts for any one recipient from any one donor does not exceed $60. Gifts valued at more than $60 are subject to regular duty and taxes on the excess value.

Revolvers, pistols, and automatic firearms are prohibited entry into Canada; all hunting rifles and shotguns must be declared.

For more information on customs and immigration regulations, contact Revenue Canada, Customs and Excise at ☎ (604) 666-0545 or call Immigration Canada at ☎ (604) 666-2171.

Taxes in Canada

A Goods and Services Tax (GST) of 7 percent is added to the price of most purchases in Canada. Visitors can obtain an instant rebate of the GST for goods taken out of the country and for accommodations, up to $500 in Canadian dollars, at participating duty-free shops at airports and border crossings. Or visitors can file for a refund from Revenue Canada by submitting receipts and proper paperwork; the visitor must leave the country within sixty days of purchase, and the application must be filed within a year of expenditures.

On top of the GST, provinces apply sales tax of 7 percent on goods and a 10 percent tax on liquor. There is also a 10 percent accommodation tax on hotel rooms.

Visitors can also apply for refunds of sales taxes in Manitoba (Provincial Sales Tax, or PST) or Québec (Tax de vente du Québec, or TVQ).

For information on GST rebates from within Canada, call ☎ (800) 668-4748. From outside of the country, call ☎ (902) 432-5608.

Legalities and Finances

Speed limits across Canada are posted in kilometers per hour. (To convert to miles per hour, multiply by 0.62.)

A typical speed limit on a multi-lane highway is ninety or one hundred kilometers per hour, or about fifty-five or sixty-three miles per hour.

Gasoline is sold by the litre. One litre is about 1.05 U.S. quarts; therefore, four litres is about 5 percent larger than a gallon.

The emergency telephone number for police, fire, and ambulance is 911 in much of Canada; where that number is not in use, just dial 0 and advise the operator that you are reporting an emergency.

Canadian postage stamps must be used on all mail posted in Canada going to points within the country or to foreign destinations. In mid-2001 rates for letters were $0.46 within Canada, $0.55 to the United States, and $0.95 to other countries.

The nation's currency is based on the Canadian dollar, made up of 100 cents. Coins include five-cent, ten-cent, twenty-five cent, one-dollar, and two-dollar pieces. The gold-colored dollar coin has a picture of a common loon bird on one side and from that it draws its nickname: the loonie. In 1996 a two-tone, two-dollar coin was introduced with a picture of a polar bear; it's nickname: the twonie.

Nearly all major credit cards are accepted across Canada; in fact they may be more acceptable than at many locations in the United States. You can use credit cards to pay parking meters in some places, for most admission tickets, and nearly all purchases.

Time Zones

Canada spreads across six time zones.

Pacific Time Zone: The Yukon Territory and all of British Columbia except its extreme southeastern corner are on Pacific Time, the same as in California.

Mountain Time Zone: The Northwest Territory and the western portion of Nunavut, all of Alberta, and the western half of Saskatchewan observe Mountain Time, sharing the hour with Montana and Wyoming and the south-central United States.

Central Time Zone: Eastern Saskatchewan, all of Manitoba, central Nunavut, and the western third of Ontario observe Central Time, with clocks set the same as in Minnesota, Wisconsin, and Illinois.

Eastern Time Zone: The Eastern Time Zone includes central and eastern Ontario, all of Québec, and far eastern Nunavut. This zone is the same as is observed on the east coast of the United States.

Atlantic Time Zone: The Atlantic Time zone includes Labrador, New Brunswick, Prince Edward Island, and Nova Scotia. Clocks here are set one hour later than the eastern zone.

Newfoundland Time Zone: Finally, there is Newfoundland, which marches to its own clockbeat. Newfoundland Time, observed only on the island, is half an hour later than Atlantic Time.

Therefore, 8 A.M. in Vancouver is 9 A.M. in Calgary, 10 A.M. in Winnipeg, 11 A.M. in Ottawa and Montréal, 12 noon in Halifax, and 12:30 P.M. in Saint John's, Newfoundland.

All of Canada, with the exception of Saskatchewan, observes daylight saving time, beginning on the first Sunday in April; clocks are moved ahead one hour. On the last Sunday in October, clocks are adjusted to Standard Time by moving them back one hour.

Canadian Holidays

On statutory holidays, also known as bank holidays, most public buildings, schools, and offices are closed. On many holidays, with the exception of Christmas Day, museums and attractions are open. Be sure to call ahead to check on hours, though. Official holidays include the following:

New Year's Day	January 1
Good Friday	Per calendar (March 29, 2002; April 18, 2003)
Easter Monday	In Québec, per calendar
Victoria Day	Next to last Monday in May (May 20, 2002; May 19, 2003)
Saint-Jean Baptiste Day (Québec National Holiday)	Québec, June 24
Canada Day/Heritage Day	July 1
Labour Day	First Monday in September (September 2, 2002; September 1, 2003)
Thanksgiving Day	Second Monday in October (October 14, 2002; October 13, 2003)
Remembrance Day	November 11
Christmas Day	December 25
Boxing Day	December 26

CANADA

Chapter 2
Canada's Climate

The climate varies significantly across the vast reaches of Canada, but in general, temperatures are lower than those across the United States in any particular month.

On the east coast the Maritime Provinces and Québec generally have cool winters with heavy winter rain and snow; snowfall can be very heavy in the Great Lakes and St. Lawrence River regions. Heavy fog is common in the fall and spring along the coast.

The interior prairie provinces generally experience cold, dry winters and hot summers.

The Pacific coast generally has the most temperate climate in Canada with heavy rainfall for much of the year and abundant snow in the mountains. Vancouver Island's west coast, along the ocean, receives an exceptional amount of rain, giving it a temperate rain forest climate that has produced the oldest and tallest trees in Canada: western red cedars 1,300 years old and Douglas firs 300 feet in height.

To the north the winters are very cold and very long, the summers short and moderate. In the Arctic region temperatures rise above freezing for only a short period of time in the heart of summer. The boreal forests in the north are covered with snow for more than half the year. Precipitation is generally light, except along the Labrador coast.

Calgary, Alberta

The winds can howl in Calgary in January, but they can also bring in a thawing Chinook wind from the west. The rainy season is from May to September, with an average of two to three inches of precipitation each month.

Month	Average High (°F)	Average Low (°F)
January	28	9
February	31	12
March	39	20
April	51	30
May	61	39

June	68	47
July	72	51
August	71	49
September	63	41
October	54	31
November	37	18
December	29	11

Edmonton, Alberta

Edmonton cools down mightily from November through March, although temperate periods are common in the winter. The wettest period of the year is from May through September, with an average of 3.5 inches of rain in June, July, and August.

Month	Average High (°F)	Average Low (°F)
January	19	2
February	23	4
March	34	16
April	50	29
May	62	39
June	68	46
July	71	50
August	69	47
September	61	39
October	51	29
November	31	13
December	21	3

Halifax, Nova Scotia

The climate in Halifax is tempered by the ocean currents and winds. You can expect some amount of rain or snow almost every day, with an average of twenty-five days of precipitation per month in December and January; the driest months are July through September, when it is wet only about half the time.

Month	Average High (°F)	Average Low (°F)
January	29	14
February	29	14
March	36	22
April	47	32
May	57	41
June	67	50
July	73	57
August	73	57
September	65	50
October	54	40
November	44	32
December	34	20

Montréal, Québec

Montréal experiences a wide range of temperature extremes, with a cold, snowy winter and a summer that regularly tops 80 degrees. The city also receives about three inches of rain or melted snow each month; the wettest months run from June to December; the first half of the year is only slightly behind.

Month	Average High (°F)	Average Low (°F)
January	21	7
February	24	10
March	35	21
April	51	35
May	65	47
June	73	56
July	79	61
August	76	59
September	66	50
October	54	39
November	41	29
December	27	13

Ottawa, Ontario

The nation's capital experiences similar weather to that of Montréal, further east on the St. Lawrence.

Month	Average High (°F)	Average Low (°F)
January	21	6
February	24	9
March	35	20
April	52	35
May	65	47
June	74	55
July	79	61
August	76	59
September	66	49
October	54	38
November	40	28
December	26	12

Saint John, New Brunswick

The seaside climate of Saint John is relatively temperate, and wet. In November, December, and January an average of 5.5 to 6 inches of precipitation—mostly snow—falls. In the summer months there's an average of about 4 inches of rain.

Month	Average High (°F)	Average Low (°F)
January	26	9
February	28	10
March	36	20
April	46	31

May	58	41
June	66	49
July	71	54
August	71	54
September	63	47
October	53	38
November	43	29
December	32	15

Saint John's, Newfoundland

Another maritime climate, Saint John's is just as wet as New Brunswick and Nova Scotia, but a bit warmer in winter and cooler in summer.

Month	Average High (°F)	Average Low (°F)
January	30	17
February	29	16
March	33	21
April	41	29
May	50	35
June	59	43
July	67	52
August	66	52
September	60	47
October	50	39
November	42	31
December	34	23

Toronto, Ontario

Toronto has a typical northeastern weather pattern, although occasional lake effect snowstorms can bury the area suddenly. The wettest period of the year is from April through September.

Month	Average High (°F)	Average Low (°F)
January	28	15
February	29	15
March	39	24
April	52	35
May	65	45
June	73	54
July	79	60
August	77	58
September	68	50
October	56	39
November	44	31
December	33	20

Vancouver, British Columbia

Vancouver has a well-tempered climate; the city can be quite comfortable in the winter when rain (lots of it) lands in the valley and snow (lots and lots of it) falls on the mountains to the north. You can expect six inches or more of precipitation of one form or another from November through January. Drier months—still wetter than most anywhere else—are May through September.

Month	Average High (°F)	Average Low (°F)
January	42	33
February	46	35
March	50	38
April	55	42
May	61	48
June	66	53
July	70	56
August	70	56
September	65	52
October	56	45
November	47	38
December	43	34

Victoria, British Columbia

Victoria is tempered by ocean currents and winds. Expect more than five inches of precipitation from November through January. The period from May through August is relatively dry. The mountains in the central region of Vancouver Island receive prodigious amounts of snow most winters.

Month	Average High (°F)	Average Low (°F)
January	44	34
February	46	35
March	51	37
April	56	40
May	61	45
June	66	50
July	70	52
August	70	52
September	66	48
October	57	43
November	48	37
December	44	35

Winnipeg, Manitoba

Winnipeg experiences a cold but relatively dry winter and a moderate but relatively wet summer.

Month	Average High (°F)	Average Low (°F)
January	10	−6
February	16	0

March	29	13
April	50	29
May	66	42
June	72	52
July	78	57
August	75	54
September	64	44
October	51	32
November	30	16
December	14	−1

Yellowknife, Northwest Territories

You want cold? Yellowknife is among the coldest of Canada's cities, with average low temperatures registered in negative double digits from December through February; winter highs in those months usually stay south of the zero mark. There is, though, relatively little rain or snow. Expect a bit more than an inch of rain in the wetter months of July through October.

Month	Average High (°F)	Average Low (°F)
January	−7	−21
February	−2	−18
March	10	−9
April	32	13
May	50	33
June	63	47
July	69	54
August	63	50
September	50	39
October	33	24
November	12	0
December	−4	−17

Celsius to Fahrenheit Conversion

The Celsius temperature scale used in Canada and much of the rest of the world sets the freezing point of water at 0 and the boiling point at 100 degrees. (Most of us have somehow managed to learn to live with a system that has water freezing at 32 degrees Fahrenheit and boiling at 212 degrees; go figure.)

To convert a Celsius reading to Fahrenheit, multiply the Celsius temperature times 9/5 and add 32 degrees.

(If you prefer working with digits rather than fractions, multiply Celsius by 1.8 and add 32 degrees.) For example, a reading of 30 degrees Celsius would work out to (30×1.8)+32, or a toasty 86 degrees Fahrenheit.

To go the other direction, from Fahrenheit to Celsius, first subtract 32 from the reading and then multiply by 5/9 (or 0.56).

For example, to convert a wintry reading of 25 degrees Fahrenheit, the formula would be: (25−32)×.56, or a chilling reading of −4 degrees Celsius.

Chapter 3
Getting Around Canada

Canada is the world's second-largest country but it ranks only twenty-eighth in population size. Its 29 million people are scattered across 3.9 million square miles, a population density of about seven persons per square mile.

Connecting the disparate parts of the huge country, stretching 3,400 miles from the Atlantic to the Pacific, has always been difficult. Much of the upper two-thirds of the nation is wilderness, mountain ranges, the inland sea of Hudson Bay, and lakes. And then add to the challenge the difficult winter conditions that snows under roads and airstrips and freezes rivers, canals, and lakes.

For much of the north the primary form of long-distance travel is by small airplane, landing on simple airstrips or on the water in floatplanes.

Major airlines fly into Canada from the United States and other countries; the largest airports are in Montréal, Toronto, Calgary, and Vancouver.

Canada has 37,193 miles of coastline, including 1,875 miles of inland waterways (excluding island coastlines). Ferries ply the waters of the inside passage of British Columbia and from Vancouver to Vancouver Island; on the east coast, ferries connect the mainland to the islands of the Atlantic Provinces.

The Saint Lawrence Seaway, a triumph of engineering, allows ocean vessels to travel deep into the continent. Some 2,300 miles long, one of the world's longest inland waterways, it stretches from the Atlantic Ocean to the western end of Lake Superior. The entire seaway is navigable about nine months of the year; icebreakers keep the waterway open year-round as far as Montréal.

Road Travel

Today there are nearly 200,000 miles of surfaced roads and 330,000 miles of unpaved roads across the country. The Trans-Canada Highway, completed in 1962, is the longest national highway in the world at 4,860 miles.

The Mackenzie Highway heads north from Alberta into the Northwest Territories; a branch splits off to Yellowknife. The Liard Highway connects from upper British Columbia to Fort Simpson, connecting to the Mackenzie. And the famed Alaska Highway runs from western Alberta through northeast British Columbia and southern Yukon Territory into Alaska.

Rail Service

The extension of the rail lines into British Columbia was part of the deal that brought the western provinces into the Confederation. Today the Canadian Railway network is one of the world's largest, incorporating almost 44,500 miles of rail lines.

The Canadian National (CN) Railway and the Canadian Pacific (CP) Railway operate most national rail freight services.

VIA Rail Canada is Canada's national passenger rail service, providing service from coast to coast. The company operates some 350 trains per week in the densely populated Québec–Ontario corridor, tourism-oriented service in the western part of the nation, and service to some of the more remote sections of the northern and western interior.

Principal lines run from Halifax in Nova Scotia across New Brunswick to the Gaspé peninsula, down to Québec, Montréal, and Ottawa and link up to the Canadian cross-country service from Toronto to Vancouver.

Other links head north from Winnipeg to Churchill in Manitoba and northwest from Jasper to Prince George and Prince Rupert in remote British Columbia.

VIA Rail Canada is an equivalent to Amtrak in the United States, operating on about 8,750 miles of track across the nation, most of it owned by freight carriers CN and CP.

Bookings are also available online at 💻 www.viarail.ca. In Canada, you can call ☎ (888) 842-7245. From the United States, tickets are sold through Amtrak and travel agents.

The flagship cross-country train service is the Canadian, which runs from Toronto to Vancouver. In 2001 the train left Toronto on Tuesday, Thursday, and Saturday mornings, arriving in Vancouver three days later. Heading eastward, the train left Vancouver Friday, Sunday, and Tuesday nights.

The most spectacular portion of the trip lies between Jasper and Vancouver; passengers can book just that portion. The Canadian enters Jasper National park twenty miles west of Edson about midday. Before dusk the train will climb 3,718 feet above sea level to cross the Continental Divide through Yellowhead Pass, surrounded by snow-topped peaks that reach to 12,000 feet above river canyons, frozen lakes, and ice-blue glaciers and snowfields.

Between Redpass and Jackman the train comes within sight of Mount Robson, the highest peak in the Canadian Rockies at 12,972 feet.

The Canadian stops in Jasper three times per week in each direction on its long journey between Vancouver and Toronto.

The Skeena ("River of Mists" in the native Gitksan language) is an all-daylight trip from Jasper to Prince Rupert on the Inside Passage of British Columbia, a 725-mile route past Mount Robson, down the western slope of the range with its giant cedars and hemlocks, and across the mostly roadless expanse of interior British Columbia to the Skeena river valley and on to Prince Rupert.

The train departs Jasper at midday three times a week and stops to spend the night at Prince George before continuing to the coast at daybreak.

In the east the Chaleur connects Montréal to the end of the Gaspé peninsula along the Baie des Chaleurs with three trips in each direction per week.

The Ocean journeys overnight from Montréal through the rural South Shore of Québec and on to New Brunswick and Halifax. From there you can connect to ferries and buses that continue further on to Prince Edward Island and Newfoundland.

VIA Rail offers several ticket passes that offer good values for travelers who want to use the train for long-distance travel.

Canrail Pass

Valid for twelve days within a thirty-day period on all VIA trains, as well as connecting bus service between Moncton and Saint John N.B. and between Charny and Québec City. The pass is good for basic economy-class accommodations; tickets can be upgraded to sleeping compartments or VIA 1 class by paying a surcharge. For information, call ☎ (800) 561-3949 or consult 🖳 viarail.ca.

The following rates were in effect in mid-2001; prices are listed in Canadian dollars:

	Low Season January 1–May 31 October 16–December 31	High Season June 1–October 15
Adult	$411	$658
Youth (2–17)	$370	$592
Student with ISIC card	$370	$592
Senior (60 and older)	$370	$592
Extra travel days	$ 36	$ 56

International Student Identification Cards (ISIC) are available to students up to twenty-five years old at accredited colleges. For information, call ☎ (800) 226-8645.

North America Rail Pass

Good for thirty consecutive days of unlimited travel on all VIA Rail and Amtrak trains in Canada and the United States. Train reservations are required. The pass is good for coach/economy accommodations; tickets can be upgraded to sleeping car, VIA 1 class, or Amtrak Custom Class, Club, or Metroliner by paying a surcharge.

The following rates were in effect in mid-2001; prices are in Canadian dollars:

	Low Season January 1–May 31 October 16–December 31	High Season June 1–October 15
Adult	$702	$1,004
Youth (2–17)	$632	$892
Student with ISIC card	$632	$892
Senior (60 and older)	$632	$892

Chapter 4
A Very Brief History of Canada

The first humans to arrive in Canada are believed to have crossed over from Asia some thirty thousand years ago on a land bridge that existed between Siberia and Alaska. Some of the visitors settled in today's Canada while others moved on to the south, all the way down the coast to South America.

First contact between the native peoples and Europeans probably occurred about a thousand years ago when Icelandic Norsemen settled for a brief time on the island of Newfoundland; the remains of that settlement are preserved today at L'Anse aux Meadows.

European exploration of Canada would not begin for another six hundred years. In 1497, just five years after the first voyage of Columbus, John Cabot arrived in Newfoundland on behalf of Great Britain. In the 1530s French explorer Jacques Cartier made the first of his trips up the Saint Lawrence River seeking the Northwest Passage, a waterway across the American continent to the rich markets of the Orient. English explorers Sir Martin Frobisher in the 1570s and Henry Hudson (sailing for the Dutch) continued the fruitless search in 1610.

The French built trading posts mostly along the Saint Lawrence River, the Great Lakes, and the Mississippi River; the English installations were mostly around Hudson Bay and along the Atlantic coast.

Although the early explorers did not find the route to China and India, they did find rich fishing grounds off the Atlantic Coast and huge populations of fur-bearing animals, mostly beaver, fox, and bear.

At the time of European settlements there were six distinct groups of Native Peoples in Canada. They were in the Arctic; the sub-Arctic from Newfoundland to British Columbia; the plateau of south-central British Columbia; coastal British Columbia and the ocean islands of the west coast. And there were the Plains peoples from the prairies to the foothills of the Rocky Mountains, the eastern woodlands tribes along the upper Great Lakes, the Saint Lawrence River, and the Atlantic Provinces.

War and disease reduced the native population of Canada from about 350,000 at the time of first contact to less than 100,000 by the time of the formation of the Dominion of Canada. Although many tribes were forced to move to reservations (known as "reserves" in Canada), there was much less violence between the natives and the colonists than there was across the border in the developing United States.

The first permanent French and English settlements were begun in the early 1600s. French fur-trading settlements were established in eastern Canada, and Samuel de Champlain lead the way to the establishment of the city of Québec on the Saint Lawrence River in 1608. Champlain had the ear of Cardinal Richelieu, chief adviser to Louis XIII in France, and that support also eventually led to the establishment of Montréal in 1642 as well as more explorations into the interior.

The colony of New France struck alliances with its trading partners, the Algonquin and the Huron. This angered the Iroquois Confederacy, rivals of the Huron; in the late 1640s they had begun a series of attacks on the colony that lasted nearly twenty years before New France was able to build forts and standing armies to withstand the assaults.

Though the settlements were mostly commercial operations for traders, they nevertheless were representatives of their European governments. As Britain and France quarreled in Europe, disputes arose between their outposts in North America.

After the British were triumphant on the Plains of Abraham in Quebec City in 1759 the Treaty of Paris (signed at Ghent in Belgium, and also referred to as the Treaty of Ghent) gave the English control of all of the former French territory east of the Mississippi. (Excluded were the tiny islands of Saint Pierre and Miquelon, off the island of Newfoundland; today they are still a department of France.)

Abandoned by France, the 65,000 French-speaking inhabitants of Canada struggled from the start to retain their traditions, language, and culture. In 1774 Britain sought to bring the French colonists into a unified colony with the Quebec Act, granting official recognition of French civil laws and guaranteed religious and linguistic freedoms.

As the situation became uncomfortable for English Loyalists in America, many migrated north to Canada, settling mainly in Nova Scotia, New Brunswick, and in Ontario along the Great Lakes. The exodus accelerated after the United States won independence from Britain in the Revolutionary War of 1776 to 1781.

With the country building a significant population for the first time, Britain established in 1791 mostly English-speaking Upper Canada (now Ontario) and Lower Canada (mostly French, with Québec at its core). Each had its own representative government, though they still were very much colonies of the mother country.

Skirmishes and disputes between Britain and the United States continued for much of the next fifty years, with numerous battles and near-wars taking place along the Saint Lawrence River, Québec, and along the border between Maine and New Brunswick.

The skirmishes broke out into open warfare in 1812. During the Napoleonic Wars in Europe between France and Britain from 1793 to 1815 both countries were accused of violating the maritime rights of neutral powers, seizing vessels that violated blockades established by each country.

After a number of years in which the U.S. Congress banned trade with European nations, trade was reopened in 1810 with the requirement that France and Britain end their blockades. The British refused to comply, and in June 1812 the United States declared war on Britain.

Aided by friendly native peoples, British troops captured Detroit, Michigan in late 1812. In 1813 American forces reoccupied Detroit. The British Royal Navy blockaded much of the east coast of the United States, all but ending foreign trade.

After incursions into Québec by U.S. troops British troops retaliated in 1814 with a march deep into the United States, burning Washington, D.C. (In September of 1814 Francis Scott Key watched the bombardment by British ships of an American fort in Baltimore; in commemoration, he wrote the words to what became the National Anthem.) The British suffered major defeats at Baltimore and Lake Champlain in Vermont and New York, and peace negotiations began in July 1814.

Local rebellions in Upper and Lower Canada against the English-speaking power structure in 1837 and 1838 led to the joining of the two colonies as the united Province of Canada. Problems continued, including a resurgence of religious quarrels with the Protestant British in Upper Canada objecting to Roman Catholic French influence in local affairs and the French in Lower Canada trying to block English efforts to anglicize the colony.

In 1848 Canada was given the right to govern itself, but remained part of the British Empire and an instrument of the mother country's foreign policy.

The other British colonies of Nova Scotia, New Brunswick, Prince Edward Island, and Newfoundland grew independently. But after the end of the U.S. Civil War in 1865 there were fears the resurgent power to the south would eventually seek to annex Canada to the north. At the same time there was a realization that the unified country was almost ungovernable.

In 1867 the British Parliament passed the British North America Act, and on July 1, 1867, Canada East, Canada West, Nova Scotia, and New Brunswick joined together under the terms of the British North America Act to become the Dominion of Canada, still under British rule. Prince Edward Island and Newfoundland did not join in the new confederation.

Led by Sir John Macdonald, the country's first prime minister, Canada began its expansion to the west and northwest. Rupert's Land, extending south and west for thousands of miles from Hudson Bay, was purchased by Canada from the Hudson's Bay Company, which had been granted the vast territory by King Charles of England in 1670.

In 1869 Louis Riel led an uprising of the Métis (descendants of French trappers and explorers and native people) against Canada in what became known as the Red River Rebellion; they objected that the transfer of Rupert's

Land was trampling on their ancestral rights to the land. Riel was forced to flee the country, but in his absence a compromise was reached in 1870 that gave his followers much of what they sought. A new province, Manitoba, was carved from Rupert's Land.

British Columbia, a Crown colony since 1858, decided to join the Dominion in 1871 on the condition that it would be linked by railroad to the rest of the country. Prince Edward Island followed suit in 1873.

In 1885 Riel returned to Canada to lead another rebellion, this one sought land rights in Saskatchewan. The uprising ended badly for Riel when he was captured; he was tried for treason, found guilty, and hanged in that year.

In 1896 gold was discovered in Klondike Creek just to the east of Alaska, leading to the massive Klondike Gold Rush of 1897 and 1898. The territory of Yukon was officially established in 1898 to ensure Canadian jurisdiction.

In 1905 two new provinces were carved from Rupert's Land: Alberta and Saskatchewan; the remainder of the huge tract of land became the Northwest Territories.

Newfoundland preferred to remain a British colony until 1949, when it became Canada's tenth province.

In 1992 the federal government agreed to create a vast self-governing homeland for the Inuit people, splitting off a huge piece of land in the gigantic Northwest Territories. The territory, named Nunavut ("our land"), became an official part of Canada in 1999.

Today native peoples in Canada speak more than fifty languages in addition to numerous dialects.

In 1913 immigration to Canada peaked with 400,000 people coming to the country, mostly from the British Isles or eastern Europe. After World War II major waves of immigrants have come from southern Europe, Asia, South America, and the Caribbean islands.

Today's population is about 30 million, with about one-third of it British in origin and one-quarter of it French in origin. Native peoples and Métis make up about 4 percent of the population, about 1.2 million people.

More than three-quarters of the population live in and around cities.

Canada's Government

Canada is a constitutional monarchy, an independent nation that the Queen of England rules but does not govern.

A federal form of government oversees ten provinces and three territories; there are two official languages, English and French.

Until 1982 Canada's Constitution was a British statute, the British North America Act of 1867; and until 1982 its amendment required action by the British Parliament.

From the time of its first colonization by the French and British, Canada has been part of a monarchy. In 1867 Canada became a self-governing "Dominion" in the British Empire. Independence came in 1931, under terms of the Statute of Westminster.

In 1867 the "Fathers of Confederation" gathered in Charlottetown, Prince Edward Island, to develop a federal form of government.

The central, or federal, government has responsibility for national defense, interprovincial and international trade and commerce, fisheries, immigration, the banking and monetary system, and criminal law. The courts have also given the federal Parliament control of aeronautics, telecommunications, shipping, and railways.

The regional, or provincial, legislatures have responsibility for education, property and civil rights, the hospital and health care systems, administration of justice, and natural resources within their borders.

Today Elizabeth II, Queen of England, is also Canada's Queen; she delegates her mostly ceremonial powers to a Governor General, appointed by the British government to serve in Ottawa.

Changing of the guard at the Parliament in Ottawa

Photo courtesy National Capital Commission

Canada's current government is based on the British system. The Parliament comprises the Queen (represented by the Governor General), the Senate, and the House of Commons.

The Senate, also known as the Upper House, is similar to the British House of Lords. The 105 members of the Senate are appointed, not elected, and are intended to be divided primarily among the main population centers of the country, which are Ontario, Quebec, the West, and the Atlantic Provinces.

The House of Commons is the major law-making body. It has one member from each of the 301 constituencies or electoral districts of the nation.

A new House of Commons must be elected at least every five years. Candidates usually represent a political party; the leader of the party that wins the largest number of seats is asked by the Governor General to become Prime Minister and form a government, choosing members of a cabinet of twenty-five ministers with various functions and powers.

Political Contentions

The Constitution of 1867 had a serious flaw—it left out a formula for constitutional amendment. It was necessary to address the British Parliament in London each time a change was needed. It was hoped the 1931 Statute of Westminster would address the problem; however, it did not.

It took until 1981 before the federal government and the provinces (except Quebec) agreed to a means to amend the Constitution in Canada. The new process was adopted at a time of increasing tension between Québec and the English-speaking remainder of the country.

The 1987 an agreement called the Meech Lake Accord sought to address Québec's objections by including provincial participation in the appointment of Supreme Court judges and senators, giving increased powers to the provinces in immigration matters and adding a constitutional declaration that Quebec is a "distinct society." However, the Meech Lake Accord was never implemented because it did not obtain the legislative consent of all provinces and the federal government, as required under the 1982 amending formula.

In 1992 another round of constitutional reform lead to the Charlottetown Agreement, which was supported by the Prime Minister, all ten provincial premiers, the two territorial leaders, and four national Aboriginal leaders. It provided for a reformed Senate and changes to the division of legislative powers between the federal and provincial governments. It also supported the right of Canada's aboriginal people to inherent self-government and recognized Quebec as a distinct society. The agreement, though, was rejected by voters in a national referendum.

Chapter 5
Traveling for Less

Don't call me cheap. Call me long distance.

In most years my family can take two or three lengthy vacations for the same amount of money most others spend on a single trip.

You can, of course, pay full price for travel or even more than full price. And you have the constitutional right to waste hours of precious vacation time waiting in line for a boring, overhyped attraction.

Me, I prefer to make the very most of my time and money. I wait for airline fare wars, I rent hotel rooms at off-peak rates, and I clip coupons like the ones you'll find in this book.

Let me lay out the *Econoguide* Rules of Travel:

1. Plan your vacations carefully but remain flexible on dates of travel to obtain the best deals.
2. Research off-peak travel periods and consider weather conditions. Look for a golden coincidence of good prices and good conditions.
3. Learn how to ask for and receive the best prices.

About Airlines

Let's get real. Do you prefer one airline over another because it offers a better quality sandwich-in-a-bag, plumper pillows, or three whole inches of extra legroom?

The way I figure it, one major airline is pretty much like any other. Sure, one company may offer a larger plastic bag of peanuts while the other promises its flight attendants have more accommodating smiles. Me, I'm much more interested in other things:

1. Safety
2. The most convenient schedule
3. The lowest price

Sometimes I'm willing to trade price for convenience; I'll never risk my neck for a few dollars.

But that doesn't mean I don't try my hardest to get the very best price on airline tickets. I watch the newspapers for seasonal sales and price wars, clip coupons from the usual and not-so-usual sources, consult the burgeoning world of Internet travel agencies, and happily play one airline against the other.

Alice in Airlineland

There are three golden rules to saving hundreds of dollars on travel: be flexible, be flexible, and be flexible.

• Be flexible about when you choose to travel. Go to Canada during the off-season or low-season when airfares, hotel rooms, and attractions offer substantial discounts.

• Be flexible in choosing the day of the week you travel. You can often save hundreds of dollars by changing your departure date one or two days. Ask your travel agent or airline reservationist for current fare rules and restrictions.

The lightest air travel days are generally midweek, Saturday afternoons, and Sunday mornings. The busiest days are Sunday evenings, Monday mornings, and Friday.

In general, you will receive the lowest possible fare if you include a Saturday in your trip, buying what is called an excursion fare. Airlines use this as a way to exclude business travelers from the cheapest fares, assuming they will want to be home by Friday night.

• Be flexible on the hour you make your departure. There is generally lower demand—and therefore lower prices—for flights that leave in the middle of the day or very late at night.

• Be flexible on the route you will take and your willingness to put up with a change of plane or stopover. Once again, you are putting the law of supply and demand in your favor. A direct flight from Los Angeles to Montreal for a family of four may cost hundreds of dollars more than a flight from Los Angeles that includes a change of planes in Chicago or Minneapolis.

• Don't overlook flying out of a different airport, either. For example, metropolitan New Yorkers can find domestic flights from La Guardia, Newark, or White Plains. Suburbanites of Boston might want to consider flights from Worcester or Providence as possibly cheaper alternatives to Logan Airport. In the Los Angeles area, there are planes going in and out of LAX, Orange County, Burbank, and Palm Springs to name a few airports. Look for airports where there is competition: try Birmingham instead of Atlanta, or Louisville instead of Cincinnati, for example.

Look for airports that are served by low-cost carriers.

• Plan way ahead of time and purchase the most deeply discounted advance tickets, which are usually noncancelable. Most carriers limit the number of discount tickets on any particular flight; although there may be plenty of seats left on the day you want to travel, they may be offered at higher rates.

In a significant change in recent years, most airlines have changed "nonrefundable" fares to "noncancelable." What this means is that if you are forced to cancel or change your trip, your tickets retain their value and can be applied against another trip, usually for a fee of about $75 to $100 per ticket.

• Or you can take a big chance and wait for the last possible moment, keeping in contact with charter tour operators and accepting a bargain price on a "leftover" seat and hotel reservation. You may find that some airlines will reduce the prices on leftover seats within a few weeks of departure date; don't be afraid to check regularly with the airline, or ask your travel agent to do it for you. In fact, some travel agencies have automated computer programs that keep a constant electronic eagle eye on available seats and fares.

• Take advantage of special discount programs such as senior citizens' clubs, military discounts, or offerings from organizations to which you may belong. If you are in the over-sixty category, you may not even have to belong to a group such as AARP; simply ask the airline reservationist if there is a discount available. You may have to prove your age when you pick up your ticket.

• The day of the week you buy your tickets may also make a price difference. Airlines often test out higher fares over the relatively quiet weekends. They're looking to see if their competitors will match their higher rates; if the other carriers don't bite, the fares often float back down by Monday morning. Shop during the week.

Other Money-Saving Strategies

Airlines are forever weeping and gnashing their teeth about huge losses due to cutthroat competition. And then they regularly turn around and drop their prices radically with major sales. I don't waste time worrying about the bottom line of the airlines; it's my own wallet I want to keep full. Therefore, the savvy traveler keeps an eye out for airline fare wars all the time. Read the ads in newspapers and keep an ear open to news broadcasts that often cover the outbreak of price drops. If you have a good relationship with a travel agent, you can ask to be notified of any fare sales.

The most common times for airfare wars are in the weeks leading up to the quietest seasons for carriers, including the period from mid-May to mid-June (except the Memorial Day weekend), between Labor Day and Thanksgiving, and again in the winter with the exception of Christmas, New Year's, and President's Day holiday periods.

Study the fine print on discount coupons distributed directly by the airlines or through third parties such as supermarkets, catalog companies, and direct marketers. In my experience, these coupons are often less valuable than they seem. Read the fine print carefully, and be sure to ask the reservationist if the price with the coupon is higher than another fare for which you qualify.

Consider doing business with discounters, known in the industry as consolidators or, less flatteringly, as "bucket shops." Look for ads in the classified sections of many Sunday newspaper travel sections. These companies buy the airlines' slow-to-sell tickets in volume and resell them to consumers at deep discount prices.

Look for ads for ticket brokers and bucket shops online and in the classifieds in *USA Today* and the "Mart" section of the *Wall Street Journal*.

Some travel agencies can also offer you consolidator tickets. Just be sure to weigh the savings on the ticket price against any restrictions attached to the tickets: they may not be changeable, and they usually do not accrue frequent flyer mileage, for example.

Don't be afraid to ask for a refund on previously purchased tickets if fares go down for the period of your travel. The airline may refund the difference, or you may be able to reticket your itinerary at the new fare, paying a $75 or $100 penalty for cashing in the old tickets. Be persistent: if the difference in fare is significant, it may be worth making a visit to the airport to meet with a supervisor at the ticket counter.

Beating the Airlines at Their Own Game

In my opinion, the airlines deserve all the headaches we travelers can give them because of the illogical and costly pricing schemes they throw at us—deals such as a fare of $350 to fly ninety miles between two cities where they hold a monopoly, and $198 bargain fares to travel three thousand miles across the nation. Or round-trip fares of $300 if you leave on a Thursday and return on a Monday, but $1,200 if you leave on a Monday and return on the next Thursday.

But a creative traveler can find ways to work around most of these road-blocks. Nothing I'm going to suggest here is against the law; some of the tips, though, are against the rules of some airlines.

Here are a couple of strategies:

Nested Tickets. This scheme generally works in either of two situations—where regular fares are more than twice as high as excursion fares that include a Saturday night stay over, or in situations where you plan to fly between two locations twice in less than a year.

Let's say you want to fly from Boston to Vancouver. Buy two sets of tickets in your name. The first is from Boston to Vancouver and back. This set has the return date for when you want to come back from your second trip. The other set of tickets is from Vancouver to Boston and back to Vancouver; this time making the first leg of the ticket for the date you want to come back from the first trip, and the second leg of the trip the date you want to depart for the second trip.

If this sounds complicated, that's because it is. It will be up to you to keep your tickets straight when you travel.

Some airlines have threatened to crack down on such practices by searching their computer databases for multiple reservations. Check with a travel agent for advice.

One solution: buy one set of tickets on one airline and the other set on another carrier.

Split Tickets. Fare wars sometimes result in super-cheap fares through a connecting city. For example, an airline seeking to boost traffic through a hub in Dallas might set up a situation in which it is less expensive to get from Los Angeles to Montreal by buying a round-trip ticket from Los Angeles to Dallas, and then a separate round-trip ticket from Dallas to Montreal.

Be sure to book a schedule that allows enough time between flights; if you miss your connection you could end up losing time and money.

Stand Up for Standing By

One of the little-known secrets of air travel on most airlines and most types of tickets is the fact that travelers who have valid tickets are allowed to stand by for flights other than the ones for which they have reservations; if there are empty seats on the flight, standby ticketholders are permitted to board.

Here's what I do know: if I cannot get the exact flight I want for a trip, I make the closest acceptable reservations available and then show up early at the airport and head for the check-in counter for the flight I really want to take. Unless you are seeking to travel during an impossibly overbooked holiday period or arrive on a bad weather day when flights have been canceled, your chances of successfully standing by for a flight are usually pretty good.

Overbooking

"Overbooking" is a polite industry term that refers to the legal practice of selling more than an airline can deliver. It all stems, alas, from the unfortunate habit of many travelers who neglect to cancel flight reservations that will not be used. Airlines study the patterns on various flights and city pairs and apply a formula that allows them to sell more tickets than there are seats, in the expectation that a certain percentage will not show up at the airport.

But what happens if all passengers holding reservations show up? Obviously there will be more passengers than seats, and some will be left behind.

The involuntary bump list begins with passengers who check in late. Airlines must ask for volunteers before bumping those who have followed the rules.

If no one is willing to give up their seat just for the fun of it, the airline will offer some sort of compensation—either a free ticket or cash, or both. It is up to the passenger and the airline to make a deal. The U.S. Department of Transportation's consumer protection regulations set minimum levels of compensation for passengers bumped from a flight as a result of overbooking.

You are also not eligible for compensation if the airline substitutes a smaller aircraft for operational or safety reasons or if the flight involves an aircraft with sixty seats or less.

How to Get Bumped

Why in the world would you want to be bumped? Well, perhaps you'd like to look at missing your plane as an opportunity to earn a little money for your time instead of as an annoyance. Is a two-hour delay worth $100 an hour? How about $800 for a family of four to wait a few hours on the way home—that should pay for a week's hotel on your next trip.

If you're not in a rush to get to Canada—or to get home—you might want to volunteer to be bumped. I wouldn't recommend this on the busiest travel days of the year, or if you are booked on the last flight of the day, unless you are also looking forward to a free night in an airport motel.

My very best haul: on a flight home from London, my family of four received a free night's stay in a luxury hotel, $1,000 each in tickets, and an upgrade on our flight home the next day.

About Travel Agencies

Here's my advice about travel agents: get a good one, or go it alone. Good agents are those who remember who they work for: you. Of course, there is a built-in conflict of interest here, because the agent is in most cases paid by someone else.

Agents receive a commission on airline tickets, car rentals, hotel reservations, and many other services they sell you. The more they sell (or the higher the price), the more they earn.

I would recommend you start the planning for any trip by calling the airlines and a few hotels and finding the best package you can put together for yourself. Then call your travel agent and ask them to do better.

If your agent contributes knowledge or experience, comes up with dollar-saving alternatives to your own package, or offers some other kind of convenience, then go ahead and book through the agency. If, as I often find, you know a lot more about your destination and are willing to spend a lot more time to save money than will the agent, do it yourself.

A number of large agencies offer rebates of part of their commissions to travelers. Some of these companies cater only to frequent flyers who will bring in a lot of business; other rebate agencies offer only limited services to clients.

You can find discount travel agencies through many major credit card companies (Citibank and American Express among them) or through associations and clubs. Some warehouse shopping clubs have rebate travel agencies.

And if you establish a regular relationship with your travel agency and bring them enough business to make them glad to hear from you, don't be afraid to ask them for a discount equal to a few percentage points.

One other important new tool for travelers is the Internet. Here you'll find computerized travel agencies that offer airline, hotel, car, cruise, and package reservations. You won't receive personalized assistance, but you will be able to make as many price checks and itinerary routings as you'd like without apology. Several of the services feature special deals, including companion fares and rebates you won't find offered elsewhere.

Tour Packages and Charter Flights

Tour packages and flights sold by tour operators or travel agents may look similar, but the tickets may come with significantly different rights.

It all depends whether the flight is a scheduled or nonscheduled flight. A scheduled flight is one that is listed in the *Official Airline Guide* and available to the general public through a travel agent or from the airline. This doesn't mean that a scheduled flight will necessarily be on a major carrier or that you will be flying on a 747 jumbo jet; it could just as easily be the propeller-driven pride of Hayseed Airlines. In any case, though, a scheduled flight does have to meet stringent federal government certification requirements.

A nonscheduled flight is also known as a charter flight. Charter flights are generally a creation of a tour operator who will purchase all of the seats on a specific flight to a specific destination or who will rent an airplane and crew from an air carrier.

Charter flights and charter tours are regulated by the federal government, but your rights as a consumer are much more limited than those afforded to scheduled flight customers.

You wouldn't buy a hamburger without knowing the price and specifications (two all-beef patties on a sesame seed bun, etc.). Why, then, would you spend hundreds or even thousands of dollars on a tour and not understand the contract that underlies the transaction?

Before you pay for a charter flight or a tour package, review the contract that spells out your rights. This contract is sometimes referred to as the "Operator Participant Contract" or the "Terms and Conditions." Look for this contract in the brochure that describes the packages; ask for it if one is not offered.

Remember that the contract is designed mostly to benefit the tour operator, and each contract may be different from others you may have agreed to in the past. The basic rule here is: if you don't understand it, don't sign it.

How to Book a Package or Charter Flight

If possible, use a travel agent you know and trust from experience. In general, the tour operator pays the travel agent's commission. Some tour packages, though, are available only from the operator who organized the tour; in certain cases, you may be able to negotiate a better price by dealing directly with the operator, although you are giving up some protection for your rights.

Pay for your ticket with a credit card; this is a cardinal rule for almost any situation in which you are prepaying for a service or product.

Realize that charter airlines don't have large fleets of planes available to substitute in the event of a mechanical problem or an extensive weather delay. They may not be able to arrange for a substitute plane from another carrier.

If you are still willing to try a charter after all of these warnings, make one more check of the bottom line before you sign the contract. First of all, is the air travel significantly less expensive than the lowest nonrefundable fare from a scheduled carrier? (Remember that you are, in effect, buying a nonrefundable fare with most charter flight contracts.)

Have you included taxes, service charges, baggage transfer fees, or other charges the tour operator may put into the contract? Are the savings significantly more than the 10 percent the charter operator may (typically) boost the price without your permission? Do savings cost you time? What is that worth?

Finally, don't purchase a complete package until you have compared it to the a la carte cost of such a trip. Call the hotels offered by the tour operator, or similar ones in the same area, and ask them a simple question: "What is your best price for a room?" Be sure to mention any discount programs that are applicable, including AAA or other organizations.

Do the same for car rental agencies, and place a call to any attractions you plan to visit to get current prices.

Negotiating for a Room

Notice the title of this section; it's not called "buying" a room. Hotel rooms, like almost everything else, are subject to negotiation and change.

Here is how to pay the highest possible price for a hotel room: Walk up to the front desk without a reservation and say, "I'd like a room." Unless the No Vacancy sign is lit, you may be charged the "rack rate," which is the published maximum nightly charge.

Here are a few ways to pay the lowest possible price:

• Before you head for your vacation, spend an hour on the phone and call directly to a half dozen hotels in the price range you'd like to spend.

• Start by asking for the room rate. Then ask them for their best rate. Does that sound like an unnecessary second request? Trust me, it's not. I can't begin to count the number of times the rates have dropped when I ask again.

• When you feel you've negotiated the best deal you can obtain over the phone, make a reservation at the hotel of your choice. Be sure to go over the dates and prices one more time, and obtain the name of the person you spoke with and a confirmation number if available.

• When you show up at your hotel on the first night, see if the rates have changed. Here's where you need to be bold. Walk up to the desk as if you did not have a reservation, and ask the clerk, "What is your best room rate for tonight?" If the rate they quote you is less than the rate in your reservation, you are now properly armed to ask for a reduction in your room rate.

• Similarly, if you somehow find that the room rate drops during your stay, don't be shy about asking that your charges be reduced. Just be sure to ask for the reduction before you spend another night at the old rate, and obtain the name of the clerk who promises a change. If the hotel tries a lame excuse, such as "That's only for new check-ins," you can offer to check out and then check back in again. That will usually work; you can always check out and go to the hotel across the road, which will usually match the rates of its competitor.

Drive?, He Said

Everyone's concept of the perfect vacation is different, but for me, I draw a distinction between getting there and being there. I want the getting there part to be as quick and simple as possible, and the being there part to be as long as I can manage and afford. Therefore, I fly to most any destination that is more than a few hundred miles from my home. The cost of driving, hotels, meals en route, and general physical and mental wear and tear rarely equals a deeply discounted excursion fare.

If you do drive, though, you can save a few dollars by using the services of the AAA or another major automobile club. Spend a bit of time and money before you head out to make certain your vehicle is in traveling shape: a tune-up and fully inflated, fully inspected tires will save gas, money, and headaches.

If you plan to travel by bus or train, be aware that the national carriers generally have the same sort of peak and off-peak pricing as the airlines. The cheapest time to buy tickets is when the fewest people want them.

Renting a Car for a Trip in Canada

Rental agencies in Canada operate very similarly to American companies.

If you're proposing to cross the border—into Canada or into the United

States—with a rental car, make sure your agreement allows for this. In most cases, one-way rentals from one country to the other are not permitted.

Be sure to seek discounts from auto clubs, airline frequent flyer clubs, and other sources. Your travel agent may be of assistance in finding the best rates.

Car rental companies will try—with varying levels of pressure—to convince you to purchase special insurance coverage. They'll tell you it's "only" $7 or $9 per day. What a deal! That works out to about $2,500 or $3,330 per year for a set of rental wheels. The coverage is intended primarily to protect the rental company, not you.

Check with your insurance agent before you travel to determine how well your personal automobile policy will cover a rental car and its contents and make sure you have coverage in Canada.

I strongly recommend you use a credit card that offers rental car insurance; such insurance usually covers the deductible below your personal policy. The extra auto insurance by itself is usually worth an upgrade to a "gold card" or other extra-service credit card.

The only sticky area comes for those visitors who have a driver's license but no car, and therefore no insurance. Again, consult your credit card company and your insurance agent to see what kind of coverage you have, or need.

Be sure you understand the rental car company's policies on minimum age for drivers (generally twenty-five), and whether a second driver can take the wheel.

Although it is theoretically possible to rent a car without a credit card, you will find it to be a rather inconvenient process. If they cannot hold your credit card account hostage, most agencies will require a large cash deposit—perhaps as much as several thousand dollars—before they will give you the keys.

Be aware that the least expensive car rental agencies usually do not have their stations at the airport itself. You will have to wait for a shuttle bus to take you from the terminal to their lot, and you must return the car to the outlying area at the end of your trip. This may add about twenty to thirty minutes to your arrival and departure schedule.

Pay attention, too, when the rental agent explains the gas tank policy. The most common plan requires you to return the car with a full tank; if the agency must refill the tank, you will be billed a service charge plus what is usually a very high per-gallon rate.

Other optional plans include one in which the rental agency sells you a full tank when you first drive away and takes no note of how much gas remains when you return the car. Unless you somehow manage to return the car with the engine running on fumes, you are in effect making a gift to the agency with every gallon you bring back.

I prefer the first option, making a point to refill the tank on the way to the airport on getaway day.

Accident and Sickness Insurance

The idea of falling ill or suffering an injury while hundreds or thousands of miles away from home and your family doctor can be a terrifying thought.

But before you sign on the bottom line for an accident and sickness insurance policy, be sure to consult with your own insurance agent or your company's personnel office to see how far your personal medical insurance policy will reach. Does the policy cover vacation trips and exclude business travel? Are all international locations excluded? Can you purchase a "rider," or extension, to your personal policy to cover travel?

The only reason to purchase an accident and sickness policy is to fill in any gaps in the coverage you already have. If you don't have health insurance of any kind, a travel policy is certainly valuable, but you might want to consider whether you should spend the money on a year-round policy instead of taking a vacation in the first place.

Also be aware that nearly every kind of health insurance has an exclusionary period for preexisting conditions. If you are sick before you set out on a trip, you may find that the policy will not pay for treating the problem.

Part II
British Columbia

Chapter 6
British Columbia

If British Columbia (BC) was a country by itself, it would be celebrated for its spectacular beauty, diverse culture, and, not the least, for its sheer size.

You'll find huge mountain peaks, Pacific beaches, thousands of square miles of pristine wilderness, coastal rainforests, and gigantic frozen glaciers and snowfields. You'll also discover Vancouver, one of the most handsome, cosmopolitan port cities; across the Strait of Georgia on Vancouver Island, Victoria is a picture-perfect port that feels like one of the last outposts of the British Empire.

British Columbia is Canada's west coast. To the east is the province of Alberta; to the north is the Yukon Territory and the western portion of the Northwest Territories. On the south are three American states, Washington, Idaho, and Montana. In the extreme northwest corner of the province is the 554-mile-long panhandle of Alaska.

More than three-quarters of the province's land area is mountainous. The Rocky Mountains run the length of British Columbia on a diagonal southeast to northwest. On either side of that central spine are the Columbia, Monashee, Cariboo, Selkirk, Purcell, Cassiar, Omineca, and Skeena ranges. More than half of the land is 4,200 feet above sea level or higher.

In the moist coastal areas stand thickets of massive Douglas fir and western red cedar. In the higher and drier interior are vast forests of pine, spruce, and hemlock. All told, almost 60 percent of the province is forest. And more than 90 percent of the land in British Columbia is Crown land, meaning it is owned and managed by the provincial government.

And of course, British Columbia is *large* at some 366,000 square miles—almost four times as large as Great Britain and twice the size of Japan—which leaves a tremendous amount of space for about 3.3 million people. Most of the population is clustered around Vancouver and across the Strait of Georgia around the capital of Victoria.

The abundant water of the rivers and streams of British Columbia discharge about 2.2 million gallons of water for every resident of the province each year; the liquid asset is used in hydroelectric dams for electricity, as well as for irrigation and drinking water.

BRITISH COLUMBIA

In the Coastal Mountains about ninety miles above Vancouver is the Whistler Blackcomb resort, one of the world's best ski resorts and a major summer recreation draw as well. Across the strait on Vancouver Island are several other significant ski areas that draw prodigious amounts of snow.

The southwest corner includes hundreds of islands and mountainous fjords along a coastline that folds in on itself to meander more than 16,780 miles. Off the coast lies Vancouver Island, which stretches some 280 miles from the U.S. border northwest.

Vancouver Island could be an island nation of its own; about the size of Holland, Vancouver Island features a spine of mountains, dozens of interesting fishing villages, vast nature preserves, and a deep water international port. At its southern tip is Victoria, the capital of British Columbia, with a population of more than 300,000 in the metropolitan area. The next largest city is Nanaimo, about sixty miles away, with a population of more than 71,000.

Most of the communities on Vancouver Island are on the east coast along the sheltered Inland Passage that leads from Vancouver north to another inland waterway on the protected side of the Alaskan islands. The east side is also the home of some magnificent, lush forests, and the main industry of the island involves forestry.

The exposed west coast of the island is mostly uninhabited with few roads and there are some impressive beaches; the Alberni Inlet cuts more than halfway through the island to the community of Port Alberni.

History

Nomadic tribes lived in British Columbia in the south near present-day Vancouver and the Fraser River Valley as well as in the northern interior.

Many were killed off by diseases—such as smallpox and venereal diseases—that were imported into the area by the white man.

Russian explorer Alexei Chirkov sailed along the northwestern coast in 1741; the Russian influence in Alaska was already tenuously established. From the other direction Juan Perez Hernandez came from Mexico to the Queen Charlotte Islands soon afterward. Other Spanish explorers sailed north from Spanish America in 1774 and 1775. A number of the islands in the Strait of Georgia, including Galiano, Valdes, and Quadra, bear their names.

Then in 1778 and 1779 Captain James Cook, Great Britain's grand explorer of the Pacific, arrived in the area in search of an entrance to the Northwest Passage. Among his staff was George Vancouver, who returned in 1792 to chart the coast in detail and along the way give the settlement his name.

It was not until the mid-1800s that the developing coal and lumber industries drew settlers to lower British Columbia. With the coal and lumber came the need to transport the commodities to market, and so the Canadian Pacific Railway was built to Vancouver.

In 1858 a gold rush brought thousands to the inhospitable interior of British Columbia.

Regions of British Columbia

The **Lower Mainland** region faces the Strait of Georgia, the trough (a submerged valley) at the mouth of the inland passage between the Coast Mountains on the mainland and the mountains of the lower end of Vancouver Island. About half the population of British Columbia—nearly two million people—live in the city of Vancouver and its suburbs, including Richmond, Burnaby, Delta, Surrey, North and West Vancouver, New Westminster, and Coquitlam.

South of Vancouver, the **Fraser River** empties into the strait. The Fraser is the longest river in the province, traveling 850 miles from near Mount Robson on the western slopes of the Rockies at Alberta border, flowing first north and then looping south. It cuts the deep gorges of the Fraser Canyon before emptying into the Pacific Ocean at Vancouver.

The Fraser Canyon runs mostly north–south from the high Central Plateau at Cache Creek through the Coast Mountains to Hope and from there west out to the Pacific. A gold strike in the canyon during the 1850s was part of the Cariboo gold rush to the interior of the province. The main line of the Trans-Canada Highway follows the canyon, and railroad tracks run along each side.

The **Okanagan Region** is a rolling highland plateau between the Cascade range to the west and the Monashee mountain range on the east. Okanagan Lake runs the length of the valley, a popular summer recreation area. The dry

Downtown Vancouver nestles against Burrard Inlet and the Coastal Mountains.
Photo courtesy of Tourism Vancouver

and relatively warm climate is the center of a large fruit-growing region as well as a burgeoning wine industry.

The **Kootenay Region**, located in the southeast corner of the province, is carved into slices by the north–south Rockies, the Purcells, the Selkirks, and the Monashees. Long, thin, and deep lakes and rivers fill many of the valleys between the mountain ranges. The Columbia River rises out of a series of small tributaries from the Rocky Mountain Trench in the north at Mount Robson, the highest point in the Canadian Rockies. These tributaries feed into Kinbasket Lake, over the Mica Dam, and form the Arrow Lakes system—including Revelstoke and Arrow—before they cross the border into the United States and eventually flow to the Pacific Ocean at the Washington-Oregon border.

There are major ski areas in Fernie and Kimberly as well as a burgeoning helicopter ski industry in the remote mountains.

The high plateau of the **Central Interior** is home to the largest cattle ranches in the world. Some, like the Douglas Ranch, are hundreds of thousands of acres in size.

The commercial center of the region is Prince George, population about 76,500. The city is transected by the east–west Trans-Canada Highway and the north–south Caribou Highway that runs from Vancouver along the Fraser River.

Nearly half of the province lies in the virtually untouched north above Prince George. The Alaska Highway starts in Dawson Creek and winds more than six hundred miles northwest and into the Yukon Territory; the road was a major wartime project of Canada and the United States, built to help protect Alaska and northwestern Canada from a possible Japanese assault.

Most of the region is mountainous and isolated with no roads other than the Alaska Highway and the Liard Highway, which branches off into the Northwest Territory near Fort Nelson. The Cassiar Highway runs north to the Yukon from Prince Rupert on the Inland Passage to Alaska.

Spectacular wilderness parks here include the sprawling Spatsizi Plateau and Mount Ediza Park.

The **Inside Passage** threads a needle almost three hundred miles from the north end of Vancouver Island to Prince Rupert at the northernmost Pacific Ocean coast of the mainland of Canada. From Prince Rupert an inland waterway continues north to Juneau, Alaska.

Narrow channels pass hundreds of untouched islands, with vistas of the Coast Mountains and the misty Queen Charlotte Islands. A ferry system connects Prince Rupert and other isolated communities to Vancouver and Vancouver Island. Other boats sail from Washington state to Alaska. In the spring and summer the waters are plied by massive luxury cruise liners.

The **Queen Charlotte Islands**, north of Vancouver Island, have been shrouded in mist and

High honors. The tallest mountain in British Columbia actually lies mostly across the border in Alaska. Mount Fairweather in the northwestern corner of the province stands 15,298 feet tall; its summit lies in British Columbia. On the other side of the province is Mount Robson, partially in Alberta; at 12,972 feet it is the highest point in the Canadian Rockies.

mystery for centuries. Once almost impossible to visit, the "Misty Islands" are now served by ferry from Prince Rupert.

The traditional home of the Haida Nation, the isolation of the islands has given rise to a number of subspecies of wildlife that exist nowhere else. Shrouded in mist and rain much of the time, the western ocean coast is rocky and rugged, while the east side has some sandy beaches. In the northeast corner of the islands is the wilderness of Naikoon Provincial Park.

Waterfalls in British Columbia

Here's a trivia question: name the highest falls in Canada. If you said Niagara, you're a few thousand miles wrong. The tallest cataract in Canada is **Della Falls**, in Strathcona Provincial Park on Vancouver Island. The water drops 1,440 feet down a mountain side. Don't expect to see a street lined with tourist traps, though; for that matter, you won't find that many tourists, either. The falls are at the end of a rugged, unimproved hiking trail.

Other notable falls in British Columbia include **Takakkaw Falls** in Yoho National Park, accessible by road off the Trans-Canada Highway. Glacial meltwater drops an unbroken distance of 1,200 feet.

About three hundred miles northeast of Vancouver are **Helmcken Falls** in Wells Gray Park. In winter a massive ice cone builds up almost to the brink, 450 feet above the isolated basin.

Bridal Veil Falls, along the Trans-Canada Highway seventy miles east of Vancouver, is easily reached by car and then an easy stroll.

British Columbia's Wildlife Resources

The sprawling wilderness and mountains of British Columbia are home to a variety of birds and mammals unmatched in Canada and much of the world.

Some 112 species of mammals have been identified in British Columbia, among them seventy-four species not found in any other Canadian province. The province has large populations of moose, caribou, elk, deer, black bear, and mountain goat, and also serves as the habitat for numerous endangered species such as white pelican, the burrowing owl, the sea otter, and the Vancouver Island marmot. Some populations may number only in the hundreds.

Three-quarters of the world's Stone sheep are located in British Columbia, 60 percent of the mountain goats, half of the trumpeter swans and blue grouse, and a quarter of the planet's bald eagles and grizzly bears.

At Boundary Bay south of Vancouver the largest populations of waterfowl to winter anywhere in Canada visit the marshlands of the Fraser River delta.

Approximately 2,500 Rocky Mountain bighorns live along the eastern border of British Columbia, on the slopes of the Rocky Mountains from the U.S. border to Golden, in scattered bands north of Mount Robson, and in the Kamloops area. Another group, California bighorn sheep, prefers the south central area of the province, in the Okanagan, Similkameen, and South Chilcotin regions.

About twelve thousand Stone sheep and five hundred Dall thinhorn sheep roam the northern reaches of British Columbia.

British Columbia has more mountain goats than anywhere in Canada or the United States. Actually, it's not a true goat but is instead a close relative of the antelope or chamois of the Swiss Alps; a population of more than fifty thousand range over most of the province. They usually stick to the roughest possible terrain above the timberline or within retreating distance of the rocky bluffs of mountain ranges.

Woodland caribou number about eighteen thousand throuhout British Columbia, ranging in the north from the Coast Mountains on the west to the eastern slopes of the Rocky Mountains and in the south in the Columbia, Rocky, Selkirk and Monashee mountain ranges.

The rare Roosevelt elk, the largest elk to be found in the world, can be found in British Columbia on Vancouver Island and adjacent parts of the mainland.

There are some 180,000 moose in British Columbia, mostly in the north, but they're on the resurgence as far south as the United States border.

Some 400,000 deer in three species are spread over almost all the province. Mule deer range over the largest part of the province from the northern reaches of the high central plateau to the mountains and highlands of its south central regions. Columbia black-tailed deer are found along coastal British Columbia and its many islands. White-tailed deer range predominantly in the southeast corner of British Columbia, the Kootenays, and the Peace River district.

In addition to browsing and grazing mammals, British Columbia has its share of predators. The cougar, the largest wild cat native to British Columbia, is found in most areas of the province except on the Queen Charlotte Islands. The cougar is known by other names around the world including puma, mountain lion, deer tiger, Indian devil, and Mexican lion.

While populations number about three thousand, their secretive hunting habits mean cougars are rarely seen except where they find themselves accidentally in conflict with human settlement. During recent years a few wandering cougars have ended up wandering in residential areas of Victoria. One hid in a basement a few blocks from Victoria's Parliament Buildings and another in the underground parking garage of the Empress Hotel.

Black bears in British Columbia number some 140,000, and they range over almost every type of terrain from coastal beaches to forests to dry grassland and subalpine meadows. In the forest they like open spaces where berries can be found but they also go fishing in streams for spawning salmon.

Grizzly bears, distinguishable by the large hump of muscle on their shoulders and a slightly flattened face, are even more shy of civilization and less plentiful than black bears. They are, though, more likely to be aggressive if they are confronted by humans. About twelve thousand range over most of the province except Vancouver Island, the Queen Charlotte Islands, and the Lower Mainland.

Nonresidents of Canada are required to be accompanied by a licensed guide while hunting British Columbian big game, which includes deer, mountain sheep, mountain goat, moose, caribou, elk, cougar, wolf, grizzly bear, and black bear.

Transportation to British Columbia

The major cities of British Columbia are well-served by air, cross-country train, and ferry services.

Visitors can drive into southern British Columbia from Washington, Idaho, and Montana in the United States and from Alberta through mountain passes near Jasper, Lake Louise, Banff, and Crowsnest Pass near Fernie. (Be sure to check for road conditions in eastern and southeastern sections during the winter.)

The interior is served by a limited network of major roads. Route 97 runs north–south through the middle of the province all the way to Fort Nelson where it splits northwest as the Alaska Highway into the Yukon Territory and on to Alaska or continues north as the very basic Liard Highway into the deep remote of the central Northwest Territories.

Another north–south road is the Cassiar Highway that heads into the mostly untouched western interior and also links Prince George to Prince Rupert, which sits just below the Alaskan Panhandle on the Pacific coast.

To get to most coastal communities the best route is often by floatplane or by boat on one of the ferries that ply the inside passage from Vancouver or Vancouver Island as far north as Prince Rupert. (From there it is possible to continue by boat up the mostly roadless Alaskan coast.)

Air Travel

Vancouver International Airport is the gateway to western British Columbia, as well as Canada's hub for service to Asia and the Pacific. Located about twenty minutes from downtown, the airport is served by taxi (about $21), airport bus (about $9), and limousine (about $26).

The airport sits in a valley, with a spectacular view of Mount Baker, across the border in Washington state. For information consult 🖳 www.yvr.ca.

Carriers to Vancouver include Air Canada, American Airlines, and KLM Royal Dutch Airlines. Domestic carriers to Victoria and other points in BC as well as Alberta, Manitoba, Washington, and Oregon include AirBC (through Air Canada); Baxter Aviation, ☎ (604) 688-5136; Helijet Airways, ☎ (800) 665-4354; and West Coast Air ☎ (800) 347-2222.

There are also seaplane services from downtown near Canada Place, flying to Victoria and elsewhere in the province. One carrier is Harbour Air Seaplanes, ☎ (800) 665-0212 or ☎ (604) 688-1277 or consult 🖳 www.harbour-air.com.

Long-Distance Rail Service

Vancouver is linked to the rest of Canada by VIA Rail Canada, ☎ (800) 561-3949 from the United States; or ☎ (800) 561-8630 from Canada. 🖳 www.viarail.ca. Pacific Central Station is located at Main and Terminal streets in Vancouver.

BC Rail Passenger Services, ☎ (604) 984-5246, or ☎ (800) 663-8238 in the United States and outside of British Columbia, operates year-round service on the Cariboo Prospector between Vancouver and Squamish, Whistler, Williams Lake, and Prince George. Summer scenic daytrips on the Royal Hudson Steam Train visit Squamish; the Whistler Explorer runs from Whistler to Kelly Lake. You can also consult a web page at 🖳 www.bcrail.com.

Transportation to Vancouver Island

Visitors coming from the mainland of British Columbia can fly from Vancouver International Airport to Victoria International Airport near Sidney, a thirty-minute drive from downtown Victoria. For information, consult 🖳 www.cyyj.ca.

There are also harbor-to-harbor floatplane flights between downtown Vancouver and Victoria harbor.

BC Ferries takes passengers and cars from the Tsawwassen ferry terminal south of Vancouver with a ninety-five-minute crossing to Swartz Bay on Vancouver Island, about thirty minutes from Victoria. Total driving and ferry time is about two-and-a-half hours.

From the United States there are airport-to-airport flights from Seattle and floatplane service from Seattle directly to Victoria harbor. Car and passenger ferry service from Port Angeles in Washington state connects across the Strait of Juan de Fuca, a ninety-five-minute crossing.

Air Service to Vancouver Island

Major airlines, including Air Canada, Canadian Airlines, and American Airlines, have service to Victoria, usually after a change to smaller planes in Vancouver or Seattle.

Kenmore Air, ☎ (800) 543-9595 or 🖳 www.kenmoreair.com, flies from Seattle to Victoria and other locations in the islands. Helijet Airways, ☎ (250) 382-6222 or 🖳 www.helijet.com, connects from Vancouver International Airport.

Floatplane service from Vancouver to Victoria is offered by carriers that include West Coast Air, ☎ (250) 388-4521 or 🖳 www.westcoastair.com, and Harbour Air, ☎ (800) 665-0212 or 🖳 www.harbour-air.com.

Ferry Service from Vancouver

The highways of British Columbia's mountainous coast outside of the southwest corner near Vancouver are on the water.

There are no maintained roads above the Powell River area, just seventy-five miles or so north of Vancouver. And there is no way—other than boat or float plane—to any of the hundreds of islands in the Strait of Georgia or to the massive Vancouver Island.

Instead there are the boats of BC Ferries. The more than forty boats in the fleet operate almost entirely in protected waters, insulated from the open ocean by Vancouver Island and the many smaller islands.

Large ferries, which can carry nearly five hundred cars and more than two thousand passengers, connect the Lower Mainland to Vancouver Island. Boats run several times a day and as often as hourly in peak summer periods on some routes.

Tsawwassen, located about twenty-five miles south of the city (just over the border from Washington state) is the terminal for ferries to Swartz Bay near Victoria and to Nainamo and the Southern Gulf Islands. In recent summer seasons ferries departed in both directions every hour on the hour from 7 A.M. to 10 P.M. with a crossing time of ninety-five minutes; additional boats are available at busiest times. Service is somewhat curtailed in the winter.

Two BC Ferries on an inland passage
Photo courtesy of Tourism Vancouver Island

Horseshoe Bay, north of Vancouver, connects to Nainamo on Vancouver Island as well as to Bowen Island and the Sunshine Coast further north on the mainland. In recent years boats departed on the ninety-minute crossing at least eight times a day from 7 A.M. to 9 P.M. in summer, with fewer trips in the winter.

The prettier of the two crossings is the one through Tsawwassen, which sends the ferry on a winding path between some of the green, hilly islands of the Strait of Georgia. And several of the boats in the fleet from Tsawwassen are closer to cruise ships than workaday ferries; you'll find restaurants, observation lounges, arcades, and gift shops at sea.

For fares, routes, and schedules for BC Ferries, call ☎ (888) 223-3779 in British Columbia or ☎ (250) 386-3431 or consult 🖳 www.bcferries. bc.ca/ferries.

There is also service from Seattle to Victoria on the *Victoria Clipper* and *Princess Marguerite* catamarans. For information on that line, call ☎ (800) 888-2535 or ☎ (250) 382-8100.

BC Ferries also serves many of the small islands in the strait, either from the mainland ferry terminal at Tsawwassen or the island ferry terminal at Swartz Bay. Boats connect to Galiano, Mayne, Saturna, the Pender islands, Saltspring, Thetis, and Kuper islands. From Nanaimo ferries serve Gabriola Island, the most northerly of the Gulf Islands.

The handsome Sechelt Peninsula is part of the mainland of British Columbia north of Vancouver, but it is accessible only by small plane or boat. Known as the Sunshine Coast, it takes its name from a claim to some fourteen more days of sunshine than sunny Victoria on the other side of the Georgia Strait. BC Ferries connects from Horseshoe Bay to Langdale with a forty-minute trip.

Ferry Services from Washington State

International ferry service connects to Victoria and Sidney from Seattle and other ports in Washington.

The *Victoria Clipper*, a high-speed catamaran, carries passengers from downtown Seattle to Victoria. From May to September, the *Princess Marguerite III* carries passengers and vehicles from Seattle to Victoria.

For information on either ship, call ☎ (250) 382-8100 in Victoria, ☎ (206) 448-5000 in Seattle, or ☎ (800) 888-2535, or consult 💻 www.victoriaclipper.com.

Washington State Ferries operates passenger and vehicle ferries from Anacortes to Sidney. For information, call ☎ (250) 381-1551 in Victoria, ☎ (206) 464-6400 in Seattle, or consult 💻 www.wsdot.wa.gov/ferries.

Victoria San Juan Cruises carries passengers from Bellingham to Victoria from May to October. For information, call ☎ (360) 738-8099 in Bellingham or ☎ (800) 443-4552, or consult 💻 www.whales.com.

Black Ball Transport runs passenger and vehicle ferries from Port Angeles to Victoria. For information, call ☎ (250) 386-2202 in Victoria, ☎ (360) 457-4491 in Port Angeles, or consult 💻 www.northolympic.com/coho.

Ferry Service to Coastal British Columbia

BC Ferries' *Queen of the North* runs from Port Hardy at the north end of Vancouver Island, sailing on an all-day trip through the Inside Passage to Prince Rupert, the last significant town on British Columbia's North Coast.

The *Queen* leaves Vancouver Island to enter a short stretch of open ocean and then picks up the Inland Passage behind Calvert Island into Fitz Hugh Sound. The ferry continues through the protected Finlayson and Grenville channels, all the way to Prince Rupert just short of the Alaskan panhandle.

Grenville Channel is a narrow waterway flanked by forested mountains. It's a bit like floating through a long, green tunnel.

At Prince Rupert you can make connections to Alaska Marine Highway System ferry, which docks alongside; that system reaches to Skagway, Alaska and beyond.

You can also pick up ferries in Prince Rupert to the Queen Charlotte Islands. And Prince Rupert is also the terminus of the Trans-Canada Highway, all the way from the East Coast.

Service on the *Queen of the North* daily alternates direction in the summer; there are weekly sailings in winter. About 150 cars can be carried on the ship to Prince Rupert.

BC Ferries also operates a local service to some isolated communities on the Inside Passage between Port Hardy and Prince Rupert on a route it calls the Discovery Coast Passage. Boats leave Port Hardy on Vancouver Island making stops at Finn Bay, Namu, McLoughlin Bay/Shearwater, Klemtu, Ocean Falls, and Bella Coola.

Vehicles can be carried to many of the destinations, although except for the final stop at Bella Coola, what few roads there are do not penetrate too far into the interior and there are no roads that run along the coast.

The peaks of Garibaldi Provincial Park are snow-capped year-round

Ferry ports include Finn Bay at the mouth of Rivers Inlet, a sport-fishing mecca. Namu is near a favorite ocean kayaking area and one of the world's richest in-shore salmon fisheries. McLoughlin Bay/Shearwater is near Bella Bella, the largest native community of the mid-coast region. Klemtu, the most isolated port of call and the most northerly point on the route, is the home community of the Kitasoo people, who have preserved their culture and customs.

Not all sailings make stops at the same ports, and some schedules can take as long as twenty-four hours to complete; there are sleeper seats and showers available on board. The terminus is Bella Coola, a village about seventy-five miles inland from the coast. The ferry follows the Dean Channel to the Labouchere Channel. The very basic Route 20 winds its way east through South Tweedsmuir Park inland to Williams Lake. From there Route 97 runs south to distant Vancouver or north to Prince George and the Trans-Canada Highway.

The connection to Bella Coola allows travelers to make a round trip by water in one direction and by road in the other.

British Columbia Festivals and Events

The arts are alive and well in British Columbia, especially in and around Vancouver and Whistler, and Victoria on Vancouver Island. Following is a list of some of the best festivals and annual events. For a more complete list and specific dates, call ☎ (800) 663-6000 for a copy of the BC Calendar of Events. You can also consult 🖥 www.hellobc.com for an updated calendar of events.

February

Chinese New Year Fair and Parade. Vancouver. Commercial displays, cultural performances, and a food festival at the Pacific National Exhibition Grounds; parade in Chinatown. Admission: adult, ❶; child and senior, free.

April

Terri Vic Dixieland Jazz Festival. Victoria. The five-day Jazz Festival is one of the largest events of its kind with more than twenty-five thousand attendees, showcasing some twenty leading jazz bands from all over the world. Held in April at eight locations in Victoria. Festival and daily passes sold.

May

Canadian Northern Children's Festival. Prince George. ☎ (250) 562-4882. Puppetry, mime theater, and music at Fort George Park in Prince George. Free admission to the festival, charge for main stage performances.

Chilliwack Dixieland Jazz Festival. Chilliwack. ☎ (604) 795-3600. National and international musicians at a three-day festival at the Ag-Rec Centre and Exhibition grounds in Chiliwack. Festival passes and daily tickets sold.

New Music West. Vancouver. ☎ (604) 684-9338. 🖳 www.newmusicwest.com. Spread over twenty-five venues throughout Vancouver with some two hundred bands and a conference that attracts some 2,500 songwriters, musicians, and recording industry representatives. Admission varies by event.

Vancouver International Children's Festival. Vancouver. ☎ (604) 708-5655. 🖳 www.vancouverchildrensfestival.com. Children's theater, puppetry, music, and dance in open-air and tent performances at Vanier Park.

June

Alcan Dragon Boat Festival. Vancouver. ☎ (604) 688-2382. 🖳 www.canada dragonboat.com. Dragon boat races, performing and visual arts, a culinary festival, and children's activities at the Plaza of Nations at Pacific Place. Mid-June.

Sam Steele Days. Cranbrook. ☎ (250) 426-4161. Four days of old-time celebration that includes a parade, sports tournaments, loggers' competitions, and barbecues. Admission varies with events; many events are free.

Vancouver International Jazz Festival. Vancouver. ☎ (604) 872-5200. 🖳 www.jazzvancouver.com. Indoor and outdoor concerts and street performers in downtown Vancouver.

Jazzfest International. Victoria. ☎ (888) 671-2112. 🖳 www.vicjazz.bc.ca/jazzfest.html. Jazz, blues, and world music. Held on the second of June at various venues in Victoria, indoors and outdoors.

July

Gold Fever Follies Summer Theatre. Rossland. ☎ (250) 362-9912. Performers tell Rossland's history through song and dance at historic Miners Hall. Held Tuesday through Saturday during July and August. Admission: adult, ❷; child, ❶.

Key to Prices
- ❶ $5 and under
- ❷ $5 to $10
- ❸ $10 to $20
- ❹ $20 and more

When prices are listed as a range, this indicates various combination options are available. Most attractions offer reduced-price tickets for children and many have family rates that include two adults and two or three children.

Kaslo Summer Music Festival. Kaslo. ☎ (250) 353-7538. Jazz, classical, blues, and rhythm, and New Age music in Kaslo Bay Park. Festival passes and daily tickets sold.

Vancouver Folk Music Festival. Vancouver. ☎ (604) 602-9798. 💻 www.the festival.bc.ca. Local, national, and international performers take the stage at Jericho Beach Park. Admission prices vary by performance.

Vancouver International Comedy Festival. Vancouver. ☎ (604) 683-0883. 💻 www.comedyfest.com. A public celebration of comedy with performers from British Columbia, elsewhere in Canada, and around the world. Held in late July and early August on Granville Island. Some events are free.

August

Hornby Island Festival. Hornby. ☎ (250) 335-2734. 💻 www.hornbyfestival. bc.ca. For eleven days in August each year this is a festival of music, dance, theater, film, and exhibits held in Hornby's hand-crafted community hall and other venues. Festival passes and daily tickets sold.

Kamloops Pow-Wow. Kamloops. ☎ (250) 828-9708. 💻 www.mwsolutions. com/kib/pow_wow.htm. Celebration of First Nations culture with competitions in dancing, singing, and drumming, held at the Kamloops Reserve Special Events Centre. General admission: ❷ per day; ❹ weekend pass.

Merritt Mountain Music Festival. Merritt. ☎ (250) 860-5989. 💻 www. moun tainfest.com. A four-day event drawing the celebrities of country and western music to the Ewalt Ranch. Entertainment includes line dancing, street entertainers, amusement rides, and clowns.

September

Fringe Theatre Festival. Vancouver. ☎ (604) 257-0350. 💻 www.vancouverfringe. com. An eleven-day celebration of drama, music, comedy, and dance put forth in the Mount Pleasant area.

Vancouver International Film Festival. Vancouver. ☎ (604) 685-0260. 💻 www.viff.org. Canadian and international feature films, short films, a trade forum, seminars, and workshops. Held at movie theaters in downtown Vancouver from late September to mid-October.

October

The Vancouver International Writers Festival. Vancouver. ☎ (604) 681-6330. 💻 www.writersfest.bc.ca. Readings and debates by Canadian and international writers, a Literary Cabaret, Poetry Bash, and authors' brunch held at various venues on Granville Island.

Chapter 7
Vancouver

The impressive glass-and-steel towers of Vancouver are sometimes hard to see when your eyes are distracted by the backdrop of the mountains across the bay and the reflection of the busy cruise and commercial port of Burrard Inlet. No complaint here; Vancouver is quite simply one of the most attractive major cities in the world. In some ways it's a Western version of Hong Kong.

Vancouver has the beautiful green of Stanley Park, culture from several universities, and one of the most diverse mixes of nationalities in the world.

The largest cultural groups of Vancouver are the British, who were among the earliest settlers and developers of the West, and the Chinese, many of whom began to arrive near the end of the nineteenth century as workers on the construction of the Canadian Pacific Railway and as miners.

Vancouver's Chinatown is the largest in Canada and third largest in North America after San Francisco and New York. The older Chinese community has been augmented in recent years by an influx of people from Hong Kong (which gives one reason for the city's "Hongcouver" nickname), as well as Vietnam and other Asian countries. Other important immigrant groups include various European populations including farmers from the Ukraine.

Located on the mainland in the southwest corner of British Columbia, greater Vancouver is made up of eighteen municipalities that occupy about 1,100 square miles in and around the Fraser River delta.

The population of the City of Vancouver itself is just over 520,000 but with the surrounding area, including Richmond, Surrey, Burnaby, Delta, Coquitlam, North Vancouver, West Vancouver, New Westminster, Port Moody, and White Rock, there are more than 1.75 million people in the community.

The metropolitan hub of the City of Vancouver is located on the Burrard peninsula. To the north are the Coast Mountains, to the west the Strait of Georgia, and to the east the lush green farmlands of the Fraser Valley. About twenty-five miles away to the south is the border with the state of Washington in the United States.

Vancouver's port, sheltered from the Pacific Ocean by Vancouver Island, is North America's second busiest port, shipping coal, minerals, grain, and oil.

Climate

Moderated by Pacific Ocean currents, Vancouver's weather is the mildest in Canada with daytime temperatures averaging 70 degrees Fahrenheit in summer and 35 degrees in winter.

Spring comes early with flowers usually in full bloom by early March. Late summer and autumn days, through October, tend to be warm and sunny. Winter is the rainy season; an average rainfall of 57 inches translates into winter snow on nearby mountains but relatively little in the Vancouver area at the base of the hills and along the water.

Stanley Park

A green jewel just minutes west of downtown Vancouver, Stanley Park, at one thousand acres, is larger than New York's Central Park. Trails lead into nearly untouched wilderness and to a wide range of attractions including the Vancouver Aquarium, a miniature train, a petting zoo, and a collection of totem poles.

The road that circles the park provides spectacular views across Burrard Inlet; a seven-mile-long seawall promenade for pedestrians offers even better vistas.

At the western end of the park is the Lions Gate suspension bridge leading to the Georgia Strait and English Bay. Entrance to the park is free, but drivers must pay for parking.

Within Stanley Park the award-winning **Vancouver Aquarium** has an impressive collection of Pacific sea life including sea otters, harbor seals, and some incredible species of fish. There's also an indoor rain forest and a collection of some of the largest fresh water fish in the world in the "Giant Fishes of the Amazon" exhibit.

In 2001 the aquarium announced it would no longer capture or purchase dolphins and killer whales from the wild and would end the display of live killer whales, sending twenty-three-year-old Bjossa to SeaWorld in San Diego. In its place the facility plans to open a new exhibit of west coast animals.

The aquarium is open every day; hours vary by season and special events; be sure to make a call before you visit. Admission: adult, ❸; youth (13–18), ❸; child (4–12), ❷. For information, call ☎ (604) 659-3474 or 🖳 www.vanaqua.org.

Key to Prices
❶ $5 and under
❷ $5 to $10
❸ $10 to $20
❹ $20 and more
When prices are listed as a range, this indicates various combination options are available. Most attractions offer reduced-price tickets for children and many have family rates that include two adults and two or three children.

Vancouver's Neighborhoods

The area in the vicinity of Water, Carrall, Cordova, and Powell Streets in downtown Vancouver began as the site of the Stamps sawmill.

In 1867 John Deighton came to town as a loquacious barkeep; he was nicknamed "Gassy Jack" and eventually what was then officially Hastings became known as **Gastown**. In 1870 it was officially renamed Granville and sixteen years later incorporated as the City of Vancouver.

VANCOUVER AND VANCOUVER ISLAND

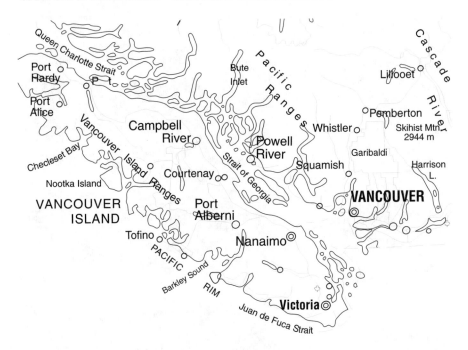

Gastown was levelled by fire in 1886 but rose again as a commercial area. Eventually it became, shall we say, the seedy side of town, including a skid row and worse.

Today most of the warehouses and shops have been converted to boutiques and restaurants; the turn-of-the-century atmosphere attracts thousands of visitors by day and cabaret patrons by night. Some of the seediness perseveres in areas to the south and east, although I doubt tourists will be shanghaied out to sea. I'm more worried about being assaulted to purchase tacky souvenirs.

Gastown's most famous object is the steam-powered clock at the corner of Cambie and Water streets; it whistles and whoops on the quarter hour and puts on a gassy show on the hour, often surrounded by visitors and their video cameras.

The Chinese are the second largest ethnic group in British Columbia after the British. North America's third largest **Chinatown**—after San Francisco and New York—is also home to the world's narrowest office building, located at the corner of Pender and Carral.

This Chinatown is a place of won-ton houses, meat stores that have windows festooned with crimson barbecued ducks and coils of Chinese sausage, and displays of exotic roots, meats, and glands. Shops sell finely lacquered pots, jade, carved wood, and embroidered dresses. Grocers here can supply just about any food item you can get in the Far East.

Little Tokyo or **Japantown** lies a few blocks beyond Chinatown on Powell Street between Gore and Dunlevy, the historical center of Japanese settlement

DOWNTOWN VANCOUVER

Horseshoe Bay Ferry Terminal · Horseshoe Bay · Cypress Provincial Park · Capilano Lake · Grouse Mountain Skyride · Lynn Headwaters Regional Park · WEST VANCOUVER · NORTH VANCOUVER · Capilano Canyon Park · Capilano Salmon Hatchery · Highview Lookout · Cypress Bowl Rd. · Upper Levels Hwy. · Capilano Suspension Bridge · Queens Rd. · Lynn Valley · St. Valley Hwy. · Passage I. · Lighthouse Park · Atkinson Lighthouse · Marine Dr. · Inglewood Ave. · Park Royal · Marine Dr. · Boulevard Park · Capilano College · BURRARD INLET · Lion's Gate Bridge · Capilano · Royal Hudson · Mission · Lonsdale Quay Market · Stanley Park · Van. Aquarium · 9 O'Clock Gun · Burrard Inlet · McGill · Sea Bus · The Ferguson Point Tea House · English Bay · Pacific Space Centre & Vancouver Museum · Canada Place · CN IMAX · Powell St. · Pacific National Exhibition Grounds · Vancouver Maritime Museum · Van. Art Gallery · Gastown Steam Clock · Hastings · UBC Museum of Anthropology · Jericho Beach Park · St. Roch Nat'l Hist. Site · GM Place · B.C. Place · Parker · University of British Columbia · Chancellor Blvd. · University Blvd. · Granville Island Market · Science World B.C. · Place Terminal · Nanaimo Ave. · Renfrew · Broadway · UBC Botanical Gardens · Pacific Spirit Regional Park · Foreshore Park · City Hall · Grandview Hwy. · Kingsway · VANCOUVER · Van Dusen Botanical Garden · Bloedel Conservatory · Queen Elizabeth Park · Mascrop St. · Central Park · Vancouver International Airport · Sea Island · Burkeville · Bridgepoint Market · Bridgeport Rd. · Fraser R. Park · Richmond · STRAIT OF GEORGIA · Queen Charlotte Channel

in Vancouver. Many of the residents were forcibly relocated to interior British Columbia during World War II. Sunrise Market at 300 Powell is a popular shopping and informal dining area.

Little India, the cultural center of the thousands of citizens of Indian descent, is on Main Street between East Forty-Ninth and Fifty-First Avenues; here some several dozen jewelry and fabric stores make up the Punjabi Market.

In its rowdy heyday as a warehouse district, **Yaletown** boasted more saloons per acre than most anywhere in the world. Today the area is home to the city's hippest galleries, shops, and loft apartments for architects, designers, and filmmakers—a Vancouver version of Tribeca or Soho.

Nearby is **False Creek**, **North False Creek**, and **South False Creek**, all former waterfront districts reclaimed for homes and shops, especially at the sprawling **Granville Island Public Market** near South False Creek.

The redevelopment of **Granville Island**, under the south end of Granville Street Bridge, started out as an attempt to convert run-down waterfront packing houses and industrial property to public markets and avant garde retail space.

Today the area is a world of stylish restaurants, art galleries, artist studios, craft shops, and theaters. Buskers add a carnival atmosphere.

The **Granville Island Information Centre** houses historical exhibits and excellent audio-visual presentations that show the development of the area. For information, call ☎ (604) 666-5784 or consult 🖳 www.granvilleisland.com.

About a mile outside of downtown, in East Vancouver, is the neighborhood of Grandview-Woodland and Commercial Drive, traditionally known as **Little Italy**. Today the area has expanded to include ethnic and cultural minorities of many origins. Here Italian gelaterias are shoulder to shoulder with reggae record shops and health food restaurants.

Once home to the rich and powerful of the Edwardian era, the inner city neighborhood of the **West End** stretches from sea to sea (Coal Harbour to English Bay) with Stanley Park on one side. Today the West End is a mix of old homes and new developments, and it is the most densely populated area of Victoria. Denman Street, a favored place to stroll, is a seven-block-long stretch of some fifty restaurants and coffee shops.

Museums and Attractions in Vancouver

For an impressive view of a great-looking city you can take a glass-enclosed elevator for a five-hundred-foot ride to the top of the Harbour Centre Tower along the waterfront in downtown. **Lookout! at Harbour Centre**, at 555 West Hastings Street, offers 360-degree views of the city, mountains, and the harbor. Admission also includes a twelve-minute multimedia show, *Once in a World, Vancouver*. A day pass includes the right to return the same day after dark. For information, call ☎ (604) 689-0421 or consult 🖳 www.harbourcentretower.com.

(And you might also want to cross over Burrard Inlet to North Vancouver and check out the view from the other side. The tram to the top of **Grouse Mountain** offers even higher views looking back toward the city. And while you're on that side of the water, you can also visit the venerable Capilano Bridge. *See details on both in Chapter 8.*)

The star collection of the city is the **Vancouver Museum**, Canada's largest civic museum, which showcases the history and culture of the city. The museum is as disparate as the wonderfully expansive province, ranging from ancient baskets to totem poles to modern Vancouver through World War I. The museum, located at 1100 Chestnut Street, is open year-round. Admission: adult, ❷; youth, ❶. For information, call ☎ (604) 736-4431 or consult 🖳 www.van museum.bc.ca.

Attached to the Vancouver Museum is a newer gallery, the **H. R. McMillan Space Centre**. This is an attractive exploration of the solar system and our attempts to visit our nearest neighbors. There are lots of hands-on exhibits and experiments. Items include hardware and uniforms that have been in space; some are related to Canada's active participation in the American Space Shuttle Program. A new program in the Planetarium Theatre is *Electric Sky*, an exploration of the Northern Lights. Joint tickets are available with the Vancouver Museum. For information, call ☎ (604) 738-7827.

A short walk away in Vanier Park is the **Vancouver Maritime Museum**, a rather low-key collection of old photographs of early Vancouver and its port along with some low-energy exhibits of artifacts. The museum is located at 1100 Chestnut Street. Admission: adult, ❷; child, ❶; senior, ❶. For information, call ☎ (604) 736-4431 or consult 🖳 www.vmm.bc.ca.

For a real sense of British Columbia's maritime history, step outside the museum and head for the water and the *Saint Roch* **National Historic Site** at 1905 Ogden Street in Vanier Park.

In the 1920s the Royal Canadian Mounted Police operated the *Saint Roch*, a wooden schooner powered by sails and an auxiliary engine. The *Saint Roch* left Vancouver in June 1940 for a crossing of the Northwest Passage; she ended up trapped in ice for two winters and did not reach Halifax until October 1942. The return trip took only eighty-six days, thus making the *Saint Roch* the first known vessel to sail a roundtrip through the Northwest Passage.

The site is open daily May to September; closed Monday September to May. Admission: adult, ❷; child, student, and senior, ❶; child (younger than 6), free; family, ❹. For information, call ☎ (604) 666-3201.

The impressive **British Columbia Museum of Anthropology** presents a world-class collection of totem poles, ceremonial objects, and artifacts in an attractive, airy structure on the University of British Columbia campus.

Cruise ships docked at Canada Place in Vancouver

Located at 6393 N.W. Marine Drive, the museum is open daily from mid-May to early September, and daily except Monday the remainder of the year. Recorded message: ☎ (604) 822-3825. Admission: adult, ❷; senior and student, ❶; family, ❹. For information, call ☎ (604) 822-5087 or consult 🖳 www.moa.ubc.ca.

For a state-of-the-art dose of "gee-whiz," there's **Science World British Columbia**, a wondrous world of hands-on science exhibits for visitors both young and old, and home to one of the largest Omnimax domed-screen theaters.

The main gallery explains physics; you can light up a plasma ball or try to blow square bubbles. In the music gallery you make music with

> **Hollywood north.**
> Vancouver has an active filmmaking industry, both for Canadian movies and for Hollywood productions that use the city and surrounding areas as a stand-in for American locales. For information on movies in production, call the B.C. Film Commission's Hot Line at ☎ (604) 660-3569.

your feet on a walk-on synthesizer. Another gallery explores natural history and yet another digs into mining in British Columbia.

The museum, nearby to the Main Street/Science World SkyTrain Station, is located at 1455 Québec Street. Admission tickets, with one or more films, range from ❷ to ❸. For information, call ☎ (604) 443-7443 or consult 🖳 www.science world.bc.ca.

In downtown Vancouver the **Vancouver Art Gallery** is a small but imposing structure home to a collection of about four thousand paintings, sculptures, photographs, prints, drawing, and objects. There's also a gallery devoted to Emily Carr's haunting post-impressionist paintings.

The imposing carved granite neo-classical structure was built as the Vancouver Courthouse in 1911. Inside, the walls are constructed of marble from Alaska, Tennessee, and Vermont; a copper-sheathed dome that has a glass oculus tops the central rotunda.

Its use as a courthouse ended in 1979; it was converted to use as the new home of the Vancouver Art Gallery in 1983.

Entry to the lobby is from Hornsby Street, through the original colonnaded link between the old courthouse and its annex, or through a new colonnade that repeats the five columns of the portico above.

Ground-floor galleries are used as the home for long-term showings of the gallery's collection of historical and contemporary art. Access to the second floor, used for major temporary exhibitions, is gained by a dramatic double staircase flanking the rotunda. The third level is primarily dedicated to the gallery's collection of works by Emily Carr and British Columbia art.

The gallery is located at 750 Hornby Street, at Robson Street. Admission: adult, ❷; senior and student, ❶; child (12 and younger), free. For information, call ☎ (604) 662-4700 or consult 🖳 www.vanartgallery.bc.ca.

For a modern multimedia experience, the **CN Imax Theatre** shows films on a five-story screen. The theater, a legacy of Expo '86, is located at the Canada Place cruise ship terminal near the SkyTrain Waterfront Station. Admission:

The miracle mile. The first time a human officially ran a distance of one mile in less than four minutes was in British Columbia, at the 1954 British Empire Games at Empire Stadium in Vancouver. Two men accomplished the feat in the same race, but Roger Bannister won at 3 minutes, 58.8 seconds. A blink of the eye behind was John Landy at 3 minutes, 59.6 seconds.

adult, ❸; senior (65+), ❷; child (4–12), ❷. Second film, $4 additional for all rates. For information, call ☎ (604) 682-2384 or ☎ (800) 582-4629, or consult 💻 www.imax.com/vancouver.

In Vancouver's thriving Chinatown the **Dr. Sun Yat-Sen Classical Chinese Garden** at 578 Carrall Street is a classical garden in the style of the Ming Dynasty, perhaps the first of its kind ever built outside China. This special place was created by artisans brought from the mother country, who used imported natural and man-made items from Suzhou, the garden city of China.

Classical gardens were originally designed by Taoist poets, intended to create a place of ordered tranquility for contemplation and inspiration. The four principal elements of the garden—in concert with the Taoist concept of opposites in balance known as yin and yang—are water, rocks, plants, and architecture.

The inscription above the entrance to the garden reads "Garden of Ease."

A gift shop at the gardens offers porcelains, books, and other items from China, elsewhere in Asia, and from local artisans. For information, call ☎ (604) 662-3207 or ☎ (604) 689-7133 or consult 💻 www.discovervancouver.com/sun.

Another impressive patch of greenery lies under glass at the **Bloedel Floral Conservatory** in Queen Elizabeth Park, a former quarry that was the source of much of Vancouver's early roadways. Here you'll find a large collection of plants, free-flying tropical birds, and colorful koi fish. The conservatory is located at Thirty-Third at Cambie Streets. For information, call ☎ (604) 257-8570 or consult 💻 www.city.vancouver.bc.ca/parks/parks&gardens/qepark.htm.

Shopping on Robson Street

Train tracks were laid along a broad street in Vancouver in 1895 and the road quickly became lined with small shops.

The street was given its name in honor of John Robson, premier of British Columbia from 1889 to 1892. After World War II it was known for a while as Robsonstrasse in recognition of the many European shopkeepers in the area.

Today Robson and the surrounding area offers a wide range of high-end retail clothing, accessory shops, and restaurants. But you'll also find many small independent shops offering an eclectic selection of art and other items.

The Robson Street Business Association maintains a website at 💻 www.robson street.bc.ca.

North Vancouver

The north side of the harbor is a very green bedroom community to Vancouver and the gateway to the Sunshine Coast and the winter and summer attractions of Whistler. It also has some interesting attractions of its own.

You can drive across the **Lion's Gate Bridge** or take a bus tour that crosses the water by water taxi.

In 1889 Scottish entrepreneur George Grant Mackay built a swinging pedestrian bridge across the rushing waters of Capilano Canyon. Today, more than a hundred years later, the bridge—updated ever so slightly—sways 230 feet above the floor of the canyon on a 450-foot crossing.

The **Capilano Suspension Bridge and Park** in North Vancouver was one of the original tourist attractions of the northwest; today it is still one of the more spectacular casual hikes you'll find anywhere.

The five-foot-wide walkway, hung from steel cables, sways from side to side and ripples up and down when the steps of tourists cross from one side to another. A sturdy handrail is on either side of the crossing; it's fun to watch some overly self-assured visitors attempt to cross without touching the rail.

On the far side of the canyon is a cool nature park that wanders through the forest to a view of a two-hundred-foot waterfall. At the entranceway is the Capilano Trading Post, a collection of native art, apparel, and souvenirs. Nearby is the Bridge House Restaurant, an old-style eatery in the former home of some of the early owners of the bridge.

The bridge, located at 3735 Capilano Road in North Vancouver, is open from 8 A.M. to dusk in the summer, and 9 A.M. to 5 P.M. in the winter. Admission: adult, ❸; student (with ID), ❷; child (6–12), ❷. Off-season rates from November through April slightly lower. For information, call ☎ (604) 985-7474 or consult 💻 www.capbridge.com.

A bit further up the road from the Capilano Suspension Bridge, the **Grouse Mountain Skyride** offers a panoramic view of the city and harbor. The enclosed tramway cabin rises 4,100 feet to the top in an eight-minute climb.

Year-round visitors can explore hiking trails at the summit, and there is an hour-long multimedia show at the **Theatre in the Sky**. In the winter there is downhill skiing with thirteen runs and a respectable 1,200-foot vertical drop. Non-skiers can take a mountaintop sleigh ride. In the summer visitors can also ride some of the ski chairlifts at the summit.

The Skyride, located at 6400 Nancy Greene Way in North Vancouver, operates daily from 9 A.M. to 10 P.M. Admission: adult, ❸; youth (13–18), ❷; child (6–12), ❷; senior, (65+), ❷; family (two adults, two children), ❹. For information, call ☎ (604) 984-0661 or consult 💻 www.grousemountain.com.

Vancouver Transportation

BC Transit covers more than 695 square miles of the Lower Mainland with bus service, a light rail service known as SkyTrain, and passenger ferry service known as SeaBus. The area is divided into three fare zones; fares are the same for any mode of transportation.

Buses run on the busiest routes from 5 A.M. to 2 A.M., and late night "Owl" service on some downtown-to-suburban routes until 4:20 A.M.

In mid-2001 fares during peak hours were $1.75 for service within one zone, $2.50 for trips that are within two zones, and $3.50 for trips that pass through three zones. Off-peak fares of $1.75 for one- and two-zone trips are in effect after 6:30 P.M. on weekdays and all day on weekends and holidays.

SkyTrain, an automated light rapid transit system, follows an eighteen-mile route between downtown Vancouver and Surrey with twenty stations along the way. SeaBus connects Vancouver with the North Shore via a twelve-minute harbor crossing. For information, call the Vancouver Regional Transit System at ☎ (604) 521-0400 or consult 🖳 www.bctransit.com.

Chapter 8
Victoria and Vancouver Island

Vancouver Island lies across the water from the city of Vancouver on the mainland, about thirty miles west across the Strait of Georgia, and north across the Strait of Juan de Fuca from Seattle in Washington state.

A mountainous spine runs along most of the length of the 280-mile-long island, breaking into long mountain fjords on the west coast that cut deeply into the island. One of them, Alberni Inlet, cuts more than halfway through the island, ending at Port Alberni.

The west coast, which faces the Pacific Ocean, is mostly uninhabited with just a few small and isolated communities. The island's major settlements and roads are clustered on the protected east coast. Lush forests of large Douglas fir and cedar thrive in the moderate, wet ocean climate.

Victoria, on the southern tip of Vancouver Island, is the capital of British Columbia, with more than 300,000 residents in the city and its suburbs. About sixty-two miles north is Nanaimo with a population of about seventy-one thousand. The island economy is based primarily on the forest industry, with several mills located up and down the eastern coast.

North of Vancouver Island lie the Queen Charlotte Islands, a scenic, mist-shrouded world little touched by modernity.

Victoria

A walk around the harbor of Victoria is a step back in time to the heyday of the British Empire.

In some ways Victoria is the most British of any major city in Canada. It's a place where they still serve high tea at the ornate Empress Victoria Hotel, and it's home to more portraits per block of the Queen (both old Victoria and today's Elizabeth II) than anywhere else I have visited in the country.

Located at the southern tip of Vancouver Island, Victoria is the most southerly and most urban of the municipalities that make up Greater Victoria.

The capital region includes Victoria, Oak Bay, Esquimalt, Saanich, Colwood, Langford, View Royal, Metchosin, Central Saanich, North Saanich, and Sidney, with a regional population of more than 330,800.

Empress Victoria Hotel, Victoria
Photo courtesy of Tourism Victoria

The modern history of Victoria dates from 1843, when Fort Victoria was built as a Hudson's Bay Company post. About fifteen years later the settlement became one of the main midway destinations and supply stations for miners seeking their fortunes in the Cariboo goldfields on the mainland. And in 1865 Esquimalt Harbour was designated as a British naval base.

But by the turn of the century Victoria was overtaken by Vancouver as an economic center. Since then, Victoria has grown more slowly than the city on the mainland while holding on to its past

Victoria has retained its designation as the capital of the province of British Columbia. Government is one of the major employers on the island. Other industries include tourism and fishing.

Bastion Square in downtown is the original site of Fort Victoria. The Maritime Museum, the Courthouse, and several other buildings from the turn of the century have been restored and currently house shops and offices.

The Empress Hotel lords over the inner harbor. The hotel maintains the tradition of railway hotels that were constructed across the West around the turn of the century. Now operated as part of the upscale Canadian Pacific group, the Empress still serves afternoon tea.

A few blocks away is Market Square, a busy packing house and warehouse from gold rush times, now home to a collection of unusual boutiques.

On the intriguingly named Pandora Street, an old feed warehouse has been transformed from an ugly duckling to the quirky but attractive Swans Hotel. The twenty-nine, two-story suites combine modern amenities with old beams. On the street level are the bustling Buckerfield's Brewery and the Fowl and Fish Cafe, which features an eclectic menu that on my visit included an ostrich stir fry (tastes like chicken).

A block further inland is Chinatown, once covering several city blocks but now mainly Fisgard Street. The street is capped by the ornate Gate of Harmonious Interest, which stands on the site of wooden gates that once barred entry to Chinatown.

Off to the side is Fan Tan Alley, a narrow passage that has shops and hidden windows and counters that are used in commerce of various sorts.

Victoria's district outdates most other Chinese settlements in Canada. It was founded in 1858, ahead of the major wave of Asian immigrants who were brought to Canada in the late 1800s to work as laborers in the building of the Canadian Pacific Railway.

Key to Prices
❶ $5 and under
❷ $5 to $10
❸ $10 to $20
❹ $20 and more

When prices are listed as a range, this indicates various combination options are available. Most attractions offer reduced-price tickets for children and many have family rates that include two adults and two or three children.

Attractions in Victoria

The premier museum of Victoria is the **Royal British Columbia Museum** located on the inner harbor. It's an impressive collection of the history and culture of British Columbia. At the museum you can walk through the streets of a pioneer town, to an old working Gold Rush waterwheel, aboard Captain Vancouver's ship *Discovery*, into a native Indian longhouse, to the bottom of the ocean, through a coastal rain forest, or along a seashore.

Outside there is a garden of BC's native wildflowers. In the summer native carvers are at work.

One of my favorite spots in all of British Columbia is a room that's full of totem poles located on the lower floor of the museum; arboreal lighting and sound effects transport you to the remotest coastal villages of the province.

The museum, founded in 1896, draws close to a million visitors per year and has burst through the seams of several structures during the years.

A recent addition is the **National Geographic Theatre**, showing Imax large-format films.

In the attached Fannin Tower, more than 10 million artifacts are housed in anthropological, biological, and historical collections for researchers.

The museum is located at 675 Belleville Street. Admission: adult, ❷; senior, ❶; child (6–18), ❶; child (6–younger), free. For information, call ☎ (250) 387-2944 or ☎ (888) 447-7977 or consult 🖳 www.royalbcmuseum.bc.ca.

For information about the Imax theater, consult 🖳 www.imaxvictoria.com.

Alongside the Royal British Columbia Museum is **Thunderbird Park**, where you'll find a collection of totem poles, many of which feature the mythical thunderbird. According to legend, thunder emanated from the movements of the bird's wings, and lightning radiated from its eyes.

The **Crystal Garden** was built in 1925 by the Canadian Pacific as a saltwater pool and lounge, an adjunct to the Empress Hotel across the road. The grand design echoed some of the great glass halls of Europe, including London's famous Crystal Palace.

At one time it was the largest indoor swimming pool in the British Empire.

The pool closed in 1971, the victim of soaring maintenance costs that included damage caused by corrosion from the saltwater pool. The community protested the loss and in 1980 the structure reopened with backing from the government of British Columbia. Today it is operated by the British Columbia Provincial Capital Commission.

Within you'll find a lush tropical paradise under glass with flamingos, butterflies, orchids, banana trees, and seasonal flowerbeds. A small collection of animals include lemurs, tiny pygmy marmosets and golden lion tamarins, and birds such as touracos, toucans, kookaburras, lorries, and ibis.

Crystal Garden is located at 713 Douglas Street. ☎ (250) 381-1277. 🖳 www.bcpcc.com/crystal. Admission: adult, ❷; child (5–16), ❶; senior (65+), ❷. A family ticket for two adults and as many as three children is $20.

Helmcken House, also next to the Royal British Columbia Museum, is the oldest home in British Columbia. Dr. John Sebastian Helmcken came to Fort Victoria in 1850, becoming the first Speaker of the Vancouver Island Assembly and one of three delegates sent to Ottawa in 1870 to negotiate British Columbia's union with Canada.

Filled with family relics, Helmcken House also has one of Canada's finest nineteenth-century medical collections, including Helmcken's medical kit. The Helmcken Family Christmas is a holiday highlight in Victoria; tickets are very difficult to obtain.

Admission: adult, ❷; senior (65+), ❶; child (6–12), ❶; child (6–younger), free. For hours and information, call ☎ (250) 356-5137 or consult 🖳 www.heritage. gov.bc.ca/helm/helm.htm or 🖳 www.tbc.gov.bc.ca/culture/schoolnet/ helmcken.

Vancouver Island has a rich maritime history well celebrated at the **Maritime Museum of British Columbia** in historic Bastion Square in Victoria's Old Town.

The museum features seventy model ships and some five thousand marine related artifacts. The passenger travel section tells the stories of the Princess, Empress, and Pioneer lines. Star of the adventure gallery is the tiny vessel *Tilikum*, which circled the globe.

Another gallery tells the story of the island's lifeline, the BC Ferry system. A commerce display shows how the development of Fort Victoria helped build the maritime industries of the west coast.

The maritime museum was established in 1954 as a naval museum on Signal Hill just outside the gates of the HMC Dockyard; it moved to its present location in 1965. The museum is located in the former Provincial Law Courts, built in 1899. In the paneled courtroom on the top floor, Chief Justice Matthew Ballie Begbie, renowned as the province's "Hanging Judge," handed down his sentences. Rising up the core of the building is an ornate open grill "bird cage" elevator, the oldest operating lift in Canada, also dating from 1899.

The museum is at 28 Bastion Square. Admission: adult, ❷; senior (65+), ❶; child (6–11), ❶; family rate, ❸. For information, call ☎ (250) 385-4222 or consult 🖳 mmbc.bc.ca.

Scottish immigrant Robert Dunsmuir built himself a castle in the 1880s, paid for with the riches he amassed as a coal baron on Vancouver Island.

The **Craigdarroch Castle** sits atop a hill on what was originally a twenty-eight-acre estate. Craigdarroch is a Gaelic word meaning "rocky oak place."

Dunsmuir spared no expense on construction. The walls are paneled with intricately carved walnut, mahogany, cedar, spruce, and other woods. Other features include magnificent stained glass windows and complex designs executed in exotic wood in the parquet floor throughout the castle's thirty-nine rooms. The massive entryway staircase leads through four floors to a glass-walled sitting room in the tower, which offers panoramic views of Victoria and the Olympic Peninsula.

Dunsmuir was the son and grandson of English coal masters; he came to British Columbia in 1851 to pursue coal for the Hudson's Bay Company. In 1869 his company managed to secure the Wellington mine near Nanaimo; Dunsmuir became one of the richest men in the province and also one of the most hated because of his tough labor practices, including his successful break-ing of an 1877 strike at the mine with replacement workers from San Francisco. His holdings eventually included railways, shipping, lumber, and iron works.

Dunsmuir died before the castle was finished, but his widow Joan lived there until her own death in 1908; at that time, her net worth was estimated at $20 million.

The castle was stripped of its furnishings and sold in a raffle in 1909. For much of the succeeding seven decades it served as a public building, including stints as the Craigdarroch Military Hospital in the aftermath of World War I,

VICTORIA

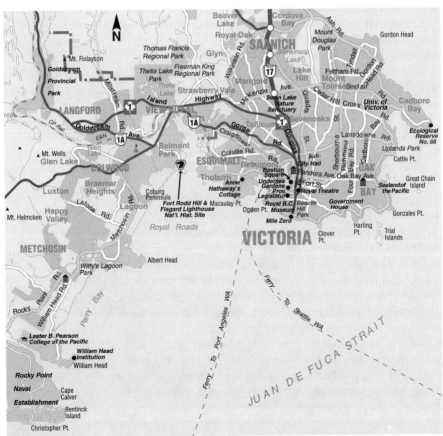

the first home of Victoria College (now the University of Victoria), the Greater Victoria School Board, and the Victoria Conservatory of Music.

The surrounding land was subdivided and now consists of a leafy suburb up the hill from the slightly funky University of Victoria district.

Since 1979 the Craigdarroch Castle Historical Museum Society has worked to refurbish the home to its former glory and recover some of the original furnishings. The hand-painted ceiling of the elaborate drawing room on the first floor included pastoral scenes; the artwork was painted over in the 1930s. In recent years a long-term project was underway to remove five layers of paint to restore the original scenes.

Self-guided tours of the castle take about an hour, and involve as many as eighty-seven steps up to the tower; there are no elevators or ramps.

Craigdarroch Castle is located at 1050 Joan Crescent, about a forty-five minute walk from town or a short taxi or bus ride. Admission: adult, ❷; student, ❶, and child (6–12), ❶. The castle is open daily from 9 A.M. to 7 P.M. in the summer and from 10 A.M. to 4:30 P.M. from September through mid-June. For information, call ☎ (250) 592-5323 or consult 🖳 www.craigdarrochcastle.com.

Several blocks south of the Legislative Buildings is the **Emily Carr House**. The home was built for the family of Victoria merchant Richard Carr in 1863; it was here in 1871 that artist and author Emily Carr was born.

Emily Carr, considered one of the most important Canadian artists, specialized in paintings and sculptures inspired by the landscape and native tribes of British Columbia.

After declining health made it impossible for her to travel she turned to writing, producing six autobiographical books. Carr never married; she died in Victoria in 1945.

The dining room, drawing room, and sitting room have been restored to period elegance from the Victorian era. Some of the rooms include possessions of the Carr family, including some of Emily's pottery and sculpture.

One room is now dubbed the "People's Gallery," presenting the work of contemporary Canadian artists.

Open from mid-May to mid-September. Admission: adult, ❷; senior (65+), ❶; child (6–12), ❶; child (6 and younger), free. For information, call ☎ (604) 356-5137 or consult 🖳 www. emilycarr.com.

The **Art Gallery of Greater Victoria** has a small but eclectic collection. Some of the holdings are housed in a mansion built in 1890 as the residence for Alexander A. Green, a Victoria banker. Perhaps with a glance up the hill toward the neighboring Craigdarroch Castle, he gave his residence the name Gyppeswyk. Green was only able to occupy his house for a year before his bank failed and he was dispossessed.

After a fire destroyed nearby Cary Castle, the mansion served as Government House, the seat of power in British Columbia for three years. During that time, in 1901, the Duke and Duchess of Cornwall and York, the future Queen Mary and King George V, visited Victoria and were entertained at a state dinner at the elegant home.

The museum's collection includes works by local favorite Emily Carr, as well as works by Canadian contemporary artists, North American and European historical artists, and a large collection of Asian artifacts. On permanent exhibition outside in the interior courtyard is a fourteenth-century Buddha head and a wooden Shinto shrine, perhaps the only one of its kind outside Japan.

The Art Gallery of Greater Victoria is located at 1040 Moss Street. Admission: adult, ❷; senior and student, ❶. Open Monday to Saturday from 10 A.M. to 5 P.M. and until 9 P.M. on Thursday. On Sunday the gallery is open from 1 to 5 P.M. For information, call ☎ (250) 384-4101 or consult 🖳 aggv.bc.ca.

Point Ellice House was built in 1862, an Italianate villa on the shores of Victoria's Selkirk Water. The house contains British Columbia's most complete collection of Victoriana in its original setting. The well-documented nineteenth-century garden is one of the best examples of a Victorian domestic garden. Costumed staff members greet visitors; events include high tea and croquet and badminton on the lawns.

The house is located on Pleasant Street, off the Bay Street Bridge, about five minutes from downtown Victoria. The site can also be reached by taking a fifteen-minute ferry ride from the Inner Harbour. Open from mid-May to mid-September. Admission: adult, ❷; senior (65+), ❶; child, (6–12), ❶; child, (6 and younger), free. For information, call ☎ (250) 380-6506 or consult 🖳 www.heritage.gov.bc.ca/point/point.htm.

The **Craigflower Manor and School House** is a recollection of life in Victoria in the mid-nineteenth century. Only the farmhouse is left of the former nine-hundred-acre Craigflower Farm, established by a Hudson's Bay Company subsidiary in 1853. Built in the 1850s the Georgian-style house has been restored to reflect that era; exhibits include farming and home life.

The restored School House, also built in the 1850s, served the children of the farm and nearby settlements. It became a museum in 1931 and is the oldest standing school building in western Canada.

The complex is located at Craigflower and Admirals Road, ten minutes from downtown Victoria. Open from June to September. Admission: adult, ❷; senior (65+), ❶; child (6–12), ❶; child (6 and younger), free. For information, call ☎ (250) 383-4627 or consult 🖳 www.heritage.gov.bc.ca/craig/craig.htm.

In Esquimalt, west of Victoria, the **Fort Rodd Hill National Historic Site** commemorates the Victoria-Esquimalt Coast Defenses that served from 1878 to 1956. Sites include three battery structures, defensive walls, gun mounts, observation posts, a World War II military hut, an underground plotting room, and prehistoric archeological features.

The site is located at the entrance to Esquimalt Harbour, about eight miles from downtown Victoria. Open from March to the end of October; call ☎ (250) 478-5849 for hours, openings at other times, and for admission charges, or consult 🖳 parkscan.harbour.com/frh. Admission to Fort Rodd Hill and Fisgard Lighthouse: adult, ❶; youth (6–16), ❶; senior (65+), ❶; family, ❸.

Near Fort Rodd Hill is the **Fisgard Lighthouse National Historic Site**, the first permanent lighthouse on Canada's west coast. Completed in 1860 it was a sentinel for mariners entering Esquimalt Harbour; it is still in operation.

Fisgard Island is also an excellent vantage point for viewing Esquimalt Harbour and marine wildlife.

Entry to the site is through Fort Rodd Hill. Open year-round with limited services in winter. Call ☎ (250) 478-5849 for hours and admission charges.

Their royal highnesses, along with some of the lowest humans of history, are on display at the **Royal London Wax Museum**, on the inner harbor of Victoria.

A walk-through of the exhibit features encounters with wax models that include the city's namesake Queen Victoria, as well as royalty of the past and present, and a recreation of the British Crown Jewels. Other sections include a Galaxy of Stars for actors of stage and screen; the Between Friends section that celebrates the friendship between Canada and the United States; some especially horrific images if you choose to enter a detour to the Chamber of Horrors; and for children, Storybook Land with characters from favorites that include *Anne of Green Gables*, the *Wizard of Oz*, and several Disney classics.

The exhibition claims a link to a branch of the Tussaud family of England and France, although the museum is not affiliated with the famed Madame Tussaud's collection in London.

The museum is located at 470 Belleville Street, in the former Canadian Pacific Marine Terminal. Built in 1924, the structure was used for decades as a ferry and steamship terminal; soldiers departed from there for World War II. It was last used for passenger service in 1963. Admission: adult, ❷; young adult and student, ❷; child, (6–12), ❶; senior, (55+), ❷. For information, call ☎ (250) 388-4461 or consult 🖳 www.waxworld.com.

Attractions on Vancouver Island

Outside Victoria, Vancouver Island's best-known attraction is **Butchart Gardens**, a world-class collection of formal and theme gardens.

Robert Pim Butchart, son of a Scottish emigrant, was born in Ontario in 1856. In 1884, at the age of 28, he married Jennie Foster Kennedy, an accomplished artist whose interests included ballooning, flying, and chemistry; on their honeymoon in England, Butchart learned the process for the manufacture of Portland cement. In 1888 he founded the Owen Sound Portland Cement Company in Ontario, pioneering the industry in Canada.

In 1902 Butchart came to Tod Inlet on Vancouver Island and then started a cement plant there two years later. The factory tapped into the growing market for the construction of permanent buildings, roads, and sidewalks on the island and the mainland of British Columbia.

Jennie Butchart took to decorating around her home with plants and flowers, and her husband supplied men from the cement plant to work on plantings. When the limestone supply from the quarry was exhausted in 1908, she began work on what was to become the sunken garden there. She also planted Lombardy and white poplars and Person plums to block the view of the cement plant.

Butchart Gardens, Vancouver Island
Photo courtesy of Butchart Gardens Ltd.

Workers brought in massive amounts of topsoil by horse cart and wheel-barrow to create garden beds on the floor of the former quarry. The project was completed in 1921.

By the 1930s the gardens were drawing thousands of visitors and had become a major tourist attraction. Today Butchart more than 1.25 million visitors come to the park each year.

The gardens have been a family operation all along, moving first to a grandson, R. Ian Ross, who remained in charge from 1939 through his death in 1997. Butchart's great-grandson, Christopher Ross, now runs the company and personally supervises the pyrotechnics for the summertime fireworks show.

The fireworks show, presented Saturday nights from early July to early September, are considered among the world's best. As many as five thousand guests pack the gardens for the show, and entrance roads often close by 5 P.M.

Theme areas include the English Rose Garden, Japanese and Italian Gardens, and the famed Sunken Garden, with its dancing fountain. Each year more than 135,000 bulbs are imported from Holland each year to add to the already dazzling spring displays.

The gardens open every day at 9 A.M. and close as late as 10:30 P.M. in the summer and during the Christmas holiday season. In the spring closing time is as early as 4 P.M., advancing to 7 P.M. by mid-June.

Butchart Gardens is located on Tod Inlet near Brentwood, about twelve miles north of Victoria. Admission prices vary by season, with highest rates from mid-June to the end of September and lowest rates from mid-January to mid-March. In 2001 admission rates were adult, ❷–❸; youth, ❶–❷; child (5–12), ❶ at all times. For information, call ☎ (250) 652-4422 or consult 💻 www.butchartgardens.com.

Tour buses travel regularly from Victoria to the gardens, and you can also take municipal buses to a stop near the entrance. **Gray Line** runs a shuttle service to Butchart Gardens from the Victoria Bus Depot behind the Empress Hotel at 700 Douglas Street for about $4 each way. You can also take a Gray Line double-decker tour bus from the front of the Empress Hotel to Butchart Gardens, with scheduled drop-off and pickup and admission to the gardens included for $24.50 for adults and $7 for children. For information on Gray Line service, call ☎ (250) 388-6539 or consult 💻 www.victoriatours.com.

The indoor tropical world of **Victoria Butterfly Gardens** was built specifically for housing and breeding butterflies and moths from all over the world. The rainforest environment is computer regulated to create the proper temperature and humidity (approximately 80 degrees Fahrenheit and 85 percent humidity) for the butterflies to carry out their life cycle and breed naturally in the garden.

Butterfly pupae are imported from butterfly farms every week to ensure a minimum of seven hundred to one thousand butterflies from thirty-five varieties are in the garden at any given time.

Pupae are displayed in the "nursery" until metamorphosis is complete and they naturally emerge from their chrysalis and eventually are released into the garden. Typical imported members of the butterfly zoo include Blue Morpho, White Tree Nymph, Monarch, Caroni Flambeau, the Blue Clipper, the Brown Clipper, and the Giant Swallowtail. The facility has also bred species on site including the Giant Owl, the Palm Fly, the Red Periot, the Tailed Jay, the Postman, the Zebra Butterfly, the Pink Rose, the Pink Cattleheart, the Great Mormon, and the Atlas Moth, the largest moth in the world.

Most of the plants in the garden are used as "host plants" that are necessary for the butterfly's life cycle or as food sources for the butterflies. Tropical plants in the garden include bougainvillea, banana plant, coconut and papaya trees, the African shield, the hibiscus, bird of paradise, passion vines, lantana, antherium, chenille, and angel's trumpet.

The gardens are located at the intersection of West Saanich Road and Keating Cross Road at the base of the access road to Butchart Gardens. The gardens are included in some packaged bus tours. You can also reach the gardens on BC Transit bus 75 from Victoria. Admission: adult, ❷; student, ❷; senior, ❷; child (5–12), ❶. Family admission is a 10 percent discount from the total. For information, call ☎ (250) 652-3822 or ☎ (877) 722-0272 or consult 💻 www.butterflygardens.com.

The **Cowichan Native Heritage Centre** in Duncan, north of Victoria midway to Nanaimo, preserves the culture of the First Nations people. On the banks of the Cowichan River you'll find a traditional Big House, a gallery of west coast art, and a modern-day multimedia presentation. Activities include storytelling, a carving shed, weaving, Cowichan sweater knitting, moccasin beading, and craftmaking. In the summer the center presents a four-hour evening feast and storytelling program.

SAANICH PENINSULA

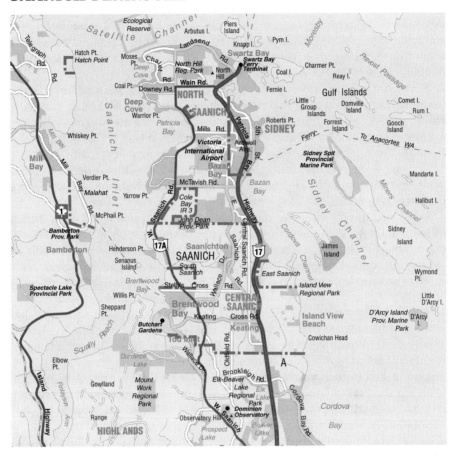

Located at 200 Cowichan Way in Duncan. Admission: adult, ❹; senior and student, ❷; child, ❶. For information, call ☎ (250) 746-8119 or consult 🖳 www. cowichannativevillage.com.

Nearby is the **British Columbia Forest Museum** where a hundred years of logging history in British Columbia are commemorated with exhibits including seven steam locomotives.

The park covers more than a hundred acres with indoor and outdoor exhibits and walking trails that detail the history of forestry in British Columbia. An original steam locomotive takes you from the entrance to the main exhibits of logging and milling equipment, passing over an old wooden trestle bridge.

The museum is just north of Duncan on the Trans-Canada Highway at 2892 Drinkwater Road, about forty-three miles north of Victoria. Open from May to September. Admission: adult, ❹; senior and student, ❷; child, ❷; child (5 and younger), free. For information, call ☎ (250) 715-1113 or consult 🖳 www.bcfor estmuseum.com.

In the former Duncan train station on Canada Avenue is a hidden treasure, the **Cowichan Valley Museum**. Displays trace the railroad history of the area as well as two extraordinary collections; one room holds the contents of a general store, frozen in time from about 1920, and the other, a hospital emergency room from not long after. The museum is open daily except Sunday. For information, call ☎ (250) 746-6612.

Northwest of Port Alberni at the end of a fjord that nearly transects the island is the **McLean Mill National Historic Site**. Here is the last surviving steam sawmill in Western Canada. You'll find a complete logging village, a millpond, dam, rainforest, and a small railway. The site on Smith Road is open from May to August. Admission: free. For information, call ☎ (250) 723-8284.

At Long Beach on the west coast of Vancouver Island, two hundred miles northwest of Victoria on Highway 4, the **Pacific Rim National Park Reserve** includes Long Beach, the West Coast Trail, and the Broken Group Islands.

Long Beach is the easiest to reach; it is a spectacular seven-mile-long stretch of sand on the Pacific Ocean. Considered one of the most beautiful stretches of ocean coast in British Columbia, huge rolling waves carry in a wealth of fascinating sealife and spread it on a broad expanse of fine golden sand.

Wickaninnish Centre, next to Long Beach, provides informative displays on the Pacific Ocean and nature tours of the beach and adjacent forests.

The forty-eight-mile-long **West Coast Trail** travels through a dense coastal rain forest of cedar, hemlock, spruce, and fir trees.

An annual Whale Festival in March and April celebrates the migration of twenty thousand gray whales along the park's shoreline.

Long Beach is open year round; the West Coast Trail is open April to October, and the Broken Group Islands from May through September. The preserve is on the west coast of Vancouver Island between Ucluelet and Tofin, about two hundred miles from Victoria. Highway 4 is the only road to the area.

Hourly, daily, and annual parking permits are available at Long Beach. Contact the park at ☎ (250) 726-7721 for more details.

West of Parksville on Highway 3 toward Port Alberni on the road to Long Beach is **Cathedral Grove**. This stand of giant Douglas fir and western red cedar is one of the few remaining on the west coast, one of the best examples of the virgin forests that greeted the first Europeans to visit the west coast. Natives regarded Cathedral Grove as a sacred place.

The tops of the tall trees form a cathedral-like ceiling high above your head while the thick tree trunks, some as old as eight hundred years, rise as pillars from a forest floor of delicate fern.

Strathcona Provincial Park is a mountain wilderness near the center of Vancouver Island. Its 520,000 acres feature mountains, valleys, lakes, alpine meadows, fast-flowing streams, and small glaciers. The trees in this area were already old when Captain James Cook of the Royal Navy landed at Nootka Sound on the west coast in 1778.

At 7,150 feet the Golden Hinde is the island's highest point. And Della Falls is the highest waterfall in all of Canada, with a 1,400-foot drop in three cascades.

Strathcona Provincial Park is off Highway 28, thirty miles west of Campbell

River. Admission: Ralph River ❹ per party; Buttle Lake ❹ per party. For information, consult 🖳 www.env.gov.bc.ca/bcparks/explore/parkpgs/strathco.htm.

The **Mount Washington Resort** ski area straddles the provincial park. The mountain is a prodigious snow magnet, although the surrounding areas have a relatively temperate climate. In a typical year some or all of the six golf courses in the Comox Valley stay open all year, permitting a combination of skiing and golfing on the same day.

The Mount Washington Resort is accessible via the Strathcona Parkway out of Courtenay. Skiers will find forty-two runs and five chairlifts, with a 1,657-foot vertical drop. Cross-country skiers can enjoy twenty-five miles of marked trails along high alpine lakes and forests. For information on the resort, call ☎ (250) 334-3234 or consult 🖳 www.mtwashington.bc.ca.

Another smaller ski area, Forbidden Plateau, nineteen miles from Courtenay, shut down in 2000 with uncertain prospects for reopening.

Other Communities on Vancouver Island

Nanaimo. On the east coast about forty miles north of Victoria, Nanaimo is the second-largest city on the island with a population of more than 71,000.

Nanaimo's economy is based on forestry, with a large pulp mill nearby and a commercial herring and salmon fishing fleet.

For tourists Nanaimo is a jumping-off point for Long Beach across the island on the west coast, for saltwater fishing in the Strait of Georgia, and for skiing at Mount Washington and Mount Arrowsmith in winter.

North Cowichan. The local economy is based around forestry. The area includes the small communities of Chemainus, Crofton, and Maple Bay, and is adjacent to the City of Duncan.

Storm waves crash on the shores of the Pacific Rim National Park
Photo courtesy of Tourism Vancouver Island

Wall murals all over the Village of Chemainus draw half a million people each year. Near Duncan, the BC Forest Museum is also attracts a major draw.

Campbell River. The small city of about thirty thousand residents sits at about the midway point of the island on the east coast, about eighty-seven miles from Nanaimo.

Campbell River claims to be the salmon capital of the world, a label also claimed by Port Alberni nearby. Campbell River is the gateway into the oldest provincial park in British Columbia, Strathcona Park, and close to skiing opportunities at Mount Washington.

A bit closer to Nanaimo are the twin communities of **Comox** and **Courtenay**, both drawing economic sustenance from the Canadian Forces Base in Comox and the forest industry. Rich agricultural land of the Comox Valley is used for dairy farming and hog, sheep, and cattle operations, as well as for numerous horse farms.

The Southern Gulf and Coastal Islands

The many islands between mainland British Columbia and Vancouver Island are a delight to explore. You're very likely, though, to have to share the scenery with whales, bald eagles hunting salmon, and tourists in search of all three.

The Southern Gulf Islands sit in the channel between Vancouver Island and the mainland of British Columbia, just above the border between Canada and the United States. They are served by the passenger and car ships of BC Ferries. The principal islands, from north to south, include Gabriola, just offshore of Nanaimo; Salt Spring; Galiano; Mayne; Pender; and Saturna.

Gabriola is an artist and writer's colony, well off the beaten path.

Salt Spring Island is very green, home to many sheep and goat farms. The population of about ten thousand is based around Ganges Village, where a weekly agricultural and handicrafts market is held as well as larger spring and fall fairs. There are more than a hundred bed and breakfasts on the island, seventy shops, and several dozen studios and galleries; road signs are keyed to a map that delivers visitors to the studios. For information about the studio tour, call ☎ (250) 537-9865 or consult 🖳 www.saltspring.com/studiotour.

Just west of Ganges Village a winding gravel road leads to the top of **Mount Maxwell**, a park with spectacular views of the region.

Salt Spring is served by ferry from Vancouver Island with large vessels from Swartz Bay to Fulford and smaller ferries from Crofton to Vesuvius. There is also service from Tsawassen on the mainland to Long Harbour.

Galiano Island was named after Spanish explorer Dionisio Alcala Galiano, who sailed the local waters more than two centuries ago. Local tribes of the Coast Salish Nation visited the island to harvest grapes, salal, and salmon berries and hunt elk, deer, and grouse. Today the island's bluffs and beaches offer places to view eagles riding the updrafts and otters, seals, and orca whales swimming just off shore; some 130 species of birds live there or visit. Jewels include **Montague Provincial Park**, which has three white shell beaches. **Dionisio Provincial Park**, at the far west tip and reachable only by boat, offers spectacular views of the North Shore mountains.

BC Ferries pull into Sturdies Bay on the island from the Swartz Bay terminal on Vancouver Island or from Tsawassen on the mainland.

For information, call ☎ (250) 539-2233 or consult ▣ www.galianoisland.com.

Mayne Island was visited by Captain George Vancouver in 1794; members of his crew camped at Georgina Point, leaving behind a coin and knife that were found more than a century later by early settlers. In the 1850s Captain George Richards of the Royal Navy surveyed the area aboard HMS *Plumper;* he named the island after his lieutenant, Richard Charles Mayne.

Early homesteaders settled in the areas around Miners Bay, named after the hopeful visitors to the area who used the island as a midway stopping point en route to the Cariboo Gold Rush of 1858.

The temperate climate of the island lead to an industry of hothouse tomatoes, including some greenhouses large enough to drive horse-drawn cultivators through the plants. Much of that industry ended when Japanese gardeners who had lived on the island were forcibly relocated to inland Canada during World War II.

Today the island's year-round population is less than one thousand. Ferries from the mainland and Swartz Bay put in at Village Bay.

For information, consult ▣ www.mayneislandchamber.ca.

Pender Island, actually two nearby islands connected by a small bridge, is reachable by BC Ferries from Swartz Bay or Tsawassen or by an inter-island connection to the terminal at Otter Bay on North Pender Island.

You'll find information at a web page run by a bed and breakfast on the island, ▣ www.penderislands.com.

Saturna Island is the southernmost of the Canadian islands in the Gulf. It includes about a dozen small bed and breakfast and cottage resorts and a few stores. BC Ferries serves the island from Swartz Bay and Tsawassen to a terminal at Government Wharf at the western tip. Winter Cove Park to the west includes trails through mixed forest and marsh and sanctuary to ducks, eagles, shore birds, seals, and otters. At **East Point Regional Park** a lighthouse marks the end of the island and the swirling currents of Boundary Pass; orca whales regularly summer just off shore.

For information, consult ▣ www.saturnatourism.bc.ca.

Scattered among the islands are hundreds of overnight anchorages and thirty-four marine parks that offer safe anchorage and moorings. Some provide fresh water supplies and sanitary facilities while others are undeveloped.

The largest marine provincial park, **Desolation Sound** on the mainland north of Powell River, includes thirty-seven miles of shoreline set against the snow-peaked Coast Mountains, a marine park of stunning beauty that is virtually unmatched in the world.

Sail and motor boats can be chartered at marinas up and down the BC coast. If you are qualified to operate a vessel, you can charter on a bare-boat basis or you can hire a boat and captain for several days or more. Some of the charter boat companies offer luxurious vessels with gourmet chefs and amenities.

QUEEN CHARLOTTE ISLANDS

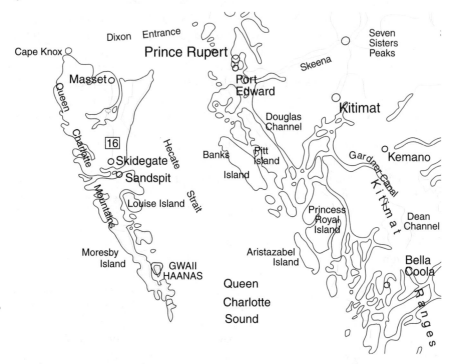

Other waterborne adventures cruise from Campbell River (served by air from Vancouver) to the Johnstone Strait to the north and among the Queen Charlotte Islands as well. Stops may include abandoned Haida villages such as Skedans, Tanu, and Ninstints. The strait is populated with large numbers of killer whales, humpback whales, Dall's porpoises, harbor porpoises, and Stellars sea lions; its shores and tidal shelves are home to sea stars, sea cucumbers, barnacles, mussels, scallops, red rock crabs, moon snails, and more.

To reach cruises further north among the Queen Charlotte Islands, visitors usually fly to Sandspit on Moresby Island.

The Queen Charlotte Islands

The 138 islands in the Queen Charlotte group cover some 1,100 square miles and feature a diverse range of vegetation zones from rain forest to alpine tundra. Thousands of years of isolation have resulted in the evolution of several distinctive island species. More than a million seabirds nest along the shoreline, and even more migratory birds pass through in the spring and fall.

Ferry service runs from Prince Rupert on the far north coast of the mainland of British Columbia. You can also fly to the islands from Prince Rupert or by floatplane from Vancouver and other points.

The **Queen Charlotte Islands Museum** in Skidegate displays Haida totem poles, ethnological and archaeological collections, as well as historical and paleontological materials. The museum at Second Beach is open daily in summer, and daily except Tuesday and Sunday the remainder of the year. Admission: adult, ❶; child (13 and younger), free. For information, call ☎ (604) 559-4643.

The **Gwaii Haanas National Park Reserve and Haida Heritage Site** in south Moresby Island in the Queen Charlotte Islands is open to a select few visitors under a program of Parks Canada and the Council of the Haida Nation.

Call ☎ (604) 559-8818 for information and reservations or write to the Gwaii Haanas National Park Reserve, Box 37, Queen Charlotte, B.C. V0T 1S0. You can also consult 📖 parkscanada.pch.gc.ca/parks/british_columbia/gwaii_haanas_marine/gwaii_haanas_marine_e.htm.

Whale Watching

The Queen Charlotte Strait off the northeast coast of Vancouver Island and narrow Johnstone Strait on the Inside Passage have the largest concentration of killer whales (*Orcina orcas*) on the planet. And the waters on the exposed west coast of the island are popular vacation spots for gray whales and humpbacks.

Whale watching companies leave from a number of ports on Vancouver Island, including the west coast ports of Tofino and Ucluelet, at the south end near Victoria and Sooke, and on the northeast coast of Vancouver Island near Port McNeill and Telegraph Cove.

And when it comes to vacationing, orcas have some very particular favorite spots including Robson Bight in Johnstone Strait where large numbers gather regularly to rub their bellies on beach pebbles. Robson Bight itself is a protected ecological reserve, but visitors can still see plenty of whales nearby.

The commercial whale watching outfits employ networks of spotters to help them deliver their promised sightings. Some operators use fast (and rough) inflatable rafts to chase out to locations where whales have been spotted.

A whale-watching expedition off Vancouver Island
Photo courtesy of Tourism Vancouver Island

Others take a more leisurely approach, using large boats that cruise waters deemed popular with whales.

And for a high-tech wrinkle, you can look for a company that offers "whale listening" using underwater microphones to eavesdrop on whale conversations.

Orcas live in "pods" of about five to twenty animals. The families are based around a dominant female, who can live to be seventy-five years old; males have a life expectancy of only fifty years. Males usually stay in the same pod as long as their mother is still alive.

In Johnstone Strait orcas are most abundant between June and October. Grey whales and humpback whales migrate up and down the Pacific coast of North America, passing Vancouver Island in the spring (starting in March) on their way north to the Gulf of Alaska, and again in the fall on their way south to the warm waters off Mexico. Some whales, though, choose to stay in the rich feeding grounds off Vancouver Island all summer.

Chapter 9
Coastal Mountains and Interior British Columbia

From Vancouver Route 99 heads due north to Whistler; on the way up the Strait of Georgia is on your left to just beyond Britannia Bay and the Coastal Mountains loom off the right shoulder.

On the site of the historic **Britannia Beach Mines**, twenty-two heritage buildings of the **British Columbia Museum of Mining** house artifacts and equipment that reflect the history of mining. There's an underground tour and demonstration of old and new mining equipment, including a gravity-fed concentrator and an area where visitors can pan for gold.

The Britannia Beach mines, thirty-two miles north of Vancouver, were once one of the major sources of copper in North America. Today mining operations have ended, but the museum offers a rare glimpse into the underground world.

The mineral wealth of the area was discovered in 1888 when a prospector shot at a deer; the animal's thrashing hooves exposed mineralized rock below the moss. Geologists determined that Britannia Mountain held copper.

In 1899 mining engineer George Robinson raised capital to exploit the riches; eventually the site came under control of the Britannia Mining and Smelting Company, a branch of the Howe Sound Company, which was to operate the mine for the next sixty years. The first ore was shipped to the Crofton Smelter on Vancouver Island in 1904. The mine reached a peak of copper production during World War I. The company town at Britannia included theaters, libraries, billiard rooms, swimming pools, and more.

On March 21, 1915, an avalanche descended on the Jane Camp at the base of the mountain, killing sixty men, women, and children. The town was re-built at a higher level on the mountain. Tragedy struck again, twice, in 1921 when Mill No. 2 burnt to the ground, and then a massive flood destroyed the small community on the banks of Britannia creek, killing thirty-seven people.

By 1929 the Britannia mines were the largest copper producer in the British Commonwealth; during the next decade, the mine also began to produce zinc and pyrite. And once again military demands for copper—this time during World War II—drove up the prices.

In 1956 a railroad line was completed from Squamish to North Vancouver, and two years later the Squamish highway was completed, ending a reliance on boats for access. During the next two decades the price of copper declined while expenses rose, and by 1974 the mine closed.

Today the mine thrives as a tourist attraction. Visitors board a mine train at the West Portal for a view of workings 1,200 feet under the ground demonstrating many of the old methods of hard rock mining. Other parts of the tour include a visit to the base of the massive Mill No. 3, built in 1922; it is one of North America's last remaining gravity-fed concentrators. Here you will also find the restored Assay Lab, which contains the museum's geology collection.

Impossible to miss is a modern-era, 235-ton super mine truck in the industrial yard; nearby are older and smaller pieces of mining equipment.

The museum is in Britannia Beach off Highway 99, about twenty-six miles from Vancouver on the road toward Whistler. Open daily May through October. Call ☎ (604) 896-2233 or ☎ (604) 688-8735 for information and for hours at other times of the year. You can also consult 💻 www.bc museumofmining.org. Admission: adult, ❷; senior (65+) and student, ❷; preschool, free; family, ❹.

Garibaldi Provincial Park is a high mountain wilderness surrounding one of Canada's deepest lakes. Lake Garibaldi, about an hour's drive north of Vancouver, formed from a natural dam of shale known as The Barrier, descends nearly ten thousand feet below the surface. The rugged, glacier-worn mountains, dominated by Mount Garibaldi, were formed during a relatively recent period of volcanic activity.

Other distinctive peaks within the park's 480,000 acres are the Black Tusk, Guard Mountain, and the Table. The park features a pristine forest of red cedar, hemlock and the majestic Douglas fir.

In the summer the park is open for camping and hiking; in the winter there are cross-country and ski touring trails.

The park is north of Squamish, east of Highway 99, forty miles north of Vancouver. For information, call ☎ (604) 898-3678, or consult 💻 www.env.gov. bc.ca/bcparks/explore/ parkpgs/garibald.htm.

Mainland BC Ski Areas

They grow them high and pile them deep in British Columbia, with more than three dozen ski areas that anywhere else in North America would be among the biggest and best. But they all have to compete with the two-headed monster of **Whistler** and **Blackcomb Mountains**, located in the town of Whistler northeast of Vancouver. By most appraisals they are the number-one ski resort in the West, an unbeatable combination of mountain, snow, and resort.

COASTAL AND INTERIOR BRITISH COLUMBIA

Chairs climb above the clouds at Blackcomb

The next time someone tells you something is stacked a mile high, think of Blackcomb with 5,280 feet of actual vertical drop. The top is a set of awesome bowls offering views of the spectacular Spearhead Range of Garibaldi Provincial Park. The bottom funnels down to a lively base ski town . . . and a short traverse across the base area you'll find the lifts that lead up to the summit of Whistler Mountain, a mere 5,020 feet high. Nothing else in North America comes even close.

One other point: although both mountains are huge, they start at a relatively low base of about 2,000 feet, with lifts topping out at 7,494 feet. This means you'll be about a mile lower than the highest mountains in Colorado and Utah, greatly reducing the effects of high altitude on visitors from lower places.

With seven Alpine bowls, Whistler is the larger of these two mammoths, but Blackcomb's upper steeps are the more awe-inspiring, if awe is what you're after.

Average annual snowfall is thirty feet at the mountaintop, and both mountains hold the snow deep into the spring. Blackcomb's glacier at the top is usually open into August.

Besides the outstanding ski facilities, there is the Resort Municipality of Whistler. The entire valley, with more than 3,500 rooms, is made up of dozens of condominium complexes, small luxury hotels, and a resort village that offers shops, restaurants, and entertainment.

The Canadian Olympic Association has chosen Whistler as the bid city for the 2010 Winter Olympics; a selection for that event is expected during 2003.

For information on Whistler, call ☎ (604) 932-3141 or ☎ (800) 766-0449 or consult 🖳 www. whistler-resort.com.

Other important ski areas in British Columbia include:

Apex Mountain Resort. Penticton. 2,000-foot vertical, fifty-six trails. ☎ (250) 292-8222 or 🖳 www.apexresort.com.

Big White Ski Resort. Kelowna. 2,656-foot vertical, 100 trails. ☎ (250) 765-3101 or 🖳 www.bigwhite.com.

Cypress Bowl. West Vancouver. 1,750-foot vertical, twenty-five trails. ☎ (604) 926-5612. 🖳 www.cypressbowl.com.

Fernie Alpine Resort. Fernie. 2,811-foot vertical, ninety-two trails. ☎ (250) 423-4655 or 🖳 www.skifernie.com.

Blackcomb and Whistler Mountains, Whistler

Grouse Mountain Resort. North Vancouver. 1,210-foot vertical, seventy-eight trails. ☎ (604) 984-0661 or 🖥 www.grousemtn.com.

Panorama Ski Resort. Invermere. 4,000-foot vertical, eighty-two trails. ☎ (250) 342-6941 or 🖥 www.panoramaresort.com.

Red Mountain. Rossland. 2,800-foot vertical, seventy-nine trails. ☎ (250) 362-7384 or 🖥 www.ski-red.com.

Sun Peaks Resort. Sun Peaks. 2,894-foot vertical, sixty-four trails. ☎ (250) 578-7222 or 🖥 www.sunpeaksresort.com.

Northwestern British Columbia

One of the more remote significant museums in Canada, the **Museum of Northern British Columbia** in Prince Rupert traces ten thousand years of human habitation on British Columbia's north coast. Included is a collection of Tsimshian, Tlingit, and Haida artifacts dating from prehistory to recent times, and the history and artifacts from the fur trade with Europeans, rail construction, and the establishment of the Port of Prince Rupert.

Located at First Avenue and McBride Street in Prince Rupert, the museum is open daily in the summer, and daily except Sunday for the rest of the year. General admission is free. Guided tours ❶ per person. Harbor tours offered in summer, ❹. For more information, call ☎ (250) 624-3207.

In Port Edward, a small community just below Prince Rupert—near the end of the British Columbia coastline where it meets the Alaskan panhandle—the **North Pacific Cannery Village Museum** is the oldest and most complete restoration of its kind in British Columbia, with exhibits on fishing and the fish processing industry, life in an 1889 cannery village, and the role of Chinese and First Nations people in the fishing industry.

Daily during July and August, and on weekends in May, June and September, visitors see *The Skeena River Story,* a play about the history of the fishery.

The museum is located at 1889 Skeena Drive in Port Edward. Open daily May to September. Admission: adult, senior, and youth (12–18), ❷; child (6–16), ❶. For information, call ☎ (250) 628-3538.

Way up north, above Prince Rupert on the British Columbia border with Alaska's Misty Fjords National Monument, the **Kitwanga Fort National Historic Site** commemorates the culture of the Tsimshian people and their history. The site encompasses *Ta'awdzep* or Battle Hill, a natural feature. On top are remains of fortified houses occupied during the historic period. Situated near an important trade route between Skeena and Nass Rivers, the site was fortified with a palisade at the beginning of the nineteenth century to enclose five houses and food storage pits.

From the fort Gitwangak people under their powerful chieftain, Nekt, waged battles to control fishing sites, protect trade routes, and enhance their prestige. The fort was abandoned after Nekt's death. Although not part of the site, totem poles located at nearby village Gitwangak tell the story of Nekt.

The site is located seventy-five miles northeast of Terrace, near the village of Kitwanga on Highway 16. For hours and admission prices call ☎ (250) 996-7191 or consult 🖳 parkscan.harbour.com/kf. Visitors must climb a long flight of stairs to reach the site.

The largest park in British Columbia is **Tweedsmuir Provincial Park** with more than 2.4 million acres of wilderness scenery, Located east of Bella Bella on the coast and Bella Coola inland. There is a canoe route with six portages from Turner Lake to Kidney Lake; canoes may be rented at Turner Lake.

For information on Tweedsmuir North in Smithers call ☎ (250) 847-7320 or consult 🖳 www.env.gov.bc.ca/bcparks/explore/parkpgs/tweed.htm. For Tweedsmuir South in Williams Lake call ☎ (250) 398-4414 or consult 🖳 www.env.gov.bc.ca/bcparks/ explore/parkpgs/tweedsmu.htm.

East of Prince Rupert in Hazleton is the **'Ksan Indian Village**, a reconstructed Gitksan Native Village such as the one that stood on the same site when the first European explorers came to the Hazelton area. Tribal houses are decorated with paintings, carved interior poles, and screens painted in traditional Northwest Coast Indian style.

'Ksan dancers perform traditional dances, and you can take a guided tour of several historic structures in the area. This is one of the few places that really provides insights into Aboriginal life before the advent of Europeans.

The 'Ksan village is located in Hazelton, 762 miles north of Vancouver by road in the interior between Prince Rupert on the coast and Prince George in the interior. For information, call ☎ (250) 842-5544 or consult 🖳 www.ksan.org.

Interior British Columbia

About one hundred miles west of Prince George is **Fort Saint James National Historic Site**, a commemoration of the role of the redoubt in the Pacific Slope fur trade. The fort, founded by Simon Fraser in 1806 during his exploration of a route to the west coast via the Fraser River, includes five original and two reconstructed log buildings.

This site, open from May through September, is also part of a research program with the Nak'azdli Elders Society that records their oral history and transcribes it into written documents for the elders. For information, call ☎ (250) 996-7191 or consult 🖳 parkscan.harbour.com/fsj.

The highest point in the Canadian Rockies is 12,900-foot-high **Mount Robson**, southeast of Prince George. Unlike many other great mountains, it is easily seen from a major road, off the Yellowhead Highway near the Alberta border.

Hiking trails lead from the highway through the Valley of the Thousand Falls to the mountain's north face, visible only from the vicinity of Berg Lake, where chunks of Berg Glacier break off and dot its surface.

From the decaying remnants of a once-bustling gold rush town, **Barkerville**, east of Quesnel, has been brought back to life as it was at the height of the gold rush days. In the 1860s, when gold was valued at $15 an ounce, more than $50 million worth was taken out of the area and Barkerville seemed headed to becoming the biggest community north of San Francisco and west of Chicago. But it all stopped as quickly as it began when the gold rush ended.

There are more than fifty buildings that predate 1900 in today's Barkerville. A museum features more than forty thousand artifacts. Interpreters offer demonstrations of mining, blacksmithing, and domestic skills and explain Victorian etiquette and British justice. In the summer season live theater is offered at the Theater Royal. Sermons are delivered in Saint Saviours Church.

Barkerville has also been the set for several western movies. For information and seasonal hours, call ☎ (250) 994-3332.

Eastern British Columbia to the Alberta Border

In southeastern BC, the **Rossland Historical Museum and Gold Mine Tour** tells the mining and social history of the area through artifacts, displays, and an underground mine tour.

Located at the junction of Highways 22 and 3B in Rossland on the border with Idaho, the museum is open from mid-May to mid-September. Admission to museum and mine tour: adult, ❸; senior and student, ❷; child (6–13), ❷; child (younger than 6), free with adult. For information, call ☎ (250) 362-7722; off-season, ☎ (250) 362-5820. 🖳 www.rossland.com/Seedo/museum.html.

Kokanee Glacier Provincial Park is a nearly undeveloped park of rugged, untouched mountains, glaciers, lakes, rivers, and forests. Most of the park is higher than 5,500 feet in the Sloan range of the Selkirk Mountains in southeastern BC. *Kokanee* is a Kootenay First Nation word meaning "red fish," a reference to the land-locked salmon of Kootenay Lake.

From Highway 3A Kokanee is about twelve miles northeast of Nelson, and from Highway 31A just north of Kaslo. Open year-round.

One of the region's most important waterfowl habitats is the **Creston Valley Wildlife Management Area** in the southeast corner of the province on the Idaho border. During migration in the spring and fall thousands of birds rest and feed at the fifteen managed ponds in the center's seventeen thousand acres. The area has more than 250 species of birds, fifty species of mammals, and thirty species of reptiles and amphibians.

Open year-round for hiking, biking, birdwatching, canoeing, fishing, or camping; the Interpretation Centre is open from mid-April to mid-October. The peak season for migration is the fall and spring. Admission: Entrance fee to the Intrepretation Centre, per person, ❶; family, ❸. For more information, call ☎ (250) 428-3260 or ☎ (250) 428-3259 or consult 🖳 www.env.gov.bc.ca/bc parks/ explore/parkpgs/kokangla.htm.

Fort Steele Heritage Town is a lovingly restored East Kootenay town of about 1890 to 1905, including more than sixty restored, reconstructed, and original buildings. You can visit an operating bakery, general store, newspaper office, confectionery, and restaurant. The Wasa Hotel has a museum with exhibits on the history of Fort Steele and the area. There's also a working steam railroad and horse-drawn wagons.

Living History Street Dramas bring to life the rise and fall of Fort Steele; interpreters portray characters such as homemakers, gardeners, and black-smiths who lived and worked in the town at the turn of the century.

Fort Steele is located ten miles northeast of Cranbrook on Highway 93–95. Open year-round. Admission: adult, ❷; family, ❹. For information, call ☎ (250) 426-7352 or consult 🖳 www.fortsteele.bc.ca.

Kootenay National Park, on the west side of the border with Alberta, is traversed by the Kootenay Parkway (Highway 93). You'll find a variety of plant life from alpine tundra in the upper reaches to stands of Douglas fir and prickly pear cactus at lower altitudes in the south. You may see Rocky Mountain bighorn sheep, mountain goats, elk mule deer, and whitetail deer.

A nature trail leads across the Vermilion River, past iron-rich clay banks, up along Ochre Creek and on to the cold mineral springs known as the Paint Pots. The iron in the water has seeped into the clays giving them a vivid orange color. Aboriginal people from both sides of the Great Divide gathered clay for decoration and trade and considered the area to be sacred.

There are more than 125 miles of hiking trails branching off the parkway.

The park is in the southeast corner of BC. The north entrance borders Banff National Park on Highway 93 South; it is located about twenty miles from Banff, Alberta. Open year-round; some facilities and services are seasonal. For information and fees, contact the park in Radium Hot Springs at ☎ (250) 347-9615 or the West Gate Information Centre (summer only) at ☎ (250) 347-9505.

The **Radium Hot Springs Pools** at the southern end of Kootenay National park are built around hot mineral springs in a beautiful mountain setting. You can soak in 40 degree Celsius (about 102 degrees Fahrenheit) water or swim in a cooler Olympic-sized pool. The pools are located near the town of Radium Hot Springs. Open daily with reduced hours in winter; for information and rates, call ☎ (250) 347-9485 or consult 🖳 www.worldweb.com/parkscanada-kootenay.

From the warmth of a hot spring to the near-permanent frost of the icefields is a short distance in southeastern BC.

More than four hundred glaciers are still at work sculpting the mountains of **Glacier National Park** above Cranbrook. With as much as seventy-five feet of snowfall each year, steep slopes and annual snowfall make it one of the world's most active avalanche zones. Snow sheds protect sections of the Trans-Canada Highway 1 and the railway from avalanches.

Half of its area is tundra where alpine meadows burst into flower for a few weeks each summer. At lower altitudes the high precipitation yields a lush rain forest of spruce and fir.

Services include guided hikes, strolls, and workshops. In the winter there is back-country skiing.

The park is located between Golden and Revelstoke on the Trans-Canada Highway 1, about two hundred miles west of Calgary. Open year-round.

For information, call the Revelstoke office at ☎ (250) 837-7500, or the Glacier Park visitor center at ☎ (250) 837-6274, or consult 🖳 parkscan.harbour. com/glacier.

A century ago the region was an awesome challenge for the builders of the Canadian Pacific Railway. At the **Rogers Pass Centre** in Revelstoke, you can learn how the builders of the Canadian Pacific Railway blazed a path through the rugged Selkirk Mountains. The interpretive center resembles part of the four miles of snow sheds constructed to protect the rail line and the highway.

The center is located on the Trans-Canada Highway 1, fifty miles west of Golden and forty miles east of Revelstoke. Open daily in summer, and from Thursday to Monday in the winter. For information and rates, call ☎ (250) 837-6274 or ☎ (250) 837-7500 or consult 🖳 www.revelstokecc.bc.ca/vacation.

A sixteen-mile drive in **Mount Revelstoke National Park** on the Summit Parkway passes through dense, old-growth rain forests of giant cedar and pine, subalpine forest, and alpine meadows and tundra. The Giant Cedars hiking trails take visitors through a stand of one-thousand-year-old red cedars.

Mount Revelstoke offers a view of the ice-clad peaks of the Monashee Range, and on the eastern horizon, the Selkirk Mountains. Running through the park are the Columbia and Illecillawaet Rivers. The park is located near Revelstoke on the Trans-Canada Highway 1, four hundred miles northeast of Vancouver and 245 miles west of Calgary. Summit Road is open late May to September. A paved parkway to the summit of Mount Revelstoke is open when clear of snow.

East of Vancouver, from Burnaby to Kamloops

At the **Burnaby Heritage Village** just east of Vancouver costumed interpreters guide visitors through an historical village museum with more than thirty buildings, recreating British Columbia from the 1890s through 1925.

Exhibits include an old Chinese herbalist shop stocked with potions, snake-skins, toads, and exotic herbs. The latest news of 1925 is available at the town printer. And children can join a class in a one-room schoolhouse, complete with a school marm.

Heritage Village is located within Deer Lake Park, off Highway 1. For information, hours, and rates, call ☎ (604) 293-6500 or consult 🖳 www.burnaby parksrec.org/villagemuseum/villagemuseum.html.

One of the best thrill rides you can take without approval from your insurance agent may be the **Hell's Gate Airtram** in Hope. The cable car makes a five-hundred-foot descent into the Fraser River Canyon to Hell's Gate where as much as 200 million gallons of water per minute flows through the 110-foot-wide gorge. At the bottom are spectacular overlooks and and the Salmon House Restaurant, famed for its salmon chowder and grilled salmon steaks.

Hell's Gate was a barrier to all but the strongest salmon as they journeyed inland to spawn. A fish-ladder built in 1945 gave them a way around the most treacherous part.

The Airtram is located 125 miles east of Vancouver on the Trans Canada Highway 1 at the Hope exit. Open mid-April through mid-October; admission ❸. For information, call ☎ (604) 867-9277 or consult 🖳 www.hellsgate.bc.ca.

The **Salmon Run on the Adams River**, about forty miles east of Kamloops, is one of the world's biggest sockeye salmon runs, a river of writhing red fish. The river is protected in its seven-mile run between Adams and Shuswap lakes.

Salmon that have fought their way up the Fraser and Thompson rivers start arriving in Adams River in October. In a dominant run on the Adams River, which occurs about once every four years, as many as two million salmon jam into the creek to spawn with up to 200,000 human visitors there to watch.

Near the town of Harrison Hot Springs, about seventy-five miles east of Vancouver, **Minter Gardens** offers ten tiered gardens with three aviaries, a petting zoo, and other entertainment. This is a place of topiary Victorian ladies, waterfalls, a living maze, and a rare collection of Penjung Rock Bonsai.

The gardens are on Trans Canada Highway 1 at 52892 Bunker Road, Rosedale. Open from April to October; for rates and information, call ☎ (604) 794-7191 or consult 🖳 www.minter.org.

South of Vancouver

The **Fort Langley National Historic Site** is a restored 1827 Hudson's Bay Company trading post. In addition to trade with natives, the Fort traded sea otter pelts to the Russians, and its salmon packing operation sold products to Hawaii and Australia. In the 1850s Fort Langley became the principal staging point in the Fraser River gold rush.

Located in Fort Langley on the Fraser River, about twenty-five miles southeast of Vancouver via the Trans-Canada Highway 1. Open daily year-round. For information and rates, call ☎ (604) 466-4005 or consult 🖳 parkscan.harbour. com/fl.

In Steveston the **Gulf of George Cannery National Historic Site** tells the tale of fish canneries in a factory that first opened in 1894 at the mouth of the Fraser River. The cannery was used until 1979. Exhibits include a canning line, demonstrations, and a film. The nearby waterfront is home to Canada's largest commercial fishing fleet.

The cannery is located thirty minutes south of Vancouver. Open daily in July and August, daily except Tuesday and Wednesday in the spring and fall, and closed in the winter. Call ☎ (604) 664-9009 for hours and rates or consult 🖳 parkscan.harbour.com/ggc.

Part III
Alberta

Chapter 10
Alberta

Alberta is the Canada of most people's imagination, a place of awesome mountains, high alpine lakes, impossibly blue glaciers, and vast oceans of snow. And somewhat incongruously, Alberta is also the home of two of Canada's most modern cities: the beefy brawn of Edmonton and the boom-and-bust energy capital of Calgary.

Along its western border are the picture-perfect mountain towns of Banff, Lake Louise, and Jasper; the last two are connected by one of the most awe-inspiring drives in the world, the Icefields Parkway.

Alberta is in some ways the Texas of Canada. A big, sprawling place that has mountains and prairies, cowboys and oil men, small towns and prosperous cities.

History

Native populations have lived in Alberta for at least eleven thousand years since around the time of the retreat of the glaciers of the last great Ice Age. Evidence of the daily lives of Alberta's earliest inhabitants—including buffalo jump sites (cliffs where the animals were lead to their deaths), hunting implements, and teepee rings—have been unearthed by archaeologists at many sites in and around Calgary.

The natives had a subsistence economy, hunting the province's plentiful buffalo and other game and gathering berries and roots.

The natives of Alberta were drastically changed almost immediately after their first contact with Europeans. The first outsiders had settled in Nova Scotia in 1604, moving on to Ontario and Québec by 1640. Traders were on the shores of Hudson's Bay in Eastern and Central Canada in the late 1600s, trading metal tools and weapons for furs and other natural treasures. The man-made goods gradually moved westward in trades among tribes.

The Canadian West, though, remained largely uninhabited by Europeans, except for a few trading posts, until the late nineteenth century.

It was developing fashion trends that drove much of the early explorations of interior Canada, led by the market for beaver hats, which were popular

ALBERTA

among European men. Heavy hunting had made the beaver nearly extinct in Europe at the same time that huge numbers of the animal were found in the New World.

The Hudson's Bay Company was granted a broad charter of privileges to about one-third of North America in 1670. In the mid-1700s the company sent representatives into the wilds of what is now Alberta to set up trading posts to seek furs from the natives. Members of the Cree nation became important middlemen in the fur trade.

American traders from Montana were also operating their own forts in Alberta, principally trading whiskey to the natives and settlers; the success of the whiskey trade also brought with it a great deal of crime and misery.

Fort Whoop-Up, near present-day Lethbridge, was the main whiskey fort in the area. There was no established government in the area, and violent lawlessness prevailed. At the same time massive hunting of the buffalo began to significantly diminish the animal's numbers. There was concern about the safety of the emerging Canadian nation, including fears of an invasion from America.

The Mounties Are Sent In

It was against that backdrop that Sir John A. MacDonald, Canada's first prime minister, created the North West Mounted Police in 1873. After a long march westward from Manitoba they headed directly to the notorious Fort Whoop-Up. Their assignment was to keep peace between the settlers and the natives, encourage more immigration, and make it safe for the construction of a transcontinental railroad.

Sales untaxed. Alberta is the only province that does not have a provincial sales tax on goods and services. There is, though, a 5 percent tax on hotel rooms, and the national Goods and Service Tax (GST) of 7 percent is levied on non-essential items.

Calgary was founded in 1875 when a detachment of the Mounties arrived and established a fort at the confluence of the Bow and Elbow rivers in a mostly uninhabited area. The territory was named by one of the commissioners of the fort after his birthplace in Calgary Bay on the Isle of Mull in Scotland. Fittingly, *calgary* is a Gaelic word meaning "clear running water," a commodity readily available in icy streams descending from the mountains.

In 1881 Calgary consisted of a Hudson's Bay Store, an I. G. Baker Company Store, the Mountie barracks, and had a population of about seventy-five.

By the 1880s the buffalo had all but vanished from the prairies.

The Hoodoos, east of Drumheller

The Railroads Open the West

Settlers brought in by the Canadian Pacific Railway (CPR), completed in 1883, set up farms. By 1891 the local population was nearly four thousand. The pioneers came from many countries including the British Isles, Scandinavia, and Ukraine; the agricultural base they established and their mix of cultures continue to this day to influence Calgary.

The CPR established its station and the townsite on its own land, naming most of the early major streets after officials of the railroad. The CPR also created and sold home lots in subdivisions—stratified by economic class—in the town. The presence of the railroad line and station helped establish Calgary as a meat packing center.

In 1905 Alberta and Saskatchewan joined the confederation as provinces. While Edmonton grew as an administrative capital city, Calgary developed as a ranching center and later as an oil town after the first discoveries of petroleum in the Turner Valley in 1914 and the larger Leduc oil field in 1947.

The railroad had another effect on the region as it established several important hotels and promoted tourism. In 1888 the CPR opened the Banff Springs Hotel, one of the largest hotels of the day with luxurious accommodations for those who came to "take the waters" at the hot springs; the Banff springs had been discovered in 1883 by railroad workers. Then in 1890 the CPR opened a small chalet on the shores of Lake Louise for visitors.

An oil refinery was built in 1923; the developing energy industry took off in the years that followed, surging during the energy crisis of the 1970s. Calgary became headquarters for many major international energy concerns and for a number of years had the highest per capita income in all of Canada, as well as the largest number of American expatriates.

The boom town atmosphere was put forth again with the 1988 Winter Olympics, which exposed Calgary to the world.

Alberta Geography

The Rocky Mountains arose as the result of the lateral movement of the North American continent, which buckled, folded, and compressed the land, eventually raising the sea floor above water level. The great sea withdrew toward the Arctic Ocean and the Gulf of Mexico; fossils of soft-bodied sea animals are still visible in rocks in high alpine areas.

Much of the present-day landscape of Alberta was formed during the last Ice Age, which ended a mere ten thousand years ago. The ice cap that covered much of the area at that time receded, scouring the land. Melting of the ice also created large flows of water, which gouged deep channels including Calgary's river valley.

The moving glaciers brought along large quantities of rocks that were frozen in the ice, depositing the debris where it melted. Some huge boulders in Alberta, known as "erratics," are unrelated to any of the local geology.

The remains of the glaciers are still very much evident in the Canadian Rockies. The most spectacular is the Columbia Icefield, which straddles the border between Alberta and British Columbia with a river of ice covering more

Moraine Lake

than 125 square miles and reaching a depth of more than one thousand feet.

The Columbia is the largest icefield south of Alaska, 233 square miles of shimmering ice and snow to the west of the Icefields Parkway, which runs from Lake Louise to Jasper.

Alberta Festivals and Events

February

Calgary Winter Festival. Calgary. ☎ (403) 543-5480. 🖥 www.calgarywinter fest.com. A celebration of winter, sport, and entertainment. Events include a Parade of Light, Mardi Gras Party on Olympic Plaza, the Patrons' Benefit Gala, and the Wheez'n Sneeze Fun Run. Admission varies with the events. Olympic Plaza, Canada Olympic Park.

May

Calgary International Children's Festival. Calgary. ☎ (403) 294-7414. 🖥 www. calgarychildfest.org. A six-day festival of children's theater, dance, puppetry, opera, dance, comedy, and music from around the world.

June

Calgary International Jazz Festival. Calgary. Nine days of big bands, blues, international beat, be-bop, and Dixieland music. Activities include dance parties, gospel music, a paddlewheeler cruise and late-night jam sessions. Held at various downtown venues. Admission varies with events.

The Works: A Visual Arts Celebration. Edmonton. ☎ (780) 426-2122. Artists and artisans from across Canada and around the world present their work in and around Churchill Square. Admission: free.

July

Banff Festival of the Arts. Banff. ☎ (403) 762-6301. Music, opera, voice, musical comedy, dance, drama, workshops, and visual arts performances. Nearly one thousand artists from Canada and around the world come together to work and perform with an international faculty of professional artists. Special feature events include the International String Quartet Competition and the Theatre Arts Festival. Held July through August each year at Banff Centre, 107 Tunnel Mountain Road. Admission: varies depending on the event.

    Calgary Folk Music Festival. Calgary. ☎ (403) 233-0904. 🖳 www.calgary folkfest.com. Local, national, and international performers are on stage at the week-long festival that includes zydeco, blues, country, jazz, rockabilly, klezmer, roots, Celtic, and folk rock. Prince's Island Park and various other venues. Admission: varies by event.

    Edmonton International Street Performer's Festival. Edmonton. ☎ (780) 425-5162. A ten-day program of street theater, spectacle, magic, dance, and music provided by magicians, clowns, jugglers, musicians, and comics in downtown Edmonton.

August

Edmonton Heritage Festival. Edmonton. ☎ (780) 488-3378. A tradition for more than twenty years with music, song, dance, food, and art from around the world. Held in Hawrelak Park. Admission: free.

    Edmonton Folk Music Festival. Edmonton. ☎ (780) 488-3378. 🖳 www. efmf.ab.ca. Held in Gallagher Park near the Muttart Conservatory in early August of each year.

    Fringe Festival. Edmonton. ☎ (780) 448-9000. 🖳 www.fringe.alberta.com. The Old Strathcona area claims the largest festival of alternative theater in North America. Events include new plays, innovative interpretations, street entertainment, theater in the park, and dance. Admission: free to festival grounds and outdoor shows. Ticket prices for indoor performances vary.

Chapter 11
Calgary

Calgary is a glittering, modern city of chrome-and-glass skyscrapers. It rises out of the prairies to the east and runs head-first into the Canadian Rockies to the west. There's a touch of the oil-fueled brashness of Dallas tempered by cowboy realism.

The entire city has sprung up in just over a century, with much of its growth occurring in the last few decades. The oil industry soared in the 1970s during the energy crisis, then fell back to earth in the 1980s. The energy business has had a slow but steady resurgence in recent years. Today something like three out of four jobs in Calgary are in some way related to the energy industry.

Calgary welcomed the world to the XV Olympic Winter Games in 1988 with facilities at the Canmore Nordic Centre, Nakiska ski resort, and the Canada Olympic Park just outside of town. The Calgary Winter Festival celebrates winter activities and commemorates the Olympics every February.

The population of Calgary is about 842,000. Many young singles are drawn to the city for the high-tech and high-pressure jobs; at various times Calgary has also had the largest population of Americans living in Canada.

Around Town

Hot in the summer and generally cold in the winter, Calgary sometimes benefits from a wintertime Chinook wind that blows in like a hot air heating system.

Many downtown buildings include connections to enclosed pedestrian walkways and bridges, known as the Plus 15 Walking System (so-called because they're at least fifteen feet above ground).

The town grew up around the place where the Bow and Elbow rivers come together. Metropolitan Calgary is divided into a four-quadrant grid. The Bow River separates North from South, and Centre Street–Macleod Trail splits the city into East and West.

Most of the downtown is located in or near the S.W. quadrant. A rough outline of downtown would run from the Bow River on the north, Ninth Avenue on the south, Centre Street to the east, and Eighth Street to the west.

CALGARY, BANFF, AND EDMONTON

The Calgary Stampede

The biggest hoopla in this brash city is the famed Calgary Stampede, which draws about 250,000 excited spectators and participants for two weeks in July.

The Stampede is one of the world's biggest rodeos as well as a huge agricultural fair, but it's also a lot more than that. To some observers it's a spectacle on the Roman scale, without the Christians and lions but including gladiator races in the form of chuckwagon sprints.

It all starts with a grand parade with the streets of Calgary overflowing with observers; the front curb positions are usually gone well before dawn. A typical two-hour parade features something like seven hundred horses, a few thousand marchers, and more than 150 floats and bands.

The parade route runs westward along Sixth Avenue from Second Street S.E., then south on Tenth Street S.W. and finally eastward on Ninth Avenue.

In downtown Olympic Plaza (Rope Square during the festival) offers a free pancake breakfast along with Western entertainment from concerts to square dancing to mock gunfights. Each night most of the city goes gaga with music, dancing, gambling, fireworks, and a general party atmosphere at every turn.

The Stampede Park includes a carnival with rides and games, a Native Village with exhibits and demonstrations by members of the Five Nations (Blackfoot, Blood, Sarcee, Stoney, and Piegan), county-fair-like agricultural displays, and various stages for events such as the World Blacksmith Competition.

Park admission: ❸; extra charges are levied to enter the stadium for races and special events.

At the daily rough-and-ready rodeo you'll find saddlebronc and bareback riding, calf roping, wild cow milking, steer wrestling, and what may be the most dangerous event, bull riding.

The chuckwagon races pit four teams of four horses in an all-out sprint for the finish line of a track that is five-eighths of a mile long.

Each evening there's a ninety-minute spectacular on the outdoor stage that includes singers, dancers, musicians, and variety acts.

The International Stock Show harkens back to the agricultural roots of the first Stampede. Events include the world champion blacksmith's contest, a steer classic, championship auctioneers, cutting horse competitions, and more than a dozen pure-bred livestock shows that feature everything from huge heavy horses to pet-sized miniature horses, which are no more than thirty-four inches tall.

Stampede grandstand admission: ❹, including admission to the park itself. Two-day tickets are also available.

Tickets for the best seats and some entire events sell out well in advance of the Stampede. You can order tickets through the Calgary Exhibition and Stampede office; for information, call ☎ (403) 261-0101 or ☎ (403) 261-0500. Tickets are sold through Ticketmaster at ☎ (403) 777-0000, ☎ (403) 269-9822, or (800) 661-1767.

The Stampede is held in early or mid-July, with the Stampede Parade on the first Friday of the event. For information, call ☎ (403) 261-0101, ☎ (403) 261-0500, or consult ▤ www. calgarystampede.com.

All's fair. The Stampede began as an annual agricultural fair in 1886. In 1912 four wealthy local ranchers financed the Calgary Stampede as a one-time event; they were brought together by one Guy Weadick, a professional trick roper. The festival was revived in 1919 but it wasn't until 1923 that the Stampede became an annual event.

Overlooking the Stampede. One way to sneak a peek at the events and celebrations of the Calgary Stampede is to visit Stampede Park the night before the parade for the "sneek-a-peek," which is a combination of a dress rehearsal and an opening ceremony that attracts tens of thousands of people.

Attractions in Calgary

The **Glenbow Museum** in the heart of downtown Calgary is a must-see. Western Canada's largest museum, it is renowned for its display of artifacts depicting the cultural history of the settlement of western Canada, a mineralogy gallery, and a display of military history of many stripes from knights in armor to Japanese samurai outfits to equipment of the two world wars.

The lobby of the Glenbow features "Aurora Borealis," an interpretation of the Northern Lights in acrylic and brushed aluminum, accompanied by an eerie light and music program.

The Warriors Gallery presents an eclectic collection of weapons from crossbows and AK-47 assault guns to ancient armor of English and German knights to the "spiritual armor" of First Nations warriors.

The source. Glenbow is named after benefactor Eric Harvie's ranch; like many of the wealthiest of Calgary, he made his fortune from bubblin' crude.

A traditional ceremonial place is shown at the Otter Flag Tipi. When it was installed in the 1970s workmen needed help from the wives of the elders—the traditional homemakers—to make it stand properly. Nearby is a spectacular headdress that includes ninety-six eagle feathers trimmed with ermine tails. Other treasures include a collection of navel cord amulets. A child's umbilical cord, which is preserved in a beaded case, was tied to a knot of the native's hair for good luck.

A collection about the prairie includes some of the things the early settlers brought with them. They include woks and a foot-operated dental drill carried by Chinese workers who helped build the Canadian Pacific Railway.

One gallery shows items from the dismal 1930s, when a combination of the Great Depression, the arrival of the Russian Thistle weed, and a mass invasion of grasshoppers—all capped off by a crippling drought—brought misery to the prairies. Items include a child's sweater made from old socks and a flour-sack brassiere.

The museum, located within the Convention Centre complex across from the Calgary Tower at 130 Ninth Avenue S.E., is open every day, with late hours on Thursday and Friday nights. The summer is the busiest season. Admission: adult, ❸; student and senior, ❷; child (6–12), ❶. For information, call ☎ (403) 268-4100 or ☎ (403) 268-4209, or consult ▣ www.glenbow.org.

On a clear day or night the view from way above at the **Calgary Tower** covers the modern buildings of downtown, the ski jump towers of the 1988 Winter Olympics, and in the distance the snow-covered Rockies.

There's a one-minute elevator ride, or 762 steps for the ambitious, to the top of the 620-foot-tall tower. You can stop to ogle from the Observation Terrace or sit down at the Panorama Dining Room, which makes a one-hour revolution as you dine on fine fare.

A ticket for the elevator costs ❷ for adults and the observation gallery is open from 8 A.M. until 11 P.M. year-round. Call for updates to hours and fees. The tower is located at 101 Ninth Avenue SW. For information, call ☎ (403) 266-7171 or consult a web page at ▣ www.calgarytower.com.

The **Calgary Zoo, Botanical Gardens** and **Prehistoric Park** is just outside downtown on St. George's Island. Canada's largest zoo, and one of the best in North America, the world-renowned institution is home to more than 1,400 animals, thousands of species of plants, and an unusual Prehistoric Park populated with life-sized models of dinosaurs.

One of the stars of the show is Kamala, an Asian elephant who wields a paintbrush. The paintings are sold to support the zoo. I don't know much about art, but there is a certain unschooled exuberance to her abstracts.

Recent additions include the Canadian Wilds exhibit, which immerses visitors in a natural landscape of the Aspen Woodlands, the Canadian Rockies, and the Boreal Forest. There are underwater viewing ports to watch polar bears, walk-through greenhouses for tropical birds, and night-for-day rooms where visitors can observe nocturnal creatures at their liveliest.

Admission: October to April, adult, ❷; child (2–17), ❶; child (younger than 2), free. May to September, adult, ❸; child (2–17), ❷; child (younger than 2), free. The Prehistoric Park is open June through September only. For information, call ☎ (403) 232-9300 or consult 💻 www.calgaryzoo.ab.ca.

At the **Calgary Science Centre** you can travel through space or through a DNA molecule. This lively hands-on museum is also home of the Pleiades Mystery Theatre and the Science Theatre.

Exhibits include ExploreAsaurus, which turns visitors into paleontologists with the chance to dig up fossils, crawl around in an egg, and come face to face with a ferocious meat eater. Oil From a Stone shows how new technologies are used to get more oil out of the ground.

The museum is located at 701 Eleventh Street SW. Admission: adult, ❷; youth (13–18), ❷; child (3–13), ❶. Prices include access to all exhibits and one Discovery Dome Show. Additional Discovery Dome Shows are ❶. For information, call ☎ (403) 221-3700 or consult 💻 www.calgaryscience.ca.

You'll learn more than you ever thought to ask about grain at the **Grain Academy**, an industry-sponsored celebration of the grain industry in Alberta from its beginnings with the early settlers to the modern techniques of today.

The academy is located at the Round-Up Centre in Stampede Park. Admission: free. For information, call ☎ (403) 263-4594 or consult 💻 www.agricore. com/about/graina.html.

The **Aero Space Museum of Calgary** offers one of the largest collections of aircraft, engines, and artifacts in North America, tracing the history of Canadian aviation. The museum has extensive research materials including technical manuals, drawings, and photographs. Facilities include workshops where technicians restore planes.

The museum building is a former Royal Air Force drill-hall from the 1940s.

Permanent exhibits include a "Histories of Flight" gallery, which highlights the evolution of flight, and an exhibition of original drawings by Flight Lieutenant Ley Kenyon titled the "Great Escape," which illustrates the escape of seventy-six officers from Stalag III during World War II.

The museum is located at #10, 64 McTavish Place NE., near the Calgary International Airport. Open daily. Admission: adult, ❷; student and senior, ❶; child (7 and older), ❶; child (younger than 6), free; family, ❸. For information, call ☎ (403) 250-3752 or 💻 www.asmac.ab.ca.

The City of Calgary's **Inglewood Bird Sanctuary** includes trails through river and forest and along a lagoon. More than 250 species of birds have been identified here, as well as three hundred species of plants. Local stars include

Downtown Calgary to the east

bald eagles, great horned owls, and flocks of ducks, geese, and other water-birds. Animal residents include mule deer, beavers, and muskrats.

A visitor center offers maps of walking trails and presents occasional talks about the wildlife.

The sanctuary is east of downtown, just past the zoo, at Ninth Avenue and Sanctuary Road S.E. Open daily from dawn until dusk. Admission: free, but there are fees for guided hikes led by professional naturalists. For more information, call ☎ (403) 269-6688 or consult 🖳 www.calgaryparks-rec.com/parks_pathways/bird_sanctuary/default.asp.

The **Museum of the Regiments** offers a glimpse at some of Western Canada's military history including the Royal Canadians (the regiment, not the dance band, and officially known as Lord Strathcona's Horse), King's Own Calgary Regiment, Princess Patricia's Canadian Light Infantry, and the Calgary Highlanders. The museum also displays dioramas, models, miniatures, and artifacts.

Located at 4520 Crowchild Trail S.W., the museum is open daily except Wednesday from 10 A.M. to 4 P.M. Admission: free, but a donation of $5 per adult is requested. For information, call ☎ (403) 974-2850 or consult 🖳 www.nucleus.com/~regiments.

On the maritime side the **Naval Museum of Alberta Society** is a commemoration of the Royal Canadian navy since its formation in 1910. The collection includes artifacts from fighter aircraft that flew from the deck of Canadian ships, ship models, and guns. Free admission. The museum is located at 1820 Twenty-

CALGARY

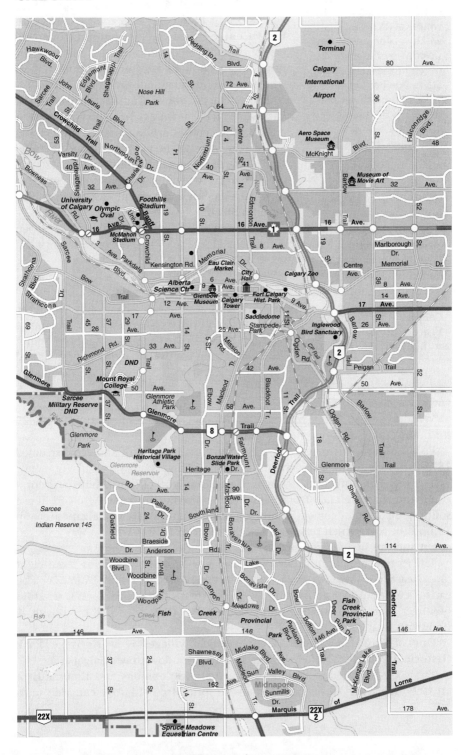

Hats on. One of the symbols of Calgary is the white cowboy hat. A white version of the classic cowboy hat made its debut in the Calgary Stampede Parade of 1947 and has been present at most ceremonies in Calgary ever since. In fact, when distinguished visitors and celebrities come to Calgary, they're not likely to receive the key to the city; instead, they're sworn in as an honorary Calgarian and given a large white cowboy hat as a badge of honor.

Calgary Convention & Visitors Bureau. ☎ (800) 661-1678.

fourth Street S.W. For information, call ☎ (403) 242-0002 or consult ▣ www.navalmuseum.ab.ca.

The bright blue cone atop the **Chinese Cultural Centre** marks the location of Chinatown, just outside of the downtown core. Many of the residents and workers are descendants of workers who came to build the railways in the 1880s.

The Calgary Chinese Cultural Centre, at 197 First Street S.W., features a museum of priceless artifacts and ceramic arts, an arts and crafts shop, and special events. The building is modeled after the Temple of Heaven in Beijing, built in 1420 and used exclusively by the Emperors for prayer to their patron deities. The seventy-foot-high ceiling includes 561 dragons and forty phoenixes.

Admission to the museum: general, ❶. Open daily from 11 A.M. to 5 P.M. For information, call ☎ (403) 262-5071.

The **Eau Claire Market** is something of a distant cousin to London's Covent Garden. Centered around a fresh food public market adjacent to the Bow River and Prince's Island Park is a wide range of restaurants and carts as well as specialty shops. The market itself is a lively warehouse of stalls and buskers. The market is located at Second Avenue and Second Street S.W. For information, call ☎ (403) 264-6460 or consult ▣ www.eauclairemarket.com.

Within the Eau Claire Market is an **Imax Theatre**. Call ☎ (403) 974-4629 for hours and admission rates.

Fort Calgary Historic Park, an historic riverside park and reconstructed 1875 fort, tells some of the colorful stories of Calgary's past.

The fort was built by the North West Mounted Police as home base for a command that stretched from Edmonton in the north to Fort Macleod in the south, a distance of some 350 miles. The present-day city of Calgary grew up around the fort, which remained in operation until 1914 when it was knocked down and the site covered over by railroad tracks and buildings.

The forty-acre park in the crook of the Bow and Elbow rivers is about eight blocks east of downtown at 750 Ninth Avenue S.E. Open daily from May 1 to early October. Admission: adult, ❷; senior (65+) and youth (7–17), ❶; child (younger than 6), free. For information call ☎ (403) 290-1875, or consult ▣ www.fortcalgary.ab.ca.

One of Canada's largest living historical villages is at **Heritage Park Historical Village**, about ten miles southwest of downtown Calgary.

The sixty-acre village includes more than 150 exhibits and thousands of artifacts depicting Western Canadian life prior to 1915. You can ride on a steam train, a horse-drawn wagon, or sail across a reservoir on the restored paddlewheeler SS *Moyie*. Hundreds of costumed volunteers and staff bring the park to life with shops, bakeries, and crafts demonstrations, and the reborn Wainwright Hotel offers old-style meals.

The C-Train runs to the Heritage Park station, where there's a bus ride to the park. The park is open daily from 9 A.M. to 5 P.M. mid-May to early September, and weekends and holidays from September through early October. Admission: adult, ❸; child (3–16), ❷, family, ❹. A free pancake breakfast is served between 9 A.M. and 10 A.M.

The park is located at 1900 Heritage Drive S.W. For information, call ☎ (403) 259-1900 or call ☎ (403) 259-1910 for recorded information. You can also consult web pages at 🖳 www.heritagepark.ab.ca.

Calaway Park is the largest outdoor amusement park in western Canada with twenty-five rides including the Corkscrew roller coaster, the Mountain Scrambler, and the Rocky Mountain Rail.

Located six miles west of Calgary on the TransCanada highway. All rides are included in admission. Call for hours and prices. The park is open weekends from mid-May to mid-June, and then daily until the end of August, returning to weekend operation until mid-October. Admission: adult, ❹; student and senior, ❸; child (2 and younger), free; families, ❹.

For information, call ☎ (403) 240-3822 or consult 🖳 www.calawaypark.com.

Sports and Recreation

The ski jump towers from the 1988 Olympic Winter Games are visible from many parts of the city of Calgary. Today they are the centerpiece of the **Canada Olympic Park**, which includes a small skiing hill, bobsled and luge tracks, a museum, ice skating, miniature golf, and a wide range of other winter and summer activities.

The ninety-meter ski jump is the highest point in Calgary. In the couse of the Olympics some thirty thousand cheering fans stood in the bowl at the bottom of the hill.

The designation as a ninety-meter hill is based on the distance most jumpers are expected to travel. The jump is now used for training because today's competitors are outjumping the hill, reaching 111 meters or more.

Skiing at the hill runs from October to March or early April with 90 percent of the snow produced by machine. The slopes are open during the week from 10 A.M. to 10 P.M. and on the weekends until 5 P.M.

The chilling plant runs most of the year, which permits use of the luge track for training in the summer, even when temperatures soar up to eighty-five degrees.

The bobsled run includes the famed Kreisel Turn, a 270-degree turn where riders are subjected to as much as 5 Gs of force. If the turn looks familiar, you may be replaying in your mind the famous crash of the Jamaican bobsled team. The surprise hit film about the team, *Cool Runnings*, was partially filmed at the Canadian Olympic Park, and the sled used in the movie is on display at a museum in the park.

Unlikely hero. Among the stars of the Calgary Olympics was Eddie Edwards, better known as Eddie the Eagle. The not-very-talented jumper constituted the entire British ski jumping team. He is best remembered for some very spectacular crashes, but in the process he managed to set a British record for the ski jump of sixty-eight meters, a record that remains unbroken and unchallenged by his countrymen.

The track drops about 350 feet over about a mile, with sleds reaching a top speed of as much as eighty miles per hour.

If you're not of Olympic caliber, you can get pretty close with a ride on the **Bobsleigh Bullet**, a one-person padded sled that follows the track by itself. The short but intense thrill costs about $45 and is offered during the winter only. In the summer there is the Road Rocket ride, which also costs $45. You can also arrange for luge lessons or rent a skeleton sled for a quick spin.

Jumpers practice year-round, changing in the spring from snow to a bristled carpet surface in the warmer months. In the summer the surrounding hills are also available for mountain biking.

Above the ski lodge is an Olympic museum with artifacts and interactive demonstrations. You can try out your timing on a bobsled start, utilize your logic on a ski racing gate layout, and test endurance and strength as demonstrations of the skills required of downhill skiers and ice skaters.

A virtual reality bobsled simulator reproduces the real track outside, featuring fourteen banked turns, including the 270-degree Kreisel Turn.

The park is located at 88 Canada Olympic Road S.W. For information and rates, call ☎ (403) 247-5452 or consult 🖳 www.coda.ab.ca/COP.

When the weather gets really rough, many Calgarians go inside to places such as the **Southland Leisure Centre**, a year-round recreation park that has ice arenas, an indoor climbing wall, a huge wave pool, and the Southland Screamer, a twisting, turning waterslide in the dark. The facility is at 200 Southland Drive S.W. For information and rates, call ☎ (403) 251-3505 or consult 🖳 www.calgaryparks-rec.com/recreation/leisure.

Another undercover park is the **Village Square Leisure Centre** at 2623 Fifty-sixth Street N.E. Here you'll find more than five acres of indoor attractions including a wave pool, the six-story-high Thunder Run Waterslide, and other activities. For information and rates, call ☎ (403) 293-4884 or consult 🖳 www.calgaryparks-rec.com/recreation/leisure.

West of Calgary in the foothills of the Canadian Rockies, **Spruce Meadows** is a renowned equestrian facility, home to three major show jumping championships: The National, The North American, and The Masters. The Masters is the richest show jumping championship in the world, with more than $1.5 million in prize money.

Admission: adult and senior, ❶; child (younger than 12) free. Additional charge for special events. For information, call ☎ (403) 974-4200 or consult the Web at 🖳 www.sprucemeadows.com.

Skiing in the Rockies

Calgary serves as the gateway to half a dozen world-class ski areas including Lake Louise, Sunshine Village, Nakiska, Marmot Basin, and Fortress (across the border in British Columbia).

Calgary Area Sports Teams

The **Calgary Flames** of the National Hockey League play home games in the twenty-thousand-seat Canadian Airlines Saddledome in Stampede Park, which borders McLeod Trail Northbound and Seventeenth Avenue S.E. The arena can be accessed off Olympic way or Fifth Street S.E.

There is limited parking on the grounds. Your best bet is to park at an LRT lot and take the train. Exit at the Stampede Park stop, a short walk to the Dome.

The Flames are in the Western Division of the NHL, along with the arch-rival Edmonton Oilers, the Vancouver Canucks, and the Colorado Rockies. For information about the team, consult 💻 www.calgaryflames.com.

The **Saddledome** box office can be reached at ☎ (403) 777-4630; seats are also sold through TicketMaster at ☎ (403) 777-0000 or consult 💻 www.pen growthsaddledome.com.

The **Calgary Cannons** baseball team, a minor league AAA affiliate of the Chicago White Sox plays seventy-two home games at Burns Baseball Stadium. For information, call ☎ (403) 284-1111 or consult 💻 www.calgarycannons.com.

The **Calgary Stampeders** football club of the Canadian Football League team and winner of the 1998 Grey Cup has games at McMahon Stadium from July to the end of November. For information, call ☎ (403) 289-0205 or consult 💻 www.stampeders.com.

Calgary Visual and Performing Arts

The **Centre for the Performing Arts**, known to locals as The Centre, is home to the Calgary Philharmonic Orchestra ☎ (403) 571-0270, Theatre Calgary ☎ (403) 294-7440, and the Alberta Theatre Project ☎ (403) 294-7475.

The Centre is located at 205 Eighth Avenue S.E. For information, call ☎ (403) 294-7455 or consult 💻 www.theartscentre.org.

The **Alberta Ballet Company** performs at various locations. For information, call ☎ (403) 245-4222 or consult 💻 www.albertaballet.com.

The **Calgary Opera** performs at Jubilee Auditorium at 1415 Fourteenth Avenue N.W. The season runs from October to April. For information, call ☎ (403) 262-7286 or consult 💻 www.calgaryopera.com.

Alberta Theatre Arts presents contemporary theater at the Martha Cohen Theatre, 229 Ninth Avenue S.E. For information, call ☎ (403) 294-7475 or consult 💻 www.culturenet.ca/atp.

The **Pleiades Theatre** at 701 Eleventh Street S.W. is an intimate 220-seat showplace at the Science Centre used for Mystery Series. For information, call ☎ (403) 221-3707 or consult 💻 www.pleiadestheatre.com.

At Fort Macleod, the **Empress Theatre Society** puts on shows at the Empress, a restored theater of about 1912 used for live presentations. For information, call ☎ (403) 553-4404 or consult 💻 www.empresstheatre.ab.ca.

For entertainment of a more speculative sort, there are three casinos in Calgary, including the **Stampede Casino** located in the Big Four Building in Stampede Park.

Getting to Calgary

Calgary International Airport is about twenty minutes from the city center. For airport information, call ☎ (403) 735-1200, ☎ (403) 735-1372 or consult ▤ www.calgaryairport.com.

It's about a $30 taxi ride into town. You can also ride to town on the more reasonable **Airporter Bus**, which makes stops at a number of major downtown hotels; for information, call ☎ (403) 531-3909.

Airlines serving Calgary include Air B.C., Air Canada, American Airlines, Canadian Airlines International, Delta Airlines, Horizon Airlines, Northwest Airlines, and United Airlines.

A number of bus and car services link Calgary Airport directly to the winter and summer resorts of Banff and Lake Louise. You'll find their counters in the Arrivals section of the airport.

Bus service goes to the Greyhound terminal, west of downtown at Eighth Avenue SW and Sixteenth Street. For information, call ☎ (403) 265-9111 or (800) 661-8747.

Other bus services include: Airporter, from Calgary Airport to major downtown hotels, ☎ (403) 531-3909; Brewster Transportation, from Calgary to Banff and Jasper, ☎ (403) 762-6767; Laidlaw, to Banff and Lake Louise, ☎ (403) 762-9102, ☎ (800) 661-4946; and Red Arrow Express, to Edmonton, ☎ (403) 531-0350, ☎ (800) 232-1958.

Transport Within Calgary

Calgary Transit offers a system of buses and Light Rail Transit trains through the metropolitan area. The C-Train is free through the heart of downtown along Seventh Avenue S.W. from Tenth Street S.W. to Third Street S.E. Listen to the announcements to know when you are leaving the free zone. For other areas and for trips that enter or leave downtown, the fares are $1.60 for adults and $1 for children ages six through fourteen; free transfers are available between buses and trains. And Calgary Transit offers discounted ticket books and day passes.

For information on train and bus routes and schedules, call the customer service center or the transit information line at ☎ (403) 262-1000 or consult ▤ www.calgarytransit.com. You can also visit the center on weekdays at 240 Seventh Avenue S.W.

Hotels in Calgary

There are nearly ten thousand hotel and motel rooms in Calgary with about four thousand rooms in the downtown core.

Finding a place to stay in Calgary is ordinarily not a difficult task, with the exception of Stampede time in mid-July when it is very difficult, if not impossible, to do so. If you're bound to visit in July, be sure to book well in advance and be prepared to pay top rates or to stay some distance from town, or both.

There's a cluster of moderate-to-inexpensive motels near Sixteenth Avenue N.W. and the Crowchild Trail that have declared themselves members of "Motel Village." They're a good alternative to downtown accommodations.

You can seek assistance in finding a place to stay by contacting the Visitor Information Services of the **Calgary Convention and Visitors Bureau.** The bureau is located at the base of the Calgary Tower at 101 Ninth Avenue S.W. Call (800) 661-1678 or locally to ☎ (403) 263-8510.

The visitors bureau also operates a web page at 🖳 www.discoveralberta.com.

You can also contact the **Bed & Breakfast Agency of Alberta** for information about their members at ☎ (403) 543-3900.

One bargain offering: the sprawling **University of Calgary** offers visitors low-priced accommodations in dorm rooms during the summer. Rates are even lower if you can produce a current student ID from another college. The university is a bit out of town in the northwestern suburbs. For information, call ☎ (403) 220-3203.

Dinosaur Country

Drumheller is a strange outpost of time in the "dinosaur country" of the Red Deer River Valley, about ninety-five miles northeast of Calgary.

Alberta's badlands, gouged out of the prairie by ancient rivers and ice, was once the domain of the dinosaur. The exposed rock of the Badlands reveals more than 70 million years of geological history in a mysterious moonscape.

The badlands, named by earlier settlers who found the soil "bad" for farming, was later found to be quite rich in fossil beds and coal. The Dinosaur Trail, a twenty-nine-mile loop starting in Drumheller, passes through points of interest in the Red Deer Valley and to the Bleriot Ferry, one of the last cable ferries in Alberta.

Coal was first mined in 1910. At one time more than 120 mines were active in the area. The Hoodoo Drive leads to old coal towns East Coulee and Rosedale.

It is also possible to take a scheduled bus from Calgary to Drumheller, although connections make a one-day roundtrip difficult.

The badlands of Alberta were sculpted by wind, water, and glacial erosion during the course of millions of years.

Scientists say the area in and around Drumheller has yielded more complete dinosaur skeletons from the Cretaceous period of about 64 million to 140 million years ago than anywhere else on Earth.

You can make a stop at the **Visitor Information Office** near the bus terminal in Drumheller for more information.

From Calgary head north on Highway 2 toward Edmonton, onto Highway 72 and then Highway 9 east. The town itself is all but hidden in a canyon below the main road.

In Drumheller is the **Royal Tyrrell Museum of Palaeontology**, home of one of the world's foremost collections of dinosaur specimens. The museum offers some of the best collections of dinosaur skeletons on earth including a rare complete reconstruction of the fearsome tyrannosaurus rex and a 100-million-year-old skeleton of a giant sea creature that was uncovered in the oil sands of northern Alberta. In fact the museum claims the world's largest gathering of complete dinosaur skeletons with some fifty in the collection and nearly 100,000 specimens of various types and sizes.

Most of the dinosaurs are presented in displays that give a sense of Alberta's setting tens of millions of years ago. An indoor garden houses living descendants and close relatives of the plants that grew during the age of the dinosaur 65 million to 350 million years ago.

The museum is named after Joseph Tyrell, who discovered the first remains of a dinosaur in the Alberta badlands in 1884; the creature was named the Albertosaurus.

The Tyrell is about four miles northwest of downtown Drumheller on North Dinosaur Trail in Midland Provincial Park, about ninety minutes northeast of Calgary. Open daily from May to September; daily except Mondays for the remainder of year, except holidays. Admission: adult, ❷; senior, ❷; youth (7–17), ❶; child (younger than 6), free; family, ❹. For information, call ☎ (403) 823-7707 or ☎ (403) 294-1992 or consult 💻 www.tyrrellmuseum.com.

About twelve miles east of Drumheller is the **Historic Atlas Coal Mine**, the last of 139 commercial coal mines in the Drumheller Valley. All of the above-ground workings—tipple, washhouse, mine office, and residences—have been restored. The tipple (where coal was sorted into sizes, stored, and then shipped) is the last of its kind in Canada. Interpretive programs concentrate on the history of mining, and the valley's social history. Tipple tour requires a moderate climb to the top of a six-story-high structure. The mine is off Highway 10. Open mid-May to mid-October. Admission: adult, ❶; family, ❸; extra fee for tipple tour. For information, call ☎ (403) 822-2220 or consult 💻 www.atlascoalmine.ab.ca.

Heading further south from Drumheller, southwest of Calgary, you'll come to **Dinosaur Provincial Park** in the Alberta Badlands. The park in the Red Deer River Valley is one of the world's richest fossil fields; dinosaur skeletons have been discovered dating back 75 million years. To protect the fossils much of the park is now accessible only through interpretive tours and hikes. The Field Station of the Royal Tyrrell Museum is located here; in specific areas, visitors may watch fossil preparation "in the field."

Access to much of the park is limited to conducted tours. Bus tours, offered six to ten times daily, wind through the Badlands, making stops among the hoodoos and other unusual rock formations.

The park is about thirty miles northeast of Brooks on the Trans-Canada Highway 1; a three-hour drive from Drumheller. Open May to late October. Admission to the park is free. Museum admission: adult, ❷; senior, ❷; youth, ❷; child (younger than 6), free. For information, call ☎ (403) 378-4342 or consult 💻 www.gov.ab.ca/env/parks/prov_parks/dinosaur.

Day Trips Amongst the Dinos

The badlands include two interesting day car trips. The **Dinosaur Trail** departs Drumheller for a thirty-mile loop through the area. The trail follows Highway

838 to scenic views of Horsethief Canyon and Horseshoe Canyon; there are walking paths down to the bottom of the canyons paved with millions of fossils.

The **Hoodoo Drive** is a fifteen-mile journey on Highway 10 into the phantasmagorical hoodoos southeast of Drumheller. The hoodoos are mushroom-like sandstone formations left behind by the ravages of time. Also on the road is the Atlas Mine, a coal mine preserved as an historical site. The Hoodoo Drive includes a side road to Wayne, home of the Last Chance Saloon.

Attractions West and South of Calgary

The **Western Heritage Centre** at the Cochrane Ranche Provincial Historic Site is a commemoration of the first large-scale cattle operation in western Canada. The ranch was a 189,000-acre spread established in 1881. Interpretive guides offer programs, displays, special events and tours.

The site is nineteen miles west of Calgary near Cochrane near the junction of Highways 1A and 22. The visitor center is open May to September, daily from 10 A.M. to 6 P.M.; the ranch site is open year-round. Admission is free, but donations are accepted. For information, call ☎ (403) 932-3242 (summer) or ☎ (403) 932-2902, or consult 💻 www.whcs.ab.ca.

All the way west of Calgary in Medicine Hat on the border with Saskatchewan, the **Clay Products Interpretive Centre** claims to have the world's largest display of Medalta pottery and Hycroft china, a major collection of turn-of-the-century pottery manufacturing equipment in North America, and the only known circular kiln in Canada. Open from May to October. Admission: adult, ❶; student and senior, ❶. The center is located at 703 Wood Street. For information, call ☎ (403) 529-1070 or consult 💻 www.medalta.org.

Medicine Hat is believed to have gained its name because of a Cree medicine man who lost his headdress in a battle with the Blackfoot. His followers beheld the hatless holy man as a bad omen and they surrendered, which was probably not the best move; according to legend, they were immediately killed.

In more modern times Medicine Hat became known for the gaseous riches that lay beneath the town. Railroad engineers drilling for water in 1883 instead found a vast field of natural gas; author Rudyard Kipling declared the town to have "all hell for a basement."

Southeast of Medicine Hat, **Cypress Hills Interprovincial Park** is Alberta's second largest park. The Hills rise from the flat prairie to an altitude of 1,464 meters. More than two hundred species of migratory birds and mammals, reptiles, and fish are found in the park. Park staff offer interpretive programs that explain the geography and history of the park, both in the amphitheater and on nature trails.

Activities include swimming, picnicking, fishing, canoeing, summer and winter camping, fifteen trails for biking, hiking, and cross-country skiing through mixed and lodgepole pine forests. For information, call ☎ (403) 893-3782 or consult 💻 cypresshills.com.

About sixty-two miles south of Calgary below Longview, the **Bar U Ranch National Historic Site** commemorates the history of ranching in Canada and of the ranch itself. The area includes a former North West Mounted Police detachment and the Pekisko Post Office with thirty-five buildings. Bar U Ranch is off Highway 22. For information, call ☎ (403) 395-2212 or consult 💻 www. parcscanada.gc.ca/parks/alberta/bar_u_ranch/bar_u_ranch_e.htm.

And then there is the famously named **Head-Smashed-In Buffalo Jump** near Fort Macleod, about ninety minutes south of Calgary. This one takes a bit of explanation. What we have here is one of the oldest, largest, and best-preserved buffalo jumps in North America, a cliff where for at least six thousand years the people of the Plains stampeded buffalo to their death. Blackfoot hunters would gather herds of buffalo to an enclosed basin and them stampede the animals in the direction of the cliff.

About the name: it memorializes an eighteenth century brave who apparently decided that a good spot to watch the stampede was from the base of the cliff. He was joined there by several hundred plummeting buffalo and met his death.

The site includes an interpretive center, trails, and an archaeological dig in the summer. At the base of the cliff is a thirty-foot-deep bed of ash and bones built up over thousands of years of use. The pit is full of artifacts ancient and more recent, but visitors are not permitted to remove any objects.

The site is about ten miles west of Highway 2 on Secondary Highway 785 near Fort Macleod. Open daily with evening hours in the summer. Admission: adult, ❷; student, ❷; child (7–17), ❶; child (younger than 6), free; family, ❸. For information, call ☎ (403) 553-2731 or consult 💻 www.head-smashed-in.com.

Also in Fort Macleod is the **Fort Museum** at the site of the first outpost of the North West Mounted Police. The museum recreates the early Mountie story, interwoven with details of the pioneer and aboriginal life.

The Fort's Royal Canadian Mounted Police Mounted Patrol performs the Musical Ride four times daily during July and August, wearing replica uniforms.

Open daily May 1 to mid-October, weekdays only for the remainder of the year; closed between Christmas and New Year's. Admission: adult, ❷; student and senior, ❷; child (younger than 6), free. Located at 219 Twenty-Fifth Street. For information, call ☎ (403) 553-4703.

Just north of the U.S. border, about thirty miles south of Fort Macleod and two hundred miles south of Calgary is the **Remington-Alberta Carriage Centre** where you will find one of North America's largest and finest collections of horse-drawn vehicles, with more than sixty on display. Visitors learn how buggies and carriages are made, try harnessing a horse, circle the wagons at a prairie campfire, and see quarterhorses, Clydesdales, and other breeds.

Open daily. Admission: adult, ❷; senior and youth (7–17), ❶; child (younger than 6), free; family, ❸. Horse-drawn vehicle rides: adult and senior, ❶; child (4–17), ❶; child (3 and younger), free; family, ❸. Located at 623 Main Street. For information, call ☎ (403) 653-5139 or consult 💻 www.remingtoncentre.com.

Due south of Calgary on the border with the United States, the **Waterton Lakes National Park** is a relatively small but rich national park where the mountains meet the prairie, joined along the southern border by a sprawling American park. More than half of Alberta's plant species is found in its grasslands, meadow, forests, and marshes. Upper Waterton Lake, the largest of Waterton's signature chain of lakes, is the deepest lake in the Canadian Rockies.

The park provides habitat for wildlife such as bison, deer, moose, elk, bighorn sheep, bear, cougars, and wolves. Each fall visitors witness a major migration of waterfowl.

In ancient times the area was an important hunting area for the Kootenai tribe, and several hundred archeological sites dating as far back as nine thousand years have been identified in the park. The Kootenai were pushed aside by the Blackfoot in the eighteenth century, and they were in turn forced to move by expanding white settlements in the nineteenth century.

In 1932 the park was joined with Montana's Glacier National Park to form the Waterton-Glacier International Peace Park, the first cross-border park.

Activities include hiking, camping, cross country and back country skiing, snowshoeing, and wildlife viewing. Guided boat tours are offered on Upper Waterton lake in season.

Located about thirty-five miles south of Fort Macleod and 166 miles southwest of Calgary via Highways 5 or 6. Admission about ❶ per person or ❸ for a group pass for as many as ten visitors. For information, call ☎ (403) 859-2224 or consult ▣ parkscanada.pch.gc.ca/waterton.

West of Fort Macleod on the border with British Columbia is the **Bellevue Underground Mine** where you can put on a miner's helmet and lamp and follow the corridors taken by coal miners from 1901 to 1961. You'll travel down nearly a thousand feet of the old West Canadian Collieries mine tunnel. The mine is off Highway 3 in the Town of Bellevue in the municipality of Crowsnest Pass. Mine tours are conducted mid-May to mid-September and by reservation at other times of the year. Admission: adult, ❸; student and senior, ❷; child (7 and younger), free. For information, call ☎ (403) 562-7388.

Nearby is the **Frank Slide Interpretive Centre** in Blairmore Crowsnest Pass. Here you can learn the tragic story of a rockslide and avalanche down the east slope of Turtle Mountain in the Crowsnest Pass area in 1903. Some 90 million tons of rock obliterated the town of Frank in ninety seconds, killing at least seventy people and burying the entrance to a coal mine. The center presents the story with a film and exhibits on the history of the Crowsnest Pass settlement and the technology of underground coal mining. Open daily. Admission: adult, ❶; student, ❶; senior, ❶; child (younger than 6), free. For information, call ☎ (403) 562-7388 or consult ▣ www.frankslide.com.

The city of Lethbridge, southeast of Calgary, is another beneficiary of the petrochemical industry, as well as some of the best farmland in the province.

The **Sir Alexander Galt Museum** tells the story of Lethbridge from the first contact with the aboriginal people to the discovery of coal, the coming of the Canadian Pacific Railway, the building of the Lethbridge Viaduct, irrigation, and post-war immigration. Galt was a nineteenth-century financier for one of the region's early mines. The museum is located at the west end of Fifth Avenue South, off Scenic Drive. Call ☎ (403) 329-7300 for hours. Admission free.

Just outside Lethbridge is **Fort Whoop-Up**, a reconstruction of Alberta's most notorious whiskey trading post that was established in 1869 by American merchants. The center features details of the trade in furs and "fire water" between Americans and the Blackfoot Confederation. The North West Mounted Police brought the trade to an end in 1875. Guided tours of the fort and guided train tour of the river valley are offered. Mid-winter programs include ice sculpturing and demonstrations of historic winter activities. Admission: adult ❶; student ❶; child (5 and younger), free; family ❸. For information, call ☎ (403) 329-0444.

The peaceful, formal setting of **Nikka Yuko Centennial Gardens** in Lethbridge's Henderson Lake Park was created as a symbol of Japanese-Canadian friendship and by extension as an apology for the internment during World War II of some twenty-two thousand Canadians of Japanese heritage.

The Helen Schuler Coulee Centre and the **Lethbridge Nature Reserve** include the floodplain forests, coulee slopes, and prairie grasslands of the Oldman River region. The reserve includes a sanctuary for many plants and animals, including desert flora and fauna such as the prickly pear cactus, rock wren, and prairie rattlesnake. The lush cottonwood forests along the river support wildlife that includes the great horned owl, porcupine and white-tailed deer. There are hands-on exhibits and self-guided trails. The site is at Third Avenue and Scenic Drive, north of the CPR High Level Bridge, Indian Battle Park. Open daily from June to September. Admission: free. For information, call ☎ (403) 320-3064.

In the valley of the Milk River southwest of Cypress Hills, **Writing-on-Stone Provincial Park** preserves ancient petroglyphs inscribed on the smooth sandstone cliffs. The etchings of men, horses, guns, bows, and shields were made by nomadic Shoshone and Blackfoot.

You can also visit **Van Cleeve Coulee**, a nesting and perching ground for golden eagles and prairie falcons and a wildlife sanctuary. The park is decorated with hoodoos, once believed to harbor spirits. Activities include guided tours to the petroglyphs, hikes, walks, and audiovisual presentations.

The park, twenty-five miles southeast of Milk River on Highway 501, is open May to mid-October. The campground is open year-round. For information, call ☎ (403) 647-2364.

Between Lethbridge and Medicine Hat, the **Museum Society of Etzikom** and the **Canadian National Historic Windpower Centre** present hundreds of artifacts from the early homesteading days in southern Alberta. Outside, fifteen restored windmills recall the history of windpower as a force in Canada's history. The museum is in Etzikom, sixty miles southwest of Medicine Hat on Highway 61, the RedCoat Trail. Open June to early September. Admission: free. For information, call ☎ (403) 666-3737.

Chapter 12
Edmonton

Edmonton is less of a tourist draw than Calgary or Banff, although not for lack of effort.

Edmonton, the capital of the Province of Alberta, has:

- A world-class museum of culture and anthropology
- An out-of-this-world science and space center
- A step back into the past at a restoration of a frontier trading post and fort
- A huge indoor water park
- An indoor NHL-sized skating rink
- An outrageous roller coaster (indoors, of course)
- A reproduction of Columbus's *Santa Maria*
- Four working submarines on an indoor lake
- More than eight hundred trendy shops within a few square blocks
- At least a hundred varied places to eat within twenty minutes walk of each other.

That's the good news. The strange news: the last seven out of the ten are in one place, the almost indescribable West Edmonton Mall.

In this chapter you'll learn there is a lot more to Edmonton than the mall, but it is also impossible to ignore the place as its big enough to be a city of its own and is the number-one tourist draw in town.

About Edmonton

Located on the banks of the North Saskatchewan River near the geographic center of Alberta, greater Edmonton is home to more than three-quarters of a million people. From a small trading post in the late 1700s it is now Canada's fifth-largest city and the hub of Alberta's extensive oil, gas, coal, forestry, and agricultural industries.

Modern-day Edmonton was built with the proceeds from a changing mix of natural treasures: from furs to gold to land to coal, oil, and gas.

Edmonton's History

Humans have been in and around Edmonton for at least ten thousand years;

Edmonton, the provincial capital of Alberta

local deposits of quartzite were mined by natives for tools and weapons. Fur traders arrived in the eighteenth century; they were drawn in part because of the rich populations of fur-bearing animals in the region and because it was a place where the territories of the Cree and Assiniboine in the north and the Blackfoot of the south came together. The three tribal nations were often bitter enemies, but the trading post at Edmonton became a sort of neutral zone where they could sell their furs to the North West Company.

It was that lucrative fur trade that brought the explorers westward. In 1795 the North West Company built Fort Augustus, near the present-day town of Fort Saskatchewan. In October of that same year William Tomison established a nearby trading post for the fiercely competitive Hudson's Bay Company.

Tomison named the fort Edmonton House after Edmonton in England, the birthplace of Sir James Winter Lake, at that time the deputy governor of the Hudson's Bay Company.

The two companies opened up the area as they traded with the Cree from the north for beaver pelts, otter, martin, and fox, and with the Blackfoot from the south for buffalo meat, bear, fish, and muskrat furs. The two forts moved at least four times, usually side-by-side for protection, until they merged as Edmonton House in 1821. In 1830 the fort was moved to the site of today's Legislature Building grounds, where it remained until it was dismantled in 1915.

When the Hudson's Bay Company sold its governing right to the Dominion of Canada in 1870, vast tracts of land were made available for purchase for the first time. Settlement soon began just outside the walls of the stockade.

The first trans-Canada railway was run through Calgary instead of Edmonton in 1891, a decision that seemed destined to make to bring an end to Edmonton's development.

Edmonton visitor information. ☎ (800) 463-4667.

But it was the discovery of gold in the Yukon in 1897 that put Edmonton on the map. Newspapers told explorers that Edmonton could outfit them for the "All Canadian Route," an overland route to the Yukon and the gold fields that avoided the extreme difficulties of Alaska and the Chilkoot Trail. Unfortunately the All Canadian Route was an extremely difficult if not impossible trail itself, and many prospectors turned back and hundreds perished. Many disappointed gold seekers stayed in Edmonton to homestead.

The settlement incorporated as a city in 1904 with a population of about nine thousand. Alberta became a province of Canada the next year, and despite opposition from Banff, Vegreville, and especially Calgary, the new capital was placed in Edmonton.

Edmonton prospered during the 1930s and earned its nickname "Gateway to the North" as bush pilots transported vital medical supplies, food, and mail to isolated northern communities. During World War II Edmonton's strategic location was significant as a point on the easiest supply route to Alaska. Construction on the Alaska Highway, an important wartime project, began in 1942 with Edmonton serving as a major transportation and supply center.

On February 13, 1947, the Leduc Number One Well, twenty-five miles southwest of Edmonton, gushed forth a fountain of black crude oil. That discovery made Edmonton the "Oil Capital of Canada." Thousands of oil and gas wells were subsequently drilled within a one hundred-mile radius of the city.

Edmonton is one of the coldest big cities anywhere (any wonder why there's a huge indoor mall and waterpark?), and in some ways it feels as though it's still an unfinished frontier town. Some of its history can still be seen in the Old Strathcona district, where heritage buildings have been preserved as boutiques, galleries, restaurants, and bars.

Attractions and Museums in Edmonton

Fort Edmonton brings back the original 1846 Hudson's Bay Trading Post, using many of the old construction materials and techniques. The most important building is the Big House, the home of the Chief Factor of what was known as the Saskatchewan District.

You'll also find a remembrance of Edmonton in its early days in 1885, a reconstructed Jasper Avenue as the capitol city in 1905, and the city as it was during the 1920s. Visitors can ride on a 1919 steam train, street cars, wagons, ponies, and a stagecoach.

Located southwest of the city on the North Saskatchewan River, the park is open from mid-May to September. City buses let off passengers about a ten minute walk from the fort. Admission: adult, senior, youth (13–17), ❷; child, ❶. For information, call ☎ (780) 496-8787 or consult the Web at 🖳 www.gov.edmonton.ab.ca/fort.

EDMONTON

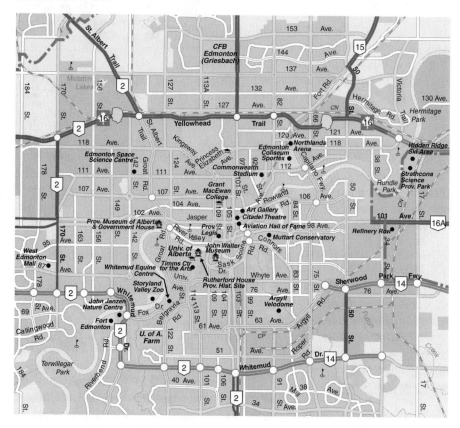

The culture and history of the entire area is gathered at the **Provincial Museum of Alberta**, a very traditional but very well presented collection from ancient fossils and tools to the First Nations to today's people and animals.

The Habitat Gallery recreates locations in the provinces' four natural regions: grassland prairie, parkland, mountain, and boreal forest. The Natural History gallery tells the geological history from dinosaurs to the Ice Age. The Native Peoples Gallery traces the history of aboriginal people in the province. And the 19th and 20th Century Gallery portrays the settlement of the west and the province's growth.

A recent expansion added the Gallery of Aboriginal Culture with exhibits that take visitors back eleven thousand years in Alberta. Artifacts range from ancient stone tools to nineteenth century garments to contemporary objects. The museum's collection of Blackfoot, Cree, and Athapaskan items is among the best in Canada. And kids of most ages are sure to appreciate the Bug Room and the Discovery Room.

The museum is located about three miles west of downtown at 12845 102 Avenue in Edmonton's western suburbs. Admission: ❶–❷. For information, call ☎ (780) 453-9100 or consult 💻 www.pma.edmonton.ab.ca.

The **Edmonton Space and Science Centre** in Coronation Park offers insights into the heavens with educational displays, films in the Devonian Imax Theatre, and planetarium shows in the Margaret Zeidler Star Theatre.

At the *Challenger* Centre visitors can take part in a simulated Space Shuttle mission. A computer lab offers explorations of the latest in high-tech machines. And there is also an observatory for up-and-coming astronomers.

The museum, located at 11211 142nd Street, is open daily except non-holiday Mondays. Admission: adult, ❷; child (3–12) ❶. For information, call ☎ (780) 451-3344 or ☎ (780) 451-9100 or consult 🖳 www.edmontonscience.com.

The **Valley Zoo** in Laurier Park caters mostly to younger visitors and has a fairly large collection of animals with a special section that has nursery rhyme characters, camels, ponies, and train rides. The zoo, located at Buena Vista Road and 134th Street, is open daily in summer; winter hours are limited. Admission: adult ❷; senior and child, ❶. For information, call ☎ (780) 496-6911 or consult 🖳 www.gov.edmonton.ab.ca/comm_services/city_ op_attractions/valley_zoo.

The glass pyramids of the **Muttart Conservatory** hold the sometimes frigid outside at bay, keeping alive indoor tropical and temperate worlds. The conservatories include plants, trees, and a small number of birds from places very different from the clime of Edmonton. The museum, at 9626 96A Street, is open daily. Admission: adult, senior, and child ❶. For information, call ☎ (780) 496-8755.

The **Edmonton Art Gallery** specializes in abstract formalism of the 1970s and Canadian historic art that includes painting, sculpture, photographs, prints, and drawings. Located at Sir Winston Churchill Square at 102nd Avenue and Ninety-ninth Street. Admission: adult, student, senior, child younger than 12, ❶. For information, call ☎ (780) 422-6223 or consult 🖳 www.gov.ed monton.ab.ca/comm_services/city_op_attractions/muttart.

On the third floor of the central police station, the small **Edmonton Police Museum and Archives** tells the story of law enforcement in Alberta from before the Royal Canadian Mounted Police (RCMP) to today. Exhibits include the old jail cells, tools of the police trade, and a stuffed rat that was an RCMP mascot. Admission: free. The museum is located at 9620 103A Avenue. For information, call ☎ (780) 421-2274.

Old Strathcona Historic Area

The original terminus of the rail spur that ran north from Calgary, Strathcona, grew as an independent town until it was incorporated into Edmonton in 1912.

Strathcona lies across the river from Edmonton and is reachable by a stroll across the North Saskatchewan River on the Waterdale or High Level bridges or by public transit.

The area in and around Eighty-second Avenue (Whyte Avenue) and 104th Street includes many buildings that date from around 1891. You'll find dozens of restaurants, boutiques, museums, and theaters.

There are a few small museums in Strathcona that have a special appeal to some; in other words, if this is what you're looking for, here's a fine example.

In a rebuilt version of the original Strathcona railroad station of 1891 you'll find the **C & E Railway Museum**, which offers a collection of railway memorabilia. The museum, at 10447 Eighty-Sixth Avenue, is open in summers only, and donations are accepted. For information, call ☎ (780) 433-9739.

The **Telephone Historical Information Centre** is a collection of all things telephonic, housed in Strathcona's original phone exchange building of 1912, at 10437 Eighty-Third Avenue. Open daily except Sunday. For information, call ☎ (780) 441-2077.

A City Under Glass

Edmonton's biggest tourist draw is not your ordinary K-mart and a food court.

This is the big kahuna of shopping malls, not just the biggest one in Alberta, or in Canada for that matter; some 20 million people pass through its doors each year. The **West Edmonton Mall** is the world's largest cathedral to modern commerce, enclosing some 5.2 million square feet with more than eight hundred stores and services including eight major department stores, nineteen movie theaters, and 110 eating establishments.

That might be enough to earn the mall more than its share of superlatives. But wait, there's more: the mall has an amusement park with twenty-five rides and attractions, a water park with the world's largest indoor wave pool, an ice skating rink, a dolphin lagoon, a submarine voyage on the world's largest indoor lake, and for some reason, an exact replica of Christopher Columbus's flagship the *Santa Maria*. Oh, and an indoor bungee jumping tower, a miniature golf course, a bingo hall, a dinner theater, and a gambling casino.

This is a place P. T. Barnum would be proud of. The monster indoor mall sprawls over the equivalent of about forty-eight city blocks; if that's beyond your strength (or will) you can rent a scooter to make your tour. And if you don't want to leave at the end of the day, you can rent a room at the luxury 354-room **Fantasyland Hotel**, which is attached to the mall. About half of the rooms are decorated in nine different theme fantasies: Roman, Hollywood, Arabian, Victorian Coach, Canadian Rail, Polynesian, Truck, Igloo, and African Safari.

This is nothing less than a city within the city, with more than twenty-four thousand people employed therein. Close to half of every dollar spent in Edmonton by visitors is left behind here; amazingly, there are still a few downtown stores and even a few downtown malls still in operation.

The mall includes just about every type of store you may want; in fact, the place is so big that a few companies have more than one storefront just in case you come in at the wrong end of the mall. (There are fifty-eight different entrances at last count.)

And believe it or not, the mall keeps expanding. The **Playdium** arcade and an **Imax** theater opened in 1999. Future plans include installation of a year-round rooftop golf driving range, a day spa, and a second hotel.

The five-acre **World Waterpark** includes twenty-two slides and attractions, the Raging Rapids inner tube ride, three children's play areas, and the world's only indoor bungee jump. Admission: peak season rates (mid-June to just after Labor Day, and the month of December) are adult, ❹; senior, ❸; child (3–10), ❷; child (younger than 2), free; family, ❹. In the off-season from mid-September to early June, except for December, the park offers discounted Early Bird tickets. During quiet periods, not all of the slides may be in operation; be sure to call for hours and seasonal rates. ☎ (780) 444-5310.

The **Submarine Voyage** takes visitors on a thirty-five-minute ride beneath the surface of the world's largest indoor lake. The twenty-four-passenger, self-propelled submarines tour a setting that includes real coral and more than one hundred types of marine life. And just for the record the four subs in the West Edmonton Mall make up a fleet just a bit less impressive than the six underwater boats of the Canadian Navy. A Deep Sea Adventure ticket includes a submarine ride, admission to the Sea Life Caverns aquarium, and the Dolphin Show. Admission: adult, ❷; child and senior, ❷; family, ❹. For information, call ☎ (780) 444-5300, ext. 3.

The **Ice Palace** NHL-sized ice arena used as a practice rink by the Edmonton Oilers and figure skating groups. At other times visitors can take to the ice.

World Waterpark at West Edmonton Mall
Photo courtesy of Edmonton Tourism

Galaxyland Amusement Park claims the title as the world's largest indoor amusement park. Star attractions include Mindbender, a fourteen-story-high triple loop rollercoaster; Galaxy Twister, a gravity-defying thrill ride; and the Drop of Doom freefall. Admission: adult, ❹; child, ❸; family, ❹. For information, call ☎ (780) 444-5391.

Nearby the amusement park is some entertainment for adults found in the **Palace Casino**.

The dark and lively **Bourbon Street** is home to nightclubs and bars. Red's is a family entertainment center that offers twenty-eight lanes of ten-pin bowling, twenty-five billiard tables, an arcade that has one hundred cutting-edge games, and a nightclub.

Mall stores are usually open weekdays from 10 A.M. to 9 P.M., on Saturday from 10 A.M. to 6 P.M., and on Sunday from noon to 5 P.M. Bars, restaurants, and attractions have varying hours of operation.

West Edmonton Mall is located at the junction of Eighty-seventh Avenue and 170th Street. The #10 bus connects downtown to the mall.

For information, call ☎ (800) 661-8890 or ☎ (780) 444-5200 or consult ▧ www.westedmontonmall.com.

The Klondike Days

The rivalry between Edmonton and slightly smaller and much brasher Calgary includes the **Klondike Days Exposition**, Edmonton's smaller and less brash answer to the wildly successful Calgary Stampede.

Klondike Days is held in the second half of July each year in Northlands Park. The event includes a parade with floats, mascots, marching bands, and drum corps. The musical groups make a return appearance at the Goldrush Musical Showcase at Clarke Stadium.

The exposition itself includes the Klondike Chuckwagon Derby with four days of competition among several dozen teams; the King of the Klondike frontier competition has events that include log sawing and chopping, axe throwing, and rope climbing. There's also the Sunday Promenade, a civic tradition of entertainments all around town that are attended by many dressed in 1890s-era finery. And then you have a midway with more than fifty rides and seventy-five game booths.

For information, call (888) 800-7275 or consult ▧ www.klondikedays.com.

Sports and Recreation Near Edmonton

The North Saskatchewan River Valley, running through the center of Edmonton, is an oasis of parkland. Within the Capital City Recreation Park there are eighteen miles of paths for hikers, bikers, and joggers.

Overall Edmonton has one of the largest and most continuous areas of urban parkland in North America, encompassing more than eighteen thousand acres. For information, call the **River Valley Centre** at ☎ (780) 496-7275.

Bike rentals are available **from Auscon Sports and Recreation.** ☎ (780) 439-1883.

Shopping Adventures Outside the Mall

There is also commercial life outside the West Edmonton Mall. In the heart of downtown are **Edmonton Centre** with 140 stores, **Eaton Centre** (one hundred stores), **ManuLife Place** (sixty stores), **Commerce Place**, **Hudson's Bay Company**, **Holt Renfrew**, and **Eaton's**.

At the **Boardwalk Market**, at 102nd Avenue and 103rd Street, two historic warehouses have been converted into space for dozens of small businesses and restaurants.

Between 102nd Avenue and 109th Avenue on 124th Street and the High Street (102nd Avenue and 125th Street) is a varied urban shopping district of individual stores, boutiques, restaurants, and small galleries.

Edmonton Arts and Entertainment

Edmonton's live theater is centered around the **Citadel Theatre** complex. The Citadel is located downtown at Ninety-ninth Street and 101A Avenue, ☎ (780) 425-1820.

The **Mayfield Dinner Theatre** at the Mayfield Inn and Suites, 16615 109th Avenue, is home for many prominent performers. For information, call ☎ (780) 483-4051 or 🖳 www.mayfielddinnedmonton.com.

The **Edmonton Opera**, ☎ (780) 429-1000 or 🖳 www.edmontonopera.com, and the **Alberta Ballet**, ☎ (780) 427-2760 or 🖳 www.albertaballet.com, perform at the Northern Alberta Jubilee Auditorium at Eighty-Seventh Avenue and 114th Street.

The 1,900-seat Francis Winspear Centre for Music is home to the **Edmonton Symphony** as well as a wide range of musical performances from classical to country, folk to jazz. For information on the symphony, call ☎ (780) 428-1108 or consult 🖳 www.edmontonsymphony.com.

Discounted tickets to events at many Edmonton venues are sold at **Tix on the Square** near the Citadel Theatre. Full-price (plus service charge) seats for most events are available through Ticketmaster, ☎ (780) 451-8000.

Winter Activities in the Edmonton Area

Groomed cross-country skiing trails are available at a number of Edmonton parks. Among the best within the city are Kinsmen, Riverside, Gold Bar, and Millcreek. All are situated along the North Saskatchewan River valley, joined by a system known as the **Capital City Recreation Park**. This permits skiers to enjoy ten miles of connected trails. For information, call ☎ (780) 496-2966 or ☎ (780) 496-7275.

Or you can get off your tired dogs and let the huskies pull you through the snow. Operators of dog sleds include Frontier Adventure Tours, ☎ (780) 915-6458, and Mukluk Kennels, ☎ (780) 963-1493.

And then there is Skijoring. First of all, give yourself a point if you know the definition of this activity; give yourself a few dozen more points if you are willing to try cross-country skiing being towed behind a pack of dogs. Try Aus Can Recreation at ☎ (780) 439-1883.

City parks and facilities offer many places for outdoor ice skating; most rinks and lakes in the city have changing rooms. Facilities include rinks at City Hall and the Legislature Grounds. For information, call the **River Valley Centre** at ☎ (780) 496-7275.

A number of operators offer romantic horse-drawn sleigh rides through the parks and countryside; most companies require group bookings but you may be able to join in with a group. Fort Edmonton Park, ☎ (780) 496-8778; MP Stables, ☎ (780) 457-1865; Ukrainian Cultural Heritage Village, ☎ (780) 662-3640; Strathcona Country, ☎ (780) 464-4242; and Whitemud Equestrian Center, ☎ (780) 435-3597.

Snowmobiling is not permitted within city limits but is readily available on public and private trails. Two nearby operators are Rocky Mountain Tours, ☎ (780) 448-5860, and Frontier Adventure Tours, ☎ (780) 915-6458.

Sledding hills are available in most parks with a family area at Mill Woods Winter Park at Twenty-third Avenue and Sixty-sixth Street. For information, call ☎ (780) 496-7275.

Spectator Sports

Commonwealth Stadium seats more than sixty-one thousand spectators for special events. The facility served as the site of the Commonwealth Games in 1978, the World University Games in 1983, and the Grey Cup Football Championships in 1984 and 1997.

The **Skyreach Centre**, at 7424 118th Avenue, is home to the city's National Hockey League team, the five-time Stanley Cup Champion **Edmonton Oilers**. For information, call ☎ (780) 414-4650 or consult 💻 www.edmontonoilers.com.

Hayfields near Pincher Creek outside of Edmonton

The city's professional baseball team, the **Edmonton Trappers** of the Triple A Pacific Coast League, play at **Telus Field**. For information, call ☎ 780-451-8000 or consult 🖳 www.trappersbaseball.com.

Seats for most sporting events in Edmonton are available through Ticketmaster, ☎ (780) 451-8000.

Attractions South and East of Edmonton

About twenty-six miles east of Edmonton restored churches, homesteads, and rural town buildings tell the story of Ukrainian immigrants and development of East Central Alberta from 1892 to 1930. The **Ukrainian Cultural Heritage Village**, on Yellowhead Highway 16, is open year-round. Admission: adult, ❷; child, ❷; child (younger than 6), free; family, ❹. For information, call ☎ (780) 662-3640 or consult 🖳 collections.ic.gc.ca/ukrainian.

About fifty miles due south of Edmonton, the **Reynolds-Alberta Museum** focuses on the technology of the prairies over the past 150 years. Exhibits include a steam engine, early tractors, and a luxury sedan. The museum is also home to Canada's **Aviation Hall of Fame**. Located between Red Deer and Edmonton off Highway 2 or 2A, just west of Wetaskiwin on Highway 13. For information, call ☎ (780) 352-5855 or consult 🖳 www.gov.ab.ca/mcd/mhs/ram/ram.htm.

In Red Deer, about seventy miles south of Edmonton, the **Kerry Wood Nature Centre** offers guided walks, a wildflower garden, interactive computer games, and a computerized "helicopter tour" of the area. Alongside the center is the **Gaetz Lakes Sanctuary**, a Federal Migratory Bird Sanctuary. More than two hundred species of birds and thirty species of mammals roam the area. The Allen Bungalow is an Edwardian residence with gardens. Admission: donations accepted. For information, call ☎ (403) 346-2010 or consult 🖳 www.city.red-deer.ab.ca/kerry.

Nearby is the **Fort Normandeau Historic Site and Interpretive Centre**, which focuses on human history from the mid- to late 1800s, including the aboriginal, Métis, and European cultures. Visitors can also book flat-water raft trips on the Red Deer River. The facility in Red Deer is open May to September. Admission: donations accepted. For information, call ☎ (403) 347-7550 or consult 🖳 www.city.red-deer.ab.ca/kerry/ftnorm.htm.

About five miles north of Markerville and about thirty minutes southwest of Red Deer off Highways 592 and 781, the **Stephansson House Provincial Historic Site** preserves the pioneer home of Stephan G. Stephansson, one of Iceland's greatest poets. Most of his Canadian output was created in this house after 1889. Costumed interpreters give guided tours, demonstrate wool spinning, baking, household chores, and read his poetry. Open from mid-May to September. Admission: free. For information, call ☎ (403) 728-3929 or consult 🖳 www.gov.ab.ca/MCD/mhs/steph/steph.htm.

Moving west from Red Deer toward the mountains you'll come to the **Rocky Mountain House National Historic Site**, a commemoration of the trading posts that linked the Pacific Slope fur trade and the eastern supply routes. The site includes archaeological digs, films, and interpretive programs. In the summer an aboriginal village demonstrates of traditional crafts such as tanning and beading. The site is about five miles west of the village of Rocky Mountain House on Highway 11A, forty-five miles west of Red Deer. For information, call ☎ (403) 845-2412 or consult 🖳 parkscanada.pch.gc.ca/parks/alberta/Rocky_ mountain_house.

Attractions North and West of Edmonton

The **Mission at Lac La Biche**, established by the Oblate missionaries in 1853, includes a convent, rectory, church, and three smaller buildings. The mission, now a national historic site, had Alberta's first commercial wheat and grist mill, its first printing press, and its first sawmill. *Lac La Biche* means "doe lake" in French.

The mission is about 120 miles northeast of Edmonton, northwest of Lac La Biche, off Highway 55. Open mid-April to mid-September. Admission: adult, ❷; child, ❷; family, ❹. For information, call ☎ (780) 623-3274 or consult 🖳 www. laclabicheregion.ab.ca/Attractions.html.

Some two hundred miles due north of Edmonton, the **Fort McMurray Oil Sands Interpretive Centre** explores the Athabasca oil sands, the world's largest single oil deposit. Exhibits depict the geological history of the area and the history and technology of oil sand mining and processing. An outdoor display of mining equipment includes "Cyrus," a seven-story-high, bucket-wheel excavator.

The center is located at 515 MacKenzie Boulevard in Fort McMurray. Admission: adult, ❶; child, ❶; child (younger than 6), free; family, ❸. For information, call ☎ (780) 743-7167 or consult 🖳 www.gov.ab.ca/mcd/mhs/fmosic/ fmosic.htm.

And way, way up north, **Wood Buffalo National Park** straddles the border between Alberta and the Northwest Territories. Canada's largest national park covers an area larger than Switzerland. Wood Buffalo is a boreal forest that has meandering streams, shallow lakes, bogs, sinkholes, and large gypsum cliffs.

Home to some two thousand bison—the largest free-roaming herd in the world—the park is also the summer nesting ground of the world's only wild flock of whooping cranes, a bird that has a two-meter wingspan. The area is also an intersection of four major waterfowl flyways.

The river delta of the Peace and Athabasca rivers is an important spawning ground for goldeye and walleye fish and home to hundreds of thousands of ducks, geese, and other waterfowl that migrate through the delta.

The park's landscape features sinkholes, underground rivers, caves, and sunken valleys. Interpreters give talks, bison creeps, and salt plains walks. Private outfitters host overnight guided tours, hiking and boating.

Visitor Reception Centres are located in Fort Smith, Northwest Territories, and Fort Chipewyan, Alberta. Road access is from the Mackenzie Highway. Open year-round. Phone ahead for conditions and fees. Call the Wood Buffalo National Park Visitor Reception Centre information line at ☎ (867) 872-7960, Fort Chipewyan ☎ (780) 697-3662, or consult 🖳 parkscanada.pch.gc.ca/parks/ nwtw/wood_buffalo.

About two hundred miles northeast of Edmonton, **Cold Lake Provincial Park** is situated along one of the largest lakes in the province, on the border between Alberta and Saskatchewan. The mixed-wood boreal forest peninsula at the southern end of the lake provides a habitat for populations of waterfowl, western grebes, and more than two hundred other species of birds.

Observation platforms for wildlife viewing are situated along Halls Lagoon. There are nine trails for novice to intermediate hikers and cross-country skiers, campgrounds, picnic sites, a boat launch, and a white sand beach.

The park is east of Cold Lake off Highway 28. For information, call ☎ (780) 639-3341 or consult 🖳 www.gov.ab.ca/env/parks/parkinfo/col.html.

About fifteen miles west of Edmonton the restored **Father Lacombe Chapel** includes religious artifacts that date from the mid-nineteenth century. In 1861 Father Lacombe and his helpers built a modest log structure to serve the needs of St. Albert Roman Catholic Mission.

The chapel is in St. Albert, off Highway 2 North on St. Vital Avenue. Open mid-May to September. Admission: free. For information, call ☎ (780) 459-7663 in summer; ☎ (780) 427-3995 in winter, or consult 🖳 www.gov.ab.ca/mcd/mhs/lacombe/lacombe.htm.

Getting to Edmonton

Edmonton is well-served by air and train service from points in Canada; some flights come directly from the United States. The **Yellowhead Highway** passes through the city heading east and west, and Highway 2 is a high-speed connection south to Calgary and on to points in Idaho and Montana. Roads are more limited to the north.

Air Travel

Edmonton International Airport is served by major airlines including AirBC, Air Canada, Canada 3000, Canadian Airlines International, Delta Airlines, Horizon Air, Northwest Airlines, NWT Air, and WestJet. For airport customer service information, call ☎ (780) 890-8382.

The airport is about eighteen miles south of the city off Highway 2, the Calgary Trail. A one-way taxi from the city center costs about $30. The **Sky Shuttle Airport Service** takes groups of passengers to and from downtown for about $11 one way and $18 round-trip. For information, call ☎ (780) 465-8515 or (888) 438-2342, or consult 🖳 www.edmontonairports.com.

Train and Bus Service

Although the original trans-Canada train bypassed Edmonton and went insetad to Calgary, today the tables are turned. Edmonton has the only passenger service, on **VIA Rail**'s "Canadian" route with connections to Toronto, Winnipeg, Saskatoon, Jasper, and Vancouver. The terminal is located in downtown at 12360 121st Street. For information, call ☎ (800) 835-3037, or consult 🖳 www.viarail.ca.

Greyhound Canada, located downtown at 10324 103rd Street, offers service across Canada, with connections to the United States. For information, call ☎ (780) 413-8747, ☎ (800) 661-8747, or consult 🖳 www.greyhound.ca.

Bus service from Edmonton to Red Deer, Calgary, and Fort McMurray is available from **Red Arrow Express** at 10014 104th Street. For information, call ☎ (780) 424-3339, or ☎ (800) 232-1958, or consult 🖳 www.redarrow.pwt.ca.

The Edmonton Street Grid

The street system in Edmonton is laid out on a grid. Streets run north and south; avenues run east and west.

Streets are numbered starting from the southeast corner of the city. The higher the avenue number, the further north. There are a few named roads just to make things interesting. The main east-west road is Jasper Avenue, also known as 101st Avenue.

Addresses sometimes string together intersections. For example, 10014 104th Street could also be stated as number 14 100th Avenue at the intersection with 104th Street.

As the city continues to expand to the east and south, Edmonton has begun to describe locations with a quadrant system. The map is divided at Quadrant Avenue and Meridian Street into four quarters. Most of the downtown is in the N.W. quadrant.

Distinctive features of the Edmonton street system include the traffic circles (in Great Britain they're known as "circuses" and in parts of the United States "rotaries"). Wherever and whatever they are called, they can be daunting to the uninitiated.

Here are the rules of the road: when approaching a traffic circle, make sure you are in the correct lane. Use the right lane if you plan to exit at the first or second exit around the circle. Use the left lane if you are leaving at the second or third exit. While you are inside the circle, the vehicle on the outside must always yield to the vehicle on the inside.

Now here's the kicker: pay attention to any signs that may give you different instructions for the circle.

Public Transportation in Edmonton

Edmonton has both bus and light rail transit (LRT) services.

The **Edmonton Transit Downtown Information Centre** is located at 100A Street and Jasper Avenue, and open weekdays. For information, call ☎ (780) 496-1611, or consult 🖳 info.gov.edmonton.ab.ca/transit. You'll find an information booth at the Church LRT station on Ninety-ninth Street.

In 2001 fares were $1.75 for adults, and $1.25 for children from ages six to sixteen and seniors older than age sixty-five. A day pass is a good deal if you will be making multiple stops during a day of sightseeing; price: adults, ❶.

Chapter 13
Banff, Lake Louise, and Jasper

Picture a landscape of craggy snow-covered peaks at every turn. In the valleys electric-blue glaciers hang like prize ribbons; below, waterfalls of one-hundred-year-old melted ice cascade into deep, pristine lakes. Elk and caribou are on patrol at lower levels; way above, mountain goats cling to impossible crevices.

Down below there are only minimal invasions of human civilization in the ancient hills. A castle-like chateau sits at one end of a small town hemmed in on all sides by mountains. In another place another chateau lords over a lake fed by a glacier.

The picture in your mind is the Canadian Rockies northwest of Calgary: Banff, Lake Louise, and Jasper. It's a place that constitutes a permanent source of reverie in my mind.

Banff

The town of Banff, about seventy-five miles from Calgary, lies within the pro-tected bounds of the **Banff National Park**. Established in 1885 Banff is the oldest and most-visited national park in Canada, spreading over more than 2,500 square miles. Included within the park are Lake Louise, nestled below the Victoria Glacier; Moraine Lake, in the valley of the Ten Peaks, and the unreal turquoise waters of Peyto Lake.

The town of Banff is the gateway to all of the activities of the park; there are very few areas within the huge region where development is permitted and scarcely a spadeful of earth can be turned in Banff without permission from the park authorities. The busiest time of the year in Banff is June to September, but the town comes back to life in the winter as a base for skiers heading for spectacular resorts that include Banff Mount Norquay, Sunshine Village, and Lake Louise.

Overhanging the town is Mount Rundle, a jagged uplift to 9,700 feet.

In 1885 the discoverer of a hidden cave above the present site of Banff described it as if he had stumbled upon a "fantastic dream from a tale of Arab-ian Nights." Warm mineral springs from within lead to an emerald pool outside. The **Cave and Basin National Historic Site** marks the birthplace of Canada's

Sunshine Village near Banff

Photo by Malcolm Carmichael
Courtesy of Sunshine Village

National Park system. Open all year. Admission: adult, ❶. For information, call ☎ (403) 762-1566 or consult 💻 www.worldweb.com/Parks Canada-Banff/cave.html.

At the same west end of town the **Sulphur Mountain Gondola** offers year-round rides to the top at 7,500 feet in four-seat gondolas; views cover all of Banff and surrounding peaks. Open year-round except for mid-December to late January, the gondola is about two miles from the town on Mountain Avenue. Admission: adult, ❷; child (6–15), ❷; child (5 and younger), free. For information, call ☎ (403) 762-2523 or consult 💻 www.banffgondola.com.

Sunshine Village, located about fifteen miles outside Banff, is a jaw-dropping Shangri-la of a ski resort. Visitors park their cars down in the valley and ride six-passenger gondolas that wend their way three miles through untouched wilderness to the base of the spectacular Goat's Eye Mountain and further along to the automobile-less base village.

It starts snowing in the valley in October and sometimes ends by summer, with an average of thirty feet of the stuff each year. All that white stuff attracted the Trail Riders of the Canadian Rockies, who built a winter cabin there in 1928 on the Continental Divide. The first skiers hiked up the hill, but in 1941 a rope tow was installed on Strawberry Hill.

Key to Prices
❶ $5 and under
❷ $5 to $10
❸ $10 to $20
❹ $20 and more
When prices are listed as a range, this indicates various combination options are available. Most attractions offer reduced-price tickets for children and many have family rates that include two adults and two or three children.

Most of the land lies in Alberta although parts of the resort meander across the line to neighboring British Columbia. In 1995 Sunshine nearly doubled in size with the opening of Goat's Eye Mountain, an extraordinary bald mountain that comes nearly to a point. For information, call ☎ (403) 762-2523 or consult 💻 www.skibanff.com.

Johnston Canyon, sixteen miles west of Banff toward Lake Louise, is a narrow passageway along Johnston Creek. There are two waterfalls in the canyon; the upper falls are more than one hundred feet high. Both are mostly frozen in the winter. It's a relatively easy hike of less than a mile to the lower falls, and then another three miles to the upper cascade and the Ink Pots, six springs that bubble out of the ground year-round.

In the winter you can make an icewalk to the same spot, but you'd do well to invest in a pair of ice grips for your shoes. Several sightseeing companies offer guided tours through the canyon with ice grips as part of the package.

Lake Louise

Named for Queen Victoria's daughter, Princess Louise Caroline Alberta, Lake Louise is more than a mile above sea level. At the east end of the lake is **Chateau Lake Louise**, an imposing formal hotel; at the other end are Mount Victoria and the Victoria Glacier, which ends in a waterfall into the lake.

In the winter the chateau clears a skating rink on the lake, the most handsome setting for sliding or a game of pickup hockey I have ever experienced. You can also bundle into a horse-drawn sleigh for a tour of the lake on a pathway that leads to the frozen waterfalls. We rode along with the big horses to the end of the lake at sunset and then looked back in awe at the Alpenglow on the mountain as the sun set at the ski resort.

The **Lake Louise Ski Area** is Canada's largest ski area and one of the biggest in North America, measured in total skiable acreage, length of runs, number of named and groomed runs, amount of off-piste adventure, and amount of novice terrain. For information, call ☎ (403) 522-3555 or consult 💻 www.skilouise.com.

The resort delivers more than three thousand vertical feet of skiing, but the top altitude is below ten thousand feet, sparing most visitors from altitude

Lake Louise as summer approaches

CALGARY, BANFF, JASPER, AND EDMONTON

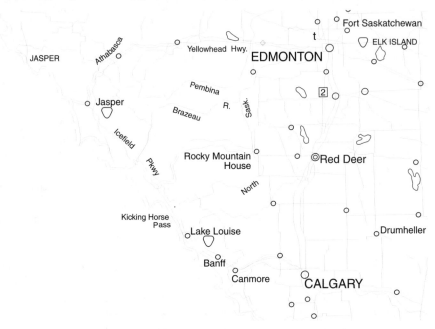

woes. And a Continental Divide climate provides consistent temperatures and dry, fluffy powder snow for most of the long, long season.

Lake Louise has a lot to offer including some wonderful bowls and chutes on the back side of the main mountain and unbelievable black-diamond plunges on the south face. The quiet side is in the back bowls, which lie over the lip at the end of the Top of the World high-speed quad at the summit of Mount Whitehorn. A set of chutes opens when the conditions are just right, and there is a W-shaped intermediate cruiser, dubbed Boomerang, that will hook you; otherwise there are enough wide but steep bowl plunges to keep you busy all day.

The view of Pyramid Peak from the top of the ski resort is beyond compare. Non-skiers can enjoy some of the same thrill by taking a trip on the Lake Louise gondola in the summer; the lift operates from early June through the end of September. Admission: adult, senior, and student, ❷; child (6–12), ❷; child (5 and younger), free.

The resort's extraordinary **Lodge of the Ten Peaks**, a huge alpine post-and-beam log cabin, is open for breakfast and lunch.

Besides the somewhat pricey Chateau, there are very few places to stay in Lake Louise itself; most skiers commute in from Banff.

From Lake Louise to Jasper

Jasper National Park, the largest park in the Canadian Rockies at 4,200 square miles, is occupied primarily by elk, bighorn sheep, deer, bear, coyote, moose, and mountain goat. The rugged scenery includes the deeply gouged Maligne canyon and picturesque Maligne Lake.

The greatest attraction of the park is the **Icefields Parkway**, a 160-mile drive from Lake Louise to Jasper that passes nearby the vast Columbia Icefield and the Athabasca Glacier, one of six glaciers that cover 125 square miles of the park. It is, quite simply, one of the most spectacular drives in the world, with each turn offering a new source of wonder from towering mountains, sheer rock faces, and miles of ice. It can also be a very tricky drive—on one visit in February we drove five hours in alternating heavy snow, fog, and ice the entire length. I somehow managed to keep our rented four-wheel-drive on the road. The next day the sun came out and the roads were dry but it took a few days before I could unclench my fists.

Running through the park is the **Athabasca River**, which rises from the **Columbia Icefield** to flow more than 750 miles north to join the Mackenzie River and eventually empty into the Arctic Sea. On the banks of the river is the **Jasper House National Historic Site**, where in 1827 the Hudson's Bay Company set up a trading house.

The Athabasca River cuts through hard, quartz-like rock to form the Athabasca Falls. There's a bridge and platforms at key viewing points twenty miles south of Jasper on Icefields Parkway at the junction with 93A. Open year-round, weather permitting. For information, call ☎ (780) 852-6176.

Another highlight is the thunderous **Sunwapta Falls**, where the Sunwapta River plunges down a steep canyon gorge before joining the Athabasca River.

Columbia Icefield off Icefields Parkway

Road closed. Highway 1A from Lake Louise to the Great Divide south of the ski area was closed permanently in 1999 to promote the movement of wildlife. The road runs parallel to the Route 93 highway. In coming years, further closings of sections of the road are possible.

Nearby is **Mount Edith Cavell**, an eleven-thousand-foot peak famed for its Angel Glacier, moraines, the Cavell Meadows, and alpine wildlife. An exhibit and interpretive trail follow the moraine and lakeshore. A longer hike leads to alpine meadows that offer an array of wildflowers and birds. The narrow switchback road to the area opens after the snow melts in late spring and closes after the first big snowfall, usually sometime in October. Local companies provide daily tours. For information, call ☎ (780) 852-6176. For hostel reservations, call ☎ (780) 852-3515.

For information on the park, call ☎ (780) 852-6176. You can visit the **Icefield Visitor Centre** in the summer for an overview of area attractions. For information, call ☎ (780) 852-7030 or consult 🖳 www.worldweb.com/parkscanada-jasper/on-line_tour/icepark.html.

Edith Cavell was a heroic British nurse who was executed as a spy by German forces during World War I.

Near Jasper, visitors can take the **Jasper Tramway** up to the alpine tundra on The Whistlers to glimpse life above the tree line.

The park's glaciers are among the most accessible anywhere in the world. One way to take full advantage is to ride a specially designed big-wheel vehicle that goes out on the ice. **Columbia Icefield Sno Coach Tours** operate from May 1 to October 15, weather permitting. Tickets: adult ❹; child (6–15) ❷; child (5 and younger) free. For information, call ☎ (403) 762-6735.

The Town of Jasper

The town of Jasper sits 230 miles west of Edmonton and 275 miles northwest of Calgary. The little town has 4,500 year-round residents; the surrounding park sees 2.5 million visitors a year.

Jasper dates back to 1811 when David Thompson, a renowned Canadian explorer and mapmaker, established a base there while he was searching for a fur-trading route through the Rockies.

The town sits in a narrow river valley, spreading only about five streets wide and less than a square mile in area. At the south end the Icefield Parkway (Route 93) enters from Lake Louise and Banff; at the north end Route 16 exits toward the Jasper Park Lodge, Maligne Lake, and Edmonton.

Winterstart/Scrooge Days offer savings in the early season before Christmas with discounts at participating hotels, restaurants, and Ski Marmot Basin. **Jasper in January** is a two-week winter festival that includes ice skating parties, food fairs, races, and special deals at hotels and Ski Marmot Basin.

Jasper is the jumping-off point for many summer and winter activities.

Licensed mountaineering guides take visitors to a climbing area in **Jasper National Park**. Pyramid Lake, at the base of the Majestic Pyramid Mountain, is regularly cleared for leisure skating and hockey. There are also outdoor areas at Mildred Lake and Lac Beauvert at the Jasper National Lodge.

About five miles up the Maligne Lake Road from Jasper, the Maligne River plunges into a steep-walled gorge of limestone bedrock at **Maligne Canyon**. Ten miles further down the same road is Medicine Lake, a lake that empties almost entirely every year. There is no surface outlet; instead, the water flows underground for many miles, emerging in such distant places as Maligne Canyon and Lac Beauvert.

At the end of the road some forty miles from Jasper is **Maligne Lake**, the largest in Jasper National Park and one of the most beautiful sights in the Rockies. In late May and June the elusive Harlequin Duck may be seen from the viewing bridge. For information on the area, call ☎ (780) 852-6176 or consult 💻 www.jasperview.com/parkscanada/malignecanyon.html.

Banff Lake Louise Tourism Bureau. ☎ (403) 762-8421.
Banff Visitor Centre. ☎ (403) 762-1550.
Jasper Tourism. 💻 www.explorejasper.com.
Parks Canada. 💻 www.worldweb.com/parks canada-jasper.
Marmot Basin. 💻 www.skimarmot.com.
Alberta Hotel Association. 💻 www.albertahotels.ab.ca.

One of the more exciting tours from Jasper is a **Maligne Canyon Ice Walk**, a rare opportunity to walk on the frozen floor of an alpine canyon within Jasper National Park. On our tour we came to frozen waterfalls that included Angel Falls and Queen of the Maligne and we ducked into ice caves. Tours are conducted by day or moonlight. Maligne Tours has an office in Jasper where you'll be outfitted with boots and ice grips and driven to the canyon. For information, call ☎ (780) 852-3370 or consult 💻 www.malignelake.com.

About seventy-five miles west of Jasper is Valemount, BC, which has a vast network of trails deep into the Robson Valley.

Nearly two hundred miles of trails make Jasper one of the largest cross-country skiing areas in Canada, with groomed trails through beautiful valleys and deep into the mountains. About twenty miles southwest of Jasper at an elevation of 6,500 feet lies the incredible **Tonquin Valley**; a trip there is a gradual climb of about fifteen miles and offers intermediate to expert nordic skiers the chance to experience one of Canada's most magnificent views.

When I skied **Marmot Basin** I got the feeling the locals would just as soon no one else knew their not-so-little secret. This is a whale of a ski area spread across the wide basin below Marmot Peak and Marmot 2, about half an hour south of Jasper. The road up the valley to the base is a bit like a back road in the Alps; until a dozen years or so ago, skiers would park miles away and ascend to the lifts in tracked buses.

Marmot Basin has fifty-three trails, some spectacular open bowls, and nearly three thousand vertical feet of skiing with a breathable top elevation of 8,534 and an annual snowfall of thirteen feet. The snow is reliable—sometimes there's too much of it—and lift lines are rare. We skied there after a prodigious early morning powder dump, losing sight of our skis for much of the time on the hill; a high point was a gourmet lunch, in ski boots. Food at the ski area is catered by the tony **Jasper Park Lodge** on Lac Beuvert, the fanciest digs in town. There are 442 rooms in cedar chalets and original log cabins.

For information on the ski area, call ☎ (780) 852-3301 or consult 🖳 www.ski marmot.com.

In summer outdoor activities include rafting on the Athabasca, Maligne, Sunwapta, or Fraser rivers with conditions ranging from gentle floats to wild whitewater plunges. For a guaranteed relaxing plunge you can visit the **Miette Hot Springs**, the hottest springs in the Canadian Rockies and one of the most spectacular settings for an outdoor hot tub anywhere.

Guided horseback rides are organized by a number of companies in Jasper to locations that include the Tonquin Valley, Skyline Trail, and North Boundary. Day trips are available; some outfitters put together two-week pack trips into the wilderness.

Jasper National Park is one of the few parks in North America that permits mountain biking, with a variety of designated trails for the novice through expert rider.

In town the Astoria Hotel reaches back to the heyday of the railroad. Its thirty-five guest rooms have been brought completely up to date.

The Sawridge Hotel Jasper was designed around a huge three-story fireplace and sky-lit atrium, with 154 rooms and suites. For a more rustic setting in summer the Alpine Village includes forty-one log chalets and several deluxe cabins on the Athabasca River. The Patricia Lake Bungalows are on the shores of striking Patricia Lake at the base of Pyramid Mountain.

The Whistlers mountain peak overlooks the town of Jasper and offers a view of mountains in all directions. The summit, accessible by trial or by the **Jasper Tram**, is at eight thousand feet. At the top you can explore the alpine zone, watch ground squirrels, pikas, marmots (the "whistlers"), and occasionally an elusive ptarmigan. Access is about four miles south of Jasper, just off the Icefields Parkway. The Tram operates from about April to mid-October, weather permitting. For information, call ☎ (780) 852-3093 or consult 🖳 www.jaspertramway.com.

Heading west about twenty-five miles from Jasper into British Columbia on Route 16 (the Yellowhead Highway), you'll come to Mount Robson, the highest peak in the Canadian Rockies at 12,850 feet.

Within the 840 square miles of **Mount Robson Provincial Park** are steep canyons, glacier-fed lakes, rivers, and streams, waterfalls, and forests. The headwaters of the Fraser River begin as a modest trickle in the southwest corner of the park. Another impressive mountain, Mount Fitzwilliam, is nearby on the Yellowhead Highway 16. For information, call ☎ (250) 566-4325 or consult 🖳 www.env.gov.bc.ca/bcparks/explore/parkpgs/mtrobson.htm.

Part IV
Saskatchewan and Manitoba

Chapter 14
Saskatchewan

Saskatchewan derives its name from the Cree word *kisiskatchewan*; applied to the Saskatchewan River it means "river that runs swiftly."

For nearly a hundred years Saskatchewan's farmers have struggled to make visitors stop their swift passage through the province and learn its charms. That's not an easy task, for the attractions of the province are pretty well hidden within the flat and featureless miles of wheat fields and undeveloped forests.

Saskatchewan is the only province that has entirely man-made boundaries. About a quarter-million square miles in size, the province stretches eight hundred miles from north to south.

Half the province is covered by forest, one-third is farmland, and one-eighth is fresh water. The major river systems are the North and South Saskatchewan, Assiniboine, and Churchill. They all flow northeast, emptying into Hudson Bay.

The Clearwater River has some of the best whitewater rafting in North America, wild and very remote. The province has nearly 100,000 freshwater lakes, the majority of them north in the rugged Precambrian shield.

The principal industry of Saskatchewan is agriculture; farmers produce more than 54 percent of Canada's wheat. Other industries include mining, construction, manufacturing, oil and petroleum, and tourism.

Saskatchewan Festivals and Events

May

Mosaic. Regina. ☎ (306) 757-5990. 🖳 www.reginamosaic.com. A citywide festival of culture with artisans, folk dances, music, song, and food from around the world. Held in late May or early June at various venues around Regina. Admission: fees depend on event.

Yorkton Short Film and Video Festival. Yorkton. ☎ (306) 782-7077. 🖳 www.yorktonshortfilm.org. North America's longest running short-film festival; the weeklong event includes daily screenings, workshops, tours, and a street festival known as "Cinerama." The event is held at various venues in Yorkton. Admission: fees depend on the event.

SASKATCHEWAN

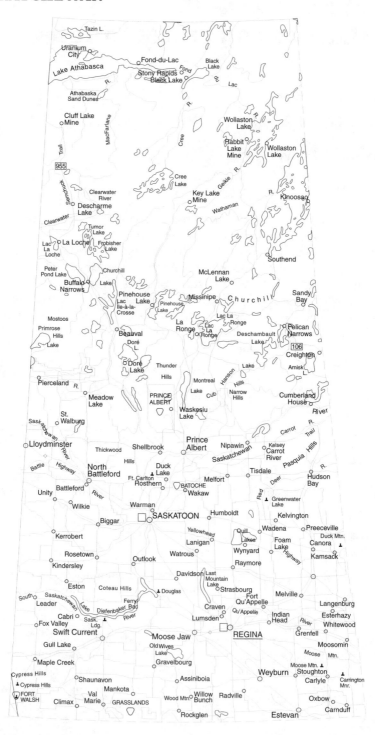

Tazin L.

Uranium City

Lake Athabasca

Fond-du-Lac

Black Lake

Stony Rapids
Black Lake

Fond

Lac

Athabaska
Sand Dunes

Cluff Lake
Mine

MacFarlane

Trail

955

Sechtchuck

Clearwater
River

Descharme
Lake

Clearwater

Cree

Cree
Lake

Wollaston
Lake

Rabbit
Lake
Mine

Wollaston
Lake

Kinoosao

Key Lake
Mine

Wathaman

Geikie

R.

Tumor
Lake

Lac
La Loche
Loche

La Loche

Frobisher
Lake

Peter
Pond Lake

Buffalo
Narrows

Churchill

Lake

McLennan
Lake

Southend

Pinehouse
Lake

Lac
Ile-à-la-
Crosse

Pinehouse
Lake

Missinipe

Churchill

Sandy
Bay

Mostoos

Primrose
Hills

Lake

Beauval

Doré
L.

Doré
Lake

Thunder

Hills

La
Ronge

Lac La
Ronge

Lac
La
Ronge

Deschambault
Lake

Pelican
Narrows

106

Creighton

Amisk

Pierceland

R.

Meadow
Lake

PRINCE
ALBERT

Montreal
Lake

Cub

Hanson

Lake

Narrow
Hills

Cumberland
House

River

St.
Walburg

Waskesiu
Lake

Sask.

Saskatchewan

River

Lloydminster

Thickwood

Hills

Shellbrook

Prince
Albert

Nipawin

Saskatchewan

Kelsey
Carrot
River

Carrot

Trail

R.

Pasquia

Hills

Battle

Highway

North
Battleford

Duck
Lake

Ft. Carlton

Rosthern

Tisdale

Deer

Hudson
Bay

Unity

Battleford

River

BATOCHE

Wakaw

Melfort

Red

Greenwater
Lake

Wilkie

Warman

Humboldt

Kelvington

Biggar

SASKATOON

Kerrobert

Yellowhead

Lanigan

Quill
Lakes

Wadena

Foam
Lake

Preeceville

Duck Mtn.

Canora

Kamsack

Rosetown

Kindersley

Outlook

Watrous

Wynyard

Highway

Raymore

Davidson

Last
Mountain
Lake

Strasbourg

Melville

Eston

Coteau Hills

Douglas

South

Saskatchewan

Lake

Leader

Ferry

Diefenbaker

Bay

Fort
Qu'Appelle

Langenburg

Esterhazy

Cabri

Sask.
Ldg.

River

Craven

Qu'Appelle

Indian
Head

River

Whitewood

Fox Valley

Swift Current

Lumsden

REGINA

Grenfell

Gull Lake

Moose Jaw

Old Wives
Lake

Moosomin

Maple Creek

Gravelbourg

Moose

Mtn.

Cypress Hills

Cypress Hills

FORT
WALSH

Shaunavon

Mankota

Val
Marie

Climax

GRASSLANDS

Wood Mtn

Assiniboia

Willow
Bunch

Radville

Weyburn

Moose Mtn.
Stoughton

Carlyle

Carrington
Mnr.

Oxbow

Rockglen

Estevan

Carnduff

A snow-covered farm in Codette

June

Northern Saskatchewan International Children's Festival. Saskatoon. ☎ (306) 664-3378. Music, storytelling, theater, dance, clowning, and puppetry by Canadian and international groups. Held in Kiwanis Park in downtown Saskatoon. Admission: ❸; evening gala concerts, ❸.

Regina International Children's Festival. Regina. ☎ (306) 352-7655. 🖳 www.tourismregina.com/regina_childrens_festival.htm. Theater, arts, and a parade over four days in early June in and around Wascana Centre in Regina. Admission: free to the site; some performances have admission charges.

Saskatchewan Jazz Festival. Saskatoon. ☎ (306) 652-1421. 🖳 www.sask jazz.com. Blues, gospel, dixieland, worldbeat, and fusion. Nearly four hundred local, national and international artists perform more than 170 concerts during this annual weeklong event. Held at venues throughout downtown Saskatoon. Admission: fees vary by event.

July

Shakespeare on the Saskatchewan. Saskatoon. ☎ (306) 653-2300. 🖳 www. zu.com/shakespeare. Innovative staging and settings for Shakespeare's works; past shows have put Hamlet in a punk rock setting and King Lear in the modern world of big business. Held during a six-week period from early July to mid-August in a tent adjacent to the Mendel Art Gallery at the foot of the Twenty-fifth Street Bridge.

A potash processing plant on the plains of Saskatchewan

August

Folkfest. Saskatoon. ☎ (306) 931-0100. 🖳 www.folkfest.sk.ca. A three-day, multicultural celebration that offers culinary specialties, traditions, and music of Saskatoon's diverse community. Held at various venues.

Saskatoon International Fringe Festival. Saskatoon. ☎ (306) 664-2239. 🖳 www.interspin.com/fringe. Ten days of alternative theater, buskers (street performers), improvisation theater, and original plays. Held at various indoor and outdoor venues.

Chapter 15
Regina

The metropolitan area of Regina seems to sprout from the flat prairie that surrounds it. Regina was the original seat of government of the Northwest Territories. It became the capital when Saskatchewan became a province in 1905.

The Cree, who used the banks of what is now Wascana Creek to dry buffalo hides, named the area *Oscana*, which means "pile of bones." European settlers thought otherwise, renaming the developing city Regina, Latin for "queen," in honor of Queen Victoria.

Today Regina is the headquarters of the Saskatchewan Wheel Pool, the world's largest grain-handling cooperative. Among Canadians and worldwide fans of Nelson Eddy films, Regina is also famous as the home of the RCMP Training Academy in Regina, Canada's school for Mounties.

Wascana Centre is a 2,300-acre oasis of green on the prairie and is home to the Royal Saskatchewan Museum, the Saskatchewan Science Centre, the Saskatchewan Legislative Building, and other attractions.

The **Royal Saskatchewan Museum** traces twelve thousand years of aboriginal culture in its First Nations Gallery. The Earth Sciences Gallery goes back even farther, following 2.5 billion years of the geological evolution of what is now Saskatchewan. One interesting exhibit examines the technology of stone tools, from the selection of stones to the design and manufacture of weapons and projectile points. The museum is located at College Avenue and Albert Street. Open year-round. Admission: donations accepted. For information, call ☎ (306) 787-2810 or consult 🖥 www.royalsaskmuseum.ca.

Nearby, the **Saskatchewan Science Center** has more than a hundred hands-on exhibits and demonstrations, plus the **Kramer Imax Theatre**. Discovery Jones's Fantastic Farming explores the province's agriculture and weather.

The science center is located at Winnipeg Street and Wascana Drive. For information, call ☎ (800) 667-6300 in Canada or ☎ (306) 522-4629, or consult 🖥 www.sciencecentre.sk.ca.

The **RCMP Centennial Museum**, the official museum of the upright Mounties, celebrates their role in Canada's history through displays of equipment, weapons, uniforms, photos, and other memorabilia of the past hundred years.

REGINA

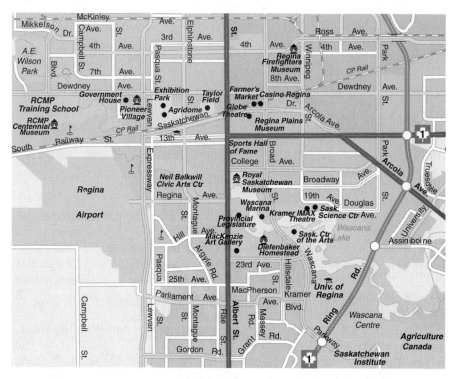

The RCMP Sergeant Major's Parade is held Monday and Thursday afternoons on the Parade Square, weather permitting, or in the Drill Hall. RCMP Sunset Retreat Ceremonies are held Tuesday evenings in the summer.

The museum is located at the RCMP Training Academy on Dewdney Avenue West. Admission: free. For information, call ☎ (306) 780-5838 or consult 🖳 www.rcmpmuseum.com.

Historical and contemporary works by Canadian and international artists are at the **Mackenzie Art Gallery**, nearby the Royal Saskatchewan Museum at 3475 Albert Street. Admission: free. For information, call ☎ (306) 522-4242 or consult 🖳 www.mackenzieartgallery.sk.ca.

Attractions West and North of Regina

The **Western Development Museum** traces the role of aviation, railways, road, and water travel in the development of the West. The collection includes antique cars, early snowmobiles, and vintage aircraft. The museum is located in Moose Jaw, about forty miles west of Regina, at the Junction of Highways 1 and 2. For information, call ☎ (306) 693-5989 or consult 🖳 www.wdmuseum.sk.ca.

Twenty miles north of Moose Jaw, the **Buffalo Pounds Provincial Park** is known for its free roaming buffalo herd. The region around the Nicolle Flats Interpretive Area is also a stopover for a variety of waterfowl. For information, call ☎ (306) 693-2678 or consult 🖳 www.serm.gov.sk.ca/parks/buffalopound.

Regina rises from the prairie

On the Alberta-Saskatchewan border, the **Cypress Hills Interprovincial Park** includes the highest land formation between the Rocky Mountains and Labrador, rising nearly two thousand feet above the surrounding countryside.

Facilities include year-round cabin rental and boat and canoe rental. The park is eighteen miles south of Maple Creek, on Highway 21. For information, call ☎ (306) 662-5411 or consult 🖳 www.serm.gov.sk.ca/parks/cypresshills.

There are, by the way, no cypress trees in the park; French Canadian explorers referred to pine trees as *cyprès*.

A bit further south from Maple Creek, the **Fort Walsh National Historic Site** features a restored 1875 North West Mounted Police redoubt constructed to stop the illegal American whiskey trade and mediate with the Sioux, who had followed Chief Sitting Bull across the Canadian border after the Battle of Little Big Horn. The fort has been restored to its appearance in 1882, and Farwell's trading post has been reconstructed and furnished in the style of 1872.

The fort is thirty-five miles southwest of Maple Creek on Provincial Road 271. Open May to the end of September; closed Monday and Tuesday. For information, call ☎ (306) 662-2645 or consult parkscanada.pch.gc.ca/parks/saskatch ewan/fort_walsh.

South of Regina

The place where Sitting Bull and his Sioux followers crossed the border from Montana to take refuge from the U.S. Army after the battle of the Little Big Horn in 1876 is now preserved as **Grasslands National Park**.

Grasslands is an original mixed-grass prairie ecosystem. The West Block features the Frenchman River Valley, a glacial meltwater channel that has deeply

The Legislature Building in Regina

dissected plateaus, coulees, and erosion features. The East Block centers on the Kildeer badlands of the Rock and Morgan Creek areas, representing the Wood Mountain Upland. The West Block is accessible by one, main, dry-weather road.

Access to the East Block is limited, with only a small part accessible in dry weather. Check with the **Visitor Information Centre** in Val Marie or the **Rodeo Ranch Museum** for road conditions and access routes.

The park is in southwestern Saskatchewan, near the Montana border; access is by Highway 4 and Highway 18. For information, call ☎ (306) 298-2166 or consult 🖳 parkscanada.pch.gc.ca/parks/saskatchewan/grasslands.

Theater and Entertainment in Regina

A history-lover's visit to Regina might not be complete without a visit to the *Trial of Louis Riel*, a summertime tradition at the Schumiatcher Theatre.

Louis Riel was tried for treason as one of the leaders of the 1885 Northwest Rebellion in which he lead Métis and Indian people in an armed uprising against the Canadian government in a dispute over land rights. Using original transcripts, the final court argument is re-enacted with the audience acting as the jury. (For the record, Riel was found guilty of treason, and he died on the gallows in November in 1885.)

One of Canada's longest running productions, the trial is presented several days a week from late July through the end of August at the theater within the Mackenzie Art Gallery at 3475 Albert Street. Admission: by donation. For information, call ☎ (306) 522-4242.

Other Regina arts offerings include the Globe Theatre on Twenty-fifth Street, which performs new works by Saskatchewan playwrights.

Chapter 16
Saskatoon

Saskatoon is, by a whisker, the largest city in Saskatchewan, but it's often overshadowed by the capital city of Regina.

Saskatoon was established as a temperance settlement by John Lake and other members of the Temperance Colonisation Colony from Ontario. According to legend a local Cree brought the colonists a handful of the purple berries that grew along the South Saskatchewan River. Lake was so impressed with the fruit, presumably for non-alcoholic uses, that he changed the name of his settlement from Minnetonka to Saskatoon, a mispronunciation of *misaskwatomin*, the Cree name for the wild berries.

The colony became a city in 1906. Today it's known as "The City of the Bridges" because of the many crossings of the river. It is no longer a temperance zone, but you still can get a slice of Saskatoon pie.

Attractions

At the **Western Development Museum** in Saskatoon you can walk the streets of a restored Saskatchewan town of the early twentieth century. Demonstrations include farming techniques.

There are other Western Development Museums in Saskatchewan; Moose Jaw, Yorkton; and North Battleford.

The museum, located at 2610 Lorne Avenue South, is open daily; closed Monday from January to March. Admission: adult, ❷; senior, ❶; child, ❶; preschool child, free; family, ❹. For information, call ☎ (306) 931-1910 or consult 🖳 www.wdmuseum.sk.ca/stoon.html.

A larger restoration is **Wanuskewin Heritage Park**, about three miles due north of Saskatoon. *Wanuskewin* is Cree for "seeking peace of mind."

Key to Prices
❶ $5 and under
❷ $5 to $10
❸ $10 to $20
❹ $20 and more
When prices are listed as a range, this indicates various combination options are available. Most attractions offer reduced-price tickets for children and many have family rates that include two adults and two or three children.

SASKATOON

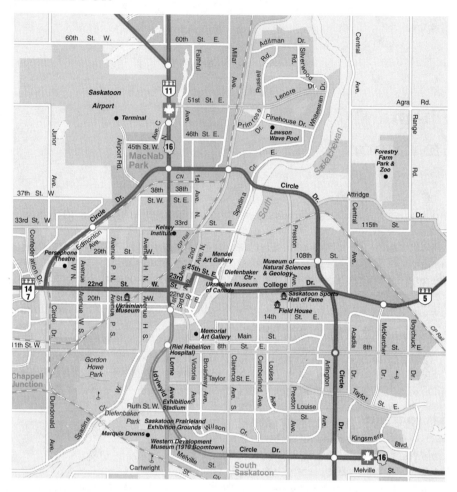

An interpretive center tells the six-thousand-year-old story of the Northern Plains people through exhibits, archaeology digs, demonstrations, and performances. The visitor center is perched on the edge of a valley overlooking Opimihaw Creek and a bison kill site. As you approach the center you walk along a buffalo drive lane that has life-sized bronze sculptures depicting the hunt.

Nineteen pre-contact sites have been discovered within the 290-acre park, some older than 1400 B.C. There is a rare boulder alignment known as a medicine wheel, tepee rings that mark ancient campsites, and a buffalo pound and kill sites where animals were processed.

Facilities include camping in a tepee or tent, traditional storytelling, outdoor cooking, and explorations of the life skills of the Northern Plains Indian culture. In the winter activities include sled dog races and craft courses.

The park is located on Highway 11. Admission: general, ❶; family, ❹. For information, call ☎ (306) 931-6767 or consult 🖳 www. wanuskewin.com.

Saskatoon, a city of bridges

At the **Batoche National Historic Site**, fifty-five miles northeast of Saskatoon, you'll find the remains of the village of Batoche on the banks of the South Saskatchewan River, the last battlefield in the Northwest Rebellion of 1885.

Métis leader Louis Riel selected Batoche, then a community of about five hundred people, as the headquarters of his provisional government. The site includes the trails, homes, church, and battlefield. Segments of the trenches used during the battle are still visible.

The site is in Batoche, off Highway 11. For information, call ☎ (306) 423-6227 or consult 🖳 parkscanada.pch.gc.ca/parks/saskatchewan/batoche.

Heading northwest from Saskatoon about a hundred miles, you'll come to the **Fort Battleford National Historic Site**, a restored North West Mounted Police fort. The redoubt was built in 1876 and operated until 1924. Buildings include the Commanding Officer's residence and the officers' quarters. The stockade and bastions are reconstructed, and the barracks include an interpretive display about the Northwest Rebellion of 1885. The fort is on the Yellowhead Highway 16. For information, call ☎ (306) 937-2621 or consult 🖳 parks canada.pch.gc.ca/parks/saskatchewan/fort_battleford.

At **Fort Carlton Provincial Historic Park**, the stockade and several structures are restored to the style of the 1860s and 1870s. Four reconstructed buildings illustrate the Hudson's Bay Company Post in the 1860s. The lifestyle of the Plains Cree is interpreted in cooperation with area First Nations Bands. The park is sixteen miles west of Duck Lake on Provincial Highway 212, about fifty miles southwest of Prince Albert on Provincial Highways 11 and 212. Open from May to early September. Admission: adult, senior, youth, ❶. For information, call ☎ (306) 953-2322 (in winter) and ☎ (306) 467-5205 (year-round), or consult 💻 www.serm.gov.sk.ca/parks/historic.

Way up north of Prince Albert, the last major city of Saskatchewan, is **Prince Albert National Park**. The park's million acres are home to an abundance of wildlife that includes deer, elk, moose, woodland caribou, wolf, lynx, otter, bison, black bear, and 235 species of birds. The park has one of the few free-roaming herds of plains bison in Canada, a colony of nine thousand white pelicans, and rare fescue grassland.

The park includes nature trails; book well in advance for guides. Recreational activities include hiking, horseback riding, paddlewheeler cruises, boating, fishing, canoeing, backpacking, cycling, cross-country skiing, snowshoeing, and camping.

The park is forty-seven miles north of Prince Albert, near the geographic center of the province; it is accessible on Highway 2 and 264, or Scenic Route Highway 263. The Interpretive Centre is open daily from the end of June to September. For information, call ☎ (306) 663-4522 or consult 💻 parkscanada. pch.gc.ca/parks/saskatchewan/prince_albert/.

Chapter 17
Manitoba

Manitoba is the farthest east of the prairie provinces, a mostly untouched buffer between the population centers of Ontario and eastern Canada and the mountains of the west.

Like much of Canada, nearly all of the population of Manitoba lives in the lower third of the province; in the nearly virgin north the province includes more than 100,000 lakes, including two of the largest in the world. And way up top, Manitoba includes a cold shoreline on Hudson Bay.

When you see the incredible watery wilderness of the north, you can understand why the Cree and Ojibwe named the place Manitoba, the place where the spirit lives.

Winnipeg

The most important city of Manitoba is Winnipeg, population 650,000. This is a very green place with nearly 1,200 acres of parkland and a reputation of having more hours of sunshine than any other major city in Canada.

Winnipeg has had a history as a trading center for more than six thousand years. First Nations traders would travel down the river systems, across the prairies, and into what is now the United States. Archeologists say they traded at the place where the Red and Assiniboine Rivers meet; in modern Winnipeg the location is known as **The Forks**.

Europeans did the same when Pierre de la Verendrye founded Fort Rouge at The Forks in 1738. The fort did not last long, but in 1804 the Northwest Company built Fort Gibraltar at almost the same place; in 1821 the Hudson's Bay Company built Fort Garry nearby.

Today The Forks is just a few blocks away from the Winnipeg Commodity Exchange, where grain contracts have been exchanged for more than one hundred years.

Attractions in Winnipeg

You can track the history of Winnipeg—and the rest of the planet—back a few billion years or so at the **Manitoba Museum of Man and Nature**. The muse-

MANITOBA

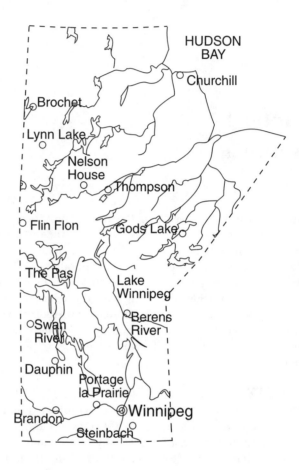

um tracks the prehistory of the area through the 1920s and then out into space with a science center and planetarium.

The Manitoba Museum is part of the Manitoba Centennial Centre, which also houses the Centennial Concert Hall. The complex is located at 190 Rupert Avenue on Main Street in downtown Winnipeg, across from City Hall and in the historical Exchange District. The museum galleries and science gallery are open daily in the summer, and daily except Monday the remainder of the year. Admission: adult, ❷; youth and senior (65+), ❶. Additional fees for admission to science gallery and planetarium shows.

For information, call ☎ (204) 956-2830 or ☎ (204) 943-3139 or consult 🖳 www.manitobamuseum.mb.ca.

Also in downtown is the **Saint Boniface Museum**. This former Grey Nuns convent of 1846 is the oldest structure in Winnipeg and the largest oak log Red River frame building in North America. The building offers a collection of artifacts pertaining to French Canadian and Métis culture.

WINNIPEG

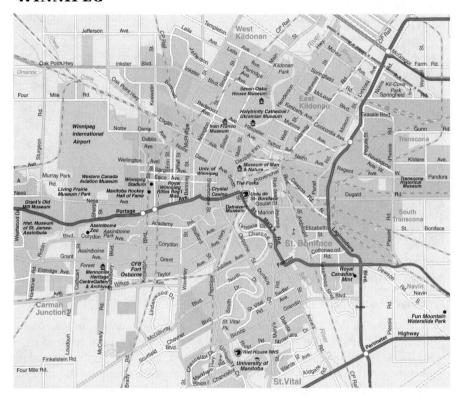

The museum is opposite The Forks National Historic Site near the Saint Boniface Cathedral, at 494 ave Taché. Open weekends only from October to May, daily for the remainder of the year. Admission: adult ❶; family ❸. For information, call ☎ (204) 237-4500.

The **Winnipeg Art Gallery**, founded in 1912, features galleries of contemporary, historical, decorative, and modern Inuit art. The museum, at 300 Memorial Boulevard, is open daily, except in the winter when it is closed Monday. Admission: adult ❶–❷. Wednesday free. For information, call ☎ (204) 786-6641 or consult 🖳 www.wag.mb.ca.

Alongside Winnipeg International Airport in a former hangar, the **Western Canada Aviation Museum** displays historical aircraft, artifacts, and a hands-on children's exhibit. There's also a Stinson airplane simulator. The museum is at the end of Elice Avenue, then north on Ferry Road. Admission: adult ❶–❷; family ❹. For information, call ☎ (204) 786-5503 or consult 🖳 www.wcam.mb.ca.

Fort Whyte Centre is a forest oasis in the city, an exploration of Manitoba's prairie grassland, wetland habitats, and wildlife. Exhibits include an Aquarium of the Prairies and floating marsh boardwalks. The site, located at 1961 McCreary Road, is open daily. Admission: general, ❶; child younger than 2, free. For information, call ☎ (204) 989-8355 or consult 🖳 www.fortwhyte.org.

Winnipeg by night
Photo courtesy of Travel Manitoba

Attractions North of Winnipeg

Oak Hammock Marsh and Conservation Area lies in the middle of the central North America flyway, and birders and naturalists have spotted more than 260 kinds of birds and twenty-five species of mammals. Activities include walkabouts and tours on foot and by canoe. The area is about twenty minutes north of Winnipeg, north of Highway 67 on Provincial Road 220. Admission: adult ❶–❷; family ❹. For information, call ☎ (204) 467-3300.

Two hours north of Winnipeg on an arm of land that extends into lower Lake Winnipeg, **Hecla Provincial Park** is made up of a group of wooded islands that have rocky shorelines. Named after an Icelandic volcano, the area is well populated with wildlife and a thick aspen forest. The park is located on the central flyway migration route for birds. Also in the park is Hecla village, a restored Icelandic village.

The island is connected to the mainland by a causeway; a ferry runs from Gull Harbour to Black Island, a bit farther out. The park is on Highway 8, northeast of Riverton. For information, consult 🖳 www.gov.mb.ca/natres/parks/regions/cen tral/hecla.html.

Northwest near Saskatchewan is **Riding Mountain National Park**, famous for its large black bear, moose, elk, deer, and wolves. A herd of bison lives in an enclosure. The park rises from the prairie to more than 2,450 feet as part of the Manitoba escarpment. Agassiz Tower offers a panorama of prairies to the north.

Riding Mountain is 192 miles northwest of Winnipeg on Highway 10, sixty-two miles north of Brandon. For information, call ☎ (204) 848-7275 or consult 🖳 parkscanada.pch.gc.ca/parks/manitoba/riding_mountain.

And far north along the border with Saskatchewan and almost beyond the

NORTH OF WINNIPEG

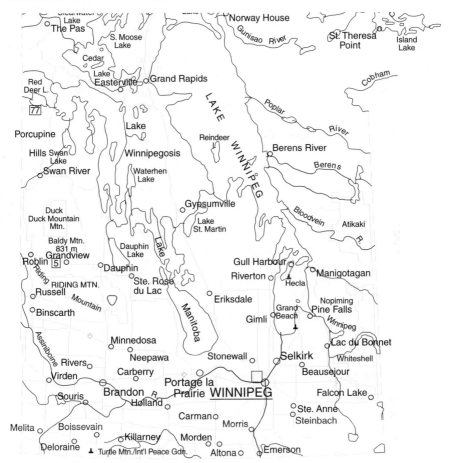

influence of modern civilization are **Clearwater Provincial Park** and above it **Grass River Provincial Park**. Clearwater, not surprisingly, is known for deep, unusually clear, blue water. A hiking trail leads to The Caves, deep crevices created by huge slabs of rock that broke off shoreline cliffs more than 400 million years ago when Manitoba was covered by a warm, shallow sea.

Clearwater is thirteen miles north of The Pas, on Provincial Highway 287. Admission: park permit ❶; in 2001, a season's yearly pass for Canada's provincial park system was $20. For information, call ☎ (204) 627-8217 or consult 💻 www.gov.mb.ca/natres/parks/regions/northern/clearwater.html.

Grass River has offered refuge to travelers for thousands of years as evidenced by rock paintings found along some of the rivers and streams. In the park are some 150 small lakes linked by a 118-mile canoe trail. The area is home to a variety of waterfowl, caribou, deer, moose, and other animals. For information, consult 💻 www.gov.mb.ca/natres/parks/regions/northern/grass_river.html.

Attractions South of Winnipeg

In the southwest corner of the province, along the longest unguarded border in the world, the **International Peace Garden** is a 2,300-acre park shared by Canada and the United States. Gardens are planted in mirror images, symbolizing the modern-day peaceful coexistence between the two countries.

The garden is fifteen miles south of Boissevain on Highway 10. Open daylight hours as season changes. Admission in 2001 was $10 per vehicle. For information, call ☎ (204) 534-2510 or consult 🖥 www.peacegarden.com.

Attractions East of Winnipeg

About fifty-five miles east of Winnipeg along the border with Ontario are three spectacular parks, one somewhat developed and the others nearly untouched.

Whiteshell Provincial Park is the largest and most popular of the three provincial parks in the region; it occupies a thousand watery square miles of the Pre-Cambrian Shield. There are some two hundred lakes in the park; West Hawk Lake, believed to have been formed by a meteor impact, is popular with scuba divers. There are horseback trails and downhill skiing slopes. The park is north of the Trans-Canada Highway 1 at the border with Ontario. For information, consult 🖥 www.gov.mb.ca/natres/parks/regions/eastern/whiteshell.html.

Farther north, above Whiteshell, is **Nopiming Provincial Park**, served by road access from Lac du Bonnet, about forty-four miles west. For information, consult 🖥 www.gov.mb.ca/natres/parks/regions/eastern/nopiming.html.

And there is **Atikaki Wilderness Park**, Manitoba's only wilderness park. There is no road access; the park is accessible only by water or air. Inside are rushing rivers, lakes, massive glacial boulders, and huge Jackpine forests.

Within the park the Bloodvein River is a wilderness perfect for canoeing with rapids and falls in its upper areas and peaceful flows along the lower reaches.

Manitoba Festivals and Events

June

Jazz Winnipeg Festival. Winnipeg. ☎ (204) 989-4656. 🖥 www.jazzwinnipeg.com. International, national, and local musicians in a week-long festival at outdoor stages. Admission: varies with the events; some events are free.

July

Manitoba Highland Gathering. Winnipeg. ☎ (204) 757-2365. 🖥 mbhg.tripod.com. Competitions in drumming, piping, and highland dancing, York boat races, sheep herding, and shearing. Held the first Saturday of July at Selkirk Park, twenty-three miles northeast of Winnipeg.

Part V
Ontario

Chapter 18
Ontario

Canada is a nation of water as much as land, and Ontario is truly defined by the water that surrounds it, runs through it, and cascades over waterfalls within it.

In fact, Ontario's very name comes from an Iroquois word meaning "high rocks near the water," quite possibly the very first advertising slogan for Niagara Falls.

Ontario is formed to its south by Lake Superior, Lake Michigan, Lake Huron, Lake Erie, and Lake Ontario. Oceangoing vessels pass over the lakes and connecting canals from as far away as Chicago to the Saint Lawrence River at Ontario's southeastern border, continuing east through Montréal, Québec City, and out to the Atlantic Ocean.

Up north, the remote wilderness is fronted by Hudson Bay and James Bay, which open onto the Arctic Circle.

Geology of Ontario

Ontario was shaped by receding ice about ten thousand years ago. Glaciers gouged huge holes in the earth, leaving the landscape pitted and scratched and creating an abundance of lakes, rivers, and waterfalls, including the most famous of them all, Niagara Falls.

Two-thirds of the province is covered by the Canadian shield, the oldest rock on earth; Precambrian granite is hundreds of millions of years old.

The glaciers also created the Great Lakes, the largest body of fresh water in the world, and etched 2,400 miles of shoreline from the Saint Lawrence River to Thunder Bay.

Northern Ontario is rich in minerals and forests. Southern Ontario, with its fertile soil and its proximity to markets in the United States, is the primary agricultural and manufacturing region of Canada.

Ontario, a territory nearly as large as France, Germany, and Italy combined, is almost the exact center of North America. In its northern coast the 412,582-square-mile province reaches a higher latitude than the beginnings of the Alaskan panhandle. Its southern extremity sits on the same latitude as northern California and Rome.

ONTARIO

The southern border of the province is shaped by the Great Lakes: Superior, Michigan, Huron, Erie, and Ontario, the largest chain of lakes in the world, containing about 20 percent of the world's fresh water.

Ontario's History

Thousands of years ago Ontario was inhabited by the First Nations people including many members of the Iroquois nation, who were the source of many of the names of lakes, towns, and cities in the province.

By the 1500s the natives had established an early democratic government with trading and other alliances among the tribes.

In 1610 Etienne Brulé reached the interior of Ontario while exploring for a route to the west. He is believed to be the first outsider to set eyes on Niagara. Brulé was followed by other French settlers, including Jesuit priests and fur traders.

French presence in the Ottawa Valley goes
back to 1615 when Samuel de Champlain was
commandant of Québec City, and undertook
first explorations of the area. The first European

Ontario tourism. 🖳
www.ontario-canada.com.

settlement was at L'Original in 1764. The French population grew during the
late 1800s when French Canadians migrated to mill towns and lumber
workings on the Ontario side of the river. The French influence strengthens as
you head eastward toward Ottawa and the Québec border.

British colonization began in 1775 when a wave of refugees fled north in
advance of the American Revolution. The United Empire Loyalists, as they
were known, occupied the region from Québec to Lake Huron. Incorporated
into the British Empire, the area was designated Upper Canada and placed
under control of John Graves Simcoe. An English soldier and Ontario's
founding governor, he established the first parliament in 1792.

The lakes were an integral part of the defense of the colony in the
eighteenth and nineteenth centuries with a series of redoubts including Fort
Henry, Fort York, Fort George, Fort Erie, Fort Malden, and Fort Saint Joseph
helping protect British and Canadian interests from American invaders.

After Simcoe abolished slavery, Ontario became a haven for slaves who fled
from the American south along the Underground Railroad of the mid-1800s.

In 1857 Ontario joined with Québec, New Brunswick, and Nova Scotia to
create Canada. The nation's first Prime Minister was a Scottish-born lawyer
from Kingston, Ontario, John A. Macdonald.

The Heritage of the First Nations

The people of the First Nations arrived in what is now Ontario more than ten
thousand years ago, following herds of caribou.

Today Ontario is home to members of more than 132 nations of Aboriginal
peoples including the Iroquois, Ojibway, Chippewa, Odawa, Pottawatomi, Cree,
and Algonquin. There are a number of interpretive centers and special events
throughout the province including Serpent Mounds Park, Petroglyphs Provincial Park, the Woodland Cultural Centre, and Manitou Mounds.

Getting to Ontario

The principal airports of the province are in Toronto and Ottawa.

Toronto's main airport, **Lester B. Pearson International**, is about fifteen
miles northwest of downtown. Taxi service costs about $40. Scheduled bus
service, about a forty-five-minute ride, costs about $15. For information, con-
sult 🖳 www.lbpia.toronto.on.ca. Some domestic flights use the small **Toronto
City Centre Airport**, on an island in Toronto's harbor.

Ottawa International Airport is about fifteen miles south of the capital
city. A taxi ride costs about $20. Scheduled bus service connects to downtown
hotels for about $10. For information, consult 🖳 www.ottawa-airport.ca.

By car, the lower half of Ontario is well-served by highway. Coming from
the United States, principal border crossings are at Buffalo or Niagara Falls,

within easy reach of Toronto. Lake Ontario stands in the way of direct access from New York State to the middle of the province; a major border crossing near Ottawa is above Watertown, New York on U.S. Route 81.

Ontario Festivals and Events

January

Ontario Winter Carnival Bon Soo. Sault Ste. Marie. ☎ (705) 759-3000. 🖳 www.bonsoo.ca. Late January. Ten days of indoor and outdoor events and activities. Fireworks, snow sculptures, skiing, skating, curling, snowpitch, snow volleyball, snowmobiling, and Canada's original Polar Bear swim, plus Fantasy Kingdom, a winter playground of professionally sculpted snow.

February

Toronto Winterfest. Toronto. ☎ (416) 338-0338. 🖳 www.city.toronto.on.ca/ winterfest. Mid-February. Ice skating shows, giant fantasy snow playground, entertainment, midway.

    Winterlude. Ottawa and Hull. ☎ (800) 465-1867 or ☎ (613) 239-5000. 🖳 www.capcan.ca/winterlude. Early February. Figure skating, snow and ice sculptures, concerts, and fireworks. Skate on the Rideau Canal, the world's longest skating rink, a five-mile stretch.

March

Canada Blooms. Toronto. ☎ (416) 447-8655. 🖳 www.canadablooms.com. Mid-March.One of the top flower and garden shows in North America, held at the Metro Toronto Convention Centre.

May

Canadian Tulip Festival. Ottawa. ☎ (800) 668-8547. 🖳 www.tulipfestival.ca. Mid-May. A legacy of the wartime friendship between Canada and Holland when the Dutch Royal Family spent an enforced exile in Ottawa; there are 100,000 tulips in bloom.

June

Benson & Hedges Symphony of Fire. Toronto. ☎ (416) 442-3667. Mid-June to mid-July. An international fireworks competition set to music over Lake Ontario. Waterfront reserved seating is available through TicketMaster at ☎ (416) 870-8000 for about $25 per person, including park admission.

    Desh Pardesh. Toronto. ☎ (416) 340-0485. 🖳 home.ican.net/~desh. Mid-June. Southeast Asian culture.

    Festival of Nations. Chatham. ☎ (519) 360-1998. 🖳 www.wincom.net/ chatham/festival.htm. Late June–early July. Canada Day weekend.

    Franco-Ontarian Festival. Ottawa. ☎ (613) 741-1225. Late June. Musical festival.

    Greater Hamilton Tattoo. Hamilton. ☎ (905) 546-4222. Early June. Copps Coliseum. Military bands, choirs, musicians, and dancers.

International Dragon Boat Festival. Toronto. ☎ (416) 598-8945. 💻 www. dragonboats.com. Mid-June. More than 160 teams race their 38.5-foot dragon boats off Centre Island. The race commemorates one of the more important cultural events in the Chinese calendar, the sacrifice of the poet/philosopher Qu Yuan, who committed suicide by drowning himself to protest the corrupt regime of a Chou emperor.

Metro International Caravan. Toronto. ☎ (416) 977-0466. Late June to early July. More than a week of pageants, shows, food, and drink celebrating the world's traditions and cultures.

Multicultural Festival of the Nations. Windsor. ☎ (519) 255-1127. Mid-June.

Royal Canadian Big Band Music Festival. London. ☎ (800) 461-2263. 💻 www.execulink.com/~bigband. Late June.

Toronto Downtown Jazz Festival. Toronto. ☎ (416) 928-2033. 💻 www.to jazz.com. Late June to early July. More than two thousand international artists perform jazz at several dozen venues in downtown Toronto.

July

Bancroft Rockhound Gemboree. Bancroft. ☎ (613) 332-1513. 💻 www.com merce.bancroft.on.ca/gemboree.htm. Late July or early August. Canada's largest mineral and gem show.

Caribana. Toronto. ☎ (416) 465-4884. Mid-July to early August. A festival of Caribbean music and culture at various locations. Includes ferry cruises, the Olympic Island Music Festival, a children's carnival, the King and Queen of the Bands, and all-day parade.

Festival Italian. Guelph. ☎ (519) 821-1110. Early July.

Kingston's Buskers' Rendez-vous. Kingston. ☎ (613) 542-8677. Mid-July. International street performers festival. Jugglers, fire eating acts, and more.

Northern Lights Festival Boreal. Sudbury. ☎ (705) 674-5512. 💻 www.nlfb. on.ca. Canada's longest continuously running bilingual multicultural outdoor music festival, held in Bell Park in early July.

Ottawa International Jazz Festival. Ottawa. ☎ (613) 241-2633. 💻 jazz.ott awa.com. Late July. Ten-day event that involves 450 national and international jazz artists at more than one hundred locations.

The Great Rendez-vous Festival. Thunder Bay. ☎ (807) 473-2344. Mid-July. Re-enactors celebrate fur trade history at Old Fort William.

Toronto Fiesta Italia. Toronto. ☎ (416) 698-2152. Mid-July.

Toronto Harbour Parade of Lights. Toronto. ☎ (416) 410-9787. 💻 www. paradeoflights.com. July 1. As many as a hundred decorated boats, each supporting a charity, light up the night in celebration of Canada Day.

Toronto Outdoor Art Exhibition. Toronto. ☎ (416) 408-2754. 💻 www.tor ontooutdoorart.org. Mid-July. North America's largest and longest-running outdoor fine art festival, with more than five hundred juried artists at Nathan Phillips Square.

August

Canadian National Exhibition. Toronto. ☎ (416) 393-6000. 🖳 www.the ex.com. Late August to early September. Canada's largest annual event, a sort of super county fair with entertainment, food, a midway with more than seventy rides, and the Canadian International Air Show.

Fergus Scottish Festival and Highland Games. Fergus. ☎ (519) 787-0099. 🖳 www.sentex.net/~scottish. Mid-August.

Festival of Friends. Hamilton. ☎ (905) 525-6644. 🖳 www.creativearts.on.ca. Early August. Canada's largest free festival of music and crafts, in Gage Park.

September

Algoma Fall Festival. Sault Ste. Marie. ☎ (705) 949-0822. 🖳 www.soonet.ca/ festival. Early September to late October.

Celtic Festival. Fort Henry. ☎ (613) 542-7388. 🖳 www.foodandheritage. com/celticfh.htm. Early September.

Owen Sound Celtic Festival. Owen Sound. ☎ (888) 675-5555. 🖳 www.oscelt icfestival.com. Mid-September. Music, dancing, and Pratie Oaten, a traditional potato harvest.

Toronto International Film Festival. Toronto. ☎ (416) 968-3456 or ☎ (416) 967-7371. 🖳 www.e.bell.ca/filmfest. Ten days of premiers, galas, and marathon movie presentations. Mid-September.

October

Oktoberfest. Kitchener. ☎ (519) 570-4267. 🖳 www.oktoberfest.ca. Mid-October. Largest German festival outside the motherland.

November

Royal Agricultural Winter Fair. Toronto. ☎ (416) 263-3400. 🖳 www.royal fair.org. The Coliseum & National Trade Centre. World's largest indoor agricultural and equestrian competition, plus the Royal Horse Show. Early November.

December

Candlelight Stroll. Niagara-on-the-Lake. ☎ (905) 468-4263. Early December.

First Night. Toronto. ☎ (416) 362-3692. A family-oriented, alcohol-free New Year's Eve celebration at various venues.

Pow-Wows

First Nations Pow-Wows are held in summer and fall and feature traditional drumming, music, dancing, and crafts.

Grand River Champion of Champions Pow Wow. Ohsweken. ☎ (519) 758-5444. 🖳 www.grpowwow.com. Late July.

Toronto International Pow-Wow. Toronto. ☎ (519) 751-0040. Last weekend in November.

Wikwemikong Annual Competition Pow Wow. Manitoulin Island. ☎ (705) 368-3021. Early August.

Chapter 19
Ottawa, Kingston, and the
Thousand Islands

Ottawa, a neat and tidy capital city, won the honor as the seat of government of Canada almost by accident. The original choice, Kingston, was right on the border with the upstart United States, and threats to the city resulted in a move north to Montréal in 1842. Fifteen years later the Americans seemed to be on the move again, and the capital was taken further inland to a place some wags said would be impossible for anyone to find.

Actually, Ottawa benefited from the existence of the Rideau Canal, which had been constructed at great human and capital cost from 1826 to 1832 to help isolate British shipping from those pesky Americans, avoiding the exposed routes along Lake Ontario.

In any case the government came to Ottawa in 1857.

The city perches above the juncture of the Ottawa River and the Rideau Canal. Gothic towers and spires of Parliament Buildings dominate the cityscape. Ottawa, Canada's capital region, is one of the world's fastest-growing high-tech industry communities.

The Ottawa River runs west to east through the metropolitan area. The north shore is the mostly French city of Hull, in the Province of Québec, and the south shore is the predominately English-speaking national capital of Ottawa in Ontario.

The main bridge across the Ottawa River is the Pont du Portage from Wellington Street in Ottawa to center city Hull.

Downtown Ottawa is in turn divided into east and west sections by the Rideau Canal.

To the west Wellington Street includes many government buildings and Parliament Hill. On the east side of the canal Rideau Street is the main drag, running into the residential and commercial districts including the Rideau Centre mall and the Byward Market, which dates back to the 1840s, and today offers farmer's markets and crafts sales.

Ottawa feels in many ways like a small-scale version of London. The Ottawa River stands in for the River Thames, and it takes only a little stretch of imagi-

The Parliament and government buildings of Ottawa

nation to see the seat of government on Parliament Hill as a version of Westminster Palace in Merry Olde England.

As befits a capital city, Ottawa also offers some excellent national museums.

Ottawa's History

Ironically, the first permanent settlers in the area of Canada's capital were a group of American families led by Philemon Wright, who had left Massachusetts in 1800 because of their unpopular Loyalist leanings.

The settlers had traveled up the Outaouais River, named after a local tribe of Algonquins. The first name for the settlement was Wright's Town, which eventually became Hull, now in the Province of Quebec.

The massive Rideau Canal project was under the direction of Colonel John By of the Royal Engineers; the town that grew up on the south shore of the river to support the work was named Bytown. In 1855 the town was big enough to call itself a city and changed its name to Ottawa, an English version of Outaouais.

In 1857 Queen Victoria named Ottawa as the nation's capital.

Around Ottawa

The **Parliament Buildings** are open for tours year-round, and there are viewing galleries to see the House of Commons and Senate when they are in session. Admission: free. For information, call ☎ (800) 461-8020 or ☎ (613) 239-5000 or consult 🖳 www.parl.gc.ca/information/visitors/indoor/center-e.htm. In the summer season, tickets are distributed at an information tent outside.

OTTAWA AND HULL

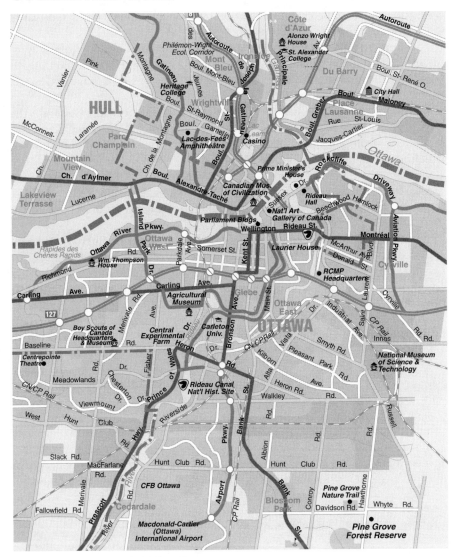

Just as in Britain, one of the highlights is Question Period in the Commons, which takes place every afternoon and on Friday mornings. For information, call ☎ (613) 992-4793. There's also a formal changing of the guard each day at 10 A.M. in the summer season.

Construction on the ornate Gothic-style buildings began in 1860. The home of the Commons and Senate was built in 1920 to replace an earlier structure destroyed by fire in 1916.

The Peace Tower, added in 1927 as a memorial to World War I, includes an observation gallery; the structure includes stone brought from the battlefields of Europe.

All of the Parliament Buildings have been under renovation for several years; work is expected to be completed in 2001. Among the work was a renewal of the bright copper roofs of the buildings.

Law students offer tours of the **Supreme Court of Canada** from May to August and by reservation at other times. The court is at Kent and Wellington Streets. For information, call ☎ (613) 995-5361 or consult 💻 www.scc-csc.gc.ca/visitcourt/index_e.html.

Rideau Hall is the official residence of the Governor General, the representative of the Queen in Canada. The home includes five public rooms; the seventy-nine-acre park setting includes formal gardens and greenhouses, which are open for tours on special occasions. The Governor General's Foot Guards and the Canadian Grenadier guards are posted outside the main gate of Rideau Hall in summer. Tours are offered year-round. The residence, located at 1 Sussex Drive, is open year-round. Admission: free. For information, call ☎ (800) 465-6890 or consult 💻 www.gg.ca.

A cultural highlight of the capital city is the **National Gallery of Canada**. Founded in 1880 it is home to the world's largest collection of Canadian art plus an extensive international collection. Located at 380 Sussex Drive, it is open year-round. Admission is free to the permanent collection. For information, call ☎ (613) 990-1985 or consult 💻 national.gallery.ca.

Founded as a branch of the British Royal Mint, the nearby **Royal Canadian Mint** struck its first coin in 1908. The mint refines about 70 percent of Canada's gold at its refinery. No longer producing every-day coinage, today the mint produces Maple Leaf investment coins in silver, platinum, and gold. Public tours are offered from early May to the end of August. Admission: adult, ❶. The mint is located at 320 Sussex Drive. For information, call ☎ (613) 993-8990 or consult 💻 www.rcmint.ca.

At the Bank of Canada the **Currency Museum** explores the evolution of money from shells to glass beads to coins and bills. The museum, located at 245 Sparks Street, is open year-round. Admission: free, no cash necessary. For information, call ☎ (613) 782-8914 or consult 💻 www.bankofcanada.ca/museum.

Key to Prices
❶ $5 and under
❷ $5 to $10
❸ $10 to $20
❹ $20 and more
When prices are listed as a range, this indicates various combination options are available. Most attractions offer reduced-price tickets for children and many have family rates that include two adults and two or three children.

The **National Museum of Science and Technology** traces our body of knowledge from early tools to outer space with stops along the way to explore vintage cars, locomotives, communications devices, computers, and much more. The museum, located at 1867 Saint Laurent Boulevard South, is open year-round. Admission: adult, ❷–❸. For information, call ☎ (613) 991-3044 or consult 💻 www.science-tech.nmstc.ca.

The **National Aviation Museum** concentrates on the evolution of flying machines and the role they played in the development of Canada. More than one hundred aircraft are on display as well as engines, aviation artifacts, dioramas, and aviation art. The museum, at Aviation and Rockcliffe

Museum of Civilization in Hull, Quebec, across the river from Ottawa

parkways, is open year-round. Admission: adult ❸. For information, call ☎ (613) 993-2010 or consult ▆ www.aviation.nmstc.ca.

The **Canadian Museum of Contemporary Photography**, an offshoot of the National Film Board, has a collection of more than 158,000 images, with a changing exhibition. The museum at 1 Rideau Canal, between the locks and the Château Laurier hotel, is open year-round. Admission: free. For information, call ☎ (613) 990-8257 or consult ▆ cmcp.gallery.ca.

The dinosaurs live on at the **Canadian Museum of Nature**, where you'll also find displays on Canada's birds, mammals, plants, and minerals. You can descend into a simulation of a gold mine, stroll along the Bay of Fundy, or walk beneath the gaping jaws of a dinosaur. Located at Metcalfe and McLeod Streets, the museum is open year-round. Admission: free. For information, call ☎ (613) 566-4714 or consult ▆ www.nature.ca.

Across the river in Hull, the **Canadian Museum of Civilization** rises from the shoreline of the Ottawa River, evoking the birth of the continent sculpted by wind, rivers, and glaciers. The museum includes extensive collections on the early peoples and ethnic diversity of Canada.

Highlighting the early settlers and ethnic diversity, Canada Hall traces one thousand years of social history. Grant Hall celebrates the rich cultural heritage of Pacific North West Coast Native Peoples. Temporary exhibitions feature folk art and traditions. The museum also features an Imax cinema.

Located at 100 rue Laurier in downtown, the museum is open year-round. Admission: general, ❷; child (2–12), ❶. For information, call ☎ (819) 776-7000 or consult ▆ www.civilization.ca/cmc/cmceng/welcmeng.html.

The Rideau Canal

After the disastrous War of 1812 the Duke of Wellington advised that the British government in Canada do something to help defend against the possibility of future clashes with the Americans. He proposed construction of an inland canal to link the military centers of Kingston and Ottawa, avoiding the more vulnerable Saint Lawrence River, which ran along the border between the two countries.

Construction of the 126-mile canal took six years and many lives. Completed in 1832 it includes forty-seven locks and twenty-four dams. The canal climbs 275 feet over the Canadian Shield and then drops 160 feet to Lake Ontario.

The canal was never used for its intended military purpose. After a period of use carrying freight, the canal is now given over to recreational uses. Cruise boats ply its length, and visitors can rent house boats.

Today it is the oldest continuously operating nineteenth-century canal in North America. Most of its locks are still operated by hand. For information, call ☎ (800) 230-0016 or ☎ (613) 283-5170 or consult 💻 www.rideau-info.com/canal.

The **Bytown Museum** at the Ottawa Locks on the Rideau Canal behind the Château Laurier explains the social, military, and economic history of Ottawa when its nickname was "Bytown." The exhibits focus on Colonel John By, the engineer of the Rideau Canal, and the canal's builders. The museum is open year-round. Admission: adult, ❷–❸. For information, call ☎ (613) 234-4570 or consult 💻 collections.ic.gc.ca/bytown.

In Smiths Fall, about an hour southwest of Ottawa, the **Rideau Canal Museum** is set in historic stone buildings along the canal. Exhibits explain the canal's construction, workings, and the flora and fauna of the area. The museum, at 34 Beckwith Street South, is open from May to October. Admission: general, ❶. For information, call ☎ (613) 284-0505 or consult 💻 www.rideau-info. com/canal/attraction.html.

Nearby is the **Smiths Falls Railway Museum**, located within a restored Canadian Northern railway station. Exhibits depict railroad history in Canada; you can stroll through heritage railway cars. And you can ride the rails to the Bascule Railway Lift bridge overlooking the Rideau Canal. The museum, located at 90 William Street West, is open from May to the end of October. Admission: adult, ❶. For information, call ☎ (613) 283-5696 or consult 💻 www. magma.ca/~sfrm.

Whitewater Rafting

The Ottawa River, ranked among the best rafting rivers in North America, is big and fast with huge-volume rapids in the spring. The largest rapids, the Coliseum, churn up twenty-foot-high waves in full flow, a torrent every bit as big as the Colorado River's Lava Falls. The river runs with as much as 150,000 cubic feet of water per second.

The flow of the Ottawa River is regulated by Ontario and Québec Hydro. The river setting includes islands, granite walls, coves, and secluded beaches, all framed by towering pines.

Several major rafting companies have riverside resorts that offer camping and cabin accommodations. Some also offer gentler family float trips.

Wilderness Tours. ☎ (800) 267-9166. 💻 www.wildernesstours.com.

Equinox Adventures. ☎ (800) 785-8855. 🖳 www.equinoxadventures.com.
Owl Rafting. ☎ (613) 646-2263, ☎ (613) 238-7238. 🖳 www.owl-mkc.ca/owl.

Kingston and the Thousand Islands

The "Limestone City" of Kingston was built at the watery crossroads where the southernmost end of the Rideau Canal meets Lake Ontario at the mouth of the Saint Lawrence River, about ninety miles south of Ottawa.

The city's strategic location at the western gateway to the Thousand Islands led to the growth of shipbuilding and defense installations during the 1800s. Kingston was chosen as the first capital of Canada in 1841, a distinction it held for just a year before it was decided that it would be safer to move the seat of government further inland and away from the pesky Americans just a few miles away.

> **Kingston Economic Development Corporation.** ☎ (613) 544-2725, www.kingstonarea.on.ca.

The area was discovered by French explorer Robert Cavalier Sieur de La Salle in the late 1600s, and the settlement began with the erection of Fort Frontenac. In 1758 the British captured the fort, and Kingston came under their control.

The War of 1812 between British and American forces lead to the fortification of Kingston, including Fort Henry. The Rideau Canal system was completed in 1826, in part as a means to create a reliable supply route from Kingston to what is now Ottawa should the Americans blockade the Saint Lawrence River.

The first Canadian Parliament was opened in Kingston in 1841. Because of renewed disputes between the British and the Americans, the decision was made to move the national seat of government away from the border; in 1844 the capital was moved first to Montréal and in 1867 to Ottawa.

The city's nickname of "Limestone City" comes from its many gray stone buildings that have been well preserved over the years. The nearby waters at the mouth of Lake Ontario are popular with sailors, and Kingston was the site of the 1976 Summer Olympics sailing event, part of the Montréal Olympics.

The **Bellevue House** national historic site features interpreters in period costumes welcoming visitors to the home of Canada's first Prime Minister, Sir John A. Macdonald. The house and grounds have been restored to their appearance in 1840. Located at 35 Centre Street, the site is open daily from April 1 through the end of October. For information, call ☎ (613) 545-8666 or consult 🖳 parkscanada.pch.gc.ca/parks/ontario/bellevue_house.

You can explore some of Canada's inland nautical heritage at the **Marine Museum of the Great Lakes**. Moored outside is the three-thousand-ton ice breaker *Alexander Henry* of the Canadian Coast Guard. The museum, located at 55 Ontario Street at Lower Union, is open weekdays from January to May, and daily from June to October. Admission: adult, senior, and student, ❶; family, ❸. For information, call ☎ (613) 542-2261 or consult 🖳 www.marmus.ca.

Nearby is the **Pump House Steam Museum**, a collection of steam engines small and large in an 1850s waterworks. Located at 23 Ontario Street, the site is open June through September. For information, call the Marine Museum of the Great Lakes, or consult 🖳 www.marmus.ca/marmus/pumphouse.html.

KINGSTON AND THE THOUSAND ISLANDS

The fully restored nineteenth-century citadel of **Fort Henry** features performances by the famous Fort Henry Guard, complete with cannon fire, guns, and fife and drum. Located off Highway 2 East below Highway 15, the restoration is open mid-May to the end of September. Admission: adult, ❷; child, ❶. For information, call ☎ (613) 542-7388 or consult 🖳 www.parks.on.ca/fort.

In the 1860s Fort Henry was the massive military stronghold of British forces. Today you can watch soldiers, tradesmen, women, and children carry out life as it was in those days. Listen to fife and drums and watch infantry and artillery perform during the daily Commandant's Parade on the parade square. Have your children enlist as young soldiers.

Built in 1846 as part of the fortifications of Kingston, the **Murney Tower Museum** is a British-style Martello tower used as military housing for more than forty years. Operating as a museum since 1925 the three floors display a collection of military and domestic artifacts of nineteenth-century Kingston. Located at King Street West at Barrie, the museum is open daily from mid-May through September. For information, call ☎ (613) 544-9925 or consult 🖳 www.heritagekingston.org/khs/murney.html.

The **Kingston Archaeological Centre** offers a collection and library about the eight-thousand-year history of human occupation of the Kingston area.

The center is located in a waterfront brewery complex. Donations accepted. Open weekdays from 9 A.M. to 4 P.M. For information, call ☎ (613) 542-3483 or consult 🖳 web.ctsolutions.com/carf/document/kac.html.

A small but interesting collection of rocks, minerals, and fossils (including the skull of a duckbill dinosaur) are on display at the **Miller Museum of Geology** at Queen's University in Miller Hall, Union at Division Streets. Open weekdays. Admission: free. For information, call ☎ (613) 533-6767 or consult 🖳 geol.queensu.ca/museum/museum.html.

At **Kingston Mills Blockhouse**, a working blockhouse on the Rideau Canal, visitors can watch boats pass through the locks. Admission: free. Located off Kingston Mills Road north of Highway 401 at exit 619 or 623. For information, call ☎ (800) 230-0016 or ☎ (613) 283-5170, or consult 🖳 www.rideau-info.com/canal/history/locks/h46-49-kingstonmills.html.

The Thousand Islands

No one seems to know exactly how many islands there are in the Saint Lawrence between Ganonoque and Brockville to the east, but there sure are a lot of them. Most are small, some are little more than a rock in the river, and some of the islands are in a foreign land.

But for more than a hundred years this lovely stretch of the river has been a favored summer vacation destination for Canadians and Americans.

You can take a cruise among the islands with departures from Kingston and Ganonoque. Among the sites is **Boldt Castle**, an elaborate summer home constructed in the late nineteenth century for George Boldt, the owner of New York's famous Waldorf Astoria Hotel. Little expense was spared, including reshaping the island as a heart, but the home was never finished and ended up abandoned.

By the way, Boldt's chef named the Thousand Island salad dressing after his boss's would-be home.

Boat lines in the area include:

Gananoque Boat Line. ☎ (613) 382-2144 or ☎ (613) 382-2146 for twenty-four-hour information, or consult 🖳 www.ganboatline.com.

Rockport Boat Line. ☎ (800) 563-8687 or 🖳 www.rockportcruises.com.

Saint Lawrence Cruise Lines. ☎ (800) 267-7868 or consult 🖳 www.stlawrencecruiselines.com. Multi-day luxury cruises on replicas of old packet boats from Kingston to Ottawa, Montréal, and Québec City.

The well-respected **Thousand Islands Playhouse** in Gananoque presents shows from May to October in a century-old theater. For information, call ☎ (613) 382-7020 or consult 🖳 www.1000islandsplayhouse.com.

In Mallorytown in the heart of the Thousand Islands tourist area, the **Saint Lawrence Islands National Park** offers exhibits and a boat launch. Open from mid-May to mid-October. Admission: adult, ❶. For information, call ☎ (613) 923-5261 or consult 🖳 parkscanada.pch.gc.ca/parks/ontario/st_lawrence_islands.

Chapter 20
Toronto

The Hurons called the harbor at the west end of Lake Ontario the "meeting place," or Toronto. Well before the arrival of Europeans, the natives beat a path from the harbor through the wilderness to Lake Huron.

The French were the first to settle in the area with a small redoubt named Fort Rouillé; they were expelled by the British in 1759 but it wasn't until after the American Revolution that Loyalists came north and established a town.

Today's neat and clean big city of Toronto grew up around Yonge Street, which was a military road of the late 1700s constructed to replace a canoe portage route between the two lakes. The British named the town that first grew there York; it regained the name Toronto when the settlement was incorporated as a city in 1834.

Along the way York was raided and severely damaged by an American raiding party during the War of 1812; in retribution a British force headed south for Washington to burn much of that city.

The rebuilt city of York prospered as a fiercely pro-British manufacturing and commercial center. The conservative cultural and social atmosphere of the town continued into the middle of the twentieth century, when Toronto became directly connected to the rest of the world by Saint Lawrence Seaway. In the 1980s the growth of Separatism in the neighboring province of Québec brought an influx of new blood, money, and more liberal philosophies.

Getting Around Toronto

As befits its conservative image, Toronto's street map could just about be printed on graph paper; the city is laid out in an almost perfect grid of streets. Yonge Street is still the principal road of the city, heading due north from the waterfront, pointing toward Georgian Bay and further north toward James Bay near the top of the province. A few blocks west of Yonge on the harbor is the CN Tower, visible from almost everywhere in the city.

Toronto has more than eighty ethnic communities; most grew after the Seaway opened and the city became, in essence, an Atlantic port. Toronto's districts include Chinatown, Little Italy, Greektown, and Little India.

TORONTO

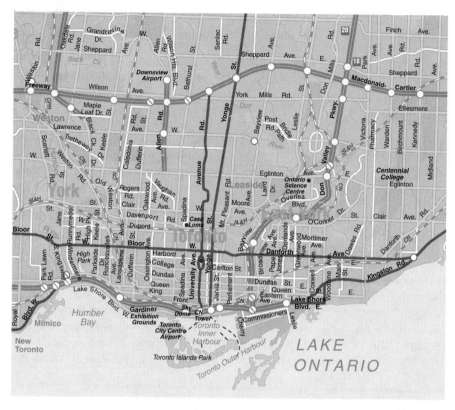

The city's version of the Underground City is the "Path," a seven-mile maze of corridors and malls linking downtown hotels and offices. The indoor walkways, with more than 1,100 shops, boutiques, and restaurants, are well appreciated in the heat of summer and the howling winds of a lakefront winter.

The **Toronto Transit** subway system has two lines with sixty stations across the metropolitan area. The Yonge/University/Spadina line runs in a U-shape from Finch Avenue south, down the length of Yonge Street to Union Station, and then north along University and Spadina avenues to Wilson Avenue. The Bloor/Danforth line runs along Bloor Street and Danforth Avenue to Main Street and then northeast to Kennedy Road.

For information on subway, bus, trolley, and streetcar lines, call the Toronto Transit Commission at ☎ (416) 393-4636 or consult 🖳 www.city.toronto.on. ca/ttc. The system sells day passes and multi-day passes at a discount.

The **Harbourfront Light Rail Transit** operates trams from Union Station to Queen's Quay and from there to Spadina Avenue along the waterfront.

Museums and Attractions

A self-declared wonder of the modern world, the **CN Tower** has certainly made its mark on Toronto—it's all but impossible to overlook. Built in 1976 as a communications tower, it is still the world's tallest structure—there are quibbles about whether the spire at its top is part of the building or just an antenna. In any case, the tower stands at 1,815 feet and five inches. A set of observation decks, including one with a glass floor, stand at the 1,122-foot level.

Also within is the 360 Revolving Restaurant, a simulator theater, a laser tag arena, and other entertainments.

The tower is located at 301 Front Street West, near the waterfront. Open year-round. Admission: adult, senior, child, ❸–❹. Ticket packages include elevator, films, and rides. For information, call ☎ (416) 360-8500 or ☎ (416) 601-4707 or consult 🖳 www.cntower.ca.

Canada's largest museum is the **Royal Ontario Museum** (ROM), and like the country, it's a sprawling mix of all kinds of delights. The museum combines art, archaeology, and science; the core of the original collection came from private gatherings. There are more than 6 million objects and specimens ranging from dinosaurs to one of the best Chinese collections in the western world.

Key to Prices
❶ $5 and under
❷ $5 to $10
❸ $10 to $20
❹ $20 and more
When prices are listed as a range, this indicates various combination options are available. Most attractions offer reduced-price tickets for children and many have family rates that include two adults and two or three children.

Toronto tourism information. ☎ (416) 203-2600. 🖳 www.torontotourism.com.

Admission to the ROM includes admission to the George R. Gardiner Museum of Ceramic Art across the street. The museum is located at 100 Queen's Park Boulevard, at Bloor Street in downtown. Open year-round. Admission: adult, ❷; senior, ❷; child (6–17), ❶; child (5 and younger), free. For information, call ☎ (416) 586-8000 or consult 🖳 www.rom.on.ca.

Next door is the **Children's Own Museum** at the former McLaughlin Planetarium at the Royal Ontario Museum.

The **Ontario Science Centre** features interactive exhibits on sport, space, food, chemistry, transportation, and more. The museum, which also includes an Omnimax Theatre, is located at 770 Don Mills Road in North York, west of downtown. Open year-round. Admission: adult, ❸; youth, ❷; child, ❶. For information, call ☎ (416) 696-1000 or consult 🖳 www.osc.on.ca.

Another mega-museum is the **Art Gallery of Ontario**, nearly a city block in size. Some fifty galleries showcase thousands of works in all media that span six hundred years. The Henry Moore Sculpture Centre houses more than one thousand of Moore's works, including one room that displays about twenty of his human form sculptures.

Next door is **The Grange**, a Georgian mansion built in 1817 that is the oldest brick house in Toronto and the Art Gallery's first home. The home, decorated with period furniture and art, is staffed by costumed guides.

The museum is located at 317 Dundas Street. Open year-round. Admission: by donation, ❷ suggested, which includes entrance to the museum and The Grange. For information, call ☎ (416) 979-6648 or consult 🖳 www.ago.on.ca.

Downtown Toronto looking toward Lake Ontario

But when it comes to true national treasures, for many Canadians there is nothing to compete with a battered old silver cup of undistinguished design. It's the Stanley Cup, the emblem of sovereignty in the National Hockey League, and it is on display for much of each year at the **Hockey Hall of Fame**.

The museum includes hockey sticks, pucks, uniforms, and other memorabilia plus state-of-the-art exhibits and interactive technology. At the end of the visit you'll find yourself in the Bell Great Hall with the Honoured Members Wall—the hall of fame—and a staggering collection of NHL trophies, including the Stanley Cup. (The cup is on the road in the championship city each year after the conclusion of the playoffs in June.)

The museum is located at 30 Yonge Street on the concourse level of BCE Place at the corner of Yonge and Front Streets. Open daily. Admission: adult, ❸; senior and youth (4–18), ❷; child (3 and younger), free. For information, call ☎ (416) 360-7765 or consult 🖳 www.hhof.com.

Fort York brings back the place where Toronto was founded in 1793; the city was twice taken by American troops in the War of 1812, and the Battle of York was fought here in 1813. The site, with a large collection of original buildings of the time, includes guides in period costumes, fife and drum music, military drills and demonstrations. The fort is on Garrison Road at Fleet Street. Open year-round. Admission: general (6–12), ❶; child (5 and younger), free. For information, call ☎ (416) 392-6907.

The sugar industry was an important one in Ontario's history, and the **Redpath Sugar Museum** tells you more than you ever thought to ask about the sweet stuff. The museum, at 95 Queens Quay East, is open year-round. Admission: free. For information, call ☎ (416) 366-3561.

Just west of downtown in Downsview is the **Black Creek Pioneer Village**, a restoration that brings to life a rural Victorian village of about 1860. Country roads and boardwalks lead to more than thirty-five homes and workshops, as well as public and farm buildings. The village is at 1000 Murray Ross Parkway in Downsview, off Highway 400. Open May to December. Admission: general, ❷; child (5–15), ❶; child (4 and younger), free. For information, call ☎ (416) 736-1733, ext. 209.

Attractions

The Imax/Omnimax technology was pioneered in Canada, and the **Omnimax Theatre at the Science Centre** is a state-of-the-art cinema, located at 770 Don Mills Road. For information, call ☎ (416) 696-1000 or consult 💻 www.osc.on.ca/WhatsPlaying/omnimax/omni.html.

The **Bay/Adelaide Cloud Forest Conservatory** is an indoor forest in Toronto's financial district that depicts the layers of a high-altitude cloud forest of Central and South America and South Asia. You'll enter a ground plane of shade plants, ascend to a tree fern level, and then make your way to the sky canopy. Open weekdays from 10 A.M. to 3 P.M. For information, call ☎ (416) 392-1111 or consult 💻 www.city.toronto.on.ca/parks/parks_gardens/bayadelaidegdns.htm.

Set in the historic Allen Gardens in downtown Toronto, the **Palm House** is styled in the grand tradition of British glass pavilions. Completed in 1909 it contains a large collection of tropical plants and succulents. It is home to the Victorian Flower Christmas Show each December. Palm House is located within Jarvis, Gerrard, Sherbourne, and Carlton Streets. The building is open daily. Admission: free. For information, call ☎ (416) 392-7288 or consult 💻 www.city.toronto.on.ca/parks/parks_gardens/allangdns.htm.

Museums of (or for) the Strange

The Academy of Spherical Arts. How's that for a highfalutin name for a collection of billiard tables? Some of the pieces of furniture, though, are true masterpieces, including one that was exhibited at the Paris Exhibition in 1900. The academy is located at 38 Hanna Avenue. For information, call ☎ (416) 532-2782 or consult 💻 www.sphericalarts.com.

The **Arthur Conan Doyle Collection** at the Metro Reference Library of Toronto is one of the world's best collections of Sherlockiana. The Victorian décor even captures the ambiance of Sherlock Holmes' fictional home at 221B Baker Street in London, complete with the violin on the mantel, a deerstalker on the rack, and slippers on the floor. Highlights of the collection include nine rare editions that make up the Sherlock Holmes Canon and an 1887 edition of *A Study in Scarlet*. The library is located at 789 Yonge Street. For information, call ☎ (416) 393-7000.

Then consider the **History of Contraception Museum**, the only museum of its kind in the world, which is probably not surprising. But if this is what you're looking for, here's a fine example: the exhibit of nearly six hundred items

Baseball trivia. Babe Ruth hit the first home run of his professional career on Hanlan's Point on the Toronto Islands. The nineteen-year-old pitcher threw a one-hit, 9–0 shutout in a minor league game against the Toronto Maple Leafs on Sept. 5, 1914, hitting a three-run homer in the process. A plaque on the island commemorates the event; the Island Airport now occupies the former location of the stadium.

The Toronto Islands are 640 acres of parkland, with lagoons, marinas, cycling paths, beaches, and quaint little 1930s cottages.

Rock shrine. The Hard Rock Cafe in Toronto was the first location for the chain. In 1978, two Torontonians opened a restaurant downtown, taking a name from a popular Doors album, Morrison Hotel/Hard Rock Cafe. By 1980, local groups and touring artists began donating autographed guitars, gold and platinum records, and other artifacts to mount on the wall.

includes such artifacts as ancient dung-and-honey tampons, dried beaver testicles, and animal membrane condoms. The collection is supervised by Ortho-McNeil, a modern maker of contraceptive products. The museum is located at 19 Greenbelt Drive in North York. For information, call ☎ (416) 449-9444.

And if that's not nearly far enough out for you, make a stop at the **Merril Collection of Science, Speculation and Fantasy**. Known as the "Spaced Out Library," this collection of some fifty-four thousand items includes material about science fiction, parapsychology, UFOs, and other subjects on the fringe. The library is located at 239 College Street, Third Floor. For information, call ☎ (416) 393-7748 or consult 🖳 www.tpl.toronto.on.ca/merril/home.htm.

Another Toronto exclusive, the **Bata Shoe Museum Collection**, includes the footwear of the rich and the infamous from the Spice Girls to actresses, defectors, and corrupt politicians. The museum, run by the Bata Shoe company, purchased Ginger Spice's shoes in 1998, adding to a collection that includes the black leather shoes worn by Mikhail Baryshnikov when he defected from the Soviet Union to Canada in 1974 as well as a few of Imelda Marcos's pumps.

The museum is located at 327 Bloor Street West. Open year-round. Admission: adult ❷; senior, student, child (5–14), ❶; child (5 and younger), free. For information, call ☎ (416) 979-7799.

Every modern city needs a Medieval-style castle; **Casa Loma** was built in 1914 by financier Sir Henry Pellatt at what was then a stupendous cost of more than $3 million.

The castle includes towers, secret passages, and restored gardens. Self-guided audio tours are included in the admission fee. Casa Loma is located at 1 Austin Terrace on Spadina Avenue north of Davenport Road. Open year-round. Admission: adult, ❷. For information, call ☎ (416) 923-1171 or consult 🖳 www.casaloma.org.

Arts and Entertainment

Toronto's theatrical scene is one of the most active theater centers in the English-speaking world after New York and London. Broadway style shows are featured in some of Toronto's recently restored heritage theaters. Productions are mounted by more than 125 theatrical companies at more than forty stages.

The **Canadian National Exhibition**, known locally as "the Ex" is the largest and oldest annual agricultural fair in Canada, spreading over eighteen days at the end of the summer and ending on Canadian Labor Day in September. The fair includes midway rides, an air show, musical performances, and botanical gardens. For information, call ☎ (416) 597-0965 or consult 💻 www.theex.com.

The **Elgin and Winter Garden Theatre Centre**, built in 1912, is said to be the last operating double-decker theater complex in the world.

While the turn-of-the-century Elgin Theatre is opulent and beautiful by itself, it's the Winter Garden, seven stories above, that steals the show. Described as one of the world's first "atmospheric theatres," the room includes a ceiling of thousands of real leaves, columns disguised as tree trunks, a glowing moon, and trellised walls.

Live theatrical performances are presented; guided tours uncover artifacts, original vaudeville scenery, and backstage areas.

The theater is located at 189 Yonge Street in downtown, opposite Eaton Centre. Open year-round for tours. Admission: adult, senior, and student ❷. For information, call ☎ (416) 314-2874 or consult 💻 www.heritagefdn.on.ca/Confer ence-Theatres/theatres.htm.

Another active theater is the **Hummingbird Centre for the Performing Arts**, located at 1 Front Street East at Yonge Street. ☎ (416) 393-7474 ext. 242. Among companies that make their home there is the National Ballet of Canada; for ballet information, call ☎ (416) 345-9686 or consult 💻 www.hum mingbirdcentre.com.

The **Toronto Centre for the Performing Arts** includes two theaters and a recital hall used for musical productions and concerts; the theater is located at 5040 Yonge Street in North York, just northwest of downtown. For information, call ☎ (416) 733-9388 or consult 💻 www.tocentre.com.

Roy Thomson Hall is home to the **Toronto Symphony Orchestra**. The theater is located at 60 Simcoe Street. For information, call ☎ (416) 593-4822, ext. 225 or consult 💻 www.tso.on.ca.

In Scarborough, north of downtown, the **Metropolitan Toronto Zoo** is home to some five thousand animals; the Zoomobile helps visitors get around the 710-acre park. Open year-round. Admission: adult, ❸; child, ❷. For information, call ☎ (416) 392-5900 or consult 💻 www.torontozoo.com.

Air Canada Centre is the modern home to the Toronto Maple Leafs of the National Hockey League and the Toronto Raptors of the National Basketball Association. For information about the arena and purchase tickets to many events, consult 💻 www.theaircanadacentre.com.

For **Toronto Maple Leaf** tickets and information, call Ticketmaster at ☎ (416) 872-5000 or 💻 www.ticketmaster.ca. You can also consult 💻 www.torontomaple leafs.com.

For **Toronto Raptors** tickets and information, call Ticketmaster at ☎ (416) 872-5000 or 💻 www.ticketmaster.ca. You can also consult 💻 www.nba.com/raptors.

The **SkyDome**, the world's first stadium to have a fully retractable roof, is home to the Toronto Blue Jays. It is also used for major concerts. For information about the arena and tickets for many events, consult 🖳 www.skydome.com.

For **Toronto Blue Jays** tickets, call ☎ call (416) 341-1234 or consult 🖳 blue jays.mlb.com. In recent years, tickets have been readily available.

Toronto City Hall is a civic showplace built around a large public square used for art shows, festivals, concerts, seasonal farmers markets, and civic ceremonies. In winter the large reflecting pool is converted to an ice skating rink. Henry Moore's sculpture *The Archer* is located near the entrance to the square. The building is at 100 Queen Street West, at the corner of Queen and Bay Streets. Open year-round. For information, call ☎ (416) 392-7341.

Harbourfront Centre Toronto, a waterfront setting for cultural events, performances, and wintertime ice skating is at the foot of York Street. For information, call ☎ (416) 973-3000 or consult 🖳 www.harbourfront.on.ca.

And there is a regular schedule of events at **Ontario Place**, an entertainment complex that includes three man-made islands with canals, lagoons, and viewing areas, a sixteen-thousand-seat amphitheater, a marina, and the Cinesphere Imax theater. Located at 955 Lakeshore Boulevard West, Ontario Place is open from May to October. For information, call ☎ (416) 314-9811 or consult 🖳 www.ontarioplace.com.

Little India is the commercial center for the Indian population of Toronto; its six blocks of restaurants, grocers, music stores, and shops include more than twenty boutiques specializing in traditional saris and other brightly colored silk fashions. The area is busiest on Sunday. Little India is located in the east end of Toronto, along Gerrard Street East, between Highfield and Coxwell Avenues.

The Toronto Skydome

East of Toronto

The rocky highlands and rolling farmlands to the east of Toronto were a haven to Loyalist settlers who fled north from America after the Revolutionary War. They founded new cities, towns and villages along the region's waterways; cleared spruce forests to build and till their crops.

Just above Toronto the **Markham Museum** preserves twenty-five acres of historic homes, shops, a railway, blacksmith shop, and a church. Located at 9350 Highway 48, the museum is open year-round. Admission: general, ❶. For information, call ☎ (905) 294-4576 or consult 🖳 www.city.markham.on.ca/Comm Serv/commculture/museum/default.htm.

A pleasant drive of about fifteen miles east along the lake to Oshawa brings you to an early automotive capital of Canada. **Parkwood Estate and Gardens** is the fifty-five-room home and estate of R. S. McLaughlin, the first magnate of Canadian General Motors. The humble abode is furnished with antiques and appointments of the 1930s; the grounds include formal gardens, sculptures, and a greenhouse. The estate, open year-round, is located at 270 Simcoe Street North. Admission: ❷–❸. For information, call ☎ (905) 433-4311 or consult 🖳 www.city.oshawa.on.ca/tourism/parkwood.html.

Not coincidentally, nearby is the **Canadian Automotive Museum** with a collection of some ninety antique vehicles, sixty of which are on display at all times. Some of the vehicles are one of a kind. The museum, located at 99 Simcoe Street South, is open year-round. Admission: general, ❶. For information, call ☎ (905) 576-1222 or consult 🖳 www.city.oshawa.on.ca/tourism/can_mus.html.

North of Oshawa in Lindsay the **Academy Summer Theatre** is in its fourth decade, occupying the century-old Academy Theatre. The season runs from mid-June to the end of August. For information, call ☎ (705) 324-9111.

The Kawartha Lakes region draws its name from a First Peoples word meaning "bright waters and happy land." It was home to the Mississauga when European explorers first arrived; at **Petroglyphs Provincial Park** scientists have found evidence of earlier settlements dating back a thousand years or more. The park, thirty-five miles northeast of Peterborough off Northey's Bay Road, is open May to October. Admission: adult, ❷; child, ❶. For information, call (888) 668-7275, ext. 1, or consult 🖳 www.ontarioparks.com/petro.htm.

To the east of the Kawartha Lakes the town of **Peterborough** sits on the **Trent Severn Waterway**, a 240-mile-long waterway that follows a complex path to link Trenton on Lake Ontario to Severn on Georgian Bay of Lake Huron. Built more than a century ago to carry small boats and barges for commerce to the inland, it has been supplanted by the Welland Canal from Lake Ontario to Lake Erie. Today the system is used exclusively for recreational boating; there are cruises that follow the path, and visitors can rent houseboats.

The waterway uses small rivers, some stretches of man-made canal, and portions of the Kawartha Lakes, and Lake Simcoe. The water level is regulated by some 125 dams. Communities along the way provide accommodation, shopping, summer theater, special events, and attractions. The canal is operated from mid-May to mid-October.

The **Peterborough Hydraulic Lift Lock** features a visitor center where you can watch one of the highest water lifts in the world, a sixty-four-foot rise. The center is open from April 1 to mid-October. Admission: general, ❶. For information, call ☎ (800) 663-2628 or ☎ (705) 750-4950.

Nearby is the **Canadian Canoe Museum**, home to more than five hundred canoes and kayaks. The museum, at 910 Monaghan Road, is open-year round but by appointment only in the fall and winter. Admission: donation. For information, call ☎ (705) 748-9153 or consult 🖳 www.canoemuseum.net.

If you're a fan of movie star Marie Dressler, a detour south to Cobourg on the shore of Lake Ontario is in order. The **Dressler Home** preserves the cottage birthplace of the Oscar-winning actress, born in 1869 as Leila Von Koerber. She left Ontario at age fourteen, making her name as a vaudeville performer. She starred on Broadway in 1892; her first film success was a 1914 Mack Sennett feature-length comedy, *Tillie's Punctured Romance*. She won the Oscar for Best Actress in 1931 for *Min and Bill*, playing opposite Wallace Beery. She died in 1934. Each October Cobourg presents the Marie Dressler Annual Film Festival.

The house, located at 212 King Street West, is open year-round. Admission: free. For information, call ☎ (905) 372-5481.

Southwest to Hamilton

Hamilton, an industrial city of 320,000 with a port on Lake Ontario, is the Pittsburgh of Canada—the country's iron and steelmaking capital. The **Hamilton Military Museum** in Dundurn Park collects Canadian military history from about 1800 through the early twentieth century with displays including uniforms and weapons of the War of 1812, the Boer War and World War I. The museum, at 610 York Boulevard, is open year-round. Admission: adult, student, senior, child, ❶; family, ❷. For information, call ☎ (905) 546-4974.

Dundurn Castle is the restored 1855 home of Sir Allan MacNab, one of Canada's early Premiers. The mansion includes forty Victorian rooms and a surrounding park with guided tours by costumed staff. Open year-round, the castle is located at 610 York Boulevard. Admission: adult, senior, and student, ❷; child (6–12), ❶. Admission to the castle also includes admission to the Hamilton Military Museum. For information, call ☎ (905) 546-2872 or consult 🖳 www.hpl.hamilton.on.ca/Collections/landmark/Dundurn.shtml.

In Mount Hope, west of Hamilton, you'll know you're at the **Canadian Warplane Heritage Museum** when you spot a CF-104 Starfighter Jet climbing into the sky from the parking lot. The museum includes twenty-five restored bombers, fighters, and trainers flown by the Canadian Military from WWII to the jet age. The collection includes the only flying Lancaster Bomber in North America. You can test your skills on the many interactive displays. The museum, at 9280 Airport Road, is open year-round. Admission: general, ❷; child (7 and younger), free. For information, call ☎ (905) 679-4183 or consult 🖳 www.warplane.com.

Chapter 21
Niagara Region

The falls at the outflow of Lake Erie into Lake Ontario is one of the most famous places on earth, although many people don't realize that about half of Niagara Falls lies in Canada.

The Niagara River is actually a strait, a body of water flowing about thirty-five miles between Lake Erie and Lake Ontario. The difference in elevation between the two lakes is 326 feet, with about half of that drop occurring at the Falls. The water passing over the Falls drains an area of 264,000 square miles that includes Lakes Erie, Michigan, Huron, and Superior. Downstream of the falls, the water continues on to Lake Ontario, the Saint Lawrence River, and on to the Atlantic Ocean.

The drop at the Canadian Horseshoe Falls is 170 feet into the Maid of the Mist pool. At the American Falls, the water drops between 70 and 110 feet to the base.

Niagara Falls is a cataract on the move. The force of the tens of millions of gallons of water passing over the top causes large sections of the rock to erode and fall into the basin each year. About twelve thousand years ago Niagara Falls was located seven miles downstream of its current position; until the early 1950s the Falls were eroding at the rate of about three feet per year. In more recent times engineers have installed diversion channels to spread the flow more evenly and reduce erosion to about one foot in ten years.

Some of the water bypasses the falls and instead heads through tunnels to the Sir Adam Beck #2 Generating Station on the Canadian side or to the Robert Moses Niagara Power Plant downstream on the American side. Under an international agreement, water removed from the river upstream is shared equally for hydroelectric generation by the two countries.

The Falls are at their highest volume of about 100,000 cubic feet per second from April to the end of October from about 8 A.M. to 10 P.M. At other times and for the remainder of the year, dams reduce the volume by about half.

Since 1925 the Falls have been lit up at night as a tourist operation. Now under the control of an international commission, the lights shine every night until as late as 1 A.M., depending on the season. A total of twenty-one Xenon

181

NIAGARA FALLS

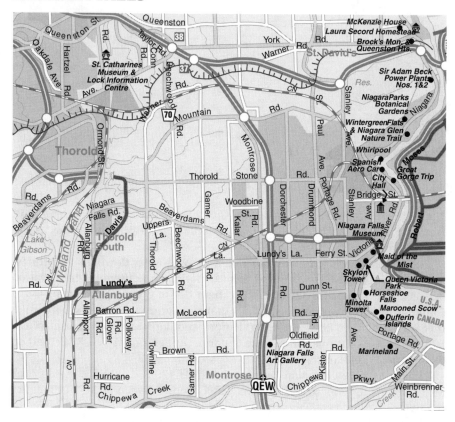

lamps with as much as 250 million candlepower are employed; eighteen are located at the Illumination Tower beside the Victoria Park Complex and three more near the base of the Falls opposite the American Falls.

A Niagara History

The Niagara area was one of the important terminuses on the Underground Railroad in the mid-nineteenth century. Neither a railroad nor underground, this was a network of sympathizers who helped escaped slaves make their way from southern states in the United States to safe haven in Canada.

Some forty thousand slaves followed the North Star to Canada, many of them passing through Niagara Falls, Fort Erie, and Saint Catharines to settlements a bit further north of the border and out of the reach of American bounty hunters, many of whom crossed the border in search of slaves. After the end of the Civil War about half of the slaves returned to the south in hopes of reuniting with their families.

For some reason daredevils have chosen to go over Niagara Falls willingly. In 1901 Annie Taylor was the first person to conquer the falls in a barrel; bruised and battered, she waited for the fame and fortune, but neither came. In 1920

Englishman Charles Stephens put an anvil in his wooden barrel for ballast, tying himself to the weight. When the barrel was recovered, the anvil and his arm were inside; he was not.

The first Canadian to conquer the Falls was Karel Soucek in 1984; he survived the plunge but was killed soon after while recreating the drop from a platform inside the Houston Astrodome. Rhode Island bartender Steven Trotter survived a 1985 plunge in a barrel encased in inner tubes.

> **Tourism information on Niagara Falls.** 💻 www.tourismniagara.com. For information on The Niagara Parks Commission, contact the Interactive Communications Centre at toll-free ☎ (877) 642-7275, or consult 💻 www.niagaraparks.com.

The Niagara Tourist District

In some ways the west side of the Niagara River, also known as Canada, has become a very commercial extension of Buffalo, the second largest city in New York State. The Niagara Parkway runs along the cliff above the Niagara River from the Peace Bridge near Buffalo to Niagara-on-the-Lake, a resort community on Lake Ontario. Winston Churchill, who knew more than a little about hyperbole and art, called the Niagara Parkway, "the prettiest Sunday afternoon drive in the world."

One of the most famous attractions at the Falls is the *Maid of the Mist*. Small rowboats ferried passengers across the Niagara River below the Falls as far back as 1834. In 1846 the first steamboat ferry, christened *Maid of the Mist*, began carrying passengers and coaches. Two years later the first suspension bridge crossed the river valley, and the ferry was recast as a sightseeing venture. Since then millions of visitors have clambered aboard one of the small boats in the fleet that cruise right to the base of the American Falls and the basin of the Canadian Horseshoe Falls.

The boats operate from late April to late October for half-hour trips. There are boarding places on both the Canadian and American sides.

Fares in 2001 were: adult, ❸; child (6–12), ❷. For information, call ☎ (905) 358-5781 or consult 💻 www.maidofthemist.com.

One of the best (and least commercial) ways to get close to the falls is to purchase an **Explorer's Passport Plus**, available from the Niagara Parks Commission.

The pass includes the Journey Behind the Falls, the Niagara Spanish Aero Car, and the Great Gorge Adventure, plus a day-long ticket for the Niagara Parks' People Movers, which travel a loop between the falls and Queenston Heights Park.

The passport is available from mid-May to mid-October. In 2001 the Passport sold for: adult, ❹; child (6–12), ❷; child (5 and younger), free. Tickets to each attraction can also be purchased individ-

> **Key to Prices**
> ❶ $5 and under
> ❷ $5 to $10
> ❸ $10 to $20
> ❹ $20 and more
> When prices are listed as a range, this indicates various combination options are available. Most attractions offer reduced-price tickets for children and many have family rates that include two adults and two or three children.

Falls short. As famous as they are, the falls are not the highest or widest in the world, nor do they have the greatest flow of water. Ahead of Niagara Falls in all three categories is Iguazu Falls on the border of Paraguay, Brazil, and Argentina.

High voltage. On Goat Island, upriver of the Falls, a monument honors Nikola Tesla, inventor of alternating current for electricity. The immigrant from Yugoslavia was a former employee of Thomas Edison. Tesla believed that a system of alternating current was a more practical means of supplying electricity than the direct current scheme supported by Edison.

The key test of Tesla's theories came in 1896 when he used the power of Niagara Falls to generate and then transmit the electricity for what was at the time a record distance of twenty-seven miles to Buffalo. Today almost all electricity is transmitted by the means he advocated.

ually at a slightly higher total price. For information, consult 💻 www.niagaraparks.com/attract/explorer-idx.html.

Journey Behind the Falls offers an elevator descent to a thrilling view of Niagara Falls from below. Lifts descend a shaft in Table Rock House Plaza beside the Canadian Horseshoe Falls. One set of tunnels extends about 150 feet to a viewing position behind the thundering waters. The main tunnels leads to an open observation deck beside Horseshoe Falls. Guests are provided with raincoats. Purchased individually, tickets in 2001 were: adult, ❷; child (6–12), ❶.

In the busy summer season visitors can reserve a time to visit the Journey Behind the Falls by calling ☎ (905) 371-0254 locally or toll-free at ☎ (877) 642-7275 or consult 💻 www.niagaraparks.com/attract/journey-idx.html.

Two miles down river from Niagara Falls the fast-moving river enters the **Whirlpool Rapids**; eons ago this was the location of the falls themselves but relentless erosion has moved the cataract upstream. The **Great Gorge Adventure–White Water Boardwalk** includes a thousand-foot-long promenade along the edge of the river for unusual access to major river rapids. Purchased individually, tickets in 2001 were: adult, ❷; child (6–12), ❶; child (5 and younger), free. For information, call ☎ (877) 642-7275 or consult 💻 www.niagaraparks.com/ attract/gorge-idx.html.

In 1916 Spanish engineer Leonardo Torres Quevedo built the **Niagara Spanish Aero Car**, a tramway that descends from the cliffs and into the whirlpool and rapids of the Great Gorge downriver from the Falls. The Aero Car continues, little changed from the original design, suspended above a bend in the river on the Canadian side. If you are making a separate visit to the attraction, tickets in 2001 were: adult, ❷; child, ❶. For information, call ☎ (877) 642-7275 or consult 💻 www.niagaraparks.com/attract/aero-idx.html.

You can also purchase a separate ticket to ride the Niagara Parks People Mover System. In 2001 daily tickets were: adults, ❷; child, ❶. For information, call ☎ (877) 642-7275.

The principal shopping area on the Canadian side of the Falls is the **Table**

Table Rock complex at Niagara Falls, Ontario

Rock Complex, where you'll likely find more T-shirts and souvenirs than you could possibly covet.

The **Table Rock Restaurant** perches on the brink of the Canadian Horseshoe Falls; there's also a fast food eatery in the same building.

A bit more upscale is the **Victoria Park Restaurant** with views of both the American Falls and the Canadian Horseshoe Falls. A dinner buffet is offered in July and August. The nearby Victoria Park Cafeteria offers simpler fare.

The **Queenston Heights Restaurant** is on the edge of the Niagara Escarpment, a ten-minute drive downriver from the Falls along the Niagara Parkway. Fine dining offerings include Afternoon Tea and Sunday Brunch.

Queen Victoria Park, adjacent to the Canadian Horseshoe Falls, was named after the reigning British monarch at the time when the Niagara Parks Commission was established in 1885.

Offering the best view of both the American and Canadian Falls, the park is also one of the best places to watch the nightly illuminations and the Falls Friday Fireworks, which take place at 10 P.M. every Friday from mid-May to early September.

From early Spring to late Fall the park bursts into bloom with floral displays; in early May of each year the Blossom Festival Parade passes through the park.

The **Niagara Falls Botanical Gardens and School of Horticulture** is downstream of the Falls between the Great Gorge and Queenston Heights. The gardens include some 2,300 varieties of plants in indoor and outdoor displays. Admission: free. In 2001 tickets for guided tours were ❶.

See the falls now. A twenty-four-hour live video display of Horsehow Falls is available on the net at 🖳 www.falls view.com from a camera mounted on the roof of the Sheraton Fallsview Hotel & Conference Center.

Nearby is the **Floral Clock**, maintained by the Niagara Parks Commission. The floral face of the clock is changed twice a season. Built in 1950 the forty-foot-wide clock was inspired by the original floral clock in Edinburgh, Scotland. Admission: free.

The **Niagara Parks Butterfly Conservatory** is a world unto itself, the largest conservatory of its kind. Located at the Botanical Gardens five miles north of Horseshoe Falls, the dome is home to some two thousand butterflies from thirty-eight species, many produced there in breeding programs. Most of the tropical creatures come from butterfly farms in Costa Rica, El Salvador, and the Phillipines. Admission: adult, ❷; child (6–12), ❶. For information, call ☎ (905) 356-8119 or consult 🖳 www.niagaraparks.com/attract/butterfly-idx.html.

The **Niagara Parks Greenhouse** is located on the Niagara Parkway south of the Canadian Horseshoe Falls and open year-round daily from 9:30 A.M. Hours are extended during the Winter Festival of Lights. Admission: free.

There are several towers offering spectacular overlooks of the falls; the views are especially dramatic at night when the tumbling waters are illuminated.

The **Skylon Tower** is the tallest structure in Niagara Falls at 520 feet and includes the obligatory glass elevators, observation deck, and revolving restaurant. The minimum charge per adult guest in the Revolving Dining Room for lunch is $19.95 and for dinner is $31.95. The tower is open year-round. Ticket prices for the elevator ride in mid-2001 were: adult, ❷; child, ❶; guests going to the restaurant pay just $2 to ride. Located at 5200 Robinson Street. For information, call ☎ (905) 356-2651 or consult 🖳 www.skylon.com.

The **Minolta Tower** is similar in view and rates; it is located at 6732 Oakes Drive. For information, call ☎ (905) 356-1501 or consult 🖳 www.niagarafalls view.com/tower.

Niagara-on-the-Lake

The scenic Niagara Parkway continues north of the falls to Niagara-on-the-Lake, the original capital of Upper Canada from 1791 to 1796 under its original name of Newark. Not much of the town from that period remains since American troops destroyed the place during the War of 1812; what remains, though, is nicely frozen in place in the early nineteenth century.

It's a place of clapboard wooden houses, old inns, and a sense of history.

Favorite stops in the town include the **Niagara Historical Society Museum**. The museum, located at 43 Castlereagh Street, is open year-round. Admission: adult ❶. For information, call ☎ (905) 468-3912.

The **Fort George National Historic Site** recreates the British garrison that was the object of the American assault in 1813. Within the palisades are the company headquarters, blockhouses, and powder magazines. You can also take a ghost tour by torchlight. The site, just south of town, is open from April 1 to

NIAGARA-ON-THE-LAKE

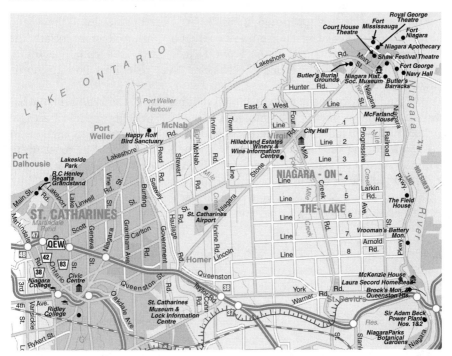

the end of November. Admission: adult, ❷; senior and child (6–16), ❶; child (6 and younger) free. For information, call ☎ (905) 468-4257 or consult 💻 parks canada.pch.gc.ca/parks/ontario/fort_george.

The cultural jewel of the lake is the **Shaw Festival**, one of the largest repertory theater companies in North America. Plays are staged at three theaters from April to October. The festival is located at 10 Queens Parade, Niagara-on-the Lake. For information, call ☎ (800) 511-7429, ext. 62 or ☎ (905) 468-2172 or consult 💻 www.shawfest.com. To contact the **Niagara Chamber of Commerce**, call ☎ (905) 468-4263 or consult 💻 www.nflschamber.com.

The Welland Canal

One of the truly amazing sites of Ontario, if not all of Canada, is that of a 750-foot-long ocean-going ship passing by just offshore of an inland city such as Toronto. The ships travel up the Saint Lawrence River past Quebec City, Montreal, Kingston, into Lake Ontario, then Lake Erie and Lake Huron and down Lake Michigan to Chicago or across Lake Superior and on to Duluth.

The huge lakes are more than deep and wide enough for the ships—the lakes are essentially inland seas.

But more than two hundred years ago merchants and mariners knew they had one big obstacle in the way: the almost two-hundred-foot-high wall of water of Niagara Falls and the rapids above and below the cataract.

The solution was the **Welland Canal**, which bypasses the Falls to connect

Lake Ontario to Lake Erie; a series of locks raises or lowers ships to overcome the 326-foot difference in elevation between the two lakes.

The canal was first proposed in 1829 by local businesses. It has been widened and improved several times since then but still follows essentially the same twenty-five-mile-long path. From Lake Ontario the canal begins at Niagara-on-the-Lake, paralleling the Niagara River to exit at Port Colborne into Lake Erie.

You can learn about the process at the **Welland Canal Centre/Saint Catharines Museum** at Lock 3. The museum includes a working model of a canal lock and other exhibits; if you're lucky you can talk to a sailor aboard one of the 750-foot-long vessels that pass through the lock outside. The museum in Saint Catherines is open year-round. Admission: adult, ❶. For information, call ☎ (905) 984-8880 or consult 🖳 www.tourismniagara.com/stcmuseum.

In the town of Welland along the canal, facades of many of the buildings include giant murals of the canal and area sights.

Chapter 22
Southern Ontario

Canada's "deep south" is the area between Lake Huron and Lake Erie where it drops down to 42 degrees latitude, making it even with New York City, northern California, and Southern European cities Rome and Barcelona.

Relative to much of the rest of Canada, this area has a mild climate and rich soil, supporting some of the best farmland in the country.

In summer the warm waters of Erie and Huron meet some of the finest freshwater beaches anywhere.

Many of the best-known towns and cities of the area draw their names directly from Britain; you can visit Windsor, London, Stratford, Kitchener, Blenheim, Cambridge . . . you get the idea.

Windsor

Windsor's location south of the border (travelers head north north from Windsor into the United States at Detroit) has put it at the center of skirmishes among British, French, and American interests dating back to the arrival of the first missionaries in the 1640s and accelerating during the War of 1812.

The city of almost 200,000 grew as a Canadian extension of the American car-making capital across the Detroit River. Although that industry has declined somewhat in Windsor, the city has benefited from a successful casino. Windsor has also managed to avoid much of the urban decline suffered by Detroit.

Casino Windsor draws about 80 percent of its patrons from the United States. After several years in temporary quarters and on a riverboat, the casino moved into a fancy new structure on Riverside Drive between Aylmer and McDougall streets. Admission is free, but visitors must be nineteen years of age or older. For information, call ☎ (800) 991-7777 or consult information at 🖳 www.casinowindsor.com.

London

The largest city in southwestern Ontario, London would very much like it if you would imagine you were a few thousand miles east in Merry Olde England.

SOUTHWEST ONTARIO

You can hop on a red double-decker bus for a tour along the Thames River that runs through town, make a stop in Hyde Park, and shop on Oxford Street.

The familiar names, though, go only so far; London is not London. It's a pleasant and successful commercial and industrial city of Canada with a First Nations history that reaches back more than eleven thousand years. And for those of a certain age, it is best known as the birthplace of Guy Lombardo.

Just outside of town the **Ska-Nah-Doht Iroquoian Village and Museum** reaches back a thousand years to reconstruct a palisaded Iroquois village, with archaeological artifacts and hiking trails. Located on Highway 2, the museum is open year-round. Admission: adult ❶. For information, call ☎ (519) 264-2420 or consult 🖳 www.lowerthames-conservation.on.ca/SkaNahDoht.htm.

The **London Museum of Archaeology** includes the Lawson Prehistoric Village, a five hundred-year old Iroquois Village that includes an on-going archaeological dig. The museum is located at 1600 Attawandaron Road, south of Highway 22. Open year-round, with reduced hours from September to April. Admission: adult, senior and student, ❶; child (3–12), ❶; family, ❸. For information, call ☎ (519) 473-1360 or consult 🖳 www.uwo.ca/museum.

The **Fanshawe Pioneer Village**, a village of more than twenty-five restored or reconstructed buildings, includes a blacksmith forging iron tools, farm animals, wagon rides, and interpretive displays and programs. The village, located at 2609 Fanshawe Park Road, is open from May to December. Admission: adult, ❷. For information, call ☎ (519) 457-1296 or consult 🖳 www.pioneer. wwdc.com.

Key to Prices
❶ $5 and under
❷ $5 to $10
❸ $10 to $20
❹ $20 and more
   When prices are listed as a range, this indicates various combination options are available. Most attractions offer reduced-price tickets for children and many have family rates that include two adults and two or three children.

You can learn more than you ever imagined about London's favorite son at the **Guy Lombardo Museum**, which features memorabilia of the bandleader and artifacts including his racing boat. The museum, at 205 Wonderland Road South, is open May to September. Admission: adult, ❶. For information, call ☎ (519) 473-9003.

Lombardo, who died in 1977, named his band the Royal Canadians, taking the name of a famed infantry regiment based in London. You can learn about the real thing at the **Royal Canadian Regiment Museum** in the 1886 Wolseley Hall. Here you'll find ornate uniforms, artifacts, and displays. The museum is on Oxford Street. Admission: free. For information, call ☎ (519) 660-5102 or consult 🖳 www.execulink.com/~thercran/museum.htm.

About forty miles west of London in the aptly named Petrolia, the **Victoria Playhouse Petrolia–Victoria Hall** has exhibits on the early oil industry of Canada. The theater offers dramatic presentations and summer stock. Located at 411 Greenfield Street, it is open all year. For information, call ☎ (519) 882-1221 or ☎ (800) 717-7694 or consult 🖳 town.petrolia.on.ca/vpp.

Stratford

The small town of Stratford, west of London toward Kitchener, took its Shakespearean connection rather lightly until the early 1950s when Sir Alec Guiness played as Richard III in a production. From that performance was born the **Stratford Festival**, today one of the world's centers of Shakespearean theater.

Actually, the festival is much more than the works of the Bard. Today it is North America's largest classical repertory theater festival with works including Shakespearean plays, classical works, modern and experimental plays, operettas, and Broadway productions. Shows are presented in three venues: the Festival, Avon, and Tom Patterson theaters.

The season runs from early May to early November. The festival is located on Highway 7 at Highway 8 East. For information, call ☎ (519) 271-4040 or consult 🖳 www.stratfordfestival.ca.

Kitchener-Waterloo

The region between London and Hamilton bears the cultural imprint of German-speaking Mennonite settlers who moved here from Pennsylvania in the 1840s. You'll find towns named Heidelberg, Breslau, New Hamburg and Berlin (now Kitchener), a robust cuisine, and an Oktoberfest.

Kitchener and Waterloo sit practically on top of each other between Stratford and Toronto, so close that locals give the area the shorthand name of K-W.

Kitchener was born as a farm center for the many Germans and Mennonites who came to the area in the nineteenth century. Not surprisingly it is now famous for the raucous **Oktoberfest** celebration that brings at least half a million visitors each year for an orgy of beer, sausages, beer, oompah music, beer, and lederhosen in about twenty festival halls. It's the biggest such festival outside Germany, held the third week of October. For information, call ☎ (519) 570-4267 or consult ▤ www.oktoberfest.ca.

Waterloo is a bit more, err, sober. It is known for two schools, the University of Waterloo and the Wilfrid Laurier University.

The **Doon Heritage Crossroads** in Kitchener is a restoration of a 1914 village that has more than twenty buildings and two farms with livestock and farm gardens. Located about two miles north of Highway 401, the site is open from May 1 to mid-December. Admission: adult, ❷; senior and child (5–12), ❶; child (4 and younger), free. For information, call ☎ (519) 748-1914 or consult ▤ www.region.waterloo.on.ca/doon.

Located in the oldest home in Kitchener, built by Pennsylvania German Mennonite settlers, the **Joseph Schneider Haus Museum** preserves the home and a traditional four-square kitchen garden. Two modern galleries feature items from the Museum's Germanic folk art collection. Located at 466 Queen Street South, the museum is open year-round. Closed Monday. For information, call ☎ (519) 742-7752 or consult ▤ www.region.waterloo.on.ca/jsh.

Just north of Kitchener in Guelph is the **McCrae House**, a limestone cottage of 1858, the birthplace of John McCrae, professor of medicine at McGill University. McCrae is best known as the author of *In Flanders Fields*, the sad antiwar poem about World War I. The poppies in the beautiful gardens bloom in June. The house is located at 108 Water Street; poppy signs lead to the museum. Open year-round. Admission: adult, student, and senior, ❶; child (5 and younger), free. For information, call ☎ (519) 836-1221 or consult ▤ www.museum.guelph.on.ca/mccraenew.htm.

Brantford

South of Kitchener in Brantford was the first North American residence of Alexander Graham Bell, preserved as the **Bell Homestead and Henderson Home**. Restored with original furnishings, the home explores Bell's invention of the telephone. Henderson House served as Canada's first telephone business office in 1877. The house is located at 94 Tutela Heights Road. Open year-round. Admission: general, ❶. For information, call ☎ (519) 756-6220.

Burlington

East of Kitchener and Hamilton, the **Royal Botanical Gardens** features 2,700 acres in bloom year-round and the world's largest lilac collection. There are more than 120,000 spring bulbs, two acres of roses, medicinal and herb gardens, a Mediterranean Garden under glass, and twenty miles of walking trails. The gardens, at 680 Plains Road West, are open from April to October. Admission: adult, senior, and student ❷; child (5–12), ❶; child (younger than 5), free. For information, call ☎ (905) 527-1158, ext. 252, or consult ▤ www.rbg.ca.

Chapter 23
Northern Ontario

Almost three-quarters of Ontario lies north of a line connecting Sault Ste. Marie, Sudbury, and Thunder Bay, although only a few thousand of the province's 10 million residents live above those three industrial centers.

The north of Ontario is a cold, stark place. Without the moderating influences of the Great Lakes, winters up north are, in a word, severe.

And there are virtually no roads above the middle of the province; the few scattered communities in Ontario's north are served by air, by boat along the coast of Hudson Bay and James Bay, and by a rail line that extends to the northeast corner of James Bay.

The **Polar Bear Express** runs from Cochrane north to Moosonee, the oldest permanent settlement in the province, on the edge of the Artic. There are no roads to connect the two towns. Once you get to Moosonee, there's not much there—not even polar bears—but the train, which takes more than four hours in each direction, offers an unusual glimpse of eastern wilderness. There's also a slower whistle-stop local train that serves tiny communities along the way. For information, call the **Ontario Northland Railway** at ☎ (800) 268-9281 or consult 🖳 www.ontc.on.ca.

The dominant geology of northern Ontario is the Canadian Shield. The same ancient glaciers that deposited rich soils in southern Ontario stripped the land down to its very bones up north, a billion-year-old granite bedrock.

The Boreal forests of the north are dominated by spruce and evergreens and populated by wolf, moose, and bear.

Mining operations in the north extract gold, silver, nickel, copper, zinc, and iron for export to world markets.

A significant portion of Northern Ontario's population is made up of Native Peoples; the area is also home to French-speaking descendants of trappers who moved into what was once the frontier of the colony of New France.

Near North (Including North Bay)

The **Algonquin Provincial Park** sits like a country of its own in Ontario's Near North, about 188 miles north of Toronto.

NORTHERN ONTARIO

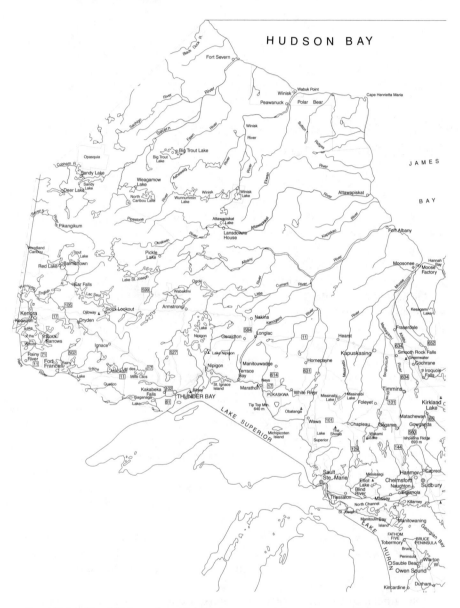

Established in 1893 as Canada's first provincial park, it includes more than three thousand square miles of mostly untouched wilderness—an area about twice the size of Rhode Island. Located on the southern edge of the Canadian Shield, the park is mostly accessible by hikers only. Route 60 cuts through the southwest corner to park headquarters where there are a few lodges and campsites. Included are hundreds of lakes and more than one thousand miles of canoe routes; in winter there are marked cross-country trails.

The Visitor Centre has exhibits on the natural and human history of the park; the small Algonquin Logging Museum tells the history of early logging. On Thursday evenings from late July to September as many as a thousand people gather in Algonquin to listen to the howls of wolf packs. **Canadian Wilderness Trips**, ☎ (416) 960-2298, offers all-inclusive, three-day Wolf Howl canoe excursions into the park.

The park is open year-round. Admission: ❷, plus $10 for a car. For information, call ☎ (705) 633-5572 or consult 🖳 www.algonquinpark.on.ca.

The town of North Bay, at the east end of Lake Nipissing, is an unremarkable working town of more than fifty thousand people; it serves as a staging point for mining communities further north and a base for wilderness vacationers. But in 1934 it became one of the best-known datelines in the world; on May 28, 1934, five identical girls were born in a log farmhouse in Corbeil, just west of town.

The children became an international sensation and literally a national treasure—the government took the children away from their parents a few months after they were born and they were raised in a glass menagerie with thousands of visitors each day paying for a glimpse.

The **Dionne Quints Museum** preserves artifacts that include clothing, toys, and news coverage from the early days of the sisters; the original log house was moved to North Bay for the convenience of modern tourists. Three of the quints still survive; they now live in Québec. The museum, open from May to October, is located at 1375 Seymour Street. Admission: ❶. For information, call ☎ (705) 472-8480 or consult 🖳 www.northbaychamber.com/quints.html.

Sudbury and Rainbow Country

Sudbury is an industrial city set amidst an other-worldly moonscape of rock and minerals; some places are so severe that they were used in 1968 as a training site for lunar explorers Neil Armstrong and Buzz Aldrin. By the time they set foot on the moon, it must have seemed a lot like walking around Sudbury.

The city of about 160,000—half French-speaking—sits on the edge of the **Sudbury Basin**, a huge dent in the Earth that may have been caused by the impact of a gigantic meteor about two billion years ago. All around are large deposits of minerals, including nickel (used in steelmaking), copper, sulphur, and large amounts of rare and valuable metals and minerals such as platinum, palladium, tellurium, gold, and selenium.

Sudbury grew primarily because of the nickel industry, mostly from one company, Inco. The smoke and sulphur belching out of smelting plants was considered the smell of jobs, although it also had the effect of poisoning much of the area.

SUDBURY

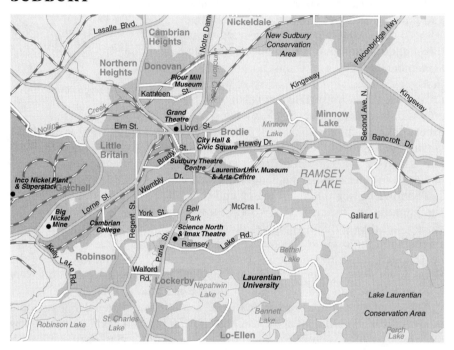

Mining continues today, although at a lower intensity than in years past; today pollution from the smelting process is funneled up huge "superstacks" that take the smoke out of the area. Unfortunately the smoke follows the prevailing west to east winds and drops in the form of acid rain on northeastern Canada and the United States, damaging forests and fish. Both governments and international groups, including U.N. agencies, have been working for decades to reduce the effects of the process.

In addition to huge smokestacks Sudbury has a most unusual municipal marker: a thirty-foot-high Canadian five-cent coin on Highway 17. (The coin is made of stainless steel, somewhat like the smaller coin in your pocket.)

Nearby the big nickel is the **Big Nickel** itself, a mine that is currently closed to tours. However, "Dynamic Earth," is a renovation project at the site that is expected to open in 2002. It will be four stories tall and offer several mining exhibits. At that time the tours down the sixty-five-foot shaft are expected to return. There's also an unusual underground garden for trees and vegetables, taking advantage of the stable and relatively warm temperatures below the earth. There is currently a self-guided surface tour of the area. Admission: general, ❶. For information, call ☎ (705) 522-3701.

A more scientific view of the industry and the region can be seen at **Science North**, an unusual hands-on museum that was carved out of a cavern in the Canadian Shield. You can learn about the geology of the Sudbury Basin and more general subjects such as meteorology (including a build-your-own hurricane), physics, and human biology. There's an Imax theater as well. The museum, at 100 Ramsey Lake Road, is open year-round. Admission to the museum: adult, senior, and child, ❸. For information, call ☎ (800) 461-4898 or ☎ (705) 522-3701 or consult 📖 sciencenorth.on.ca.

Sudbury has declared itself the "Festival Capital of the North." Its best-known festival is the **Northern Lights Festival Boreal**; Canada's longest continuously running folk festival, it is held each July. For information, call ☎ (705) 674-5512 or consult 📖 www.nlfb.on.ca.

The **Sudbury Theatre Centre** is the only professional theater company in northern Ontario. Located at 170 Shaughnessy Street, shows are offered from January to May, and September to December. For information, call ☎ (705) 674-8381 or consult 📖 www.sudburytheatre.on.ca.

Southwest of Sudbury on the shores of North Georgian Bay, **Killarney Provincial Park** offers wilderness recreation. The "La Cloche" mountains here have been a favored landscape subject for Canadian artists. The park offers camping, canoeing, hiking trails, and an outdoor theater plus snowshoeing and cross-country skiing in winter. The park, located on Highway 637, is open year-round with limited services in the winter. Admission: ❷. For information, call ☎ (705) 287-2900 or consult 📖 www.mnr.gov.on.ca/MNR/parks/kill.html.

Along the west shore of Georgian Bay, the **Thirty Thousand Islands** beckon paddlers into sheltered channels of an archipelago of smooth granite outcrops topped by lone pines. For information, consult 📖 www.greatlakes.net/tourism/rec/isle.html. Operators in the area include **White Squall Paddling Centre**, ☎ (705) 342-5324 or consult 📖 www.whitesquall.com.

Manitoulin Island

The world's largest freshwater island, eighty-seven miles long and twenty-five miles wide, Manitoulin Island sits in Georgian Bay on Lake Huron, about fifty miles southwest of Sudbury.

God's Island, or so the original Ojibwa word declares, is big enough to have about twenty small communities, some one hundred lakes, and a population of about eleven thousand, many of them Native Peoples. There are many small farms and a summer tourism economy.

A band of Ojibwa in Wikwemikong refused to cede their lands to white outsiders in 1861, and to this day the eastern tip of the island is officially not a part of Canada. In early August of each year Wikwemikong is the site of the largest powwow in the province, a three-day celebration.

From northern Ontario the island can be reached by a causeway on Route 6 off Route 17, west of Sudbury. From lower Ontario the only way in is by ferry, a thirty-two-mile trip from Tobermory at the end of Cape Hurd, about 120 miles north of Kitchener.

In Sheguiandah the **Little Current Howland Centennial Museum** presents the history of the island with seven restored buildings, an aboriginal cultural collection, a sugar shack, interpretive programs, and craft demonstrations. The museum, open from May to October, is off Highway 6. Admission: adult, senior, student (12–16), ❶. For information, call ☎ (705) 368-2367 in season and ☎ (705) 368-1374 at other times.

Sault Ste. Marie

First of all, you've got to learn how to pronounce the name of this place: It's not "salt." The local pronunciation is "Soo." The same goes for the Michigan city of the same name, which sits on the other side of the rapids on Saint Mary's River between Lakes Huron and Superior.

The **Sault Ste. Marie Canal** was dug in 1895 to bypass the rapids, completing a route to the Atlantic Ocean. In the process, the twin Soos grew as industrial and port cities.

The **Sault Ste. Marie Canal National Historic Site** explains the story of the canal and its workings, including huge wooden lock gates and antique valve machinery. The site, near the International Bridge to Sault Ste. Marie, Michigan, is open year-round. Admission: free. Tour: adult and senior, ❶; child (younger than 6), free. For information, call ☎ (705) 941-6262 or ☎ (705) 941-6205 or consult 🖳 parkscanada.pch.gc.ca/parks/ontario/sault_st-marie_canal.

On the waterfront, the **Canadian Bushplane Heritage Centre** tells the story of Canadian bush flying, Ontario Provincial Air Service, and forest fire fighting from 1878 to the present day. You can also reserve a flight.

The museum, open year-round, is located at 50 Pim Street. Admission: adult and senior, ❷; child, ❶; child (younger than 5), free. For information, call ☎ (705) 945-6242 or consult 🖳 www.bushplane.com.

About forty-five miles north of Sault Ste. Marie, the **Lake Superior Provincial Park** is renowned for its rugged beauty along the eastern shoreline. The park, near Wawa off Trans-Canada Highway 17, is open from May to October. Admission: ❷. For information, call ☎ (705) 856-2284 or consult 🖳 www.ontarioparks.com/lakes.html.

Thunder Bay

Thunder Bay is as far west as an oceangoing freighter can go in Canada, the end of a journey that can reach back to Detroit, Toronto, Montréal, Québec City, and out into the Atlantic Ocean at the Gulf of Saint Lawrence. (Ships can proceed about 120 miles further west to Duluth in that other country that lies below the border, the United States.)

Thunder Bay was a northern headquarters of the Northwest Company in 1789, and later the Hudson's Bay Company; much of the beaver pelts heading from the Canadian West to Europe passed through Fort William there. A network of railroads was put in place in the nineteenth century on the basis of a rumored silver strike, but the mine was a bust.

Thunder Bay's economy was based around its port, which used the railways to bring in grain from the prairies bound for markets around the world. For many years Thunder Bay was Canada's largest grain-handler. That business has declined over the years in favor of Vancouver on the Pacific Ocean.

The biggest tourist draw today is **Old Fort William**, which brings back to life the world's largest fur trade post as it was in 1815. Costumed historic characters portray daily life in more than forty reconstructed buildings, a farm, and an Ojibway encampment. The restoration, near downtown on Broadway Avenue, is

THUNDER BAY

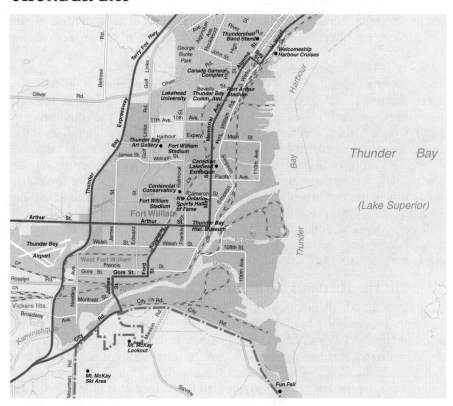

open from mid-May to mid-October. Admission: adult, ❸; senior, student, and child, ❷; child (younger than 5), free. For information, call ☎ (807) 473-2344 or consult ▦ www.oldfortwilliam.on.ca.

The **Thunder Bay Art Gallery** on the campus of Confederation College, has one of the largest collections of contemporary First Nations art. The museum, at 1080 Keewatin Street, is open year-round. Admission: adult and student, ❶. For information, call ☎ (807) 577-6427 or consult ▦ www.thunder bayculture.com.

Billed as the Niagara of the North, a 130-foot-high waterfall plunges into a steep gorge west of Thunder Bay at **Kakabeka Falls Provincial Park**. For information, call ☎ (807) 473-9231 or consult ▦ www.ontarioparks.com/kaka.html.

About seventy miles west of Thunder Bay, **Quetico Provincial Park** protects thirty Ojibway paintings on sheer rock faces. Cliffside eagle and osprey nests can be seen by canoeists paddling the same routes used by fur traders in the 1600s. More than nine hundred miles of wilderness canoe routes include links to the Boundary Waters Canoe Area Wilderness in Minnesota.

The park is south of Highway 11, midway between Fort Frances and Thunder Bay. Open year-round. Admission: donations accepted. For information, call ☎ (807) 597-4602 or ☎ (807) 929-3141 or consult ▦ www.quetico park.com.

James Bay Frontier

About 150 miles north of Sudbury on the outskirts of utter wilderness, there's the unexpected metropolis of Timmins, which is one of the largest cities in Canada.

We're talking square miles, more than nine hundred, for a municipality of about fifty thousand. Timmins brings together a large number of small mining communities in what was once one of the largest gold-mining camps in North America. There is still some gold mining, although today the emphasis is on **Kidd Creek Mines**, the world's largest producer of silver and zinc. Other mines bring out metals and minerals that include iron, copper, and talc.

At the **Timmins Underground Gold Mine Tour and Museum**, you can journey 180 feet underground into the Hollinger Gold Mine, once the richest gold mine in the Western Hemisphere. Most guides are retired miners; exhibits include restored historical buildings. The museum is open in July and August daily. In May and June, and September and October Wednesday through Sunday. Admission: general, ❸; family, ❹. For information, call ☎ (800) 387-8466, ☎ (705) 360-8510, or consult 🖳 www.timminsgoldminetour.com.

Far North: Hudson and James Bay

Accessible only by plane, **Polar Bear Provincial Park** is home to the largest concentration of polar bears in Ontario. Bears congregate along the saltwater coast of Hudson Bay and James Bay in August and September, waiting for the ice to return for their passage into the bay. At other times of the year, visitors can see Beluga whales, black bear, caribou, walrus, seals, lynx, moose, and snow geese. The park is nearly two hundred miles northwest of Moosonee. For information, call ☎ (705) 336-2987 or consult 🖳 www.ontarioparks.com/pola.html.

Part VI
Québec

Chapter 24
Québec

Québec is one of the most Gallic places outside of France, a fiercely independent province of Canada.

The largest province in Canada, Québec is almost three times the size of France itself, more than double the size of Texas, and seven times larger than all of the United Kingdom. The province extends 1,200 miles north to south; Québec's northernmost point, Cap Wolstenholme, is less than 255 miles from the Arctic Circle. Most of the province is covered by forest or water; it has 3,600 miles of shoreline.

The French character celebrates food and festivals, and Québec has an abundance of both. In fact, most of the festivals are centered around food. As it is with the rest of Canada, the vast majority of Québec's population lives within the southern hundred miles of the province.

Most of the seven million inhabitants of Québec live along the Saint Lawrence River. About seventy thousand First People belonging to ten different nations and eight thousand Inuit live in about fifty villages throughout the province.

History Lesson

Explorer Jacques Cartier, sent to the new world by the King of France, landed in the Gaspé peninsula in 1534 and claimed the land as New France; like most explorers, the fact that the Inuit and other First Peoples had been living there for thousands of years did not matter.

Cartier named the mountain overlooking the Saint Lawrence River "Mont Royal"; it is from that hill the modern city of Montréal takes its name.

In 1642 the settlement of Ville-Marie was founded as a missionary village, and from that humble beginning came the world's second-largest French-speaking city and the world's largest inland port.

Québec City, 150 miles closer to the mouth of the Saint Lawrence, was founded in 1608 when Samuel de Champlain established a fur-trading post near the Iroquois village of Stadacona. The government and religious center

QUÉBEC

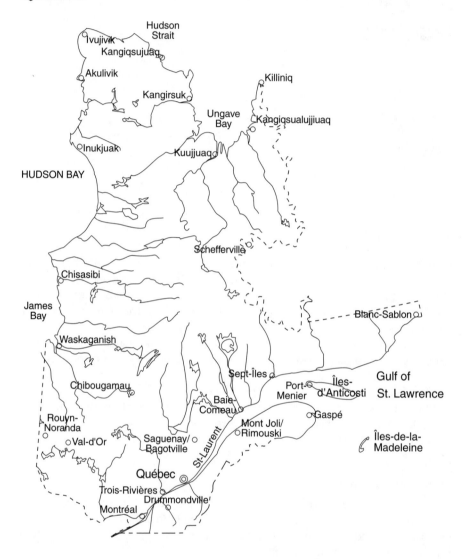

grew within the fortifications of the Upper Town on the bluff, while merchants and craftsmen settled in the Lower Town along the river.

Champlain and the French were ousted by British troops in 1629 for three years; the town and its citadel went back to French control and then served as the base for military activities in the area for the next century.

While war raged in Europe the motherland in France was otherwise distracted, and Québec City fell to the British in 1759. In 1760 British troops occupied Montréal. New France, with sixty thousand colonists, officially surrendered to Great Britain in 1763, ending French control.

Major Cities

The hub of the province is Montréal with 3.3 million residents in the metropolitan area, just slightly under half the population of the entire sprawling province.

Laval, on the other side of the Saint Lawrence from Montréal, is the second largest city in Québec.

The city of Hull is at the western border of Québec, at the confluence of the Outaouais (Ottawa) and Gattineau rivers. The location was no accident—Hull was established to support the logging industry in the early nineteenth century, and the rivers were the highways of the day. Today Hull functions as a French adjunct to Canada's national capital across the provincial border in Ottawa.

Though Québec City is a major population center with more than 500,000 residents, it has much more of a provincial feeling than cosmopolitan Montréal. It is a city that has held on to its history and the influence of the church.

First Nations in Québec

The Huron-Wendat, the Montagnais, and the Micmac make up the three major aboriginal nations in Québec.

The Montagnais live in communities on the North Shore of the Saint Lawrence, in Betsiamites, Masteuiatsh (Pointe–Bleue), and Les Escoumins in the Lake-Saint-Jean region.

The Hurons are centered around Wendake near Québec City, and the Micmac on the Gaspé Peninsula.

The Nation of Québec?

Regional tourist associations. Tourisme Québec. ☎ (800) 363-7777. 🖳 www.tourisme.gouv.qc.ca.

Abitibi-Témiscamingue. ☎ (800) 808-0706, ☎ (819) 762-8181. 🖳 www.48nord.qc.ca.

Bas-Saint-Laurent. ☎ (800) 563-5268, ☎ (418) 867-3015. 🖳 www.tourismebas-st-laurent.com.

Eastern Townships. ☎ (800) 355-5755, ☎ (819) 820-2020. 🖳 www.tourisme-cantons.qc.ca.

Charlevoix. ☎ (800) 667-2276, ☎ (418) 665-4454. 🖳 www.tourisme-charlevoix.com.

Duplessis. ☎ (418) 962-0808. 🖳 www.tourismecote-nord.com.

Îles-de-la-Madeleine. ☎ (418) 986-2245. 🖳 www.ilesdelamadeleine.com.

Lanaudière. ☎ (800) 363-2788, ☎ (450) 834-2535. 🖳 www.tourisme-lanaudiere.qc.ca.

Laurentides. ☎ (800) 561-6673,☎ (450) 436-8532. 🖳 www.laurentides.com.

Laval. ☎ (800) 463-3765, ☎ (450) 682-5522. 🖳 www.tourismelaval.qc.ca.

Montérégie. ☎ (450) 469-0069.

Montréal. ☎ (514) 844-5400. 🖳 www.tourisme-montreal.org

Outaouais. ☎ (800) 265-7822, ☎ (819) 778-2222. 🖳 www.tourisme-outaouais.org.

Greater Québec. ☎ (418) 522-3511. 🖳 www.quebec-region.cuq.qc.ca.

Saguenay–Lac-Saint-Jean. ☎ (800) 463-9651, ☎ (418) 543-9778. 🖳 www.atrsaglac.d4m.com.

There was a time in the late 1960s and early 1970s when Québec did not seem to be a very friendly place for English-speaking residents and visitors, not to mention the rest of the Canada.

For much of the history of the province, especially in the commercial and banking center of Montréal, the power and money lay mostly in the hands of the English-speaking minority, a holdover from the British era.

In the 1960s the "separatist" movement began to grow in influence in Québec. On the political side, the Parti Quebecois began to attract more followers. At the same time the Front de Libération de Québec (FLQ) took some of its cues from the terrorist organizations in other parts of the world.

In 1970 the FLQ kidnapped the British trade commissioner and Québec cabinet minister Pierre Laporte, seeking as ransom the release to Cuba of twenty-five of the group's members who were jailed for acts of violence. After the federal government refused to acquiesce, his captors, who were later caught and prosecuted, murdered Laporte.

Ottawa did, though, address some of the concerns of the French in Québec, and in 1976 the Parti Quebecois won control of the provincial government. In 1980 voters in the province were given a chance to support independence in a referendum, but the option was supported by only 40 percent of the voters.

One important effect of the terrorism and the growing political strength of the separatists, though, was an exodus of a great deal of the Anglophone power structure and some entire companies from Québec into neighboring Ontario, including Toronto and Ottawa.

The atmosphere in Québec continues to move toward separation. Another referendum in 1995 garnered just short of 50 percent.

It's unclear, though, whether Québec will ever be an independent nation of its own. Detractors say its economy and infrastructure is still very much connected to the rest of Canada.

In any case, the political situation has cooled down considerably as far as tourism in the province. English-speaking visitors to Québec are welcomed as a linchpin of the economy.

Québec Festivals and Events

January

Québec Winter Carnival. Québec City. ☎ (418) 626-3716. 🖳 www.carnaval. qc.ca. Late January to mid-February. Ice palace, ice-sculpture competitions, canoe races on the frozen Saint Lawrence River and night parades. Events at various locations in Old Québec.

March

Festival International du Film sur l'Art (International Festival of Films on Art). Montréal. ☎ (514) 874-1637. 🖳 www.artfifa.com. International festival of film and video over six days.

May

Carrefour international de théâtre de Québec (International Crossroads of Theater). Québec City. ☎ (418) 692-3131. 🖳 www.carrefourtheatre.qc.ca. Held in even-numbered years for two weeks in May. An international theater festival that showcases contemporary works.

Festival de théâtre des Amériques (Festival of Theater of the Americas). Montréal. ☎ (514) 842-0704. 🖳 www.fta.qc.ca. Avant-garde theater festival that showcases Canadian and international companies. Held every two years in downtown Montréal.

Festival international de musique actuelle de Victoriaville (Avant-garde Music Festival). Victoriaville. ☎ (819) 752-7912. 🖳 www.fimav.qc.ca. Festival of avant-garde music with twenty-five concerts held at the Colisée des Bois-Francs, the Cinéma Laurier and the Cégep de Victoriaville.

Les Coups de théâtre/Rendez-vous international de théâtre jeune public (The Montréal children's theatre festival.) Montréal. ☎ (514) 499-2929. 🖳 www.les400coups.com. An international theater festival for young people ages four to sixteen years. Held every two years, with the next festival scheduled for May of 2002.

June

Air Canada Grand Prix. Montréal. 🖳 www.grandprix.ca. Canada's only Formula 1 race, held in mid-June.

Festival International de Jazz de Montréal. Montréal. ☎ (514) 523-3378. 🖳 www.montrealjazzfest.com. Late June to early July. The greatest names in the world of jazz perform on ten outdoor stages in the streets and in concert halls.

La Fabuleuse histoire d'un royaume (The Fabulous History of a Kingdom). La Baie. ☎ (418) 697-5151. 🖳 www.royaume.com/~rleclerc. Late June to late July. A romantic portrayal of the history, culture and pride of the people of the Saguenay region, with two hundred volunteer actors.

July

Québec City Summer Festival. Québec City. ☎ (418) 523-4540. 🖳 www.festi val-ete-quebec.qc.ca. Streets, public squares, and halls come alive with music each summer with free and moderately priced concerts. Indoor and open-air concerts feature pop, rock, world music, classical music, variety shows, and street music.

Festival mondial de folklore de Drummondville (World Festival of Folklore). Drummondville. ☎ (819) 472-1184. 🖳 www.drummond.com/folklore. The World Folklore Festival brings representatives from twenty countries for ten days of music, songs, dancers, folktales, food, and crafts.

Just for Laughs Festival. Montréal. ☎ (514) 845-3155. 🖳 www.hahaha.com. As many as 500,000 spectators attend 1,500 performances by nearly 650 comedians from fourteen different countries. Downtown Montréal and in the Old Port at outdoor and indoor venues.

Les Grands Feux Loto-Québec (The Grand Fires). Québec City. ☎ (418) 523-3389. 🖳 www.lesgrandsfeux.com. Late July to early August. A fireworks and music festival at the waterfall in Parc de la Chute-Monmorency.

Tremblant International Blues Festival. Tremblant. 🖳 www.tremblant. com. Late July to early August. Performances on outdoor stages, at bars, and restaurants.

August

Festi-Jazz international de Rimouski. Rimouski. ☎ (418) 724-7844. 🖳 www. festijazzrimouski.com. End of August. More than one hundred internationally renowned jazz musicians give fifty performances in concert halls, bars, and the streets of Rimouski.

Festival international du film de Québec (Québec International Film Festival). Québec City. ☎ (418) 694-9920. 🖳 www.telegraphe.com/fifq. Late August to early September. In the heart of Québec, in the Cinéplex Odéon theater, Place Charest.

Les FrancoFolies de Montréal. Montréal. ☎ (514) 523-3378. 🖳 www.franco folies.com. Early August. A musical celebration of the French-language song in all its diversity—rock, pop, jazz, Latin and African beat; it's said to be the largest francophone cultural event in the world.

World Film Festival. Montréal. ☎ (514) 848-3883. 🖳 www.ffm-montreal. org/en. Late August to early September. More than four hundred films from more than sixty countries.

September

Festival international de nouvelle danse (International Festival of Modern Dance). Montréal. ☎ (514) 287-1423. 🖳 www.festivalnouvelledanse.ca. Late August to early September. A leading Avant-garde dance festival, integrating various disciplines, including theatre, cinema and the visual arts.

October

Festival du cinéma international en Abitibi-Témiscamingue (International Film Festival). Rouyn-Noranda. ☎ (819) 762-6212. 🖳 www.telebec. qc.ca/fciat. Late October to early November. More than eighty films of various lengths from twenty different countries.

Chapter 25
Montréal

Picture if you will a mountain in the middle of an island in a river flowing out to the Atlantic Ocean more than a thousand miles away. Then add in a major city with a thriving business district, a lively cultural scene, several excellent universities, a très chic collection of shops and galleries, and a population drawn from all over the world.

Today's Montréal is one of the most cosmopolitan cities on the planet, a mélange of French tradition. British merchants and shippers helped grow the city as a bustling trade center in the late 1600s; in modern times the city has grown by waves of immigrants from more than eighty countries from all over the world. By one account, Montréalers speak more than thirty-five languages.

Montréal is also easily accessibly by air, boat, or car. It lies only thirty-seven miles north of the U.S. border with highways leading to upstate New York and New England.

An Adventure of Discovery

In 1642 Paul de Chomedey, Sieur de Maisonneuve, founded Ville-Marie, which quickly expanded to cover the area known today as Old Montréal.

Long before it was Montréal, or even "Ville-Marie" as it was known in the early days of the colony, it was "Hochelaga," a place where native tribes came together for thousands of years before the first European set foot there.

The history of Montréal is made evident at **Pointe-à-Callière Museum of Archaeology and History**, located at an archaeological site that has yielded a treasure trove of artifacts from the earliest days of the settlement.

Nearby, an old fire station houses the **Montréal History Centre** whose permanent exhibition recalls other aspects of the city during the years.

The **Château Ramezay Museum** and the **Sir-George-Etienne-Cartier House** present the lifestyles of some of the city's wealthier residents during the seventeenth through nineteenth centuries, explored through the architecture and furnishings of the day.

MONTRÉAL

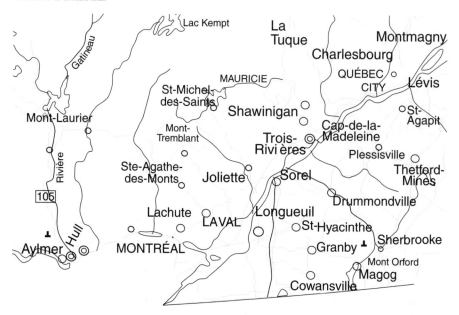

A Religious Heritage

Known as the Sailors' Church, **Notre-Dame-de-Bonsecours** chapel rests on the remnants of the wood foundation of the original chapel, which dates back to 1673. The view of the harbor from its rooftop observatory makes it easy to imagine the sailing ships of old returning from long voyages overseas.

The chapel is just one of the many religious institutions that provide a window on the history of Montréal and its strong religious heritage. Another is the **Old Saint-Sulpice Seminary**. Featuring several elements reminiscent of the architecture of the French Régime, this building was erected in 1685.

Notre-Dame Basilica symbolizes the growth of the community. Built in 1829 this masterpiece of Neo-Gothic architecture was inspired by Notre-Dame cathedral in Paris. Its interior of carved wood covered in gold leaf is a tribute to local artists. Located across the street from Place d'Armes, dominated by a statue of the city's founder, Paul de Chomedey, sieur de Maisonneuve.

A Maritime Heritage

The **Port of Montréal** is linked to some two hundred port cities around the world by some forty shipping lines. Canada's number one container port and the second on the Eastern seaboard after New York, it handles a wide range of cargo year-round and provides access to North America's industrial heartland (Québec, Ontario and the U.S. Midwest, Northeast, and Southeast), Europe, and the Mediterranean.

The Port of Montréal's Iberville Passenger Terminal also welcomes thousands of cruise ship passengers every year. A variety of short (one hour to one day) cruises and river tours are available as well. These provide spectacular views of the city from the same vantage point as the first European visitors to Hochelaga.

Thanks to its unique geographic position, by the early eighteenth century "Ville-Marie" had already grown into a prosperous fur-trading center. Then, as Montréal's development gradually shifted away from the harbor to the lower slopes of Mount-Royal, the vitality of the city's old port waned. Montréal's 350th birthday celebrations in 1992 marked the renovation of the Old Port waterfront and the gates to the Lachine Canal.

A Gastronomic Heritage

And then there is the food. Montréal, with its sidewalk cafes, quaint bistros, chic dining rooms and restaurants, can hold its own against any European city.

In addition to the French contributions to fine food, Montréal has benefitted from the influx of many ethnic groups; there are significant populations of Asians, Italians, Greeks, and Jews, each contributing to the cultural and gastronomical fabric of the city.

Transportation

Montréal has two major airports. **Aéroport de Dorval (Montréal International Airport at Dorval)** is about fifteen miles southwest of the city. Dorval handles nearly all scheduled international and domestic flights. For information, call ☎ (514) 394-7377 or consult 🖳 www.admtl.com.

Montréal International Airport (Mirabel), about thirty-five miles northwest of the city, is used primarily by charter operations. For information, call ☎ (514) 394-7377 or consult 🖳 www.admtl.com.

A taxi from Dorval into the center city costs about $30. Regular bus service, about $10 one-way, runs from the airport to a downtown terminal with free shuttles from there to many major downtown hotels. You can also take a train from Dorval to Gare Centrale, for about $5; service is hourly during the day.

Within the city of Montréal, the **Métro** subway system provides quick, reliable, inexpensive, and—dare I say it—pleasant transportation. Look for Métro signs on major streets in the city; much of Underground Montréal is attached to one or another subway stop.

There are four lines on the system; you can transfer from one to another at the Berri-UQAM station (orange, green, and yellow), Lionel-Groulx (green and orange), Snowdon or Jean-Talon (blue and orange.)

Tickets are quite reasonable, priced in mid-2001 at $2. A better deal is a *carnet* or *lisieur* of six tickets for $8.50; the coupons can be shared within a family. Children younger than eighteen travel for about half price. You can also purchase a tourist card that allows unlimited travel on subways and buses from information centers, the Berri-UQAM Métro station, and many downtown stations; the card costs $7 per day or $14 for three consecutive days.

You can also obtain a transfer, or *correspondance*, from the Métro to the bus system or vice versa.

For information about the Métro system, consult 🖳 www.stcum.qc.ca.

MONTRÉAL MÉTRO

The City of Montréal

Old Montréal, the Vieux-Port, fell into disrepair in the 1960s. It was saved and restored by a municipal commission.

In 1992 the city celebrated its 350th anniversary. The Champ-de-Mars, once a military parade ground and later a public market, was reworked, and in the process archaeologists uncovered fortifications built in the 1700s; a section of Champ-de-Mars was restored to illustrate Montréal's era as a walled city.

With tourism to the old city came a revival of commerce in the 1990s, including the construction of the World Trade Centre that sprung up as a new building behind the facades of eleven existing Victorian buildings.

The **Old Port of Montréal**, is a huge interpretive site with cultural, historical and recreational features. Access is via the rue de la Commune, between Berri and McGill streets. For information, call ☎ (800) 971-7678 or ☎ (514) 496-7678 or consult 🖳 www.oldportofmontreal.com.

The area includes street entertainers, walking tours, and wintertime ice

MONTRÉAL

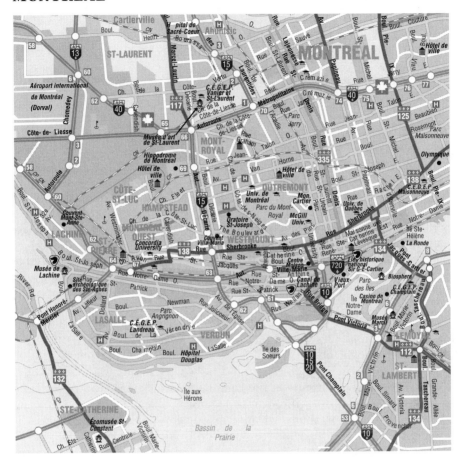

skating and sliding. From May to October a fleet of *bateau mouche* boats offer tours of the river and dinner cruises; the boats depart from Jacques-Cartier Pier at the Old Port of Montréal.

The sinuous path of Saint-Paul Street dates back to the city's early days; the stone buildings there are mainly from the nineteenth century.

Square Dorchester

Montréal's small version of Trafalgar Square in London is north of René-Lévesque Boulevard West, between Peel and Metcalfe Streets, an urban park dotted with monuments. The most imposing are the statue of Sir Wilfrid Laurier, the first French Canadian premier of Canada, and the Boer War Memorial. Also in the square is a monument to Scottish poet Robert Burns. On the north side of the square is a branch of Infotouriste, the Montréal tourist and information center. The nearest Métro stop is Peel.

The park is named in honor of Lord Dorchester, Canada's Governor General from 1768 to 1778 and 1786 to 1795.

Île Notre Dame

The Île Notre-Dame in the Saint Lawrence was created in the 1960s out of the rocks and earth dug from beneath Montréal for the construction of the Métro.

The island was used as the site for much of Expo '67, a World's Fair exposition. The rowing competitions of the 1976 Summer Olympics were also held on the island, and the Olympic Basin is today used for recreational boating. When the island was used as the site of the 1980 Floralies Internationale, a major flower show, it was crisscrossed with decorative canals and gardens, which are still maintained. The Grand Prix de Canada is held at the Circuit Gilles Villeneuve race track on the island.

But the biggest contemporary use of the island is for the **Montréal Casino**, an elegant gambling facility in the former French and Quebec pavilions built for Expo '67. One of the largest casinos in the world, the building includes more than one hundred gaming tables and nearly three thousand slot machines, as well as a gourmet dining room, a dinner theatre, three popular-priced restaurants, a theater, and a souvenir shop.

Open daily from 9 A.M. to 5 A.M., guests must be eighteen years of age or older. Informal garb such as jogging pants and cut-off shorts are not allowed.

For information, call ☎ (514) 392-2746 or ☎ 1-800-665-2274 or consult 💻 www.casinos-quebec.com.

You can reach the island through the Île-Ste-Hélène station of the Métro. A ferry runs from Jacques-Cartier pier in Old Montréal to the Parc-des-Îles from mid-May to mid-October.

Île Sainte-Hélène is another island attached by a causeway to Île Notre-Dame. The **Stewart Museum at the Fort, Île Sainte-Hélène** is a step back into four centuries of history through an extensive collection of old maps and documents, antique weapons, scientific instruments and navigational aids.

Authentic eighteenth-century military drills are performed by the soldiers of La Compagnie franche de la Marine and The Olde 78th Fraser Highlanders.

The fort is open daily from mid-May to mid-October, and daily except Tuesday the rest of the year. Métro: Île-Ste-Hélène. Admission: adult, ❷; child, ❶. For information, call ☎ (514) 861-6701 or consult 💻 www.stewart-museum.org.

Nearby, the **Biosphere** is an unusual interactive museum that highlights Canada's abundant water resources. Within the geodesic dome of the former American pavilion at Expo '67, four exhibition areas offer movies, computers, and giant scale models. A multimedia show on six circular mobile screens focuses on the importance and fragility of the Saint Lawrence–Great Lakes ecosystem, home to almost half of Canada's population and 20 percent of the world's fresh water reserves.

For information on the museum, call ☎ (514) 283-5000 or consult 💻 biosphere.ec.gc.ca/cea.

Key to Prices
❶ $5 and under
❷ $5 to $10
❸ $10 to $20
❹ $20 and more
When prices are listed as a range, this indicates various combination options are available. Most attractions offer reduced-price tickets for children and many have family rates that include two adults and two or three children.

Île Sainte-Hélène is also home to **La Ronde**, the largest amusement park in Montréal, with more than thirty-four rides as well as other entertainment. In early 2001 the city entered into an agreement to sell the rides and lease the land to Six Flags, a major U.S.-based theme park operator. As part of the transaction, Six Flags committed to invest nearly $100 million in improvements beginning with the 2002 season.

> **Montréal on-line.** 🖳
> www.tourism-montreal.org.
> A live Internet camera
> can be seen at: 🖳 www.
> montrealcam.com.

The park is open from mid-May through early September. Admission: adult ❸; child, ❸. For information, call ☎ (800) 797-4537 or ☎ (514) 872-4537, or consult 🖳 www.pdi-montreal.com/Attraits/Ronde.html.

The park is accessible by car from the Jacques-Cartier bridge, or from the Île-Sainte-Hélène Métro stop.

Chinatown

Montréal's lively **Chinatown** might be more honestly named "Asian World." Immigrants from Vietnam and Thailand have augmented the original settlers of the area, Chinese immigrants who came to Canada in the late 1860s to work in the mines and on railroad projects.

Chinatown, with an excellent selection of restaurants and shops, is centered around Saint-Laurent Boulevard and de La Gauchetière Street just above downtown Montréal. There's a pedestrian mall on de La Gauchetière Street.

Museums and Attractions

Among the jewels of downtown Montréal is the **Museum of Fine Arts (Musée des beaux-arts de Montréal)**. The museum and its annex across the street are works of art in themselves, and the galleries are crammed with an internationally renowned collection of paintings, sculpture, jewelry and other fine art.

The museum draws its lineage back to a group of wealthy collectors who founded the Art Association of Montréal in 1860. As such, it is the oldest art museum in Canada and one of the oldest in North America, founded ten years before New York and Boston had similar associations.

In 1909 the same group raised funds for the construction of a museum in the heart of the Golden Square Mile, the toniest residential district of Montréal, now the heart of downtown. The building, now the Benaiah Gibb Pavilion, opened in 1912. It's an imposing structure with a white marble façade and solid oak doors with bronze. (The bas-reliefs originally planned for the building's façade had to be redesigned because the models and the plasterworker accompanying them went down with the *Titanic* on April 14, 1912.)

It took until 1991 before a second major building could be opened, the Desmarais Pavilion across the street on Sherbrook. Old and new pavilions are linked by an underground passageway of galleries.

The core of the collection was donated to the museum by the old money of Montréal, mostly Anglophones. The eclectic assortment ranges from the Old

Masters—including works by El Greco, Rembrandt, Canaletto, Pissaro, and Monet—to items of Canadian art from the seventeenth century colony of New France to the present day. My favorite: a luminous portrait of a young girl in her seasonal finery against the brilliant leaves of autumn, in Tissot's *Octobre*.

The museum, in downtown Montréal, between rue Bishop and rue Crescent at 1379–1380 rue Sherbrooke Ouest, is open Tuesday to Sunday and Holiday Mondays. Métro: Peel or Guy-Concordia. Admission to the Museum's permanent collection is free at all times, but donations are appreciated. Admission to special exhibits: adult, ❸; senior and student, ❷; child (12 and younger), ❶; child (2 and younger) free; family, ❹. For information, call ☎ (514) 285-2000 or consult 🖳 www.mbam.qc.ca.

The **Musée d'art contemporain de Montréal. (Museum of Contemporary Art)** claims Canada's most significant collection of contemporary art. The permanent collection includes works from Canada and around the world from 1939 to the present.

The museum is atop the Place des Arts parking lot in downtown Montréal, between Jeanne-Mance and Saint-Urbain streets, at 185 rue Saint-Catherine Ouest. Admission: adult, ❷; senior and student, ❶; child (younger than 12), free. For information, call ☎ (514) 847-6212 or consult 🖳 www. macm.org.

One of the most renowned collections in North America of furniture, ceramics, glass, jewelry, graphic design, textiles, and lighting fixtures is found at the **Montréal Museum of Decorative Arts**. Collections are organized by the major movements that influenced the twentieth-century decorative arts. The museum is located in downtown at 2200 rue Crescent. Métro: Guy-Concordia. Closed Mondays except holidays. Admission: adult, ❸; student and senior, ❷. For information, call ☎ (514) 284-1252 or consult 🖳 www.madm.org.

The leading archeological museum of Montréal and one of the best of its kind anywhere, the **Pointe-à-Callière, Montréal Museum of Archaeology and History** is on the site where Montréal was founded over the city's first Catholic cemetery. The museum takes visitors through six centuries from the Indian period to the present. An underground archaeological tour includes displays of artifacts from archaeological digs all over town.

The museum is located at 350 Place Royale in the heart of Old Montréal, three streets west of boulevard Saint-Laurent, via rue de la Commune. Admission: adult, senior, and youth (13–25), ❷. For information, call ☎ (514) 872-9150 or consult 🖳 www.musee-pointe-a-calliere.qc.ca.

The **McCord Museum of Canadian History** tells the cultural history of Canada through decorative items, scientific instruments, paintings, engravings, drawings, and photographs. The museum features exhibitions that focus on life in Montréal and Québec; one particularly affecting display shows the toys of childhood. The museum also houses ethnological and archaeological exhibits about the native peoples of Canada. The McCord is located at 690 rue Sherbrooke Ouest in downtown Montréal, between McGill and University streets. Métro: McGill. Open daily except Mondays. Admission: adult, ❷; senior, ❶. For information, call ☎ (514) 398-7100 or consult 🖳 www.musee-mccord.qc.ca.

The **Redpath Museum**, part of McGill University, studies the history and diversity of the natural world with a vast collection of minerals and precious stones, ethnological and archaeological artifacts, fossils, and mounted animals. Located at 859 rue Sherbrooke Ouest. Métro: McGill. Admission: free. For information, call ☎ (514) 398-4086, ext. 3188, or consult 🖳 ww2.mcgill.ca/redpath.

The **Château Ramezay Museum** preserves a chateau built in 1705 for Claude de Ramezay, the Governor of Montréal. A superb example of urban architecture during the French Regime, exhibits showcase the economic, political, and social life of Montréal and Québec from the beginning of the colony to the end of the nineteenth century.

The chateau was headquarters for American revolutionary forces occupying the city in the winter of 1775. Benjamin Franklin and Benedict Arnold both stayed here during that time.

The chateau is located at 2280 rue Notre-Dame Est in the heart of Old Montréal, across from the City Hall near the Place Jacques-Cartier. Métro: Champ-de-Mars. Open daily in summer and closed Monday the remainder of the year. Admission: adult, ❷; child, ❶. For information, call ☎ (514) 861-3708 or consult 🖳 www.chateauramezay.qc.ca.

Also in Old Montréal is the **Centre d'histoire de Montréal (Montréal History Center)**, a collection of the history of the city from the early days of the Iroquois to the present. Exhibits explore population, transportation, housing, inventions, and technology in an urban center. The museum is located at 335 place d'Youville, between rue McGill and rue Saint-François-Xavier. Open daily in summer; closed Monday the remainder of the year. Métro: Square-Victoria. Admission: general, ❶. For information call ☎ (514) 872-3207 or consult 🖳 www.ville.montreal.qc.ca/chm/chm.htm.

The **Sir George-Étienne Cartier National Historic Site** preserved the Victorian domestic luxury of the Cartier family home of the 1860s including period bedrooms, living room, and dining room. An exhibit features events in the career of Cartier, an influential politician and Father of Confederation. The museum, in Old Montréal, is located at 458 rue Notre-Dame Est between rue Berri and rue Bonsecours. Open April to December. Admission: adult, senior, child (5–16), ❶. For information, call ☎ (800) 463-6769 or ☎ (514) 283-2282 or consult 🖳 parkscanada.pch.gc.ca/cartier.

The "Filles du Roi" were young orphan girls sent to New France to find a husband and populate the overseas colony. The **Maison Saint-Gabriel**, near Old Montréal, is a restored 1668 farmhouse built as a home for the girls. Located at 2146 Place Dublin; Métro: Square-Victoria. Closed Monday. Admission: adult, ❷; senior and student, ❶. For information, call ☎ (514) 935-8136 or consult 🖳 www.maisonsaint-gabriel.qc.ca.

Cinémathèque Québécoise is a museum of moving images with exhibits on the history and culture of cinema, television, and new media, with scheduled screenings. Located in the heart of the Latin Quarter, at 335 de Maisonneuve Boulevard East; Métro: Berri-UQAM. Open daily except Monday and Tuesday. Admission: ❶. For information, call ☎ (514) 842-9763 or consult 🖳 www.cinematheque.qc.ca.

You can explore the heavens in French or in English (check the schedule for the language of presentation) at the **Planétarium de Montréal**, located at 1000 Saint-Jacques Street West. Open daily except Monday. Admission: adult, ❷; child (18 and younger), ❶. For information, call ☎ (514) 872-4530 or consult 🖳 www.planetarium.montreal.qc.ca.

And now for something completely different: the **Just for Laughs Museum (Musée juste pour rire)** is (seriously) a museum devoted to humor, including multimedia exhibits and visitor participation. The museum is located in downtown Montréal, at the corner of Saint-Laurent and Sherbrooke Streets. Métro: Saint-Laurent. Admission: adult ❷; child, ❶. For information, call ☎ (514) 845-4000 or consult 🖳 www.hahaha.com.

Montréal Museum Pass

The most economical way to visit a variety of permanent and temporary exhibitions in twenty-five Montréal museums is a pass.

You can purchase a Montréal Museum Pass at the Infotouriste Center at 174 Notre-Dame Street East, at ticket windows of most participating museums, and at the concierge desk of some of Montréal's major hotels.

Participating museums include:
- Environment Canada Biosphère
- Canadian Centre for Architecture (CCA)
- Centre d'histoire de Montréal
- Château Dufresne
- Château Ramezay Museum
- Cinémathèque québécoise
- Écomusée du fier monde
- The fur trade at Lachine national historic site
- Just for Laughs Museum
- Léonard & Bina Ellen Art Gallery (Concordia University)
- Maison Saint-Gabriel
- Marguerite Bourgeoys museum
- McCord Museum of Canadian History
- Montréal Holocaust Memorial Centre
- Montréal Museum of Archaeology and History, Pointe-à-Callière
- Montréal Museum of Decorative Arts
- Montréal Museum of Fine Arts
- Musée d'art contemporain de Montréal
- Musée d'art de Saint-Laurent
- Musée de la ville de Lachine
- Musée des Hospitalières de l'Hôtel-Dieu de Montréal
- Musée Marc-Aurèle Fortin
- Redpath Museum
- Sir-George-Étienne Cartier National Historic Site
- Stewart Museum, The Fort Saint Helen's Island

Note that many museums are closed on Monday, and certain restrictions may apply on temporary exhibitions.

For information, call ☎ (514) 845-6873 or ☎ (800) 363-7777 outside of Montréal. In 2001 a pass valid for two days in a three-day period sold for $20.

Olympic Park Museums and Attractions

The Maisonneuve district to the north of downtown was an independent, highly industrialized city until the 1900s. Many beautiful public buildings and grand homes remain from that era; the area also includes a number of impressive parks that served as a tourist destination for Montréal residents. In 1976 the area became the center of Montréal's Summer Olympics; many facilities from that global gathering remain.

The **Insectarium** is just what it sounds like . . . and a whole lot more. Within the walls of the bug-shaped museum near the Olympic Park are thousands of live insects of every description from more than one hundred countries; even more are preserved and mounted.

For most of us it takes a few moments to get over our built-in aversion to all things creepy and crawly; and then it's over, and we find ourselves fascinated by the colors and shapes and whimsy of nature. There are insects that look like birds, like twigs and leaves, and like exotic pieces of jewelry. Some insects whistle and sing while others manage to hang absolutely motionless, waiting for the proper moment to pounce.

The Insectarium is alongside the **Botanical Garden**. It was created in 1931 and is now one of the largest in the world with ten exhibition greenhouses and more than thirty outdoor gardens. You can imbue yourself with the exotic charm of the Chinese and Japanese gardens or step through the doors of the Tree House and learn about the inside story of Quebec's forests. A sightseeing train travels to its remote corner.

The **Japanese Garden** includes a bonsai collection. The five-acre **Chinese Garden** was designed in cooperation with the city of Shanghai and features seven pavilions in Ming Dynasty style surrounding the calm waters of "Dream Lake."

The Insectarium and Botanical Garden are located at 4101 Sherbrooke Street East, about fifteen minutes east of downtown Montréal and walking distance from the Pie-IX Métro station. Both facilities are open daily. Admission: ❸–❹. Combination tickets with the Botanical Garden, Insectarium, the Montréal Tower and the Biodôme are available. For information, call ☎ (514) 872-1400 or consult 💻 www.ville.montreal.qc.ca/jardin/engl/ejardin.htm.

Within the walls of the **Biodôme** you can feel the heat and humidity of a tropical forest, the cool air of the Laurentian Forest, the underwater world of the Saint Lawrence River, and the polar habitat of the Arctic and the Antarctic.

This unusual museum, nestled in the shadow of the Montréal Tower, puts visitors into the midst of four ecological zones, each complete with plants and animals. There are tree monkeys, colorful jungle birds, porcupines, turtles, and an amazing colony of penguins and alcidae.

The museum is located at 4777 avenue Pierre-de-Coubertin. Métro: Viau. Admission: adult, senior, student, ❷; child (6–17), ❶; child (5 and younger), free.

For information, call ☎ (514) 868-3056 or ☎ (514) 868-3000 or consult 💻 www.
ville.montreal.qc.ca/biodome/ebdm.htm.

And then there is the unusual **Montréal Tower**, the world's tallest inclined
tower, which rises 550 feet over the neighborhood and offers a view of
Montréal and the Saint Lawrence River that can reach fifty miles on a clear
day. The tower was intended to hold the cables and pulley to lift the huge
retractable roof off the Olympic Stadium below, making the indoor arena part
of the great outdoors when weather permitted. However, the mechanism never
performed properly and the roof—a leaky one, no less—was fixed in place. A
huge two-level elevator climbs up the rail to an observation platform at the
top. The tower is open daily. Admission: adult, ❷; child, ❶

The **Olympic Stadium** is home of the Montréal Expos baseball team. In
recent years the team has been in financial difficulties. The good news is that
there have been tens of thousands of available seats in the stadium for games;
the bad news is that some observers don't expect the Expos to have a long
history in Montréal.

The Biodome, the Montréal Tower, and the Olympic Stadium are all in the
Olympic Park; the nearest Métro stop is Viau. For information, call ☎ (514)
252-8687.

Arts and Entertainment

Montréal boasts more than one hundred theater and musical groups and fifty
dance companies from the Montréal Symphony Orchestra and the Grands
Ballets Canadiens to the ridiculously sublime Cirque du Soleil.

The city has more than 150 concert venues, none more active than the **Place
des Arts**. Located in downtown, its five halls have welcomed some of the world's
greatest singers, dancers, musicians, and actors.

The **Montréal Symphony Orchestra** and the **Grands Ballets Canadiens**
perform at the Place des Arts at 260 de Maisonneuve Boulevard West. Métro:
Place-des-Arts. For information, call ☎ (514) 842-3402 or ☎ (800) 203-2787. For
information on the orchestra, consult 💻 www.osm.ca. The website for the
ballet is 💻 www.grandsballets.qc.ca. Ticket office: ☎ (514) 842-9951.

For general information and schedules for events at the Place des Arts, consult 💻 www.pdarts.com.

The NHL's **Montréal Canadiens** (Les Habs to the locals) play in the impressive **Molson Centre**, which replaced the venerable but crumbling Forum.
Nearly two and a half times the size of the old Forum, the team's new home
provides room for more than twenty-one thousand spectators. For information on the hockey team, consult 💻 www.canadiens.com.

The **Molson Centre** is located at 1250 rue de la Gauchetière. For information on the arena and tickets to hockey and many special events held there,
call ☎ (514) 989-2841.

The **Olympic Stadium** is home to the **Montréal Expos** baseball club. The
stadium is located at 4141 Avenue Pierre-de-Coubertin. For information on
the Expos, call ☎ (514) 846-3976 or consult 💻 expos.mlb.com.

The Canadian Football League's **Montréal Alouettes** play at **Percival Molson Memorial Stadium** on the campus of McGill University at 475 Pine Avenue West. For tickets, call ☎ (514) 871-2255 or consult 💻 www.cfl.ca/CFLMontreal.

Churches

Montréal began as a missionary colony, and the history and influence of its churches continues to this day.

Notre-Dame-de-Bonsecours holds a special place in Montréal's heart. The original 1657 structure was Ville-Marie's first church. Rebuilt in 1771 a figure of the Virgin Mary on the tower served as an important landmark for sailors on the Saint Lawrence, many of whom later came on shore to worship here. Many left behind votive offerings of model ships that still hang from church rafters; for that reason it is also known as the Sailor's Church.

The church is on rue Saint Paul near Marché Bonsecours.

The queen of Old Montréal is **Notre-Dame Basilica**, an imposing structure outside with a surprisingly delicate interior. The Catholic church is considered a masterpiece of Neo-Gothic architecture; it was completed in 1829.

The main castle-like altar (representing the Kingdom of God) is set against a painted bright blue sky on the back wall. The 3,500 seats in the church are illuminated by the light streaming through stained glass windows imported from Limoges in France; they depict the founding of Ville-Marie.

The nineteenth-century organ is one of the largest in the world with some seven thousand pipes. Organ concerts are presented most Friday nights.

Behind the altar is the **Sacred Heart Chapel**, known as Montréal's Wedding Chapel. Rebuilt after an arson fire in 1978 it presents an unusual combination of old and new.

Architects were able to save the right side of the ornate wooden chapel; the left side was re-created and a modern ceiling and altar were added. A huge bronze sculpture, *L'Arbre de la Vie* (Tree of Life), stands behind the pulpit.

The church's West Tower, known as "The Perseverance," holds a twenty-two-thousand-pound bell; and the East Tower, "The Temperance," has a ten-bell carillon. When they ring to summon worshipers, they can be heard throughout Montréal.

The designer of the church was an Irish-American Protestant named James O'Donnell; it has been said he was so inspired by his work that he converted to Catholicism.

Open year-round, guided tours are offered in the summer. Entrance to the basilica is free; there is a modest admission charge at a small religious museum. The basilica is located in the heart of Old Montréal, between rue McGill and rue Saint-Laurent, at 110 rue Notre-Dame West. For information, call ☎ (514) 842-2925 or consult 💻 www.patrimoine-religieux.qc.ca/bndmtl/bndmtle.htm.

Saint Patrick's Basilica, known to Montréalers as "The Irish Church," is straight out of the Gothic style of the fourteenth and fifteenth centuries. Finished in 1847 the interior includes huge pine columns, each formed from a single tree trunk more than eighty feet long. The church is located at 454

René-Lévesque Boulevard West. Métro: Square-Victoria. For information, call ☎ (514) 866-7379 or consult 💻 www.patrimoine-religieux.qc.ca/spatmtl/spat mtle.htm.

Not far away near Square Dorchester, somewhat in the shadow of the downtown high-rises, is **Mary Queen of the World Cathedral.** The church is a quarter-scale replica of Saint Peter's Basilica in Rome; it was completed in 1894 in what was at the time Montréal's Anglo-Protestant sector. The cathedral is on René-Lévesque Boulevard West at Mansfield. Métro: Bonaventure. For information, call ☎ (514) 866-1661 or consult 💻 www. patrimoine-religieux.qc.ca/ cmrdmf02.htm.

Saint George's Anglican Church is the oldest building on Place du Canada. A neo-Gothic gem of 1870 the interior features intricate woodwork and a tapestry from Westminster Abbey used at the coronation of Queen Elizabeth II. The church is at the corner of Peel and de la Gauchetière streets West. Métro: Bonaventure. For information, call ☎ (514) 866-7113 or consult 💻 collections.ic. gc.ca/relig/sgeoa/sgeoaexe.htm.

The largest Protestant church of Montréal is **Saint James United Church,** built in 1889 to serve the Methodists of the time. The Gothic exterior is complemented with an ornate Victorian interior. Saint James is located at 463 Sainte-Catherine Street West. Métro: McGill. For information, call ☎ (514) 288-9245 or consult 💻 collections.ic.gc.ca/relig/sjamu/sjamuexe.htm.

On the back side of Mont Royal is **Saint Joseph's Oratory,** one of the most important pilgrimage destinations in North America. Built between 1924 and 1956, the oratory is topped by a copper dome that is second in size only to Saint Peter's in Rome.

The Oratory was built at the urging of Brother André (1845–1937). André started a small chapel on Mont Royal in 1904 dedicated to Saint Joseph; visitors soon began claiming miraculous cures from being in his presence. The contributions of parishioners allowed André to begin construction of the oratory. Inside the Italianate church is a basilica—the Chapel of the Blessed Sacrament—a votive chapel where Brother André's tomb (and his preserved heart in a glass case) can be found. Two museums are dedicated to Brother André and religious art.

The observatory at the top of the basilica is the highest point in Montréal, offering a commanding view of the city.

From the gate at the foot of the hill there are three hundred steps to the door of the oratory. It is not unusual to see visitors making a pilgrimage on their knees, stopping on each step to make a prayer.

Brother André was beatified by Pope John Paul II on May 23, 1982, a step in a process that may lead to sainthood.

Saint Joseph's Oratory is located at 3800 chemin Queen Mary, about four miles from downtown Montréal by car. It is a short walk from the Côte-des-Neiges Métro stop. For information, call ☎ (514) 733-8211 or consult 💻 www. saint-joseph.org.

Universities of Montréal

McGill University is spread across sixty buildings in downtown Montréal at the foot of Mont Royal, just off Sherbrooke Street West. The English-speaking college was chartered in 1821, funded by wealthy merchant James McGill.

The **Redpath Museum**, dedicated mainly to natural history, is located on the campus. The nearest Métro stop is McGill. Guided tours of the campus are available. For information, call ☎ (514) 398-6555 or consult 🖳 www.mcgill.ca.

The **Université du Québec à Montréal** (UQAM) is a major French-speaking university with some forty thousand students. It is located in downtown at 405 Sainte-Catherine Street East near the Berri-UQAM Métro station. For information, call ☎ (514) 987-3000 or consult 🖳 www.uqam.ca.

Created by noted architect Ernest Cormier, the Art Deco main building of the **Université de Montréal** is the center of the second-largest French-speaking university in the world with about fifty-eight thousand students. The college is at 2900 Édouard-Montpetit Boulevard, near the Université de Montréal Métro stop. For information, call ☎ (514) 343-6111 or consult 🖳 www.umontreal.ca.

The Underground City

What began as a basic shopping center in the basement of a high-rise building in 1962 has grown to include more than twenty miles of climate-controlled passages that connect nearly two thousand shops, offices, restaurants, apartments, hotels, railway stations, theaters, and parking garages—all protected from the weather. The underground ties into the Métro subway system at several points.

It's an attractive and pleasant way to shop and a great way to get around in the frigid winters and hot summers of Montréal.

The city below covers close to 4 million square meters and links up with two bus terminals, ten Métro stations, 1,200 offices, 1,615 housing units, seven major hotels, Université du Québec à Montréal campus, the University of Montréal, Olympic Park, Place des Arts (performing arts center), two department stores, 1,600 boutiques, two hundred restaurants, forty banks, thirty movie theaters, and three exhibition halls.

Downtown Shopping Malls

The Underground City was born with the opening of **Place Ville Marie** at René-Lévesque Boulevard and University Street. Métro: McGill and Bonaventure. This cathedral to commerce, with more than seventy-five boutiques and restaurants, is cruciform in design, recalling the founding religious vocation of Montréal. For information, call ☎ (514) 861-9393.

The forty-seven-story **Place Victoria** was completed in 1964. It has a main lobby that is dominated by a forty-two-foot-tall stalactite made of three thousand pieces of Murano glass that hangs down four floors.

Below, shops and eateries are linked to the Radisson-Hôtel-des-Gouverneurs and the underground network. On the square there's an authentic Parisian Métro entrance in the 1900 style, a gift from the city of Paris. Place Victoria is located at 800 Place Victoria; Métro: Square-Victoria.

The **Montréal Eaton Center**, at Ste-Catherine and McGill College, is the largest shopping center in downtown Montréal with 175 stores and places to eat. The center is at 705 Sainte-Catherine Street West. Métro: McGill. For information, call ☎ (514) 288-3708.

Another hundred shops and restaurants sit beneath the **Christ Church Cathedral**; a circular stage in the central atrium is used for special events. **Les Promenades de la Cathédrale** is located at 625 Saint Catherine West. Métro: McGill. For information, call ☎ (514) 849-9925.

Place Montréal Trust, on rue Sainte-Catherine at McGill College Avenue, includes a five-story galleria with 120 fashion boutiques, restaurants (including Planet Hollywood), and specialty shops. The modern architecture contrasts with a thirty-foot-high antique bronze fountain at the base of the atrium; in the holiday season a large musical Christmas tree adorned with animated scenes and an electric train is added. The center is located at 1500 McGill College Avenue. Métro: McGill or Peel. For information, call ☎ (514) 843-8000 or consult 💻 www.shop.net/mall-fr/regions/QC/Montreal/mtrust.htm.

Linked to the Hotel Complexe Desjardins, the Place des Arts, the Palais des congrès, and the Musée d'art contemporain, **Complexe Desjardins** includes more than 120 boutiques, restaurants and bars, four movie theaters and an immense plaza used for exhibitions, shows, festivals, and circuses. The center is bounded by Sainte-Catherine Street, René-Lévesque Boulevard, Saint-Urbain and Jeanne-Mance Streets. Métro: Place-des-Arts or Place-d'Armes. For information, call ☎ (514) 845-4636.

If you're hungry a visit to **Le Faubourg Ste-Catherine** should take care of all of your needs; if you're not hungry when you arrive, you will be before you depart. Inspired in some ways by New York's Seaport Fulton Market and Boston's Quincy Market, the Faubourg Sainte-Catherine combines fruit and vegetable stands, boutiques, restaurants, and a cinema. Sunday brunch is a gastronomic tradition here. Located at 1616 Sainte-Catherine Street West, the nearest Métro station is Guy-Concordia. For information, call ☎ (514) 939-3663 or consult 💻 www.lefaubourg.com.

The **Atwater Market** dates back to 1933 and features a vegetable market plus caterers and specialty boutiques selling meats (there are seven butchers on site), fish, baked goods, and fine foods. The Lachine Canal cycling path rims the market, which is at 138 Atwater Avenue, south of Notre-Dame Street. Métro: Lionel-Groulx. For information, call ☎ (514) 937-7754.

Beneath the silver dome of the nineteenth-century landmark building **Le Marché Bonsecours (Bonsecours Market)** is a craftsman's market for fine arts and design objects. The market is also home to the Galerie des Métiers d'art du Québec.

The building was designed as a public market, for concerts and exhibitions, and as a government facility; it was used by the Canadian parliament for a short period. The market is located at 350 Saint-Paul Street East; the nearest Métro is Champ-de-Mars. For information, call ☎ (514) 872-7730 or consult 💻 www.marchebonsecours.qc.ca.

Entertainment

L'Amphithéâtre Bell includes a tony year-round indoor ice skating rink at the base of a fifty-one-story downtown skyscraper at 1000 de La Gauchietière Street West. Métro: Bonaventure. The rink is open daily except Monday and into the night from April to October; skate rentals are available. Admission: adult, ❷; senior and child (15 and younger), ❶. For information on the public skating schedule, call ☎ (514) 395-0555.

Imax, Old Port. Another outpost of the high-tech cinema group is located at Place King-Edward Pier at the corner of de la Commune and Saint-Laurent. ☎ (800) 349-4629 or ☎ (514) 496-4629 or consult 🖳 www.isci.ca/EN/imax.

Croisières du Port de Montréal. Montréal harbor cruises depart daily from Horloge Pier. For more information, call ☎ (800) 667-3131 or ☎ (514) 842-3871.

Lachine

In 1667 the religious governors of the area granted land on the west side of the island of Montréal to explorer Robert Cavelier de La Salle, who spent much of his life in search of a passage through North America to China. (Along the way he discovered Louisiana at the mouth of the Mississippi River.)

Local residents mockingly called his land "La Chine" (China), and the name stuck; some implied La Salle thought the rapids were all that stood between Montréal and China itself.

In 1689 many of the residents of the Lachine area were massacred by Iroquois warriors. A pair of forts was later built at the site to protect fur traders who were forced to portage around the rapids that blocked the Saint Lawrence at that site. Later the nine-mile-long **Lachine Canal** was built to allow boats to bypass the rapids. It served that purpose from 1825 to 1970; the Saint Lawrence Seaway replaced it as a route to the Great Lakes in 1959.

Today the canal is a green oasis and bicycle path; a small museum tells its story. Located at 711 boulevard Saint-Joseph, about eight miles from Montréal in Lachine. Admission: free. For information, call ☎ (800) 463-6769 in season or ☎ (514) 637-1291 or consult 🖳 parkscanada.pch.gc.ca/canallachine.

Nearby, the **Fur Trade in Lachine National Historic Site** tells the socio-economic importance of the fur trade of the late 1700s. The site is located at 1255 boulevard Saint-Joseph. For information, call ☎ (800) 463-6769 or ☎ (514) 283-6054 or consult 🖳 parkscanada.pch.gc.ca/fourrure.

Carillon

About twenty-five miles west of Montréal, at the **Argenteuil Regional Museum (Carillon Barracks)**, you can visit the garrison that served officers and soldiers of the British army during the Patriote Rebellions of 1837–1840. The collection in the Georgian-style buildings represents the history of the region through artifacts, tools, and furnishings. The museum is in Carillon, about fifty minutes from Montréal on Route 344, the route de la rivière de l'Outaouais. Open mid-May to mid-October. Closed Monday. Admission: adult and senior, ❶; child (12 and younger), ❶; family, ❷. For information, call ☎ (514) 537-3861.

Chapter 26
Outside of Montréal: Laval and the Laurentians

As attractive as the big city of Montréal is as a place to work and visit, sometimes you've just got to get away. Luckily, Montréalers have their own spectacular playground in the backyard: The Laurentian Mountains.

And between Montréal and the hills is Laval, the second-largest city in Québec, with charms of its own.

Laval

Laval lies twenty minutes north of downtown Montréal, situated mostly on Île Jesus, an island that sits between the Rivière des Prairies and the Rivière des Mille-Îles.

Archeologists have uncovered evidence on the island of settlements that go back for centuries. European explorers named the island Montmagny in honor of the second governor of New France. In 1636 the island was given to the Jesuits who gave it the current name of Île Jesus.

In the nineteenth century huge quantities of wood for construction purposes were exported from the region to England. Thousands of trees were harvested along the Outaouais and Gatineau rivers and placed in gigantic rafts for transport on the river in convoys known as cages.

Laval began to flourish in the late nineteenth century with the opening of the Sainte-Rose train station. The area became a favorite vacation spot for Montréalers, many of whom built summer homes in the Sainte-Rose area.

The **Cosmodôme**, home to the Space Science Centre and Space Camp Canada, is located in Laval. Interactive exhibits include an introduction to the cosmos, physical laws in space, telecommunications, and teledetection. It is located at 2150 autoroute des Laurentides (Route 15) in Laval. Admission: adult, senior, student, and child (6 and older), ❷; family passes are available. Open daily in the summer, and daily except Monday for the remainder of the year. For information, call ☎ (450) 978-3600 or consult 🖥 www.cosmodome.org.

Also worth a viewing in season is **Centrale de la Rivière-des-Prairies (Rivière-des-Prairies Generating Plant)**, a hydroelectric plant open to visitors

LAVAL AND THE LAURENTIANS

all summer. The dam was completed in 1930, bridging the river between Montréal and Laval. Free tours are offered from mid-May to mid-September. For information, call ☎ (800) 365-5229 or consult 🖳 www.hydroquebec.com.

Musée Armand-Frappier is a museum dedicated to the fight against tuberculosis, a fight led by renowned Québec scientist Armand Frappier. Located at 531 boulevard des Prairies, the museum is open weekdays through the year, with weekends added in July and August. Admission: adult, ❷; student, ❶. For information, call ☎ (450) 686-5641 or consult 🖳 www.musee-afrappier.qc.ca.

Parc de la riviére des Mille-Îles, the single largest natural park in greater Montréal, is an ecological sanctuary based around the river and its many islands, home to some two hundred species of birds and dozens of reptilian, amphibian, and mammalian species.

You can explore the area by renting a canoe, kayak, or pedalboat or go as part of a group on a *rabaska*, a huge canoe used by First Peoples. Rates are about ❷ per hour; guided excursions by rabaska are offered on weekend afternoons.

In winter the park offers more than fifteen miles of cross-country trails, sliding areas, and a half-mile skating rink. Equipment is available for rent.

For information on the park, call ☎ (450) 622-1020 or consult information at 🖳 www.parc-mille-iles.qc.ca.

Le Centre de la Nature (Nature Center) offers more than three miles of cross-country trails, a lake skating area, and sled and tubing areas. Equipment is available for rental. The center is located at 901 avenue du Parc in Saint-Vincent-de-Paul. For information, call ☎ (450) 662-4942.

Laval is also home to a large flower industry, growing about a third of all hothouse flowers in the province. Several producers open their doors for tours.

Les Serres Sylvain Cléroux (Sylvain Cléroux Greenhouses) offers guided tours weekdays from 9 A.M. to 4 P.M. The hothouses are located at 1570 rue Principale in Sainte-Dorothée. For information, call ☎ (450) 627-2471 or consult 🖳 www.resomatic.com/cleroux/index1.html.

Fleurineau-Économusée de la fleur, a major producer of dried flowers, sells more than 100,000 bouquets per year. Most of the flowers are grown on nearby land owned by the Marineau family. The factory and nearby Flower Economuseum showcasing floral crafts is open Monday through Saturday from 9 A.M. to 5 P.M. or later, and Sunday from 10 A.M.

Key to Prices
❶ $5 and under
❷ $5 to $10
❸ $10 to $20
❹ $20 and more
When prices are listed as a range, this indicates various combination options are available. Most attractions offer reduced-price tickets for children and many have family rates that include two adults and two or three children.

The facility is located at 1270 rue Principale in Sainte-Dorothée, just up the road from Les Serres Sylvain Cléroux. For information, call ☎ (450) 689-8414.

Another floral center is **Paradis des orchidées (Orchid Paradise)**, a greenhouse that specializes in orchids; there are more than forty-three thousand plants here. The facility is located at 1298 montée Champagne in Sainte-Dorothée. For information, call ☎ (450) 689-2244.

When the first faint glimmers of spring start to thaw the snows of Québec, it's time to head into the woods for a sugaring-off party at a maple syrup farm. Peak season is March and April.

Two farms that welcome visitors to sugaring-off parties are:

Cabane à sucre Lalande (Lalande Sugar Cabin), at 870 montée Laurin in Saint-Eustache. For information, call ☎ (450) 473-3357 or consult 🖳 www.lalande.ca.

Cabane à sucre Constantin Gregoire (Constantin Gregoire Sugar Cabin), at 1054 boulevard Arthur-Sauvé in Saint-Eustache. For information, call ☎ (450) 473-2374 or consult 🖳 www.constantin-gregoire.qc.ca.

For a different kind of sweet treat, you can visit the world of bees at **Intermiel**, a working honey processor where you can watch beekeepers at work and learn about pollination, honey, royal jelly, and wax. Guided tours are offered daily. Intermiel is located at 10292 rue Lafresnière in Saint-Benoit. For information, call ☎ (800) 265-6435 or ☎ (450) 258-2713 or consult information posted at 🖳 www.cloxt.com/intermiel.

The Lafrance apple orchards, **Les Vergers Lafrance (Lafrance Orchards)**, include more than twelve thousand trees that produce seventeen varieties of apples. Fruit and products that include cider, juice, and pies are available. Located at 1473 chemin Principal in Saint-Joseph-du-Lac. Open July to October on weekdays from 9 A.M. to 5 P.M. For information, call ☎ (450) 491-7859.

The Laurentians

The view on the horizon from Laval is the foothills of the Laurentians, some of the oldest mountains in the world. Just over an hour's drive from Montréal,

A snowboard exhibition at Mont Tremblant
Photo courtesy Mont Tremblant Ski Resort

the mountains include more than thirty golf courses, dozens of camp sites, water sport resorts, and more than twenty ski hills.

To drive to the mountains from Montréal, take the Laurentian Autoroute (Autoroute des Laurentides), 15 North or Route 117.

The Upper Laurentians begin about ten miles north of Mirabel International Airport outside Montréal. Geologists classify the mountains as pre-Cambrian. Not formed by volcanoes, the Laurentians are the results of upheavals and folding of the underlying crust of the earth.

Over millions of years the movement of glaciers rounded the tops of the peaks and gouged the deep valleys below.

The core of the Laurentians is the **Parc du Mont-Tremblant**, encompassing more than four hundred lakes, seven rivers and uncounted streams. Nature trails lead to the **La Chute du Diable (The Devil's Waterfall)**, which tumbles into narrow gorges. An interpretive site explains how the park area has changed from the time of the First Peoples, then the arrival of lumber companies and finally the installation of recreational facilities and the commitment to an ecological heritage.

> **Tourist bureaus.**
> **Laurentians.** ☎ (450) 436-8532 or ☎ (800) 561-6673.
> **Laval Region.** ☎ (450) 682-5522 or ☎ (800) 463-3765. www.tourismelaval.qc.ca.
> **Lanaudière Tourism.** ☎ (450) 834-2535 or ☎ (800) 363-2788. 🖳 www.tourisme-lanaudiere.qc.ca.

At the southern tip of the park is the **Mont Tremblant** ski resort, one of the finest in the east. Mont Tremblant is just one of nineteen ski areas in the hills; many of the other areas are open at night, drawing Montréalers after work; others make the most of their relative smallness, operating like country clubs.

A web of some 1,700 miles of marked and groomed snowmobile trails runs through the hills. You'll also find summertime activities that include water parks, golf courses at most every turn, and hiking trails.

The park is about eighteen miles from Sainte-Agathe. Open: year-round. Admission: free. For information, call ☎ (819) 688-2281.

As you enter into the mountains **Saint-Saveur**, about forty miles from Montréal, marks the unofficial start of the tourist attractions of the Laurentians. Here you'll find the Mont Saint-Saveur Resort, a skiing and golf center. Nearby is the Parc aquatique du Mont Saint-Saveur, a water park with your essential wave pool, lazy river, and slides. The water park is open from mid-June to early September. Admission: ❸–❹. For information, call ☎ (450) 227-4671 or consult 🖳 www.montsaintsauveur.com.

In Piedmont, **Glissades des Pays-d'en-Haut (High Country Slides)** is a winter snow tubing and rafting center that has more than six miles of slopes and trails. Located at 440 chemin Avila, the park is open from mid-December to the end of March. Admission: ❸–❹. For information, call ☎ (450) 224-4014.

Saint-Agathe-des-Monts is known for sandy beaches along Lac des Sables.

Lanaudière

To the northeast of Montréal the Lanaudière region extends from the city's outskirts to the eastern peaks of the Laurentians. The district includes a bit of most everything in the province, from the Saint Lawrence River with its rich agricultural plains to the alpine valleys, lakes, and rivers nestled between the wooded slopes of the Laurentian region.

Lanaudière was one of the first regions to be settled by French colonists.

The **Joliette Museum of Art** offers a changing exhibition of Québec and Canadian works, plus a large collection of decorative religious art objects from Québec, juxtaposed with European works from the late Middle Ages and the Renaissance. Located at 145 rue Wilfred-Corbeil in Joliette. Admission: adult, senior, and student, ❶. For information, call ☎ (450) 756-0311.

The **Parc régional des chutes Monte-à-Peine-et-des Dalles** is a regional park including a set of hiking trails along L'Assomption River; trails lead to three different breathtaking waterfalls: the swift Dalles Falls, the small and approachable Desjardins Falls, and the majestic Monte-à-Peine Falls. The park, in Saint-Jean-de-Matha, is open from mid-May to October. Admission: general, ❷.

The **Grand-Portage Gardens**, nestled in the foothills of the Laurentians, feature vegetables and flowers displayed in English and oriental arrangements of annuals and perennials. Located at 800 chemin du Portage in Saint-Didace, about ten miles from Saint-Gabriel-de-Brandon. Open mid-June to September. Admission: general, ❷. For information, call ☎ (450) 835-5813.

South of Montréal at Delson-Saint-Constant, the **Canadian Railway Museum** displays more than a hundred steam and diesel locomotives, passenger cars, freight cars, and trams. The site also includes a nineteenth-century rural railway station and a model railway exhibit. The museum, off Route 209, is open daily from May to September, with limited hours through mid-October. Admission: adult, ❷; senior and child, ❶; child (younger than 4), free. For information, call ☎ (450) 638-1522 or ☎ (450) 632-2410 or consult 🖳 www.exporail. org/musee/musee_CRM.htm.

Major Ski Areas of Québec

Laurentians

Gray Rocks. 630-foot vertical, 22 trails. ☎ (800) 567-6767. 🖳 www.grayrocks. com.

Mont Blanc. 985-foot vertical, 35 trails. ☎ (800) 567-6715, ☎ (819) 688-2444. 🖳 www.ski-mont-blanc.com.

Mont Saint-Saveur. 700-foot vertical, 29 trails. ☎ (450) 227-4671. 🖳 www. montsaintsauveur.com.

Ski Chantecler. 685-foot vertical, 23 trails. ☎ 450 229-3555.

Tremblant. 2,130-foot vertical, 77 trails. ☎ (819) 681-2000. 🖳 www. tremblant.ca.

Eastern Townships

Bromont. 1,330-foot vertical, 22 trails. ☎ (866) 276-6668. 🖳 www.skibro mont.com.

Mont Orford. 1,770-foot vertical, 43 trails. ☎ (819) 843-6548. 🖳 www.mt-orford.com.

Mont Sutton. 1,500-foot vertical, 53 trails. ☎ (514) 866-7639. 🖳 www.mt-sutton.com.

Greater Québec/Charlevoix

Le Massif. 2,525-foot vertical, 20 trails. ☎ (418) 632-5876. 🖳 www.lemassif. com.

Mont-Sainte-Anne. 2,050-foot vertical, 55 trails. ☎ (418) 827-4561. 🖳 www.mont-sainte-anne.com.

Stoneham. 1,380-foot vertical, 25 trails. ☎ (418) 848-2411. 🖳 www.ski-stoneham.com.

Chapter 27
The Eastern Townships

Les Cantons de l'Est (The Eastern Townships), is rich farmland that is an extension of the Appalachian region of upper Vermont and New Hampshire; it is Québec's garden, a place of farm towns and maple sugar shacks. It is also home to a peculiar church architecture born of the relatively modest means of the parishioners; many of the sharply angled roofs are painted silver instead of the copper metal or gold-leaf of wealthier districts around Québec or Montréal.

You'll rarely hear locals talk about the Cantons; French-speakers are apt to refer to the area as L'estrie.

All but uninhabited before 1792 because of the proximity to the American border, the Eastern Townships were first settled by English-speaking settlers. Following the American War of Independence, the lots in the Townships were granted to Loyalists and later to immigrants from Great Britain and finally to French Canadians.

Because the division of lots made available after 1791 took place under British administration, the Estrie region has a high concentration of townships (square lots) as opposed to the other regions in Québec where seigneuries (long rectangular strips of land) predominate.

The Eastern Townships

An hour's drive east from Montréal, the Eastern Townships (Cantons de l'Est) were established by Loyalists who crossed back over the border from the United States after the unpleasantness (for them) of the American Revolution. There are many picturesque small towns and farms and a few significant ski resorts, including **Mont Sutton, Mont Orford**, and **Mont-Sainte-Anne**.

The heart of the summer vacation scene is the town of **Magog**, which occupies the northern end of **Lac Memphrémagog**, which reaches across the border into Vermont. At **Saint Benoît-du-Lac**, the monks at the Benedictine monastery are famed for their small production of L'Ermite blue cheese. For information, call ☎ (813) 843-4080 or consult 🖳 www.st-benoit-du-lac.com.

Near Magog is Mont Orford, home to the substantial ski area of the same name and many summer activities. For information, call ☎ (819) 843-6548 or consult 💻 www.mt-orford.com.

The Montérégie

To the south and west of Montréal between the Ontario and New England borders and the foothills of the Appalachians, the so-called "Garden of Québec" is dotted with small hills, lakes, and rivers.

The **Coteau-du-Lac National Historic Site** preserves the remains of the first canal with locks in North America. From the Blockhaus, an octagonal-shaped defense building, visitors can view the rapids and surrounding region and learn about the history of the Saint Lawrence River. The site is located at 308A chemin du Fleuve in Coteau-du-Lac. Open mid-May to October. Admission: adult and child, (6–16) ❶; child (5 and younger), free; family ❷. For information, call ☎ (800) 463-6769 or ☎ (514) 763-5631 or consult 💻 parkscanada. pch.gc.ca/parks/quebec/coteau.

The area is also known as the "Valley of the Forts"; the French and British both built fortifications including Fort-Chambly in Chambly and Fort-Lennox on Île aux Noix.

At the **Battle of the Châteauguay National Historic Site** you can relive the victory of the Canadian army commanded by Lieutenant-Colonel Charles-Michel de Salaberry over the American troops that tried to capture Montréal in 1813. Salaberry's battalion of about three hundred managed to outmaneuver and trick more than seven thousand American soldiers.

The national historic site in Allan's Corner on the banks of the Châteauguay River includes a museum, a lookout over the battle site, and interpreters to explain the defensive strategy of the Canadians. Located in Howick, about eighteen miles from Châteauguay via Route 138, the site is open mid-May to October. Admission: adult and child (6–16), ❶; child (5 and younger), free; family, ❷. For information, call ☎ (800) 463-6769 or ☎ (514) 829-2003 in season or consult 💻 www.parcscanada.gc.ca/parks/quebec/chateauguay/en/index.html.

The **Fort Chambly National Historic Site** preserves a fortress built in the early 1700s to defend French colonists from British attacks. The fort, on rue de Richelieu in Chambly, is open March to mid-December. Admission: general (6–16), ❶; family, ❷. For information, call ☎ (800) 463-6769 or ☎ (450) 658-1585 or consult 💻 www.parcscanada.gc.ca/parks/ quebec/fortchambly/en/index.html.

The **Fort Lennox National Historic Site** preserves the history of a British island fort of the nineteenth century. Interpreters explain living conditions of the soldiers of the time and explains the purpose and strategic location of the buildings, including the powder magazine, the quarter-guard, and the barracks. The fort is reached by ferry from Saint-Paul-de-l'Île-aux-Noix, just over the border from the United States off Autoroute 21 from Montréal or exit 6 from the United States. Open mid-May to early September and weekends in September only. Admission: adult, ❷; child (6–16), ❶; family, ❸. For information, call ☎ (800) 463-6769 or ☎ (450) 291-5700 or consult 💻 www.parcscanada. gc.ca/parks/quebec/fortlennox/en/index.html.

Montérégie Tourism. ☎ (450) 469-0069

At **Parc Safari** more than a thousand animals roam free while visitors drive through encaged in their cars; guided tours are offered over FM radio. The park is in Hemmingford off Route 202, just north of the U.S. border with upstate New York.

Open May to September. Admission: adult and child (3–10), ❸; child (2 and younger), free. For information, call ☎ (800) 465-8724 or ☎ (514) 247-2727 or consult 🖳 parcsafari.qc.ca.

Only in Canada would there be a museum of snowmobiles. At the **Musée J. Armand Bombardier** there's that and a whole lot more. The science and technology museum is centered around inventor Joseph Armand Bombardier, who revolutionized recreational and emergency winter transportation with early snowmobiles. Today the company also produces airplanes and trains.

The museum is located in Valcourt, due east of Montréal and about thirty miles west of Sherbrooke, off Route 243. Admission: adult, ❷; senior and child, ❶. For information, call ☎ (450) 532-5300 or consult 🖳 www.fjab.qc.ca/jab hom_f.htm.

There's nary a snowmobile in sight, except maybe in the parking lot of the small **Musée Beaulne in Coaticook**, just above the border with Vermont. The museum's collection includes period costumes and old textiles, embroidery, lace, and quilts, housed in the Château Norton. Admission: adult. ❷. For information, call ☎ (819) 849-6560 or consult 🖳 www.museebeaulne.qc.ca.

Mauricie

On the north side of the Saint Lawrence between Montréal and Québec City, the Mauricie region includes some relatively accessible examples of nature at its extreme, including sheer rock walls, waterfalls, and deep forest.

In Trois-Rivières the **Musée des arts et traditions populaires du Québec (Museum of Arts and Traditions)** includes an unusual collection of artifacts, from toys, textiles, tools, furniture, and household objects of the early settlers to a collection of prehistoric artifacts of the Native Peoples and the first European explorers. You can also explore 160 years of the old Trois-Rivières prison, the only interpretation center that depicts prison life in Québec. The museum is off Autoroute 40. Admission: ❷–❹. For information, call ☎ (800) 461-0406 or ☎ (819) 372-0406 or consult 🖳 sites.rapidus.net/crc/CRC_pgs/P_Organs/MAT PQ.htm.

You can experience some of the daily life of steelworkers in the eighteenth and nineteenth centuries, including the blast furnace and casting room, at the **Forges du Saint-Maurice National Historic Site.** Located at 10000 boulevard des Forges in Trois-Rivières, the museum is open from May to October. Admission: adult and child (6–16) ❶; child (5 and younger), free; family, ❷. For information, call ☎ (800) 463-6769 or ☎ (819) 378-5116.

Chapter 28
Québec City

Upon his arrival in 1608 Samuel de Champlain chose to settle at "Kebec," an Algonquin word that means "where the river narrows."

Considered for many years the gateway to the northern continent, Québec City was many times the object of conquest.

In 1690 the Comte de Frontenac repelled the British forces under Admiral William Phipps and fortified the city. Then in 1759 the city fell into the hands of the English army after the battle of the Plains of Abraham; soon afterward, France ceded its colony to England.

In 1775 American forces lead by General Richard Montgomery and Colonel Benedict Arnold failed in an attempt to invade the area.

Although no further battles took place in the area, the English went on to complete the fortifications that today surround the heart of Québec, the only remaining walled city north of Mexico.

Capital of New France and then of the English colony, Québec City became the capital of the Province of Québec at the time of Canadian confederation in 1867.

Today Québec City and the surrounding area has a population of more than half a million, almost all of them French-speaking.

The striking profile of the Château Frontenac hotel rises over Cap Diamant; Dufferin Terrace, built onto the flanks of the cape, offers a breathtaking view over the old city, the Petit-Champlain, Place Royale, and the Old Port.

In the heart of Old Québec City the Ursulines Convent, founded in 1639, is the oldest educational institution for young women in North America. Nearby is the Québec Seminary, with its silver roof and towers.

Québec City is famously divided into an Upper and Lower Town. The upper area was the site of the defenses of old Québec; the lower town is exposed along the Saint Lawrence River.

There are more than twenty staircases cut into the rock face of the cliff between the upper and lower towns, including one ominously named the Breakneck Stairs (*L'escalier cassecou*). On all the stairs the trip down is not all that bad, but the prospect of climbing all the way back up is not that attractive in the heat of summer or the bitter cold of winter. The alternative for pedestrians is to take one of the *funiculars* or *ascenseurs*, inclined elevators that are built into the hill; there is a charge of a dollar or two for the privilege.

Getting to Québec City

The **Aeroport International Jean-Lesage de Québec** is twelve miles west of the city. Taxi fare to the city is about $30. Buses connects the airport to downtown and major hotels for about $10. For airport information, call ☎ (418) 640-2742 or consult 🖳 www.tc.gc.ca/QuébecRegion/nh/aeroport-jeanlesage.html.

Trains from Montréal arrive at the **Gare du Palais** in the Lower Town. Service from the Atlantic provinces to the east arrives at a terminal at Lévis across the Saint Lawrence; a ferry runs from there to the Lower Town.

By car Québec City is about 175 miles east of Montréal.

Upper Town

For many visitors the most recognizable building in Québec City is the imposing **Château Frontenac**, a landmark hotel opened in 1893 and completed with the addition of a central tower in 1924. Two historic wartime conferences were held here in 1943 and 1944, with participants including British Prime Minister Winston Churchill and American President Franklin Roosevelt.

Guided tours, led by a character in costume, are offered daily from 10 A.M. to 6 P.M. from May through mid-October and at other times of the year on Saturday and Sunday only from 1 to 5 P.M. Admission: adult and senior, ❷; child (6–16), ❶. For information, call ☎ (418) 691-2166 or consult 🖳 www.chateaufrontenac.com.

Alongside the base of the Château is the terasse Dufferin, where Champlain built Fort Saint-Louis in 1620 and where he died in 1635. His successor, Montmagny, erected a manor here, which served as the residence of the governors of New France for two decades. It was destroyed by fire in 1834. In 1838 the governor constructed at the location a boardwalk, which has since been extended during the years.

Nearby is the Frontenac Street stairway to the Lower Town, one of eleven stairways linking the two parts of town.

Above the Chateau is the **Musée du fort (Fort Museum)**, where visitors can relive the six sieges of Québec and the battle on the Plains of Abraham through artifacts, descriptions, and a huge model of Old Québec. Located at 10 rue Sainte-Anne, the museum is open daily. Admission: adult and senior, ❷; student and child (10 and younger), ❶. For information, call ☎ (418) 692-1759 or consult 🖳 parkscanada.pch.gc.ca/parks/nova_scotia/fort_anne/Fort_anne_f.htm.

The **Plains of Abraham** themselves are preserved at **Battlefields Park**. Exhibits at the Martello Tower No. 1 show aspects of military engineering; exhibits at the Martello Tower No. 2 are about astronomy and meteorology.

Battlefields Park, officially created in 1908, stretches over 250 acres and includes lush formal gardens. Shuttle service and guided tours are available.

Located at 390 avenue de Bernières, the interpretive center is open year-round while the Martello Tower and bus tour of the park are open from May to October. Admission: adult, senior, and child, ❶; child (12 and younger), free; family, ❸, depending on the choice of activities; combination ticket (includes shuttle, tour and park), ❷. For information, call ☎ (418) 648-4071.

The **Musée du Québec**, located on the Plains of Abraham, includes paintings, sculpture, photography, silverwork, and engraving. The museum showcases Québec art and international exhibitions. Admission: adult and senior, ❷; student and child (12–16), ❶; child (11 and younger), free. For information, call ☎ (418) 643-2150 or consult 💻 www.mdq.org.

Key to Prices
❶ $5 and under
❷ $5 to $10
❸ $10 to $20
❹ $20 and more
When prices are listed as a range, this indicates various combination options are available. Most attractions offer reduced-price tickets for children and many have family rates that include two adults and two or three children.

The **Musée de l'Amerique francaise (Museum of French America)** is on the historic site of the old Québec Seminary, dating back to 1663. The museum tells the story of the French history and culture in Québec.

Located at 9 rue de l'Université, the museum is open daily from mid-June to mid-September, and daily except Mondays the remainder of the year. Admission: adult, senior, and student, ❶; child (12 and younger), free; free admission on Tuesday except in summer. For information, call ☎ (418) 692-2843 or consult 💻 www.mcq.org/maf.

Alongside the seminary is the **Notre-Dame-de-Québec Basilica-Cathedral**; erected during the French regime, it was damaged during the siege of 1759 and destroyed by fire in 1922; in 1925 it was rebuilt based on the original plans.

The parish of Notre-Dame is the oldest on the American continent north of Mexico. The cathedral represents nearly 350 years of work in its decorations, including stained glass windows, paintings, sculptures, and a chancel lamp that was a gift from Louis XIV. Governor Frontenac and most of the bishops of Québec are buried in the crypt.

The cathedral is open daily. Guided tours are offered weekdays from May through November. The church is located at 20 rue De Buade. Admission: free, except during the "Act of Faith" presentations. For information, call ☎ (418) 694-0665 or consult 💻 www.patrimoine-religieux.com/ndq/ndq_en.html.

From May 1 to Canadian Thanksgiving in October, the "Act of Faith" sound and light show is presented in the basilica. The multimedia show, presented in English and French, is offered weekday afternoons and weekend evenings. Call for schedules. Admission: adult and senior, ❷; student, ❶; child (12 and younger), free.

The **Musée des Ursulines (Ursulines' Museum)** is on the site of the original house built in 1644 by Madame de la Peltrie, the benefactress of the Ursuline order. The exhibits include paintings, sculptures, embroideries, furniture, and artifacts of French and Amerindian cultures dating back to the

QUÉBEC CITY

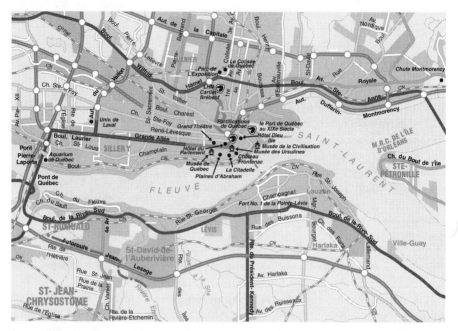

arrival of the Ursulines in 1639. Other exhibits discuss the evangelization of Amerindian girls in the seventeenth century.

Located at 12 rue Donnacona, the museum is open May to August Tuesday to Saturday, and from September to April the same days plus Sunday afternoons. Guided tours available with reservation. Admission: adult, senior, student, and child (12–16), ❶; child (11 and younger), free. For information, call ☎ (418) 694-0694 or consult 📖 www.museocapitale.qc.ca/014.htm.

Next door is the **Chapelle des Ursulines**. Though the building only dates from 1902 the interior décor of the primitive chapel erected on the site in 1723 has been preserved. The remains of the founder of the order, Marie de l'Incarnation (1599–1672) lie in the oratory adjacent to the chapel's nave. Admission: free. For information, call ☎ (416) 694-0413 or consult 📖 collections. ic.gc.ca/relig/ursul/ursulint.htm.

On the ground floor of the Québec City Hall the **Urban Life Interpretation Centre** explores the growth of the city, including a music video titled *Ballade urbaine* ("Urban Ballad"). The museum is located on the ground floor of City Hall at 43 côte de la Fabrique. Open daily from mid-June to September; closed Monday the remainder of the year. Admission: adult and student, ❶. For information, call ☎ (418) 691-4606.

Above the river the **Fortifications of Québec National Historic Site** contains the restored ramparts that surrounded Old Québec. A three-mile path dotted with gun batteries provides breathtaking views of the Saint Lawrence River. The Esplanade powder magazine, converted into an Information Center, explains three centuries of history. The site is located at 100 rue Saint-Louis near the Saint Louis Gate and the Parliament Buildings. Open from April to October. Admission: general, ❶; guided tour, ❷–❹. For information, call ☎ (800) 463-6769 or ☎ (418) 648-7016 or consult 💻 www.parcscanada.gc.ca/parks/ Québec/fortifications/en/index.html.

Nearby is **The Citadel/Musée du Royal 22e Régiment**, which is still occupied by troops. The Royal 22e Régiment Museum houses a mighty collection of weapons, uniforms, and military documents from the 1600s to the present day. The military tradition continues today with the Changing of the Guard and the Retreat. The Citadel is at the entrance of Old Québec, via the Grande Allée, just past the Saint-Louis Gate. Open year-round. Admission: adult, ❷; senior and child (7–17), ❶; child (6 and younger), free. For information, call ☎ (418) 694-2815 or consult 💻 www.lacitadelle.qc.ca.

Also nearby is the **Artillery Park National Historic Site**. A relief model of the city dating back to 1808 is on exhibit at the Arsenal Foundry, which was built in 1901. The Dauphine redoubt of 1712 offers exhibits, vaults, artillery casemates, and a formal English Tea Ceremony in the Officers' Mess. The Officers' Quarters (1818) displays period decor and antique furniture.

Located in the heart of Old Québec at 2 rue d'Auteuil, via rue Saint-Jean, next to the gate. Open April to October. Admission: adult, student, and child (6–16), ❶; child (5 and younger), free, with an additional fee for the English Tea Ceremony. For information, call ☎ (800) 463-6769 or ☎ (418) 648-4205 or consult 💻 www.parcscanada.gc.ca/Parks/Québec/artillerie/en/index.html.

Within the convent of the founders of the first hospital in Canada, the **Musée des Augustines de l'Hôtel-Dieu de Québec (Museum of the Augustine Sisters)** includes artifacts of French Canadian culture from the dawn of the colony as well as information about early medical care. One of the treasures is the chest brought by the founders of the convent in 1639. A "cabinet of curiosities" contains a collection of surgical, dental, and pharmaceutical instruments.

With prior arrangement visitors can also tour the arched cellars of the convent, which date back to 1695.

In the same building is the **Centre Catherine de-Saint-Augustin**. She was one of the pioneers of the church in Canada.

The convent is located at 32 rue Charlevoix. Open daily except Monday. Admission: free, but donations are welcomed. For information, call ☎ (418) 692-2492 or consult 💻 www.vmnf.civilization.ca/Collect/August/augus_1f.html.

Several commercial attractions also tell the story of Québec. The **Musée de cire de Québec (Québec Wax Museum)** is located within one of the city's oldest homes, dating back to 1670. Dioramas and figures tell the story of the city from Champlain to Montcalm and more. The museum, located at 22 rue Sainte-Anne, is open daily. Admission: adult and student, ❶; child (12 and younger), free. For information, call ☎ (418) 692-2289 or consult 💻 www.museo capitale.qc.ca/030.htm.

The **Québec Expérience** is a multimedia 3-D sound and light show that traces Québec's history from the time of the first explorers to modern days. The theater includes several dozen video and slide projectors on eight screens. The attraction is located at 8 rue du Trésor. Admission: adult, ❷; student, ❶; child (5 and younger), free; family tickets are available. For information, call ☎ (418) 694-4000 or consult 🖳 www.clic.net/~qe.

Lower Town

Another multimedia show, in the Lower Town of Québec across from the Old Port, is **Explore Sound and Light**. Visitors travel through time and sail with Jacques Cartier and Samuel de Champlain on their voyages, join the settlers during their first winter in Québec in 1608, and observe the first encounters between the Native Peoples and the Europeans. The show, located at 63 rue Dalhousie, near Place-Royale, is open May to September. Admission: general, ❶. For information, call ☎ (418) 692-1759.

Nearby, the **Old Port of Québec Interpretation Centre** tells the story of Québec City as the gateway to North America in the 1800s. The exhibition takes us back to the atmosphere of a bustling seaport and a thriving lumber industry. The center is located at 100 rue Saint-André. Admission: adult, ❶; child (6–16), ❶; child (5 and younger), free; family, ❷. For information, call ☎ (800) 463-6769 or ☎ (418) 648-3300 or consult 🖳 parkscanada.pch.gc.ca/vieuxport.

One of the most impressive museums in the city is the **Musée de la civilization (Museum of Civilization)**. The building's architecture is worth a visit; the modern structure echoes the steep roofs of the Old Port and incorporates several historical buildings, including the Maison Estèbe with its impressive arched cellar. There are ten exhibits about the history of Québec and on various themes that explore cultures from around the world. The museum is located at 85 rue Dalhousie, across from the Old Port, via boulevard Champlain or boulevard Charest. Admission: adult, ❷; child (12–16), ❶; child (11 and younger), free. For information, call ☎ (418) 643-2158 or consult 🖳 www.mcq.org.

Around Québec City

Heading northeast about fifteen minutes from Old Québec brings visitors to the Île d'Orléans, the largest official historic district in the province. Six villages on the island offer two dozen heritage buildings, including the old Gosselin mill in Saint-Laurent and the Mauvide-Genest manor, which now includes a museum and restaurant. The island developed as a shipbuilding center and as a market garden for the city of Québec City; the shipwrights are all but gone, but the farmers remain. The large island in the Saint Lawrence is accessible via the Pont de L'Île d'Orléans off Autoroute Dufferin-Montmorency.

Not quite Niagara but a spectacular site nevertheless, the **Parc de la Chute-Montmorency** features 270-foot-high waterfalls served by a cablecar to the top. The **Manoir Montmorency**, perched on the cliff, includes a restaurant, information center, a promenade on the edge of the cliff, and suspended bridges that take you over the canyon and falls.

The park is in Beauport, about eight miles east of Québec City and past Île d'Orléans along Autoroute 440. Open year-round. Admission: free. For cable car ride, ❷. For information, call ☎ (418) 663-3330 or consult 🖳 www.chute montmorency.qc.ca.

Further east is a sticky delight, the **Musée de l'abeille (Honey Museum)** in Château-Richer. Here's your chance to take a Bee Safari and learn about the job of a beekeeper, the never-ending work of the bee, and the by-products of a hive. The bee museum has a collection of modern and antique tools, and there are two observation hives safely blocked off behind glass.

Visitors can sample honey and *mead* (honey wine). The museum is located at 8862 boulevard Sainte-Anne in Château-Richer, about a mile from Sainte-Anne-de-Beaupré, via Autoroute 440 or via Route 138. Admission: free. For information, call ☎ (418) 824-4411 or consult 🖳 www.musee-abeille.com.

The **Sanctuary Sainte-Anne-de-Beaupré** is an enormous neo-Gothic basilica decorated with religious works including paintings, sculptures, and stained-glass windows. Visitors can also follow the Way of the Cross lined with life-sized, cast-iron figures and visit the Scalla Santa and the Memorial Chapel. The sanctuary is located in Sainte-Anne-de-Beaupré, about twelve miles east of Québec City. For information, call ☎ (418) 827-3781 or consult 🖳 collections.ic. gc.ca/relig/sabea/sabeaine.htm.

The 240-foot-high **Saint-Anne** waterfall is accessible at the **Grand Canyon des chutes Sainte-Anne**. Footpaths follow the upper ledges of the canyon, leading to three bridges suspended above the waterfall. The park is about three miles east of Sainte-Anne-de-Beaupré off Route 138. Open from May to October. Admission: ❷–❹.

The area is also home to the **Mont Sainte Anne** ski resort, one of the larger areas in the northeast with fifty-five trails. For information, call ☎ (418) 827-4561. 🖳 www.mont-sainte-anne.com.

On the Saint Lawrence River about thirty miles east of Québec City, the **Cap Tourmente National Wildlife Area** in Saint-Joachim-de-Montmorency combines the beauty of vast salt marshes, coastal plains, and mountains. The wildlife area preserves an important habitat on the migratory route of the Greater Snow Goose. The area off Route 138 is open year-round; interpretive services are offered from mid-April to late October. Admission: adult, ❷; child, ❶. For information, call ☎ (418) 827-3776 or consult 🖳 www.qc.ec.gc.ca/faune/ faune/html/nwa_ct.html.

North and West of Québec City

North of Québec City, the **Jardin zoologique du Québec (Zoological Garden of Québec)** is home to more than six hundred animals and an active animal preservation program. The zoo is in Charlesbourg, off Autoroute Laurentienne North. Admission: adult and student, ❷; child (4–13), ❷; child (younger than 4), free. For information, call ☎ (418) 622-0313 or consult 🖳 www.aquarium.qc.ca.

About five miles upriver from Québec City, the **Maison des Jésuites** (Jesuit House) in Sillery dates back to about 1730, and even then was the third residence on the site. The renovated building has a beautiful yard and garden with nearby ruins of a Native Peoples encampment and cemetery and the remains of Saint-Michel Chapel. The site was chosen in 1637 by Jesuit priests who wanted to encourage two nomadic tribes, the Montagnais and Algonquin, to settle and convert to Christianity. The site is located at 2320 chemin du Foulon in Sillery. Open mid-March to mid-December. Admission: donations accepted. For information, call ☎ (418) 654-0259 or consult 💻 www.mcc.gouv.qc.ca/reseau-archeo/partenai/jesuites.htm.

A bit further west, the **Aquarium du Québec** offers a collection of more than 260 species from Québec and around the world. The aquarium is located at 1675 avenue des Hôtels in Sainte-Foy. Open year-round. Admission: adult, ❸; senior, ❷; student, ❷; child (4–13), ❷; child (3 and younger), free. For information, call ☎ (418) 659-5266 or consult 💻 www.aquarium.qc.ca.

Chapter 29
The South Shore

Across the river from Québec city and Charlevoix, the Chaudière-Appalaches region offers some glimpses back to the days of the seigneuries during the French Régime, and the battles among the English, French, and the Americans; later it was the arrival point for many modern immigrants to Canada.

Wayside crosses dot the country roads throughout Québec and especially in the small towns on either side of the Saint Lawrence. They are reminders of a European custom and emblems of French settlement patterns. As time went by the wayside cross came to be regarded by residents as both a sign of their attachment to Catholic religious values and a safeguard against misfortune.

Tapping of maple trees for syrup, an art passed down from the Aboriginal peoples, celebrates the arrival of spring. Montérégie, Chaudière-Appalaches, Estrie, and Lanaudière are dotted with maple groves. One northeast specialty is maple syrup poured onto fresh snow.

In Lévis across from Québec City, **Fort No. 1 at Pointe de Lévy National Historic Site** preserves part of the defense system constructed between 1865 and 1872 to ward off American invaders moving northward from Maine. You can explore the tunnels and the fortified casemates and enjoy spectacular views of the area. The fort is located at 41 chemin du Gouvernement Lévis, accessible off Autoroute 20 or by the Québec-Lévis ferry from the Old Port. Open mid-May to October. Admission: general, ❶. For information, call ☎ (800) 463-6769 or ☎ (418) 835-5182 or consult 🖳 www.parcscanada.gc.ca/parks/quebec/levy.

For more than a century **Grosse Île** was the transit point for thousands of Europeans who emigrated to the New World. Most came from Ireland and the British Isles. The lengthy crossing under unsanitary conditions contributed to the spread of infectious diseases, and many thousands died on board or were ill on arrival in Canada. Overlooking L'Isle-aux-Grues Archipelago, Grosse Île was called "quarantine island" and was a mandatory stop-over before the immigrants were allowed to mix with the local population.

Grosse Île and the Irish Memorial National Historic Site preserves some of the buildings and includes displays about the history of the island. To get to

Key to Prices
❶ $5 and under
❷ $5 to $10
❸ $10 to $20
❹ $20 and more
  When prices are listed as a range, this indicates various combination options are available. Most attractions offer reduced-price tickets for children and many have family rates that include two adults and two or three children.

the site, boats run from Québec City's Old Port, or from the Boarding Dock at Montmagny or at Berthier-sur-Mer. Open May to October. Admission: ❹, including boat trip. For information, call ☎ (800) 463-6769 or consult 🖳 www.parcscanada.gc.ca/parks/quebec/grosseile.

The **Centre éducatif des migrations (Migration Educational Center)** at Montmagny is an exploration of migration: that of the Greater Snow Goose and humans to the New World. Exhibits also explore the history of the Grosse Île quarantine island.

Located at 53 rue du Bassin Nord, the museum is open June to November. Admission: adult ❷; child ❶. For information, call ☎ (418) 248-4565.

Due south of Québec City, Thetford Mines was an important geological site. The **Musée minéralogique et minier de Thetford Mines (Museum of Mineralogy and Mining)** presents a history of the mineral industry, with exhibits on mineralogy and the geology of the Appalachian mountains and the Région de L'Amiante. The museum, located at 711 boulevard Smith Sud, is open February to December. Admission: adult ❷; student (10–17) ❶. For information, call ☎ (418) 335-2123 or consult 🖳 www.mmmtm.qc.ca.

If you're so inclined you can take a guided tour of an open-pit asbestos mine and visit extraction, packing, and shipping sites at **Mining Tours in Thetford Mines**. Located at 682 rue Monfette Nord. Admission: adult ❸; student (10–17) ❷. For information, call ☎ (418) 335-7141.

Chapter 30
Lower Saint Lawrence
to the Gaspé and the Magdalen Islands

The south bank of the Saint Lawrence River, downriver from Québec City, is a narrow band that stands between the river and the upstarts across the border in America. The area is known as Bas-Saint-Laurent, or the Lower Saint Lawrence.

The small villages along the shore have lovely charms of their own and also serve as a gateway to the handsome Gaspé Peninsula and Îles-de-la-Madeleine (Magdalen Islands).

Bas-Saint-Laurent

There are museums for just about everything, so why not have one dedicated to . . . the eel. The **Site d'interprétation de l'anguille (Eel Interpretation Site)** celebrates the snakelike fish with displays, a demonstration eel trap, and smoked-eel canapés. The museum is in Kamouraska, off Route 132. The museum is in season from mid-May to late October. Admission: adult, ❷; child, ❶. For information, call ☎ (418) 492-3935 or consult 🖳 www.kam.qc.ca.

Nearby, the **Musée de Kamouraska** explores the crafts and folklore of a people who have lived by the land and the sea for more than three hundred years. Open from mid-May to mid-December. Admission: general, ❶; family, ❸. For information, call ☎ (418) 492-9783 or ☎ (418) 492-3144 or consult 🖳 www. moutonnoir.com/mukam.htm.

Baie de L'Isle-Verte National Wildlife Area is an internationally recognized wetland that provides a nesting habitat for 130 species of birds, some on the list of endangered species. It is also an important nesting and breeding area for the black duck. The area is in L'Isle-Verte, about twelve miles from Rivière-du-Loup. Open June to September. Admission: adult, ❷; student, ❶; child (younger than 12), free. For information, call ☎ (418) 827-3776 or ☎ (418) 648-7138 or consult 🖳 www.qc.ec.gc.ca/faune/faune/html/nwa_biv.html.

At the intriguingly named village of Trois-Pistoles, the **Parc de l'Aventure basque en Amérique (Basque-American Adventure Park)** pays tribute to the life and times of the Basque fishermen who hunted whales in the area around

LOWER SAINT LAWRENCE

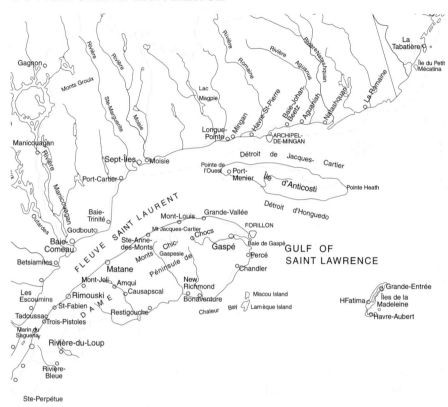

1584. There is also a documentation and genealogical center. Trois-Pistoles, by the way, does not refer to a set of three weapons, but instead to a trio of ancient Spanish gold coins. The park, off Route 132, is open June to the end of August. Admission: adult, ❷; youth and researchers, ❶. For information, call ☎ (418) 851-1556 or consult 🖳 www.icrdl.net/paba.

Local groups also organize trips to the unspoiled **Île aux Basques** in the Saint Lawrence River. This small island was once frequented by whale hunters from the Basque Country. Today it is an unspoiled and peaceful haven and a favorite spot for outings. Nearly 230 bird species and four hundred plant species have been identified on the island. For information, call ☎ (418) 851-1202 or consult 🖳 www.qc.ec.gc.ca/faune/faune/html/mbs_ile_aux_basques.html.

The **Pointe-au-Père Lighthouse National Historic Site** and **Musée de la Mer (Museum of the Sea)** is one of Canada's highest lighthouses; you can climb 128 steps to the top for a view of sea and coastline. The museum contains an exhibit on the *Empress of Ireland*, which collided with a coal carrier and sank in the Saint Lawrence River in 1914 with the loss of 1,012 lives. Pointe-au-Père is six miles from Rimouski. The site is open June to October. Admission: adult ❷; child, ❶; family, ❹. For information, call ☎ (418) 724-6214 or consult 🖳 parkscanada.pch.gc.ca/parks/quebec/phare-pointe-pere.

The Gaspé Peninsula

The Gaspé is Canada's French seacoast, a spectacular piece of Atlantic Canada with mountains, seashore, dense forests, and wildlife.

And if that's not enough, you can catch a ferry to go even farther out: the **Îles de la Madeleine (Magdalen Islands)** in the middle of the Saint Lawrence. A weekly ferry moves down the Saint Lawrence; there is more regular service from Souris on Prince Edward Island.

Some of the area's most impressive marine and arctic-alpine habitats can be found in the **Parc de la Gaspésie**, ten miles outside Sainte-Anne-des-Monts. The park includes Mont Jacques Cartier and Mont Albert, each more than three thousand feet in height. The park is open year-round.

Key to Prices
- ❶ $5 and under
- ❷ $5 to $10
- ❸ $10 to $20
- ❹ $20 and more

When prices are listed as a range, this indicates various combination options are available. Most attractions offer reduced-price tickets for children and many have family rates that include two adults and two or three children.

Admission: free. Additional fees are charged for guided tours and for guides and transportation for moose-watching. For information, call ☎ (418) 763-7811 or ☎ (888) 783-2663 or consult ▣ www.sepaq.com.

In the town of Gaspé at the tip of the peninsula at the Gulf of Saint Lawrence, the **Musée de la Gaspésie** tells the story of the region including the Native Peoples, the arrival of Jacques Cartier, and the cultural heritage of today's inhabitants. Historical interpretive trails lead to the shore of Gaspé Bay. The museum is on Route 132. Admission: general, ❶; child (younger than 12), free; family, ❷. For information, call ☎ (418) 368-1534 or ▣ www.mcc. gouv.qc.ca/region/11/pamu/musegas.htm.

Another spectacular preserve is **Forillon National Park** on the eastern tip of the Gaspé Peninsula, off Route 132. An interpretive center, open from June to mid-October, reveals secrets of the underwater world, geological features, and the flora and fauna of Forillon. The park itself is open year-round. There are entrances in Cap-des-Rosiers to the north and Cap-aux-Os to the south. Admission: adult, ❷; child, ❶. For information, call ☎ (800) 463-6769 or ☎ (418) 368-5505 or consult ▣ www.parcscanada.gc.ca/forillon.

Within Forillon National Park at the southeast tip of the peninsula, the **Grande-Grave National Historic Site** tells about life at the turn of the century at the peak of the cod fishery. You can visit a store and warehouse; and at Anse Blanchette, a family home is staffed by actors in period costumes. The site, off Route 132, is open from early June to mid-October. Admission: adult and child, ❶; family, ❷. For information, call (800) 463-6769 or ☎ (418) 892-5553 or consult ▣ parkscanada.pch.gc.ca/parks/quebec/grande-grave.

Nearby in Percé you can walk at low tide to the giant limestone **Percé Rock** offshore or take a boat trip to visit a colony of gannets at the **Parc de l'Île-Bonaventure-et-du-Rocher-Percé**. The park, off Route 132, is open from June to mid-October. Admission: free. For information, call ☎ (418) 782-2721 or consult ▣ www.qc.ec.gc.ca/faune/faune/html/rom_ile_bonaventure.html.

There are a number of small historical restorations on the peninsula, exploring the history and culture of the region and its people.

In Paspébiac along the **Baie des Chaleurs**, which separates the Gaspé from northern New Brunswick, the **Site historique du Banc-de-Paspébiac** shows the various activities of eighteenth-century fisheries, with demonstrations of the traditional maritime trades of blacksmithing, boatbuilding, and net mending. The site is open from mid-June to September. Admission: ❷–❹. For information, call ☎ (418) 752-6229 in season or ☎ (418) 752-5049 off-season or consult 🖳 www.mcc.gouv.qc.ca/region/11/pamu/bancpasp.htm.

Nearby in New Richmond, the **Gaspesian British Heritage Centre** is devoted to the British heritage in the Gaspé Peninsula, with costumed staff members and twenty buildings decorated with period furnishings. Open mid-May to mid-October. Family admission: ❷. For information, call ☎ (418) 392-4487.

At the end of the Baie des Chaleurs in Pointe-à-la-Croix on the border with New Brunswick, the **Battle of the Restigouche National Historic Site** displays archaeological treasures salvaged from the French frigate *Le Machault*, which sank during a battle with the British fleet in the summer of 1760. Exhibits include a close-up view of sections of the vessel and numerous artifacts from the hold. The site, about four miles from Campbellton, New Brunswick, via Route 132, is open from June to mid-October. Admission: adult and child, ❶; family, ❷. For information, call ☎ (800) 463-6769 or ☎ (418) 788-5676 or consult 🖳 www.parcscanada.gc.ca/parks/quebec/ristigouche/en/index.html.

L'Îles-de-la-Madeleine (Magdalen Islands)

The Magdalen Islands sit in the Gulf of Saint Lawrence. The windswept, barely developed spit of land is connected by ferry to Souris on the eastern end of Prince Edward Island. There's also a weekly ferry that connects from Montréal. A small airport receives flights from Québec City and Montréal.

The island has a surprisingly mild climate, tempered by southerly currents.

The **Museum of the Sea (Musée de la mer)** features exhibits about life in the Magdalen Islands with displays about fishing, transportation, navigation, and shipwrecks in the Gulf of Saint Lawrence and around the islands. The museum is located in Havre-Aubert. Admission: general, ❷. For information and hours, call ☎ (418) 937-5711 or consult 🖳 www.ilesdelamadeleine.com/musee.

Nearby is the **Aquarium des Îles**, exhibiting a variety of fish and aquatic species from the Gulf of Saint Lawrence including seals from Greenland as well as various fishing techniques and conservation methods. Open June 1 to mid-October. Admission: adult and child (6 and older), ❶; family, ❷. For information, call ☎ (418) 937-2277 or consult 🖳 www.ilesdelamadeleine.com/aquarium.

At the northeast end of the islands in Grosse-Île, the **Pointe-de-l'Est National Wildlife Area** explores the landscape of the Magdalen islands, a protected area representing the remains of a unique ecosystem in Québec, including the nesting habitats of a number of endangered species of birds. Open from April to November. Admission: general, ❶. For information, call ☎ (418) 648-7138 or ☎ (418) 827-4591 or consult 🖳 www.qc.ec.gc.ca/faune/faune/html/nwa_pe.html.

Chapter 31
The North Shore of the Saint Lawrence

To the east of Québec City, the regions of Charlevoix, Manicouagan, and Duplessis offer an extraordinary mix of small French towns, spectacular mountains and seascapes, and glimpses of untouched wilderness that extend northward five hundred miles to the Hudson Strait and Baffin Bay.

Geologists say much of the area was formed as the result of an ancient meteor impact.

The main road—the only one in some places—is Route 138, which extends from west of Québec City along the coast as far as Havre-Saint-Pierre where the road meets coastal wilderness. From there you can continue on by boat or plane; you can also cross the Saint Lawrence to the Gaspé Peninsula by ferry.

Charlevoix

The Charlevoix region, along the north shore of the Saint Lawrence to the east of Québec City, is a place straight out of a landscape artist's imagination with rivers, islands, and hills dotted with lovely little towns. Civilization is spread pretty thin here; just north of the communities along the Saint Lawrence begins nearly untouched wilderness that extends to the top of Hudson Bay.

The area, named after Jesuit historian Francois Xavier de Charlevoix, included early settlements at the lovely Baie-Saint-Paul on the river in the Gouffré Valley at the base of the highest range of mountains in the Laurentians.

The **Centre d'histoire naturelle de Charlevoix** explores the geological history, the flora, the fauna, the climate, and human history of the Charlevoix region. The exhibit, "Destiny from the Sky," presents the extraordinary diversity of the natural landscape of this area that was formed by the fall of a meteor. The site is off Route 138 in Baie-Saint-Paul. Admission: donations accepted. For information, call ☎ (418) 435-6275 or consult 🖳 www.charlevoix. net/rando/exposition.htm.

The **Parc des Grands-Jardins, Visitor Centre and Château-Beaumont Interpretation Centre** is a subarctic ecosystem typical of northern Québec. Naturalists take visitors along walking paths, discuss the natural history of the park, and introduce the resident herd of caribou. The park is about thirty miles north of Baie-Saint-Paul off Route 381. Open late May to late October. Admission: free. For information, call ☎ (418) 846-2057 in season or consult 🖳 www. quebecweb.com/tourisme/charlevoix/parcs/granjrdfranc.html.

Saint-Joseph-de-la-Rive was once a prosperous shipbuilding village; it was one of the first settlements in Charlevoix. Shops in town sell painted clay "santons," which depict the inhabitants of Charlevoix in their various trades.

From the harbor you can catch a ferry to **Isle-aux-Coudres**, a developed island just off the north shore of the Saint Lawrence near Baie-Saint Paul. You can visit a working watermill built in 1825 and a windmill constructed in 1836. The miller grinds wheat and buckwheat and tells stories about his ancient trade. Open mid-May to mid-October. Admission: adult, student, and senior, ❶; child (12 and younger), free. For information, call ☎ (418) 438-2184 in season or consult 🖳 www.quebecweb.com/tourisme/charlevoix/ musees/ilecdreang.html.

Also on Île-aux-Coudres at the **Musée les voitures d'eau** you can step on board a dry-docked schooner and learn about navigation on the Saint Lawrence River. Exhibits explore navigational instruments used in the early 1900s and the lifestyles of isolated communities during the winter months. Open mid-May to mid-October. Admission: general, ❶; child (12 and younger), free. For information, call ☎ (800) 463-2118 or ☎ (418) 438-2208 or consult 🖳 www.que becweb.com/tourisme/charlevoix/musees/ autoeauang.html.

Further east the valley through which the Malbaie River flows was formed by glacial erosion of a deep crater in the earth's crust, resulting in hanging valleys and steep rocky cliffs. You can learn about the unusual geology at the **Parc régional des Hautes-Gorges-de-la-rivière-Malbaie** in Saint-Aimé-des-Lacs. For information, call ☎ (418) 439-4402 or consult 🖳 www.quebecweb.com/tour isme/charlevoix/parcs/htegorgang.html.

At Baie-Sainte-Catherine, a ferry crosses the mouth of the Saguenay River. The **Saguenay-Saint Lawrence Marine Park** and the **Pointe-Noire Interpretation and Observation Centre** protects marine habitat where the Saint Lawrence estuary and the Saguenay fjord meet. From the natural lookout, you can often watch belugas and mink whales. The park, on Route 138 at Pointe-Noire, is open June to October. Admission: free. For information, call ☎ (418) 235-4703 or consult 🖳 parkscanada.pch.gc.ca/parks/quebec/saguenay_Saint-laurent.

Other whale-watching centers include Tadoussac, Cap-de-Bon-Désir and the Escoumins.

Saguenay-Lac Saint Jean

The south shore of the Saguenay river is dotted with quaint villages; residents are nicknamed "Bleuets" in honor of the abundant blueberries of the area.

Around Lac Saint Jean at the head of the river, the local cuisine includes a variation of Québec's tourtière. The Saguenay version of the meat pie is made with layers of cubed game meat and potatoes piled between two thick crusts.

Other culinary specialties of the Saint Lawrence include broadbean soup (*soupe aux gourganes*) in Charlevoix, fish chowder (*bouillabaisse*) in the Gaspé or rabbit stew (*gibelotte*) on Îles de Sorel in Montérégie.

For an unusual view of the story of the rise and fall of a town and a way of life you can visit the **Village historique de Val-Jalbert**, an open-air museum that tells of the hope generated by the construction of a pulp mill in 1901 and the subsequent migration of the workers after the mill shut in 1927. Visitors can explore the ghost town by foot or aboard a train and travel in a gondola lift for views of the surrounding countryside, including a 234-foot-high waterfall. The village is off Route 169 in Chambord, six miles from Roberval. Open mid-may to mid-October. Admission: adult, ❸; child (7–14), ❷; child (6 and younger), free. Additional fee for the gondola. For information, call ☎ (418) 275-3132.

> **Key to Prices**
> ❶ $5 and under
> ❷ $5 to $10
> ❸ $10 to $20
> ❹ $20 and more
>   When prices are listed as a range, this indicates various combination options are available. Most attractions offer reduced-price tickets for children and many have family rates that include two adults and two or three children.

At the Zoo de Saint-Félicien some one thousand animals roam free while humans are in cages. The environment includes lakes and rivers and a diversity of flora and fauna. The zoo is located at 2230 boulevard du Jardin in Saint-Félicien, about fifteen miles from Roberval. Open mid-May to late September. Admission: adult and child (12–17), ❸; child (11 and younger), ❷. For information, call ☎ (800) 667-5687 or ☎ (418) 679-0543.

Manicouagan

On the eastern side of the Saguenay River signs of civilization become farther and farther apart; the river begins to widen as it heads for the Gulf.

In the center of Tadoussac the **Centre d'interprétation des mammifères marins (Marine Mammal Center)** offers an exploration of whales and other marine mammals with interactive exhibits and listening posts. Nearby, whale-watching tours depart from the town wharf. The center is open mid-May to the end of October. Admission: ❷. For information, call ☎ (418) 235-4701.

You may be able to observe several species of whales from dry land at the **Cap-de-Bon-Désir Interpretation and Observation Centre**. The facility, about three miles east in Grandes-Bergeronnes, is open June to October. Admission: adult, ❷; senior, ❶; child, ❶. For information, call ☎ (418) 232-6751 in season or ☎ (418) 235-4703 off-season or consult 📖 www.destinationquebec.com/region/ ereg_det_manicoua.html.

Nearby, the **Centre d'interprétation Archéo Topo** explores prehistoric remains of settlements of Native Peoples dating back more than five thousand years, uncovered at two archaeological sites. Located off Route 138 near Grandes-Bergeronnes, the site is open mid-May to mid-October. Admission: adult, ❷; child, ❶. For information, call ☎ (418) 232-6286 in season or ☎ (418) 232-6302 off-season or consult 📖 www.archeotopo.qc.ca.

Car-carrying ferries cross the wide Saint Lawrence River from **Baie-Comeau** on the north shore to Matane on the Gaspé Peninsula. For information, call ☎ (418) 562-2500 or consult 📖 www.traversiers.gouv.qc.ca/matane/indexa.htm.

At Baie-Trinité the **Pointe-des-Monts Historical Lighthouse** was built in

1830 and operated until after World War II. The building now contains an exhibit on the life of lighthouse keepers. The house formerly used by the lighthouse keepers has been turned into a bed-and-breakfast. Open mid-June to mid-September. Admission: ❷; additional fee for whale-watching or fishing trips. For information, call ☎ (418) 939-2332 in season or ☎ (418) 589-8408 off-season.

The Duplessis Region

The vast wilderness of rivers and forests of the Duplessis region stretches to the eastern border of Québec, where the Saint Lawrence meets the sea.

Among the many islands of the area is **Anticosti**, which sits in the middle of the Saint Lawrence where it meets the Gulf of Saint Lawrence. The island is inhabited by beaver, moose and a herd of 125,000 white-tailed deer.

On the remote eastern end of the mainland, the **Mingan Archipelago National Park Reserve** has ensured the conservation and development of about forty islands of varying sizes located a few miles off the coast. Havre-Saint-Pierre is the end of Route 138, which has tracked the north shore of the river from Québec City and beyond; travel further east is by boat or airplane.

At Sept-Îles, the **Musée régional de la Côte-Nord et Vieux-Poste** explores the archaeological and ethnological heritage of the Côte-Nord (North Coast). The Vieux Poste is a reconstruction of an eighteenth-century Hudson Bay Company Trading Post and is surrounded by a wooden palisade; also on display are Montagnais Indian artifacts. The museum is open year-round; the Vieux Poste Vieux Poste is open daily 9 A.M. to 5 P.M. from late June to mid-August. Admission: the Vieux Poste has a small fee; the museum is free. For information, call ☎ (418) 968-2070 or consult 🖳 www.bbsi.net/mrcn/vpfranc.htm.

Perched near the end of the road in Havre-Saint-Pierre, the **Mingan Archipelago National Park Reserve** is the gateway to the unusual landscape of limestone monoliths sculpted by time, the sea, and colonies of Atlantic Puffins. At the Visitor Centre a film on the history and natural resources of the park is shown daily. To get to the offshore islands, choose from various tours offered by private transportation companies. The reserve is open mid-June to mid-September. Admission: adult and child ❶; fees ❹ for boat tours to the islands. For information, call ☎ (418) 538-3285 in season; or ☎ (800) 463-6769 in the off-season or consult 🖳 www.parcscanada.gc.ca/mingan.

Anticosti Island is accessible by plane or by boat from Sept-Îles or Havre-Saint-Pierre. For information, call ☎ (800) 463-0863 or ☎ (418) 535-0156.

The main settlement on the island is **Port Menier** at its western tip; points of interest include the cavern of the rivière à la Patate, the Vauréal and Schmitt waterfalls, and Cape Tunnel and Cape de la Table.

For tourist information, contact the Municipalité du Lac-Geneviève. at ☎ (418) 752-6229.

Chapter 32
Western Québec

Western Québec, overhanging Ontario and heading due north to Hudson Bay, is a place of big forests, many lakes, and few roads.

The Abitibi-Témiscamingue region was one of the last areas of the province to be settled; it expanded with the growth of mining, forestry, and farming. As early as the sixteenth century, fur traders were attracted to the region; drawn by the wildlife and natural resources, the *coureurs des bois* roved the vast wilderness and traded with the First Nations.

History in the Woods

On **Lake Témiscamingue**, which sits on the border with Ontario, the **Fort Témiscamingue National Historic Site** preserves an old fur-trading post. Summer events include outdoor talks, historical reenactments with period costume, and craft demonstrations. The site is also home to a stand of Eastern white cedar in twisted shapes; the locals have named it the "enchanted forest."

The fort is five miles from Ville-Marie via Route 101 South. Open June to September with limited hours during off-season. Admission: general, ❶. For information, call ☎ (800) 463-6769 or ☎ (819) 629-3222 or consult 🖳 parkscanada. pch.gc.ca/parks/quebec/temiscamingue.

You can step into the days of the Gold Rush at **La Cité de l'Or (The City of Gold)**, an historic mining town that dates from the early 1900s. Costumed staff—including former miners—help visitors don a miner's hat and an old-fashioned miner's suit, and escort them down a 1,200-foot ramp into the mine. Located in Val d'Or via Route 101 or Route 117. Open late June to early September; call for other times. Admission: adult, ❹; child, ❷. For information, call ☎ (819) 825-7616 or consult 🖳 www.citedelor.qc.ca.

Just west of Val d'Or in Malartic, you can learn more about the various minerals that make up the underground wealth of the Abitibi region at the **Musée régional des mines de Malartic (Malartic Mines Museum)**. The museum is located off Route 117. Admission: adult ❷; child, ❶. For information, call ☎ (819) 757-4677 or consult 🖳 www.museemalartic.qc.ca.

WESTERN QUEBEC

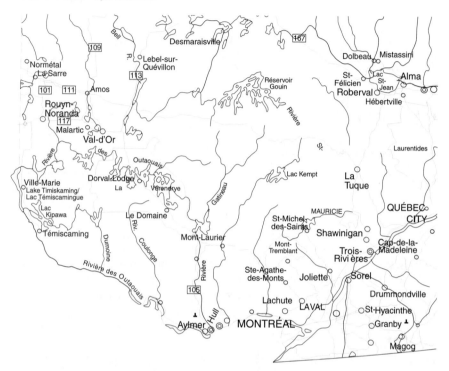

The **Maison Dumulon Historic Site** preserves an isolated general store, post office, and family home of the early 1900s with actors portraying the original owners, Jos and Agnès Dumulon. The site, off Route 117 in Rouyn—Noranda, is open year-round, with limited hours in off-season. Admission: adult, ❶; youth (12–16), ❶; child (11 and younger), free. For information, call ☎ (819) 797-7125 or consult 🖳 www.lino.com/~rsmhat/dumulon.html.

Key to Prices
❶ $5 and under
❷ $5 to $10
❸ $10 to $20
❹ $20 and more
When prices are listed as a range, this indicates various combination options are available. Most attractions offer reduced-price tickets for children and many have family rates that include two adults and two or three children.

At Angliers on the shores of Lake des Quinze, the *T. E. Draper* lies in dry dock, an historic monument built around the largest towboat used by the Canadian International Paper Company from 1929 to 1972 for towing wood. Also at the site is the Chantier de Gédéon, a reconstruction of a typical lumber camp that shows the daily life of the men preparing for log drives. Angliers is off Route 391, about twenty-two miles from Ville-Marie across the border in Ontario to the west. Open mid-June to early September. Admission: adult, ❷; child, ❶. For information, call ☎ (819) 949-4431 or consult 🖳 www.lino.com/~rsm hat/angliers.html.

Part VII
Atlantic Canada

Chapter 33
Atlantic Canada

The provinces of Atlantic Canada—New Brunswick, Newfoundland, Nova Scotia, and Prince Edward Island—are a study in extremes. This is a region of mountains that lead to forests and rough, worn rocky harbors that have been shaped by the pounding surf of the Atlantic or by astounding tides created by the unique geography of the region.

New Brunswick, on the mainland and sharing its borders with Maine in the United States and the Gaspé Peninsula of Québec, is an enchanted forest land. Its southern side faces the Bay of Fundy, where some of the highest tides in the world sweep in and out daily.

Nova Scotia is a bit of Scotland in the New World, a barrier island to the mainland with a rich history of seafaring. At its north end is rugged Cape Breton Island, part of the unhappy story of the Acadians.

Held within the protected waters to the west of Nova Scotia, the province of Prince Edward Island is Canada's smallest—but among its most densely populated—regions; it's almost impossibly green and tranquil.

Newfoundland and Labrador are two notably different pieces of the same province. Newfoundland has remnants of some of the oldest civilizations in North America, while Labrador is a northern Canadian wilderness within the reasonable reach of adventurous travelers.

Acadia

Some historians attribute the term Acadia or Arcadia to Giovanni da Verrazzano, who in the 1520s explored North Carolina to Maine, including New York harbor, but never reached as far north as Nova Scotia or Prince Edward Island. He may have been reaching back to classical Greek for the word *Arcadia*, which means a pastoral paradise, or the word may have come from an encounter with natives who used the word *quoddy* or *cadie* to describe the land around them.

Maps of the early 1520s applied the name Acadia to the land that stretched from Nova Scotia south to New Jersey in the United States. A 1548 map placed Larcadia near today's Cape Cod in Massachusetts. In 1566 an Italian mapmaker moved Larcadia to what is now Nova Scotia, seven decades before the French began settling there.

The French originally applied the name Acadia to much of the Atlantic colonies of New France, including places we today call southeastern Quebec, eastern Maine, New Brunswick, Nova Scotia, and Prince Edward Island.

The first French settlers came to Acadia in 1604 while France and Great Britain were at war in Europe. The followers of Samuel de Champlain and Pierre Sieur de Monts settled in a stockade on Saint-Croix in the Bay of Fundy. After a difficult winter cut off from the mainland by treacherous ice floes, they crossed over to the southern part of the bay and reestablished their settlement in Port Royal in 1605.

The French settlers were industrious farmers, tilling the difficult soil and erecting dikes in a system known as *aboiteaux*, which prevented high tides from soaking and ruining the main land.

During one of several changes in control of Atlantic Canada between France and England, King James I granted the land to a fellow Scot, William Alexander, naming the territory Nova Scotia or New Scotland.

Through most of the next century, though, Acadia remained in French hands. But in 1713 the Treaty of Utrecht ceded most of Acadia—all of Atlantic Canada except for Cape Breton and Prince Edward Island—from France to Britain.

In the process the Acadians were abandoned by France, leaving the British in control of prosperous French colonies. The Acadians promised to stay neutral in any dispute, but the British distrusted them.

During the second half of the eighteenth century, hostilities between France and Britain were renewed as the two countries fought for control of eastern Canada in what became known as the Seven Years War. For extra support England brought in some of its troops in New England, while France cultivated its relationship with the formidable Mi'kmaq nation. At the same time back in Britain, Roman Catholics in Britain were under suspicion as a threat to the Crown.

In 1754 the British gave the Catholic Acadians one year to decide to swear allegiance to the Crown or leave. Nearly all refused.

In 1755 the Expulsion or grand dérangement began. Families were rounded up and in many cases separated. About six thousand Acadians were deported to New England, Louisiana, France, and England. Some drowned at sea in shipwrecks.

Britain then turned its attention to the remaining Acadians in New Brunswick in settlements along the Petitcodiac River; many small villages in the Tantramar region were burned and their inhabitants driven out.

The Seven Years War ended in 1763; in 1764 a proclamation by the British governor allowed the Acadians to return to their homeland if they would take an oath of allegiance. Many made the long trip home, although a colony remained in New Orleans, where the word Acadian became *cajun*.

Chapter 34
Newfoundland and Labrador

Newfoundland and Labrador are like an eastern bookend to Canada's west coast in British Columbia; there are few major settlements, only a handful of roads, and a wondrous world of wildlife that seems to take little notice of the intrusions made by humans.

The island of Newfoundland is home to most of the 570,000 residents of the province and nearly all of its roads and infrastructures. On the mainland, Labrador sits above and alongside far eastern Québec, with a handful of settlements located along the coast and inland near Churchill Falls where a massive hydroelectric plant generates power, mostly for Québec.

Saint John's in Newfoundland claims the title as the first city in the New World and dubs Water Street the oldest avenue in North America. Several dozen vessels were anchored in the sheltered harbor forty years before the Mayflower landed a few hundred miles south in Massachusetts.

Several hundred years later Guglielmo Marconi communicated the other direction, receiving the first transatlantic wireless message from a station at the top of Signal Hill.

Saint John's is the easternmost city in all of North America. In fact, Newfoundland is so far east it is beyond the Eastern Time Zone, sitting in a halfway zone known as Newfoundland Time, half an hour later than the rest of Atlantic Canada and the East Coast of the United States.

Newfoundland

Southern Newfoundland consists of two peninsulas. The lower, moth-shaped land is known as the **Avalon Peninsula**. Avalon includes the city of Saint John's in its northeast corner.

The upper land is the **Bonavista Peninsula** and includes the colony of Bonavista where John Cabot landed in 1497, calling the place a "New Founde Land."

The center of the province, nearly untouched at its core, includes **Gander** to the northeast and southern coast settlements including the **Burin Peninsula** (gateway to the small islands of **Saint Pierre and Miquelon**, the last remaining piece of France in North America; the islands sit just off shore).

NEWFOUNDLAND AND LABRADOR

The **Northern Peninsula** juts into the Gulf of Saint Lawrence, ending at the Strait of Belle Isle across the channel from eastern Québec and lower Labrador.

History

Native peoples were on the island as the last great Ice Age receded, followed by the Innu and Inuit who established settlements several thousand years ago.

Archeologists have uncovered a one-thousand-year-old Viking settlement at **L'Anse aux Meadows** in the northern peninsula.

In 1583 England claimed Newfoundland, but for more than a century there were disputes between England, France, and other nations over the abundant fish stocks in the region. For more than four hundred years the province was the center of the world's cod fishing industry. A preparation of cod tongues continues as one of the region's specialties, along with partridgeberry pie.

Getting to Newfoundland and Labrador

Marine Atlantic oceangoing car ferries sail year-round from North Sydney, Nova Scotia, to Port-aux-Basques in Newfoundland.

In summer a ferry also sails from North Sydney to Argentia on the Avalon Peninsula. For details, call ☎ (709) 695-4266 or consult 📖 www.gateway tonewfoundland.com/port/passenger.html.

On the island, the Trans-Canada Highway, Route 1, begins in Saint John's and works its way north and then west to the ferry terminal at Port-aux-Basques. Route 1 passes most communities on the island, including Gander, Windsor, and Corner Brook. A provincial road heads north from Deer Lake to the top of the Northern Peninsula on the Strait of Belle Isle, across from Labrador.

A **Labrador Marine** ferry crosses between Saint Barbe in Newfoundland and Blanc-Sablon in far eastern Québec. Central Labrador can be reached overland from northern Quebec along Route 389 to Route 500. For information on the ferry, call ☎ (709) 877-2222.

International airports at Saint John's and Gander connect Newfoundland and Labrador to centers in Europe and North America.

Attractions in Newfoundland

History is literally in the air at the **Signal Hill National Historic Site** in Saint John's.

Originally a British fort, in 1901 Guglielmo Marconi received the first transatlantic wireless radio signal here.

Signal Hill provides a great view of the city below; it was here that flags were hoisted to announce the approach of merchant ships. The final battle of the Seven Years War between English and French armies took place here as well. For information, call ☎ (709) 772-5367 or consult 📖 parkscanada.pch.gc.ca/ parks/newfoundland/signal_hill.

The tip of Cape Spear in Saint John's is the most easterly point in North America. The **Cape Spear National Historic Site** is the location of the oldest surviving lighthouse in the province; the 1836 light has been restored, and visitors can also learn about the life of the lightkeeper and his family.

Nearby is Fort Cape Spear, a defense battery built during World War II. In spring and summer the point is also an excellent site for whale-watching, birding, and iceberg-spotting. Open from mid-May to mid-October. Admission to the ground and the lighthouse, adult, senior, and child, ❶; family, ❷. For

Newfoundland ferries.
Bell Island Ferry. ☎ (709) 895-6931
Change Island–Farewell Ferry. ☎ (709) 627-3448
Fogo Island–Farewell. ☎ (709) 627-3492
Gaultois–MacCallum–Hermitage. ☎ (709) 551-1446
Newfoundland–Saint John's Fortune. ☎ (709) 722-3892
Saint Pierre Ferry, Lake's Transport. ☎ (709) 832-0429 or ☎ (800) 832-2006.

Say it right. Most visitors try to merge the name of the province into one mashed potato of a word, saying "newfin-lind" or something like that. You can tell a native, or a knowledgeable visitor, however, by his or her deliberate pronunciation that gives equal emphasis to all three conso- nants: "new-found-land."

information, call ☎ (709) 772-5367 or ☎ (709) 772-4210 or consult 🖳 parkscanada.pch.gc.ca/parks/newfoundland/ cape_spear.

Across Conception Bay, in Brigus, the **Hawthorne Cottage National Historic Site** preserves the home of noted Arctic explorer Robert Bartlett. In 1908 Bartlett was captain of the ship that took Robert E. Peary to the North Pole.

The 1830 home is one of the last examples of picturesque or cottage orné architecture in the province.

The site is open from June to October. Admission adult, ❶; family, ❷. For information, call ☎ (709) 528-4004 or consult 🖳 parkscanada.pch.gc.ca/parks/newfound land/hawthorne_cottage.

Central Newfoundland

On the Burin Peninsula in south-central Newfoundland, the **Southern Newfoundland Seaman's Museum** covers five hundred years of fishery and marine heritage of the French, Spanish, Portuguese, Basque, and English. The museum is in Grand Bank, about 225 miles from Saint John's. For information, call ☎ (709) 832-1484 or consult 🖳 www.nfcap.nf.ca/east/GrandBank/Attract/Seaman.html.

Saint Pierre and Miquelon

The last remaining official vestige of France are the two tiny islands of Saint Pierre and Miquelon, about ten miles off the southern coast of Newfoundland.

Some six thousand French citizens live on the sandy islands speaking the French language, drinking French wine, and drawing on the French economy. The islands are a department of France, equivalent to an overseas territory.

The two islands were claimed by France in the 1500s but went back and forth with Britain over the years; they were made part of the British colonies after the Seven Years War but were turned back to France in 1783 under the Treaty of Paris.

The larger of the two islands is Saint Pierre, with most of the population. There are a handful of hotels, and good French food is de rigeur.

The islands were an important waystation in the rumrunning industry during Prohibition in the United States. Vast quantities of Canadian liquor were legally exported to Saint Pierre & Miquelon and then picked up by American privateers for illegal import.

Visitors from Canada or the United States do not need passports or visas, but should bring proof of identity. Nationals of other countries should check with their emigration authorities.

The ferry to the islands runs from Fortune, Newfoundland to Saint Pierre. For information, call ☎ (800) 563-2006.

NEWFOUNDLAND

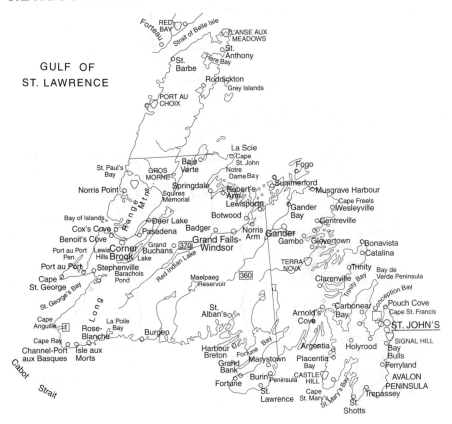

Air Saint Pierre flies from Montréal, Halifax, and Sydney; contact Canadian Airlines International for information. In the United States, the information number is ☎ (800) 426-7000.

For tourism information, call the Saint Pierre Tourist Office at ☎ (800) 565-5118 or consult 🖳 www.st-pierre-et-miquelon.com.

Bonavista Peninsula

At the end of the Bonavista Peninsula, about 188 miles from Saint John's, John Cabot landed in 1497, just five years after Columbus. The Italian navigator was sailing on behalf of the British Crown.

In Bonavista the **Ryan Premises National Historic Site** commemorates the role of the East Coast fishery in Canadian history from the early 1500s to the present. You can explore a merchant's shop, watch local craftsmen, and visit other period buildings and costumed staff. The site is open from late June through mid-October. Admission: adult, senior, and youth, ❶; family, ❷. For information, call ☎ (709) 468-1600 or consult 🖳 parkscanada.pch.gc.ca/parks/newfoundland/ryan_premises.

Nearby is the **Cape Bonavista Lighthouse Provincial Historic Site**, where interpretive staff open a lighthouse restored to its 1870 appearance. The small, squat lighthouse and building is painted in bold red and white stripes. Open from June to October. Admission: free. For information, call ☎ (709) 468-7444 or ☎ (709) 729-0592 or consult 🖳 www.manl.nf.ca/capebona vista.htm.

North Central Newfoundland

At the top of the of the Baie Verte Peninsula, the **Dorset Eskimo Soapstone Quarry National Historic Site** is an archaeological exploration of an ancient quarry of the long-ago departed Dorset Eskimos, who chiseled the stone for utensils some five thousand years ago. A botanical trail leads to a viewing area for icebergs and marine life, including seals, whales, dolphins, and seabirds. The area, in Fleur de Lys, is open year-round. Admission: general, ❶. For information, consult 🖳 www.manl.nf.ca/dorseteskimo.htm.

Way up north on the Northern Peninsula on the west coast facing the Gulf of Saint Lawrence, the **Port au Choix National Historic Site** preserves vestiges of three ancient cultures: the Dorset Eskimo, the Groswater Eskimo, and the Maritime Archaic Indian. The visitor center in Port au Choix is on Highway 430, the Viking Trail. The site is open from mid-June to mid-September. Admission: adult, senior, and student, ❶. For information, call ☎ (709) 861-3522 in the summer only, or ☎ (709) 458-2417 at other times or consult 🖳 parkscanada. pch.gc.ca/parks/newfoundland/port_choix.

At the lower end of the Gulf of Saint Lawrence coast of the Northern Peninsula, **Gros Morne National Park** is a lunar landscape formed by ancient collisions of massive tectonic plates. Boat tours explore majestic fjords and the Tablelands, a two-thousand-foot-high plateau formed from rocks from deep within the earth's mantle. The park is home to herds of caribou and arctic hare, among other wildlife. The park is about twenty-five miles northwest of Deer Lake. The park is open year-round. Admission: adult, ❷; child, ❶. For information, call ☎ (709) 458-2417 or consult 🖳 www.grosmorne.pch.gc.ca.

At the far northeastern end of the Northern Peninsula, above the entrance to the Strait of Belle Isle, Vikings explored the area one thousand years ago. At **L'Anse aux Meadows National Historic Site**, the outline of sod houses can still be seen, proving to some that explorers from Iceland and Greenland were the first Europeans to visit the New World. The visitor center includes artifacts and exhibits. The site, north of Saint Anthony off Highway 430, the Viking Trail, is open from mid-June to late September. For information in the summer, call ☎ (709) 623-2608 or ☎ (709) 458-2417 in the off-season or consult 🖳 parks canada.pch.gc.ca/parks/newfoundland/anse_meadows.

Wildlife, Preserved

Thirty kilometers south of Saint John's is the largest colony of Atlantic Puffins in North America. Venture out to the **Witless Bay Ecological Reserve** and you're likely to be surrounded by thousands of the stout little "sea parrots."

Great swimmers and fishers, the bright-billed puffins stuff themselves with capelin and other fish until they are almost too fat to fly. Eventually they make their way to the steep slopes of Gull and Great Islands where they burrow into the soil to make their nests.

There are more than three hundred species of birds here including falcons, hawks, and ospreys; northern species include murres and boreal owls; and European species include fulmars, which are rarely seen in North America.

And the area has attracted colonies of bald eagles, with an estimated four hundred nesting pairs located across the island.

One commercial tour operator to Witless Bay is **Captain Murphy's Seabird and Whale Tours**. For information, call ☎ (709) 334-2002 or consult 🖳 www. witlessbay.com.

A good birding location is Placentia Bay or Trinity Bar, two hours from Saint John's.

Cape Saint Mary's Ecological Reserve is one of the premier gannet nesting areas in North America. However, on **Gannet Island** off the coast of Labrador, you're not likely to spot a single gannet; the place was instead named after a nineteenth-century British survey ship. There are, though, some 200,000 sea birds on the island, including an estimated twenty-four thousand razorbills.

At Baccalieu Island live the largest known colony of storm petrels, some seven million in all.

Labrador

For thousands of years travelers to Labrador have not taken the journey casually. From Native Peoples to the Vikings to early European explorers, a visit to Labrador has been a difficult but rewarding trip. It still is.

There are no road maps to Labrador, which is not much of a problem because there are basically just two roads in all of its 117,000 square miles.

One gravel byway, Route 500, connects from Happy Valley–Goose Bay at the mouth of the Hamilton Inlet and traverses the interior to Churchill Falls and on to the border with Québec, near the grandly named tiny town of Labrador City.

Another road, Route 510, runs about thirty miles along the Strait of Belle Isle from the ferry terminal in Blanc-Sablon to the community of Red Bay.

Everything else is connected by boat or seaplane with most of the population of about twenty-nine thousand scattered among small villages along the coast.

Getting to Labrador

A ferry crosses from Saint Barbe to Blanc-Sablon in far eastern Québec. For information and schedules, call ☎ (709) 877-2222.

Central Labrador can be reached by road from northern Quebec on Route 389 to Route 500.

Railroad service between Sept-Iles, Québec and Schefferville in west-central Labrador is provided

Hospitality Newfoundland and Labrador
107 LeMarchant Rd.
St. John's, NF A1C 2H1 Canada
☎ (709) 722-2000
☎ (800) 563-6353

by the Iron Ore Company of Canada's **Québec, North Shore, & Labrador Railways**. For information, call ☎ (418) 944-8205.

Provincial Ferry Service boats connect to some of the more isolated points of Labrador. Summer service runs from Lewisporte, Newfoundland to Goose Bay, Labrador. For information, call ☎ (800) 563-6353 or consult 🖳 www.gov. nf.ca/ferryservices/schedules/E-bond.htm.

The Labrador Straits

The straits is the southernmost region of Labrador, across the Strait of Belle Isle from the Island of Newfoundland.

Route 510 follows the coast from Blanc-Sablon, Québec northeast to Red Bay. You'll have to float your way over to Labrador to one end or the other of the road. The Strait of Belle Isle ferry runs from Saint Barbe, Newfoundland to Blanc-Sablon. Marine Atlantic passenger ferries service Red Bay from Lewisporte, Newfoundland during the summer. You can also fly into the small airport at Blanc-Sablon from points in Québec.

Departing from Blanc-Sablon, you can drive along fifty paved miles of Route 510, the road that connects the communities on the southeastern coast.

Southern Labrador

What appears to be nothing more than a mound of rocks is actually the oldest known funeral monument in North America and among the oldest in the world. The **L'Anse Amour Burial Mound** marks the burial place of a Maritime Archaic Indian child who died about 7,500 years ago.

Artifacts found with the child's body include a walrus tusk, harpoon head, grinding tool, and a bone whistle. The items indicate the boy may have held an important status in the community. L'Anse Amour is on the Labrador Strait just over the border from Québec's Blanc-Sablon where the ferry from Newfoundland lands. The site is open year-round. Admission: free. For information, call ☎ (709) 458-2417.

Nearby, the **Point Amour Lighthouse Provincial Historic Site** preserves an important marker along the coast, the second tallest lighthouse in Canada; on a clear day you can see across the Strait of Belle Isle to Newfoundland. Exhibits include the lightkeeper's home and office, restored to the period when the light was first illuminated in 1858. Open June to October. Admission: adult, ❶; children (younger than 12), free. For information, call ☎ (709) 927-5825.

Just a bit further along the coastal road, the **Red Bay National Historic Site** preserves a Basque whaling operation from the late sixteenth century. On Saddle Island in the harbor of Red Bay, archaeologists have discovered the outlines of buildings and a cemetery.

A Spanish galleon, believed to be the San Juan, was found lying in deep silt at the bottom of the harbor in 1978. The ship is a rare surviving example of the type of ships used by Europeans to colonize the New World in the sixteenth century. The site is open from mid-June to mid-October, and by appointment at other times of the year. Admission: general, ❷. For information, call ☎ (709) 920-2176 or consult 🖳 www.parcscanada.gc.ca/redbay.

LABRADOR

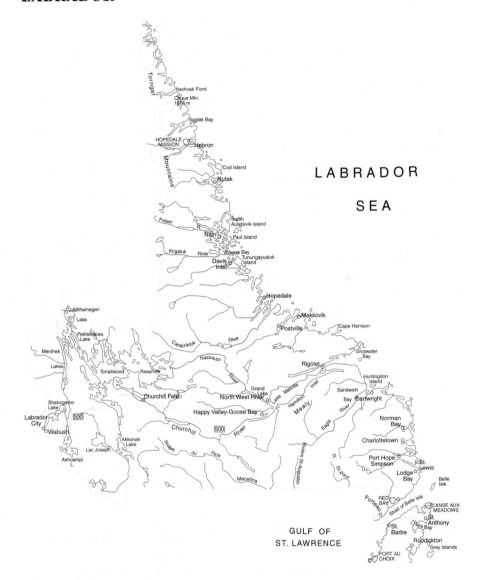

LABRADOR
SEA

GULF OF
ST. LAWRENCE

Central Labrador

Inland Labrador is a place of lakes and rivers alive with millions of fish. It is also home to a high-tech marvel, the **Churchill Falls Hydroelectric Station**. Built in the 1970s, the facility channels the Churchill River over a 920-foot drop and through underground turbines that produce enough power to supply most of New England. Tours are available by advance reservation. For information call ☎ (709) 925-3335 or consult 🖳 www.hydro.qc.ca/generation/hydro electric/churchill/churchill_falls.

The North Coast

Labrador's remote North Coast runs from Rigolet to the tip of the Torngat Mountains at the top of the province. This is a place of the Northern Lights, with natural light shows presented an average of 243 nights per year.

The Innu and Inuit people believed the North Lights were torches carried by dead ancestors to light the way for the living.

The land includes numerous sub artic islands. The rough coastline is slashed by fjords that penetrate deep inland.

Marine Atlantic's passenger ferries visit a number of North Coast communities in the summer months with ships from Happy Valley-Goose Bay to ports at Rigolet, Makkovik, Postville, Hopedale, Davis Inlet, and Nain. For information, call ☎ (800) 341-7981 or consult 💻 www.marine-atlantic.ca.

Nain is the northernmost community in Labrador, and the seat of the Inuit culture in the province. Elders still speak the Inukitut language. From Nain chartered boats visit the abandoned community of Hebron and the Hebron Fjord further north. Hebron was formerly a Moravian Mission, and a large church and other buildings still stand there.

Three mountain ranges—the Torngats, Kaumajets, and Kiglapaits—have the highest peaks east of the Rockies. Much older than the mountains to the west, geologists have found some of the oldest-known rock on the planet here.

At the southern end of the region, Rigolet is often visited by pods of seals and Minke whales. Boat trips visit their feeding areas.

Newfoundland and Labrador Festivals and Events

March

Labrador 400 International Sled Dog Race. Labrador. Dogsledders from the United States and Canada compete in the longest race east of Minnesota and third longest in North America outside of Alaska. The start and finish line is in Labrador City. The race, which usually takes five to seven days, can be observed in Labrador City, Wabush, and along the Labrador Highway.

July

North West River Beach Festival. Lake Melville, Labrador. 💻 www3.nf.sym patico.ca/townofnwr. An outdoor festival held on a sandy beach featuring traditional food such as caribou, bakeapple, and redberry dishes, and crafts such as Innu tea dolls, handcrafted moccasins, and wood and bone carvings.

August

Labrador Straits Bakeapple Folk Festival. Forteau, Labrador. Music, crafts, traditional food, square dancing at various venues.

Newfoundland & Labrador Folk Festival. Saint John's, Newfoundland. ☎ (709) 576-8508. Traditional music, dance, and storytelling festival.

The Royal Saint John's Regatta. Saint John's, Newfoundland. ☎ (709) 576-8921. Perhaps the oldest continuing sporting event in North America, held every year since 1826, using traditional British-style boats on Quidi Vidi Lake.

Chapter 35
Prince Edward Island

Prince Edward Island, known more by its initials PEI, is a crescent island in the Gulf of Saint Lawrence that's protected from the open ocean by the hook of Nova Scotia but nevertheless frozen in time.

It is a lovely place of red soil, green fields, white sand beaches, and blue sea and sky offset by gray shingle fishing villages and white clapboard farm houses. If that doesn't give you enough to form a mental image, consider the island's occasional nickname: the million-acre farm.

It's also a place where a lucky visitor can be invited to a *ceilidh*, an informal house party or community gathering centered around traditional Maritime and Gaelic music, but by no means limited to those forms—just about anything can (and will) go. Derived from a Gaelic word meaning a visit, ceilidh is pronounced *kay-lee*.

History of PEI

PEI was the native home of the Mi'kmaq, part of the Algonquin nation; they called their island Abegweit, meaning "land cradled on the waves." There is evidence of settlements on the island dating back more than ten thousand years.

In 1534 French explorer Jacques Cartier sighted the island and named it Île Saint-Jean; the lonely French and Acadian farmers who stayed behind were barely noticed until nearly two hundred years later when a larger settlement was established at Port La Joye near today's Charlottetown.

A century later little Charlottetown also earned an imposing title as the Birthplace of Canada. In 1864 politicians held the first in a series of meetings that would eventually lead to the creation of a new federation of provinces.

And finally it is all but impossible to think about PEI without considering the impact of a single work of fiction: Lucy Maud Montgomery's novel, *Anne of Green Gables*.

It was just a book, and almost a century old at that, but the charming portrait Montgomery painted of Prince Edward Island has been sustained; if anything, the island has adapted itself to be more like the book over the years. Some 350,000 visitors per year—about half of all the island's tourists—make a

PRINCE EDWARD ISLAND

pilgrimage to the Green Gables House in Cavendish. The house itself is as much a work of fiction as the book, but no matter.

(The fascination with Anne is not limited to young girls, either. The book is very popular in Japan, and Japanese tourists regularly make the very long trip to PEI.)

Modern PEI

PEI is Canada's smallest province, only about 2,200 square miles; it is also the nation's most densely populated, with about 132,000 residents, although there is still quite a bit of open space. The province is only 160 miles from end to end and about forty miles across at its widest point.

The island has been a backwater in Canada for much of the century, losing out to provinces with economies based on manufactured goods and to agricultural areas better connected to markets.

The biggest change in the modern history of PEI came in 1997 when the island was linked to the mainland in New Brunswick by the Northumberland Strait Bridge, officially named the **Confederation Bridge**, one of the world's longest at nearly eight miles and the longest to cross ice-covered waters.

The idea of connecting the island to the rest of the world was a controversial one; more than ten millennia of human occupation had adapted to the relative isolation of island living. After many years of debate, it took a plebiscite by residents before it was approved.

The bridge is an amazing sight, a thin gray ribbon extending from shore and past the curve of the horizon. In winter, ice floes move their way around the supports that are protected by ice shields.

The high-tech bridge was constructed out of precast concrete segments, which were floated out to sea and then installed on pylons by a special heavy-lift vessel. Drivers and vehicles are monitored all the way across by electronic sensors checking traffic and weather conditions. Beneath the roadway, a chamber holds electrical, telephone, and fiber-optic cables to connect PEI to the mainland.

Waterside in New London

One immediate impact of the bridge was a sharp increase in the number of tourists who make their way to PEI. In 1996, before the bridge, some 800,000 visitors came by boat. At least a million visitors are expected to cross the bridge each year.

Getting to PEI

The Confederation Bridge connects Cape Jourimain in New Brunswick to the town of Borden-Carleton, PEI. It takes about twelve minutes to drive across the two-lane structure.

A car-carrying ferry travels between Wood Islands in the southeastern corner of the island to Caribou, Nova Scotia. For information and schedules, call ☎ (902) 566-3838 or ☎ (888) 249-7245.

There is also a ferry that connects Souris in the northeastern corner of PEI to Magdalen Island, eighty-four miles away in the Gulf of Saint Lawrence.

Air service links Charlottetown to Halifax and Toronto.

The Confederation Trail

In December of 1989 the last railroad cars on Prince Edward Island were loaded onto the ferry and floated off to the mainland; with that a century of railroading on the island came to an end.

But today the railroad's right-of-way, which stretches from one end of the island to the other, has been reborn as the **Confederation Trail**, a ten-foot-wide path for hikers, bicyclists, and even wheelchairs. The builders of the

CHARLOTTETOWN

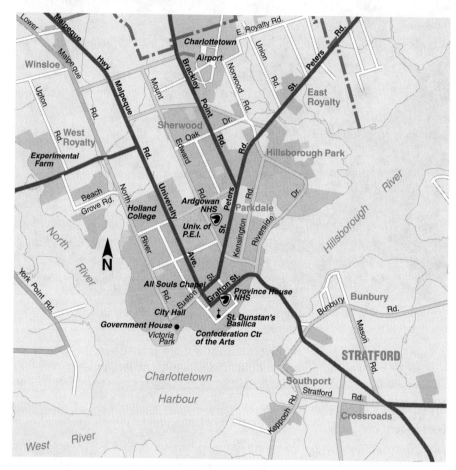

railroad went out of their way to avoid hills and valleys wherever possible; because of that, the trail winds its way across the landscape, rarely heading in a straight line for very long.

More than 140 miles have been opened, with the longest stretch about eighty miles from Kensington to Tignish in Prince County. In eastern Kings County, part of the trail hugs the spectacular north shore from Morell to Saint Peters Bay, over bridges and along the ocean.

There are rest areas and shelters every few miles, and interpretive signs explain some of the history of the area. Some of the old railway stations have been converted into museums, restaurants, or tourist information centers.

In winter the PEI Snowmobile Association grooms and marks the trails.

Charlotte's Shore: In and Around Charlottetown

The cultural capital of Charlottetown is the **Confederation Centre of the Arts**, a combination museum and theater complex. The museum includes a history of PEI and the evolution of Canada as a nation. One of the treasures, not surprisingly, is Lucy Maud Montgomery's original manuscript of *Anne of Green Gables*. In the theater the musical version of that book and other live theater is presented; the summer theater season runs from late June to early September.

The Confederation Centre is located at 145 Richmond Street. For information, call ☎ (800) 565-0278 or ☎ (902) 566-1267 or consult 🖳 www. confederationcentre.com.

On the south shore of the Charlotte Coast, not far from the Confederation Bridge, the **Victoria Playhouse Summer Festival** is presented in a restored 1912 community hall. For information, call ☎ (902) 658-2025.

Anne's Land

North Central PEI, above Charlottetown facing the Gulf of Saint Lawrence, is Green Gables land, the fictional home of Anne and the real birthplace and workplace of author Lucy Maud Montgomery. In fact, it is hard to make a step without bumping into something about Anne, Green Gables, or Montgomery. It's a bit of an obsession, but if you or your children are fans of the book, there's more than enough Anne to go around.

The **Green Gables House** of the book was inspired by a farm site once owned by Montgomery's relatives. In 1937 the house and surrounding farmland were preserved within. The Green Gables House is furnished to portray the period setting described in the novel.

Nearby walking trails with interpretive signs highlight some of Montgomery's favorite woodland haunts. The home, on Route 6, west of Route 13, is open from early May to early September. Admission: general, ❶. For information, call ☎ (902) 963-2675 or consult 🖳 parkscanada.pch.gc.ca/parks/ pei/otherhp/green_gables.

The Green Gables House is within the **Prince Edward Island National Park** on the Gulf. The park protects a system of sand dunes, beaches, sandstone cliffs, salt marshes, and freshwater ponds. Green Gables House is located in the park. Located north of Blue Heron Drive, Highway 6. Open year-round. Admission: adult, ❷; child, ❶. For information, call ☎ (902) 672-6350 or consult 🖳 parkscanada.pch.gc.ca/parks/pei/pei_np.

Nearby, you can tour **Lucy Maud Montgomery's Cavendish Home**, where the author lived from 1876 to 1911 and where she wrote *Anne of Green Gables*. The home, in Cavendish, is open for tours from June to mid-October. Admission: general, ❶. For information call ☎ (902) 963-2231 or consult 🖳 www.pe island.com/lmm.

Lucy Maud Montgomery's Birthplace in New London displays the writer's scrapbooks, wedding dress, and various Victorian pieces. Open from early June to early October. Admission: general, ❶. For information, call ☎ (902) 886-2099.

For yet another view, the *Anne of Green Gables* **Museum** on Route 20 in Park Corner is in the home of her Uncle John Campbell and Aunt Annie Campbell. Montgomery lived here at various times during her life and was married here in 1911. You can peer into Anne's Enchanted Bookcase, enjoy the beautiful grounds, and take a wagon ride with Matthew by the Lake of Shining Waters. Open from mid-May to mid-October. Admission: general, ❶. For information, call ☎ (902) 436-7329 or consult 🖳 www.cavendishpei.com/museum.html.

And for something that has absolutely nothing to do with *Anne of Green Gables*, except for the appeal to children of all ages, the Cavendish area includes a small collection of your basic tourist traps: mini-golf, go-karts, a drive-in theater, and a small amusement park.

There is an outpost of the **Ripley's Believe It or Not Museum** chain in Cavendish, presenting nine galleries of strange stuff and illusions. For information, call ☎ (902) 963-2242 in the summer or ☎ (902) 962-2022 in the winter.

Woodleigh Replicas & Gardens offers thirty replicas of Britain's castles and buildings, extensive English gardens, water gardens, and more, spread over forty-five acres of countryside. Some replicas are large enough to enter and are furnished with antiques and artifacts. Open from June to mid-October. Admission: adult, ❷; youth (13–17), ❷; child (6–12), ❶. Family rates available. Located near Burlington on Route 234. For information, call ☎ (902) 836-3401 or consult 🖳 www.woodleighreplicas.com.

The Évangéline Region

In misty Miscouche, a few miles inland from Bedeque Bay, the **Acadian Museum of PEI** tells the difficult story of the odyssey of the island's Acadian people from 1720 to the present through artifacts, narratives, and music. The museum, on Route 2, is open year-round. Admission: general, ❶. For information, call ☎ (902) 436-6237 or consult 🖳 www.teleco.org/museeacadien.

Down at the coast on the Northumberland Strait, **Le Village at Mont Carmel** is a small interpretive site where you can meet actors who portray Acadian families who arrived in 1812, walk through the restored 1820 Notre-Dame-du-Mont-Carmel log cabin church, and visit other facilities such as the blacksmith's shop and the school.

The site, located on Route 11, is open from late May through early September. Admission: general, ❶. For information call ☎ (902) 854-2227 or consult 🖳 collec tions.ic.gc.ca/cooperation/village/village.htm.

In the 1800s shipbuilding was PEI's most important industry. At Port Hill on the northern side near Malpeque Bay, the **Green Park Shipbuilding Museum and Yeo House** traces the history and the craft of shipbuilding. You can also visit ship owner James Yeo Jr.'s restored Victorian residence, built in 1865. The site is open from mid-June to September. Admission: adult, ❷; child, ❶. For information, call ☎ (902) 831-2206 or ☎ (902) 368-6000 (off season) or consult 🖳 www.pei museum.com.

Northwestern PEI

Anne, the Acadians, and shipbuilding got all the glory. But for some it is the lowly PEI spud that deserves its moment of recognition. Not that the island's principal crop doesn't get any respect at all. Witness the **PEI Potato Museum**, home of displays of farming equipment, potatoes, a community museum, potatoes, an old school house, potatoes, and an historic chapel. There are potatoes, too, including a gigantic sculpted spud out front. The museum is in Centennial Park in O'Leary, the potato capital of PEI. (The annual Potato Blossom Festival is held in the late July.) Open from June to October with special openings by reservation. Admission: adult, ❷; family, ❸. For information, call ☎ (902) 859-2039 or consult 🖳 www.peipotatomuseum.com.

Northeast PEI

Near Souris, the **Basin Head Fisheries Museum** tells the story of the fishing industry of PEI with displays of boats, gear, and a saltwater aquarium and coastal ecology exhibit. Open from June to September. Admission: adult, ❷; child, ❶. For information, call ☎ (902) 357-7233 or consult 🖳 www.peimuseum.com/basin head.shtml.

Near the northeast corner of the province, the **Elmira Railway Museum** preserves some of the history of the nineteenth- and early twentieth-century PEI railway through photographs, telegraph equipment, fare kiosks, and other artifacts. Located in Elmira, the museum is open from mid-June to September. Admission: general, ❷. For information, call ☎ (902) 357-7234 or ☎ (902) 368-6601 in the off-season or consult 🖳 www.peimuseum.com.

Prince Edward Island Festivals and Events

July

College of Piping Celtic Festival. Summerside. ☎ (902) 436-5377. Concert series, Highland and step dancing, piping and drumming, traditional Scottish heavyweight athletic competitions, children's events. Held throughout the summer at 619 Water Street East.

Eddie May Murder Mystery Dinner Theatre. Charlottetown. ☎ (888) 747-4050. Peaks Quay, from July through September.

Feast Dinner Theatre. Charlottetown. ☎ (902) 629-2321. Late June through September.

Potato Blossom Festival. O'Leary. ☎ (902) 859-2888. A celebration of the lowly spud, the main crop grown on the island, held at various venues.

Rollo Bay Fiddle Festival. Souris. ☎ (902) 687-2584. Open-air fiddle concerts, dances, and performances by entertainers from all over North America.

August

Annual Fiddlers and Followers Weekend. Cavendish. ☎ (902) 963-2221. The Maritime's best fiddle and piano players, step dancers, barbeques, and lobster parties, all at the Rainbow Valley Amusement Park.

Annual Highland Games. Eldon. ☎ (902) 659-2205. Scottish games, dances, and music.

Fête nationale des Acadiens. ☎ (902) 854-2324. One-day festival celebrating PEI's Acadian culture through historical displays, traditional music, step-dancing, Acadian food. Held in a different community each year.

Lucy Maud Montgomery Festival. Cavendish. ☎ (902) 628-4346. Ice cream social, period games, old style barn dance, readings from the author of *Anne of Green Gable*'s works.

Chapter 36
New Brunswick

Originally part of the colony of Nova Scotia, New Brunswick was split off by itself in 1784 to create a district for British Loyalists who were moving north from the unexpectedly independent United States.

By the end of the nineteenth century New Brunswick was the most prosperous part of Canada, the economic engine driven by a booming shipbuilding industry around Saint John. But the market for wooden ships collapsed early in the twentieth century when steel construction took over.

Today New Brunswick depends mostly on agriculture (lumber and potatoes) and the fisheries for its relatively meager economy; there is also a mining industry (zinc, lead, and copper) in the north.

New Brunswick is the only officially bilingual province in Canada, about one-third French-speaking (the Acadian descendants).

Getting to New Brunswick

New Brunswick is the most accessible province of Atlantic Canada, located on the mainland and connected to the Trans-Canada Highway and U.S. Interstate 95. A number of other routes enter the province from Quebec and Maine.

Saint John Harbour is a port of call for cruise ships, and a car ferry goes from Digby, Nova Scotia, to Saint John. Another ferry crosses the Northumberland Strait from PEI. The impressive eight-mile-long Confederation Bridge connects New Brunswick to Prince Edward Island.

Fredericton Area

Fredericton, the provincial capital, is a small but handsome town, well inland on the Saint John River.

The well-regarded **Beaverbrook Art Gallery** in Fredericton offers a fine collection of eighteenth- and nineteenth-century British portraiture, late Renaissance Italian, Flemish, and French decorative arts, modern British art, and historical and contemporary Canadian and provincial art. The museum was bestowed by newspaper magnate Lord Beaverbrook of New Brunswick. One of the treasures of the gallery is Salvador Dali's *Santiago el Grande*. The gallery is

Fredericton, New Brunswick

open year-round. Admission: adult, ❶; family, ❷. For information, call ☎ (506) 458-8545 or consult 🖳 www.beaverbrookartgallery.org.

About twenty miles west of the capital is the **Kings Landing Historical Settlement**, a detailed preservation of the life of the early Loyalist settlers. The seventy-building settlement depicts the social history of the Saint John River Valley from 1790 to 1910. Each of the historic homes, trade areas, and farms is restored to a different era of that period.

Located in Prince William off the Trans-Canada Highway, the settlement is open from June to mid-October; fall and spring by reservation. Admission: adult, ❸; senior and child, ❷; family, ❹. For information, call ☎ (506) 363-4999 or consult 🖳 www.kingslanding.nb.ca.

Saint John Area

During the Golden Age of Sail in the late 1800s, little Saint Martins on the southern coast of New Brunswick was one of North America's largest shipbuilding communities because the huge tides created a natural dry dock for ship construction. The affluence of that community helped build up Saint John about twenty miles southwest.

Explorer Samuel de Champlain landed nearby in 1604 on Saint John the Baptist Day; a settlement at what was called Saint John was begun in 1631. The area was incorporated as a city in 1785 by Loyalists who were turned out of their homes in America because they backed the wrong side in the War of Independence. Saint John is now the largest city in the province.

FREDERICTON

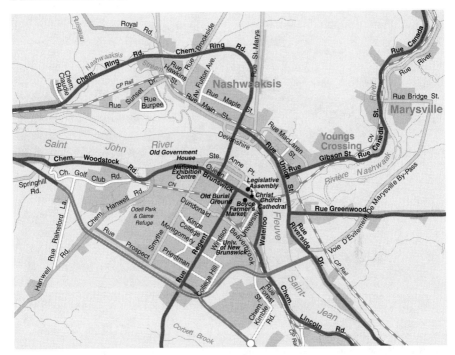

One of the natural oddities of this part of the world are the **Reversing Falls**, a phenomenon that occurs twice a day when the high tides (in some places rising to almost forty-eight feet) of the Bay of Fundy meet and overpower the Saint John River and force it to flow back upstream. An information center in Saint John at an overlook of the river describes the phenomenon; the center is open from mid-May to early October. For information, call ☎ (506) 658-2937 or consult 🖳 new-brunswick.net/Saint_John/reversingfalls/reversing.html.

At the **New Brunswick Museum** on Market Square, displays include artifacts of the province's aboriginal history to the nineteenth-century lumbering and shipbuilding industries.

Open year-round, the museum is at 277 Douglas Avenue. Admission: adult, ❷; senior and student, ❶; family, ❸. For information call ☎ (506) 643-2300 or consult 🖳 www. gov.nb.ca/0130.

Southwestern New Brunswick

This corner of the province, on the north side of the entrance to the Bay of Fundy, was made famous in the 1930s as the summer home of President Franklin D. Roosevelt on Campobello Island.

The thirty-four-room "cottage" and gardens are preserved in **Roosevelt Campobello Inter-**

Key to Prices
❶ $5 and under
❷ $5 to $10
❸ $10 to $20
❹ $20 and more
When prices are listed as a range, this indicates various combination options are available. Most attractions offer reduced-price tickets for children and many have family rates that include two adults and two or three children.

NEW BRUNSWICK

national Park. Nearby beaches, coastal trails, and a golf course are also available to visitors. The island is reachable by ferry from Deer Island; there is also a bridge from Campobello to Lubec, Maine. The grounds of the park are open year-round; the Roosevelt home is open for visitors from late May to early October. Admission: free, but donations are accepted. For information, call ☎ (506) 752-2922 or consult ▣ www.fdr.net.

The region's fishy heritage is examined in two facilities along Passamaquoddy Bay on the border with Maine. At the **Atlantic Salmon Centre** in Chamcook, an aquarium built into the stream bank lets you study the salmon nursery and see full-grown fish of twenty-five pounds or more. The site, on Route 127 East, is open from mid-May to mid-October. Admission: general, ❶. For information, call ☎ (506) 529-1384 or ☎ (506) 529-4581 off season or consult ▣ www.asf.ca/ConservCentre/conscent.html.

The **Huntsman Marine Science Centre–Aquarium/Museum** in Saint Andrews allows visitors the chance to discover the marine life of the Bay of Fundy. A favorite area is a touch pool where you can lay hands on sea cucumbers, star fish, and other marine creatures. The museum, on Brandy Cover Road, is open from May to October. Admission: general, ❶. For information, call ☎ (506) 529-1202 or ☎ (506) 529-1200 or consult ▣ www.obfs.org/OBFS_Stations/NB_Huntsman_Marine_Sci.html.

Moncton

Moncton is a bit of a backwater, both literally and figuratively, but this city at the geographic heart of the Maritimes does have its historical and cultural significance. An unusual combination of Anglo-phone, French, and Acadian cltures, Moncton is in many ways a more integrated community than Montréal or Québec City.

Tourism Moncton. ☎ (800) 363-4558, ☎ (506) 853-3590. 🖳 www.greater. moncton.nb.ca.

Moncton is the site of the largest French-speaking, Canadia college outside the province of Québec, the **Université de Moncton**, located on a campus just beyond the downtown area.

About that "backwater" label: Moncton grew up along the banks of the Petitcodiac River, which is the very end of the tidal phenomenon of the Bay of Fundy.

The **Petitcodiac** (a Micmac name for "river that bends like a bow") flows toward the ocean and empties into the Bay of Fundy. The funnel-shaped bay has among the highest tides in the world. When the incoming tide enters the bay, seawater rushes into the river channel, traveling upstream in a frothing wave that spans the river; this tidal "bore" ranges between a few inches and a few feet. Within about an hour of the arrival of the tidal bore, the level of Petitcodiac will rise by about twenty-five feet.

Timetables of the tidal bore are available through local tourist agencies. A special clock at the entrance to Bore Park displays the day's scheduled natural event. The best view of the tides is at Hopewell Cape at the mouth of the river, about twenty miles southeast of Moncton.

Just outside the city, rich farmland and rolling countryside converge on flat, lowland marshes that fan out from the banks of the Petitcodiac. Along the edge of the river are grassy, humped dykes built by early settlers to reclaim the marsh-lands and hold back the voracious Fundy tides.

Moncton was incorporated in 1855 with shipbuilding as the main industry. However, the advent of steam and iron ships—requiring more sophisticated shipyards and industries—brought growth to an end, and Moncton reverted to a village in 1862. Almost ten years later Moncton became the Atlantic regional headquarters for the Intercolonial Railway, and in 1875 the area became a town once again. This is commemorated in Moncton's motto, Resurgo, which means "I rise again." By 1890 Moncton reached city status.

Moncton Airport is located in Dieppe, about fifteen minutes from down-town, with service by major Canadian carriers. Moncton is served by VIA Rail with connections within the Maritimes and beyond to Québec and Montréal.

Bore Park, located in one of the oldest sections of the city was the site of the original Acadian settlement and was also the location of the town's dock during the heyday of the shipping industry in the 1950s. Ships carrying cargoes of flour, rum, and molasses from the West Indies or passengers and freight to Saint John tied up at wharves to wait for the next high tide.

Today the unusual setting includes park benches, and for those visitors who want to watch the arrival of the tidal bore, there are viewing platforms that overlook the river.

In summer local musicians perform in the park, with offerings from folk to string quartets.

Bridge work. The province has one of the highest concentrations of covered bridges in North America, thanks to its lumbering heritage. The Saint John River Covered Bridge at Hartland is the world's longest, some 1,270-feet in length. Hartland is northwest of Fredericton near the Maine border of central New Brunswick. Another notable crossing is the Smiths Creek Covered Bridge in Newtown between Saint John and Moncton, built in 1910.

Centennial Park in the city center is an all-season recreation area, very popular year-round. In the summer there's hiking, tennis, mountain-biking, and lawn bowling. In the winter the 450-acre park is used for cross-country skiing, skating, horse-drawn sleigh rides, and tobogganing.

The **Acadian Museum** at the University of Moncton is a center for historians, folklorists, and visitors interested in the Acadian story, with artifacts dating back to 1604. Next to the museum is the University's art gallery, which features Acadian contemporary art. Both are in the Clément-Cormier building. Open all year, donations are accepted. For information, call ☎ (506) 858-4088 or consult 💻 www.umoncton.ca/maum.

Legends of a mysterious road in the Moncton area date back to the 1800s when local farmers noticed their horses worked harder going down the hill, and their wagons ran into the horses' heels heading up. A stream alongside the road seems to run uphill.

In 1933 a local entreprenuer opened a restaurant at the top of the hill. Locals called the area various names, including Fool Hill and Magic Hill, but it was **Magnetic Hill** that stuck. Eventually the Magnetic Hill Theme Park began.

Today, visitors can drive the road—foot off the gas heading up, and with the foot on the accelerator going down. Other tourist attractions include the Magnetic Hill Railroad, a miniature train that takes passengers on a mile-long tour of the park, and **Magnetic Hill Zoo**, which has a small collection including tigers, lions, camels, a petting zoo, and a wildlife contact area that has a herd of deer. There is a nominal admission for each of the attractions.

I'm not going to spoil the fun here, but if you are wondering: what you see is not what you get.

Magnetic Hill is located at the intersection of the Trans-Canada Highway and Highway 126. For information on the Magnetic Hill Zoo, call ☎ (506) 384-9381 or ☎ (506) 384-0303 or consult 💻 new-brunswick.net/new-brunswick/moncton/zoof.html.

South of Moncton to the Bay of Fundy

A drive down the Fundy Coastal Drive leads to the beautifully rugged shoreline of Cape Enragé, Dennis Beach, Waterside, Mary's Point, and Alma. Birds and wildlife are plentiful and strong surf regularly washes up ocean treasures for beachcombers.

You can see the unusual "flowerpots" along the shore—large rocky columns eroded by the incessant tides into unusual shapes.

The place to watch the incoming tides is at Hopewell Cape south of Moncton. At low tide you can walk on the ocean floor to the base of the flowerpots; twice a day, though, the tide comes in, bringing between thirty and fifty feet of water over a six-hour period before the process reverses.

The official place to watch the water is the **Rocks Provincial Park**, off Route 114. The park is open from mid-May to mid-October. Admission: adult and senior, ❶; child (younger than 4), free; family, ❸. For information, call ☎ (506) 734-3429 or ☎ (506) 856-2940.

Further south at the entrance to Chignecto Bay at the end of the Bay of Fundy, the **Fundy National Park** includes dramatic scenery, hiking trails, and other facilities. Open year-round. Admission: adult and senior, ❶; family, ❷. For information, call ☎ (506) 887-6000 or consult 📖 parkscanada.pch.gc.ca/parks/new_brunswick/fundy.

Southeast of Moncton along the province's border with Nova Scotia at Aulac, the **Fort Beauséjour National Historic Site** preserves a star-shaped pentagon fort built by the French between 1751 and 1755 as part of their long struggle with the British for the possession of Acadia. The fort was also used during the American Revolution and the War of 1812. There is a visitor center and panoramic views of the vast salt marshes at the head of the Bay of Fundy. Open from June to October. Admission: adult and senior, ❶; family, ❷. For information, call ☎ (506) 536-0720 or ☎ (506) 876-2443 or consult 📖 parkscanada.pch.gc.ca/parks/new_brunswick/fort_beausejour.

Beaches of the Northumberland Strait

Sandy beaches border the summer-warm waters of the Northumberland Strait about twenty minutes northeast of Moncton.

Although its northern location would seem to argue against New Brunswick as a beach community, the province nevertheless claims that it has the warmest salt waters north of Virginia. This happens because the water is relatively shallow and insulated from cold currents; that doesn't mean the air temperature will necessarily be broiling in August, though.

There are twenty-eight developed beaches along New Brunswick's east coast between Dalhousie and Cape Tormentine and fifteen along the south coast. Nearest to the Moncton area are the rugged beaches between Shediac and Cape Tormentine.

Parlee Beach Provincial Park in Shediac includes full facilities and tourist attractions. Nearby are Murray Beach, Sandy Beach, and Plage L'Anoiteau.

Farther north is **Kouchibouguac National Park** on the Acadian coast, which protects miles of fragile white sand dunes and the endangered piping plover. Swimming in the relatively warm water is popular here; the park also offers canoeing, cycling, and nature trails. Kouchibouguac is also home to one of the largest tern colonies in North America and more than 220 other bird species. The park is open year-round. Admission: adult, ❶; family, ❷. For information, call ☎ (506) 876-2443 or consult 📖 parkscanada.pch.gc.ca/parks/new_brunswick/kouchibouguac.

New Brunswick Festivals and Events

July

Canada's Irish Festival on the Miramichi. Miramichi. ☎ (506) 778-8810 or ☎ (506) 778-2353. Four days of Irish music, dancing, pipes, crafts, food, and drink. The "Family Parade" involves more than 1,500 people.

Festival provincial des pêcheries. (Provincial Fisheries Festival.) Shippagan. ☎ (506) 336-8726. The Blessing of the Fleet, deep sea fishing excursions, and fishing competitions.

August

Chocolate Festival. Saint Stephen. ☎ (506) 465-5616. A celebration of sweets, centered around Ganong Brothers, Canada's oldest family-owned confectionery, and claimant of the title of inventor of the chocolate bar.

Festival acadien de Caraquet (Caraquet Acadian Festival). Caraquet. ☎ (506) 727-2787. More than one hundred performers from Acadian and Cajun communities across North America for entertainment, cultural activities, and the Blessing of the Fleet.

Festival by the Sea. Saint John. ☎ (506) 632-0086. A celebration of Canadian history, culture, and arts on stages throughout Saint John; ten days and nearly one hundred performances on stages throughout Saint John.

Miramichi Folk Song Festival. Miramichi. ☎ (506) 622-1780. The longest-running folk festival in North America; the five-day festival features Canadian and New Brunswick folk music, workshops, and family events.

September

Festival international du cinéma francophone en Acadie (International French Film Festival in Acadia). Dieppe, Moncton and Shediac. ☎ (506) 855-6050. A festival of films and videos from more than twenty-five countries.

Chapter 37
Nova Scotia

Based on the descriptions sent back by early explorers, in 1621 King James I of England called the land Nova Scotia, which means New Scotland.

For thousands of years the island had been home to the Mi'kmaq people.

It wasn't until the late 1700s that large numbers of settlers began to arrive on the island, bringing with them a bit of the Gaelic language and traditions.

The first European settlers were French artisans and entrepreneurs who arrived in 1605 and founded Port Royal on the Annapolis River, one of the earliest European settlements on the continent. But the colony was attacked by British from the Virginia Colonies in 1613; it was abandoned soon thereafter.

The British staked their claim in 1621 with a short-lived settlement. The French returned in the mid-1630s with a settlement at the site of today's Annapolis Royal, declaring it the capital of the French colony and naming it Acadie. Acadian farmers built dykes along the Minas Basin and farmed the reclaimed marshlands.

The conflicting claims of the French and British were dealt with in the Treaty of Utrecht in 1713 with the British establishing their sovereignty of all the Maritimes, except Cape Breton Island and Prince Edward Island.

After the deportation of the 1750s many Acadians returned to Nova Scotia and rebuilt in areas such as Saint Mary's Bay on the Bay of Fundy, known as the French Shore.

Nova Scotia Geography

The funnel-like shape of the Bay of Fundy and its eastern reaches of Minas Basin and Chignecto Bay cause the largest range between high and low tides in the world, sometimes as much as fifty-three feet. Tidal bores, fast-moving walls of water that signal the oncoming tidal change, are visible at Truro, Maccan, and Windsor. For an unusual thrill you can try tidal-bore rafting on the Stubenacadie River.

Halifax is the regional air travel hub, offering direct flights to destinations throughout Atlantic Canada, as well as to Toronto, Montréal, Ottawa, and major cities along the East Coast of the United States.

NOVA SCOTIA

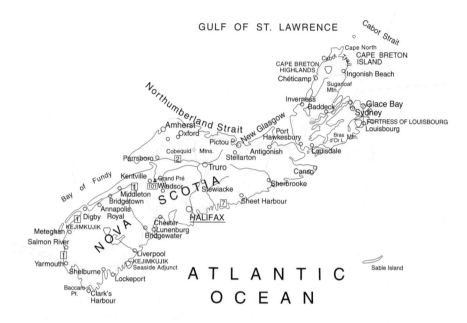

A car ferry operates between Bar Harbor, Maine, and Yarmouth, Nova Scotia. Another ferry connects Portland and Yarmouth in the summer. Travelers arriving via New Brunswick can take a car ferry from Saint John, New Brunswick, to Digby, Nova Scotia, or they can enter the province at Amherst, via the Trans-Canada Highway.

For information on ferries from Portland, Maine to Yarmouth, call *Scotia Prince* Cruises at ☎ (800) 341-7540 or consult 🖳 www.scotiaprince.com.

From Bar Harbor, Maine, to Yarmouth, service is provided by **Northumberland and Bay Ferries**. For information call ☎ (888) 249-7245 or ☎ (902) 566-3838 or consult 🖳 www.nfl-bay.com. Ferries also serve Saint John, New Brunswick to Digby, Nova Scotia, and Wood Islands, PEI to Caribou, Nova Scotia.

At the northern end of Nova Scotia lies Cape Breton Island, attached to the main part of the province by a causeway.

Tragic Remembrances

For all of its beauty, Halifax and Nova Scotia have also had their moments of unwanted renown for manmade disasters, including the sinking of the *Titanic* in the cold waters well offshore in 1912 and the crash of a fully loaded passenger jet off the coast in 1998. Probably the most horrific incident in Halifax's history occurred on Dec. 6, 1917, when two ships collided in the harbor.

The French vessel *Mont Blanc* was heading into the harbor for provisions before heading to Europe and the Allied war effort carrying explosives and ammunition, including half a million pounds of TNT. She was struck by the *Imo*, a Norwegian ship, carrying relief supplies to Belgium.

The *Mont Blanc* caught fire and drifted toward shore; a large crowd gathered on the waterfront to watch the blaze. Suddenly the TNT exploded. More than two thousand people, most of them on shore, were killed, and much of north Halifax was leveled and burned. Windows were shattered as much as fifty miles away.

By some estimations the cataclysm was the largest unnatural explosion on earth until the unhappy arrival of the atom bomb.

The *Titanic* Legacy

Artifacts recovered from the sinking of the *Titanic* are on display at the **Maritime Museum of the Atlantic**, along with memorabilia of the *Mont Blanc* disaster.

At the waterfront museum are boats, models, figureheads, and artifacts from bells to ditty bags to sailor's needles and more. Also on display is a deck chair from the *Titanic*. CSS *Acadia*, a hydrographic vessel, is regularly moored at dockside and open for viewing in the summer.

Tourism Nova Scotia. ☎ (800) 565-0000, or consult 💻 www.explore.gov.ns.ca/.

Key to Prices
❶ $5 and under
❷ $5 to $10
❸ $10 to $20
❹ $20 and more
When prices are listed as a range, this indicates various combination options are available. Most attractions offer reduced-price tickets for children and many have family rates that include two adults and two or three children.

The museum, located at 1675 Lower Water Street, is open year-round. Admission: adult, ❷; senior and child (16 and younger), ❶; family, ❸. For information, call ☎ (902) 424-7490 or consult 💻 museum.gov.ns.ca/mma.

The museum tells the story of the *Titanic* through the tales of the *Mackay-Bennet*, one of two cable ships based in Halifax that were given the grim assignment of retrieving bodies from the Atlantic waters. The ship left Halifax a few days after the sinking, followed close behind by the *Minia*.

The *Mackay-Bennet* picked up some 306 bodies from the water, earning her the unfortunate nickname of the "death ship." Of a total of 328 bodies picked up by the two ships, 209 were returned to Halifax, with the remainder buried at sea.

A temporary morgue was set up at the Mayflower Curling Rink. Those bodies not claimed by relatives were buried in three Halifax cemeteries: The Fairview Lawn Cemetery, Mount Olivet, and Baron de Hirsch. Most of the gravestones, paid for by the White Star Line, are simple black granite blocks. Some families chose to add more personal monuments. A memorial to an "Unknown Child" is located at Fairview Lawn Cemetery.

Fairview Lawn Cemetery is home to the largest number of *Titanic* graves. All the victims thought to be Protestant were buried in this nondenominational cemetery at the corner of Windsor Street and Kempt Road.

Mount Olivet Cemetery holds nineteen Catholic victims of the *Titanic* disaster, including J. F. P. Clarke, the bass player in the ship's band. The cemetery is located at 7076 Mumford Road.

HALIFAX

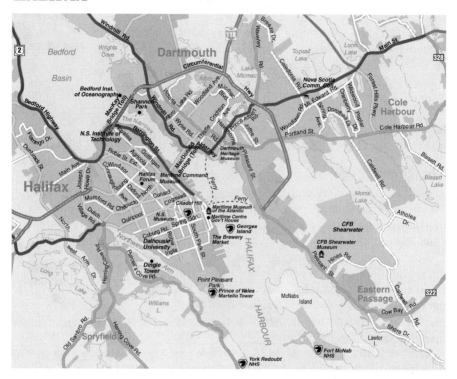

Ten male victims are buried in **Baron de Hirsch Cemetery**, a Jewish burial place at Connaught Avenue at Windsor Street.

For more information on sites related to the *Titanic* in Nova Scotia, call ☎ (800) 565-0000 or consult ▤ titanic.gov.ns.ca/index.html.

Halifax

The undercurrents of Nova Scotia, of course, run to the sea, from the original settlers to the early fishing fleets to the *Titanic*.

The ***Bluenose II*** schooner is a replica of the original *Bluenose*, a champion vessel pictured on the Canadian dime. Famous for her speed, she consistently won International Fisherman's Trophy Races with the Americans during the 1920s and 1930s. Her image has graced every Canadian dime since 1937. The ship sails from a dock at the Maritime Museum of the Atlantic in Halifax and from the waterfront in Lunenburg from late August to September. Cruises are priced at adult, ❸; child (12 and younger), ❷; family, ❸. For information, call ☎ (800) 763-1963. Reservations are required.

Halifax's role as a key naval station in the British Empire is commemorated at the **Halifax Citadel National Historic Site**. The current Citadel, completed in 1856, was the fourth in a series of British forts built on this site.

At today's restored fort costumed interpreters reenact the roles of soldiers and their families; displays include an Army museum with artifacts. The fort's gun is fired daily at noon.

Halifax draws its history from its waterfront

The fort offers spectacular views of Halifax and its harbor. The vehicle entrance to the fort is on Sackvile Street, near Brunswick Street. The restoration is open from mid-May to mid-October; the grounds are accessible year-round. Admission: adult, ❷; youth, ❶; family, ❸. For information, call ☎ (902) 426-5080 or consult 💻 parkscanada.pch.gc.ca/parks/nova_scotia/halifax_citadel.

From mastodons to whales, the **Nova Scotia Museum of Natural History** tells the living story of the province. The museum includes life-sized models of the earliest dinosaurs of Canada. Also on display are examples of Mi'kmaq quilt work. The museum at 1747 Summer Street is open year-round. Admission: adult and senior, ❶; child (5 and younger), free; family, ❷. For information, call ☎ (902) 424-7353 or consult 💻 museum.gov.ns.ca/mnh.

The **Art Gallery of Nova Scotia** shows contemporary and historic Canadian, British, and European art, as well as Nova Scotian fine art and folk art. The gallery is located at 1741 Hollis at Cheapside, Halifax. Open year-round. Admission: adult, ❶; child (12 and younger), free. For information, call ☎ (902) 424-7542 or consult 💻 www.agns.gov.ns.ca.

Living art is on display at the **Public Gardens**, the oldest formal Victorian gardens in North America. Begun in 1753 as a private garden, the seventeen-acre plot was taken over by the Nova Scotia Horticultural Society in 1836. The present layout, designed in 1875 by a former gardener to the Duke of Devonshire in Ireland, includes trees, flower beds, fountains, duck ponds, hedges, wrought iron gates, French Formal, and English Romantic style gardens.

Sunday afternoon musical performances are staged in the Gardens' Victorian bandstand.

The Public Gardens, located on Spring Garden Road at South Park Street, are open from spring to late autumn. Admission: free. For information, call ☎ (902) 490-4895.

Saint Paul's Anglican Church, on Grand Parade in Halifax, is the oldest Protestant church in Canada and Britain's first overseas cathedral. Opened in 1750 its burial vaults hold the remains of a number of well-placed British colonials, allowing the church to lay claim to the title of the "Westminster Abbey of the New World." The church is open year-round; admission is free.

Point Pleasant Park is a 186-acre park with walking paths along the coast and through forests, home to remains of several British fortifications that once protected Halifax and its harbor. The Municipality rents the land from the British Crown for one shilling a year under a 999-year lease. Located at 1749 Tower Road, the park is open year-round and admission is free.

In the 1800s a canal linked Halifax harbor with the Bay of Fundy through a seventy-mile course of lakes and locks. The **Fairbanks Interpretive Centre**, in Canal Park at Port Wallace in Dartmouth, is home to artifacts from local archaeological digs and a thirty-foot working model of a canal lock. A boat takes visitors on a half-hour tour of the Deep Cut. A similar display is located at the Shubenacadie Canal Fairbanks Centre, at 54 Locks Road in Dartmouth. For information, call ☎ (902) 462-1826.

In the late 1700s Dartmouth was the headquarters for a whaling company established when a number of Quaker families moved from the island of Nantucket, Massachusetts after the American Revolution. Today the **Historic Quaker Whalers' House** is the oldest house in Dartmouth; costumed guides explain life of the time. The site at 57–59 Ochterloney Street is open from June to early September and by appointment at other times. Admission: free. For information, call ☎ (902) 464-2253.

Peggy's Cove

South of Halifax, across Mahone Bay from Peggy's Cove, is the historic town of **Lunenberg**. The Old Town District was established in 1753; the fishing and shipbuilding community includes preserved buildings, public spaces, and an eighteenth-century European grid layout. The schooner *Bluenose* was built here.

Today Lunenburg is the base for Canada's largest fleet of deep-sea trawlers.

On the Lunenberg waterfront, the **Fisheries Museum of the Atlantic** explores shipbuilding, whaling, and the once-profitable industry of rum-running to the United States. The museum is open from May to mid-October, with some programs offered at other times of the year. Admission: adult, ❷; child, ❶. For information, call ☎ (902) 634-4794 or consult 💻 museum.gov.ns.ca/fma.

Further down the coast about twenty-five miles south of Halifax, is the picturesque village of **Peggy's Cove**; it's rare to hear it described in any other way, and for good reason. Imagine a quaint northeastern fishing village set against the pounding breakers of the Atlantic and you're thinking of this place.

In 1770 William Rodgers arrived from Ireland with his wife Peggy and set up a home on the eastern side of Saint Margaret's Bay. Peggy referred to the narrow, rocky inlet as her cove. A town was established there in 1811, and the name was immortalized. A solitary lighthouse stands on the shore. There are only about sixty residents in the town, a simple timber church, and a handful of clapboard and shingle houses and sheds along the shore.

Peggy's Cove earned some unhappy mentions in September of 1998 when it was the nearest community to the offshore crash of a Swissair jetliner, serving as the base of operations for recovery efforts.

Western Nova Scotia

The western reaches of Nova Scotia include the Evangeline Trail area and the Lighthouse Route of the southwest.

The **Ross Farm Museum** in Kentville preserves a sixty-acre farm of the 1800s. The museum includes a vintage store, an 1817 farmhouse, barns, a workshop, schoolhouse, blacksmith's shop, and cooperage. Costumed guides demonstrate spinning, woodworking, blacksmithing, wooden spoonmaking, barrelmaking, and other crafts. Located off Highway 101, the museum is open from mid-June to mid-October, with limited operations at other times of the year. Admission: adult, ❷; child (6–17), ❶; child (younger than 6), free; family, ❸; on Sunday morning admission is free until 11 A.M. For information, call ☎ (902) 689-2210 or consult 💻 museum.gov.ns.ca/rfm/.

East of Kentville on the water at Minas Basin, the **Grand-Pré National Historic Site** was the original home of the most successful Acadian settlement, which included an extensive system of dykes that reclaimed marshland as productive farms.

In 1755 more than 2,200 Acadians were deported from Grand-Pré alone, about 20 percent of all those displaced from their homes. Their fertile lands were quickly taken over by settlers from New England known as Planters.

Today's site explains the story of Acadian pioneer life and the tragedy of their expulsion. There is a statue of Notre-Dame de L'Assomption, their patron saint, and a figure of Evangeline, the fictional heroine of Henry Wadsworth Longfellow's epic about the deportation.

The site, on Grand-Pré Road near Wolfville, is open from mid-May to mid-October. The grounds are open year-round. Admission: general, ❶. For information, call ☎ (902) 542-3631 or consult 💻 parkscanada.pch.gc.ca/parks/nova_sco tia/grand_pre.

Annapolis Royal is the oldest settlement of European origin in Canada. It was founded by the French in 1605 and was the capital of British Nova Scotia from 1710 to 1749. At the end of a sheltered bay was the first successful settlement for the Acadians, after an unsuccessful attempt on the small isle of Saint-Croix.

The **Fort Anne National Historic Site in Annapolis Royal** was the site of four French forts, the oldest dating to the 1630s. The restored powder magazine dates back to 1708. You can tour the period buildings, take graveyard tours by candlelight, and examine a modern-day heritage tapestry—Queen Elizabeth II even added a few of the tapestry's three million stitches while on a visit here. The site is open from mid-May to mid-October; the grounds are open all year. Admission: adult, senior, and child, ❶; child (younger than 5), free; family, ❷. For information, call ☎ (902) 532-2397 or consult 💻 parkscanada.pch.gc.ca/ parks/nova_scotia/fort_anne.

Nearby, the **Annapolis Royal Historic Gardens** include more than a mile of winding pathways through theme gardens and displays reflecting the history of the region. For information, call ☎ (902) 532-7018 or consult 💻 www.his toricgardens.com.

Western and Southwestern Coast

The jewel of the far west in Nova Scotia is **Kejimkujik National Park**, which consists of two parcels—one inland, and one on the shore.

The main park, off Route 8, the Kejimkujik Drive, protects 240 square miles of inland lakes and forests. For thousands of years the Mi'kmaq canoed along its waterways. There is canoeing, camping, hiking trails, and an interpretive center in the park, which is open year-round. Admission: adult, senior, and child, ❶; family, ❷. For information, call ☎ (902) 682-2772 or consult 💻 parks canada.pch.gc.ca/parks/nova_scotia/kejimkujik_np.

The **Seaside Adjunct, Kejimkujik National Park** is a wild, isolated stretch of coastline along the Atlantic shore. There are sand beaches, rocky coves, and rugged hiking trails. The park is about fifteen miles southwest of Liverpool, off Highway 103. Admission: free. For information, call ☎ (902) 682-2772.

North Central Nova Scotia

The **Glooscap Trail** runs from Amherst to Windsor along the Fundy Shore, including following the Minas Basin with the world's highest tides.

The wild, isolated stretch of coastline along Nova Scotia's Atlantic shore is home to the endangered piping plover. The area offers sand beaches, headlands, rocky coves, rugged hiking trails, and sightseeing.

The **Fundy Geological Museum in Parrsboro** illuminates the ages-old story of the Bay of Fundy's eroding cliffs, which reveal evidence of 325-million-year-old fossils. Displays include some of the world's oldest dinosaur bones, models of ancient landscapes, mineral deposits, and ancient tree and animal fossils from Carboniferous Age ("coal age") forests. The museum is located at 6 Two Island Road. Open year-round. Admission: adult, senior, child (6–17), ❶; family, ❷. For information, call ☎ (902) 254-3814 or consult 🖳 museum.gov.ns.ca/fgm.

At the remote northwest reach of the province on Chignecto Bay across from New Brunswick, the **Joggins Fossil Centre** looks back 300 million years with hundreds of coal-age fossils; the collection has been augmented by younger and older specimens donated by amateur collectors from around the world. Located in Joggins, the museum is open from early June to late September. Admission: adult, ❶; child (younger than 5), free. For information, call ☎ (902) 251-2370 or consult 🖳 museum.gov.ns.ca/places/joggins/ joggins.htm.

Northeastern Nova Scotia (The Marine Drive)

The road from Halifax along the Atlantic shore toward Cape Breton winds its way through dozens of pretty coves and tiny fishing villages. There are marked and unmarked beaches and sightseeing points at most every turn.

About 120 miles from Halifax, **Sherbrooke Village** is a restored lumbering and shipbuilding community from more than a hundred years ago. The site has twenty-five buildings, including a wood turner's shop, print shop, sawmill,

North Harbor, Cape Breton

and a rural doctor's office. Sherbrooke was also a boom town for a short period of time, around the end of the nineteenth century when gold was found nearby. Located on Route 7. For information, call ☎ (902) 522-2400 or consult 🖳 museum.gov.ns.ca/sv.

At the extreme eastern tip of Nova Scotia's main island in Canso, the **Grassy Island National Historic Site** tells the story of a remote two-hundred-year-old French and British fishing settlement. The site includes the remains of fortifications from the eighteenth century and a colonial New England fishing station. Located on the Canso waterfront off Union Street, open June to mid-September. Admission: general, ❶. For information, call ☎ (902) 295-2069 or consult 🖳 parkscanada.pch.gc.ca/parks/nova_scotia/grassy_island.

Cape Breton Island

Cape Breton Island is a palette-shaped island to the northeast of mainland Nova Scotia, connected by the half-mile-long Canso Causeway. A ferry out of North Sydney also links Cape Breton Island to Newfoundland.

The art that was created with this palette is that of a mostly unspoiled, rugged land. The western shore is Scotland in the New World, one of the few places where Gaelic is still spoken and taught. The area is the cradle of Canada's Celtic fiddlers and singers. The hooked rugs of Chéticamp are world famous.

The southeast shore has been a stronghold of Acadian culture since the eighteenth century. Many communities, including Belle-Côte, Terre-Noire, and Saint-Joseph-du-Moine were settled by Acadians returning from exile after 1763.

And at the top end of the island the **Cabot Trail** passes through magnificent mountains and seaside. The paved road is named for Giovanni Cabot, who is believed to have spotted the island in 1497; the Italian navigator was exploring on behalf of the British Crown.

Fortress Louisbourg, Cape Breton

SYDNEY

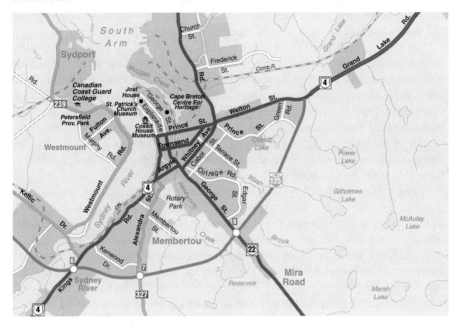

Half of the trail's 185 miles lies within Cape Breton Highlands National Park, 366 square miles of highland plateaus, coastal cliffs, windswept barrens, and deep-walled canyons.

Baddeck, on the shores of Bras d'Or Lake ("Golden Arm"), is a beautiful inland sea fifty miles long and twenty miles wide. It's an important breeding ground for the bald eagle. The native Mi'kmaq people gathered along the shores of the lake; their descendants sell fine quill work and basketry and keep their culture alive with drum and dance groups.

Sydney

Sydney is situated in the island's industrial heartland and is a major city with three-quarters of the population settled in and about it. Sydney was built around coal mines and steel plants, which belched smoke over the city until the 1950s. The closure of those plants left the city in an enduring funk.

Year-round car ferry service links North Sydney to Port-aux-Basques, Newfoundland, and in the summer, to Argentia, Newfoundland. For information, call **Marine Atlantic** at ☎ (800) 341-7981 or ☎ (902) 794-5254 or consult 💻 www.marine-atlantic.ca. You can also fly from Sydney to Saint-Pierre et Miquelon and other destinations.

Around Cape Breton

The dusky jewel of the region is the **Fortress of Louisbourg** National Historic Site, south of Sydney on Route 22.

Canada is a country that loves its restorations, and I visited dozens of them.

But it is Louisbourg that sticks in my memory. On a cold and drizzly day in late September, there was precious little to break the feeling of stepping into the year 1744 in Colonial New France.

The fortress was one of the busiest harbors in North America in the eighteenth century. Today more than fifty reconstructed buildings are populated by costumed actors who recreate the lives and activities of the residents. There are homes, a creepy jail, powder magazines, formal gardens, lively taverns, and three period restaurants. There is also an interpretive trail that explains about the native Mi'kmaqs, and guided walking tours of the area.

The restoration, south of Sydney on Rte. 22, is open from May to October; the grounds are open year-round. Admission: adult, ❸; child, ❶. For information, call ☎ (902) 733-2280 or consult 🖳 fortress.uccb.ns.ca.

Alexander Graham Bell was a resident of Cape Breton Island for the last three decades of his life, from about 1885 until his death in 1922. He lived in Baddeck, in the center of Cape Breton on Saint Patrick's Channel, which nearly cuts the island in half. Bell said Cape Breton reminded him of his native Scotland.

In Baddeck the **Alexander Graham Bell National Historic Site** includes a surprising collection of artifacts, photographs, and personal mementos. Most visitors are amazed to learn of the wide range of Bell's interests. Twenty years after he invented the telephone, he devoted much of his energy to aeronautics. On February 23, 1909, Bell's experimental airplane, the *Silver Dart*, took off from the ice of Baddeck Bay to fly the first powered, controlled flight in Canada, about half a mile. He also developed the first hydrofoil boat, which reached a top speed of about seventy miles per hour on the lake.

Also shown are some of his works on teaching deaf children.

Open year-round, the museum is on Chebucto Street (Route 205) in Baddeck. Admission: adult, senior, and youth, ❶; child (6 and younger), free; family ❸. For information, call ☎ (902) 295-2069 or consult 🖳 parks canada.pch.gc.ca/parks/nova_scotia/ alex_g_bell.

Bell's home, Beinn Bhreagh, across the bay from the museum, is closed to the public.

The 186-mile **Cabot Trail**, which begins and ends in Baddeck, is one of the most scenic highways anywhere. Opened in 1932 it was built to link the island's northern coastal isolated fishing communities.

The Keltic Lodge, Cabot Trail, Cape Breton

The **Highland Village Museum** in Iona celebrates more than 180 years

Point Prim lighthouse, Digby

of Scottish settlement in Nova Scotia with a collection of historic buildings and costumed staff members. The blacksmith and weaver create and sell their works. The museum also includes a genealogical center. Open from early June to late October. Admission: adult, senior, and child (5–18), ❶; child (4 and younger), free; family, ❸. For information, call ☎ (902) 725-2272 or consult 🖳 www.highland village.ns.ca.

At the northern end of the island, **Cape Breton Highlands National Park** includes six hundred square miles of breathtaking highlands and coastal wilderness; half of the Cabot Trail is located along the coast within the park with access to hiking trails, waterfalls, and beaches. At park headquarters in Ingonish Beach you'll find what is claimed to be the largest nature bookstore in Atlantic Canada. Open year-round. Admission: adult, senior, and youth, ❶; family, ❷. For information, call ☎ (902) 224-2306 or consult 🖳 parkscanada.pch.gc.ca/parks/ nova_scotia/cape_highlands.

Below the Highlands National Park, the **Ceilidh Trail** stretches sixty-seven miles through Cape Breton Island's Scottish fishing and farming communities along scenic Route 19. During the summer almost every town along the trail has daily get-togethers and musical concerts celebrating Celtic traditions.

Nova Scotia Festivals and Events

May

Annapolis Valley Apple Blossom Festival. A celebration of Nova Scotia's apple-growing and farming industries, held from Digby to Windsor.

On the Waterfront Festival. Dartmouth. ☎ (902) 466-2769. New works by contemporary Atlantic Canadian playwrights.

Summer-Long

Chester Playhouse Summer Festival. Chester. ☎ (902) 275-3933. Summer repertory theater and other performing arts from early July to early September.

Evangeline Musical Drama. Church Point, Université Sainte-Anne campus. ☎ (902) 769-2114. The language and soul of Acadie are brought to life in song, dance, and music in a drama based on Henry Wadsworth Longfellow's epic poem. Presented from late June to mid-September.

Festival Antigonish Summer Theatre. Bauer Theatre, Saint Francis Xavier University campus. ☎ (902) 867-3333 Box Office or ☎ (902) 867-2100. Repertory theater from late June to early September.

King's Theatre Summer Festival. Annapolis Royal. ☎ (902) 532-7704. Concerts, films, plays, craft and antique shows

Shakespeare by the Sea. Halifax. ☎ (902) 422-0295. An outdoor wooded setting at Cambridge Battery in Point Pleasant Park, in July and August.

Ship's Company. Parrsboro. ☎ (902) 254-2003 or ☎ (902) 254-3000 in season. New works reflecting the life of Atlantic Canada staged on the main cargo deck of the historic ship MV *Kipawo* and its adjoining wharf.

SoundsCapes. Performances in Louisbourg, Baddeck, Ingonish, Chéticamp, and Margaree. ☎ (902) 539-8800. From mid-June to mid-October, including traditional ceilidhs with song, fiddling, and dancing.

July

Acadian Days. Grand-Pré. ☎ (902) 433-0065. Grand-Pré National Historic Site. Acadian music, traditional dishes, arts and crafts.

Antigonish Highland Games. Antigonish. ☎ (902) 863-4275. Hundreds of musicians, dancers, and athletes perform and compete in the oldest continuously held Highland Games in the world outside Scotland. Events include workshops, outdoor tattoos, pipe bands, caber toss and heavyweight events.

Mahone Bay Wooden Boat Festival. Mahone Bay. ☎ (902) 624-8443. A celebration of the traditions and craft of boat building. Events include a three-hour competition to design, build, and then race a small boat on Mahone Bay.

Nova Scotia International Tattoo. Halifax. ☎ (902) 492-4212. More than two thousand military and civilian participants play the pipes and drums, perform in military bands, and present historical reenactments and dances.

August

Lunenburg Folk Harbour Festival. Lunenburg. ☎ (902) 634-3180. Music at the wharf, Victorian bandstand, Opera House, hilltop tent.

September

Atlantic Film Festival. Halifax. ☎ (902) 422-3456. Public screenings of current Canadian and international films and video, and juried competitions.

Atlantic Fringe Festival. Halifax and Dartmouth. ☎ (902) 435-4837. Some 250 performances held over three days and six nights at various locations. Plays from Atlantic Canada, Ontario, Québec and New England.

Part VIII
The Great Northwest

Chapter 38
Nunavut

There's a whole lot of spectacular open space in Nunavut, a place that is at the same time the newest territory in Canada and the repository of one of its oldest ongoing cultures.

Carved out of the eastern two-thirds of the Northwest Territory, Nunavut stretches from the northern end of Manitoba and Québec deep into the Arctic and the Northwest Passage, including the magnetic North Pole. It's an area as large as all of Western Europe and larger than Alaska and California combined but populated by only about twenty-seven thousand people.

Nunavut, which means "Our Land" in the Inuit or Eskimo language, sprawls across 740,000 square miles; there are just twelve miles of paved highway. Nunavut extends into Canada's Arctic into the Baffin, Keewatin, and Kitikmeot regions, spreading across three time zones.

The territory was officially born on April 1, 1999, ending two decades of political and legal struggles by the Inuit, who make up about 85 percent of the population. Canada agreed to grant self-government to settle the largest land-claims suit in the nation's history.

The new capital is Iqaluit, home to just 4,500 people. As part of the celebrations, Canada issued a new twenty-five-cent coin, designed by Inuit artists and engraved with an owl and bear.

Government ceremonies for the new territory were held in a complex of Cold War–era hangers that were originally designed to dispatch jet fighters in the event of a Soviet military threat.

A small legislative chamber in Iqaluit features sealskin-covered benches instead of desks; the building's wooden arches meet in the center in the shape of an igloo.

In addition to the two official Canadian languages of English and French, the province uses Inuktitut, which is mostly an eastern Arctic Inuit language, and Inuuinaqtun, which is mostly spoken in the western portion.

The province is almost entirely beyond the treeline and is a place of stark beauty. The winter is, of course, quite cold and dark, but there are millions of stars, the Northern Lights, sundogs, and white-outs. The summer is slightly less

NUNAVUT

cold, a place of the Midnight Sun with exotic wildflowers on the tundra and rare and unusual migratory birds, seals, muskox, caribou, and polar bear.

The Lay of the Land

Iqaluit includes a handful of mostly basic hotels with about 180 beds in total, a hospital, a museum, and some stores. All of the other communities in the territory are quite small, home to between 100 and 1,800 people each.

There are virtually no roads outside of the small communities. The only practical transportation is by small airplane. Nunavut is served by commercial carriers, including First Air, Canadian North, NWT Air, Calm Air, and Skyward. Long-distance air service is generally from Montreal or Ottawa. There is a short shipping season in the summer.

Because of the remoteness of much of the territory, the cost of travel there is high. Air service is limited and expensive and subject to cancellation or delay because of bad weather. Several cruise lines include summertime stops on tours that cross through the Northwest Passage.

Nunavut has little industry, with most of the population engaged in subsistence jobs. The territory is expected to rely on federal funds for 90 percent of its budget for some time to come, with

much of the money spent on programs to address social problems that include relatively high rates of crime, substance abuse, and suicide among the isolated communities.

Winter lasts from September through May in much of the territory, and most tourist-oriented activities are aimed at adventures on snow or ice.

The most northerly community is Grise Fjord, population 130. The mean temperature in July is a mere 50 degrees Fahrenheit, which is a lot better than January's mean temperature of 30 degrees below zero. It's a place where there is close to twenty-four hours of daylight throughout June and about half an hour a day in December. And it's a place where a typical price for two liters of milk (a bit more than two quarts) is about $7.

Virtually everything you purchase in Nunavut will cost somewhere between a bit more and a lot more than elsewhere in Canada because supplies need to be brought in from great distances.

Iqaluit, the largest town in the territory, celebrates the coming of spring with the week-long Toonik Tyme festival in late April. Events include community feasts, games and dogsled races, igloo-building contests, and entertainment.

Summer, a not-quite-so-cool period in July and August, is a time for hiking, kayaking on rivers or at sea, and visits to isolated historic sites.

Hunting is a major attraction; native groups offer hunts of polar bears and grizzly bears, albeit under a quota system.

The Baffin Region, Arctic Islands

The Baffin region includes dozens of small islands plus Baffin Island itself, which stretches from north of Labrador and the top of Québec to nearly five hundred miles north of the Arctic Circle.

Baffin is a place of ice-carved fjords, coastal bays clogged with icebergs, the world's tallest cliffs, and eastern North America's biggest mountains.

Baffin is also home to animals right out of storybooks and legends: massive walrus, giant bowhead whales, seals, white beluga whales, and the improbable narwhal with its nine-foot-long ivory tusks. On land you'll find rare Peary Caribou, herds of muskox, Arctic fox and wolves, and polar bear.

Dozens of species of unusual birds also make their home in Baffin including Peregrine Falcons, predatory Snowy Owls, the spectacular King Eider, and three species of the loon family. There are massive colonies of cliff-dwelling Thick-Billed Murres, kittiwakes, gullemots, and the continent's largest colony of tundra-nesting Snow Geese.

This far north even parts of the ocean come and go with the seasons. The frozen sea becomes a highway for dogsleds and snowmobiles in winter, and a passage for boats in the short summer. (In between, of course, it's tough sledding.)

By day the sky hosts to rainbows, rings around the sun, and sundogs. (A sundog is a parhelic halo parallel to the horizon at the altitude of the sun.)

Nunavut Tourism
P.O. Box 1450
Iqaluit, NT X0A 0H0
☎ (867) 979-6551,
☎ (800) 491-7910
🖳 www.nunatour.nt.ca.

By night the Northern Lights can fill the sky with vivid, swirling greens and pinks.

In the summer, though, you won't see much of the night. Northern Nunavut is within the land of the Midnight Sun, where for almost half the year, the sun revolves overhead instead of rising and setting.

You'll find stunning mountain scenery in the **Auyuittuq National Park Reserve** from the giant Penny Ice Caps where glaciers fill mile-deep valleys carving their way to spectacular coastal fjords. Bizarre tower-shaped peaks such as Mount Asgard line a hiking trail. For information on the reserve, consult 🖳 www.nunavutparks.com/auy.html.

For a high Arctic adventure, you can journey to lands-end on **Quttinirpaaq (Ellesmere Island) National Park Reserve**, an island that makes up Canada's northernmost land. Here the highest mountains in eastern North America tower above unusual arctic oases where wildlife and vegetation inexplicably flourish. The earliest known prehistoric sites in the Eastern Arctic are clearly visible on Ellesmere's surface. For information on the reserve, call ☎ (867) 473-8828 or consult 🖳 parkscanada.pch.gc.ca/parks/nunavut/quttinirpaaq.

The coasts are lined with stone fox traps, ancient kayak stands, and the remains of dwellings—some thousands of years old. You can learn about the ancient pre-Dorset culture, whose members used tiny stone weapons to harvest large animals from land and sea. You can delve into the ways of the legendary Tuniit people, studying the intricate ivory artifacts they left behind.

More recent history can be found at abandoned century-old whaling stations; you can follow in the footsteps of historic explorers including Martin Frobisher, John Franklin, and Henry Hudson.

In summer you can board a cruise ship for a journey among the scenic fjord coasts of Canada's High Arctic, north of 80 degrees.

There is even a place where visitors can take a rare scenic drive hundreds of miles above the Arctic Circle. A rough fifteen-mile road, one of the few in the entire province, crosses rugged Arctic tundra between the communities of Arctic Bay and Nanisik with panoramas of Admiralty Inlet.

And if this all is not far out enough, there are flights to the North Pole.

Keewatin Region, West Coast Hudson Bay

The Keewatin or Kivalliq is the center section of Nunavut, on the mainland on the west coast of Hudson Bay.

The land is part of the Canadian Shield, which was shaped by the flow of molten rock from deep within the earth and then reshaped by four successive great continental ice sheets. The continental glacier, an ice sheet nearly three miles thick, carved the rock as it advanced, and then redeposited its load as it retreated. The marks left on the land include deep grooves cut by the rocks carried by the ice and glacial polish applied by the scouring of billions of grains of sand carried in the ice. Rocks of all sizes were carried hundreds of miles and dropped in areas that seem out of place.

Streams of meltwater within the glaciers also deposited material, which remains as gravel and sand eskers snaking across the land. Eskers are important denning sites for wolves, bears, wolverines, and foxes; they also make natural landing strips for small airplanes.

The retreat of the last of the glaciers was only about six thousand years ago, and the land is still rising about an inch per year; the high point of Keewatin is now about 635 feet.

Millions of waterfowl make their homes in the south in flat lowland marshes and in the north on sheer cliffs. Tundra covers most of the land with low woody plants pruned by ice crystals in the winter and limited by the permafrost just below the surface. In summer the tundra bursts into bloom with white-tufted arctic cotton and deep magenta rhododendron.

Northern lights. The Aurora Borealis is a view of explosions on the sun, visible at extreme northern latitudes. In the Northwest Territories and Nunavut, the best displays are on clear nights from September to January. In the Yukon, the best views are in the fall and spring after sundown, but also through the summer.

Four great rivers drain the Barrenlands to the west of Hudson Bay, providing a favorite path for canoeists and hikers. Although the land is known as Barrenlands, it is in fact far from barren and is home to polar bears, foxes, seals, walrus, whales, migrating birds, and a wide range of flora and fauna.

Kitikmeot Region: The Northwest Passage

The Kitikmeot extends east and west along mainland Canada's Arctic Coast and includes many Arctic Islands. The principal settlements are Cambridge Bay, Coppermine, Holman, Gjoa Haven, Pelly Bay, and Yaloyoak, with a total population of about six thousand.

As in most Arctic regions, summer temperatures can range from a low of the freezing mark to the sixties. Except for a small area on the mainland, the Kitikmeot region is completely beyond the treeline and north of the Arctic Circle, which results in twenty-four hours of daylight for most of the summer and twenty-four hours without sun for a portion of the winter. The return of the sun is a time for celebration in many communities in the region.

Historic parks and sites commemorate expeditions to search for the Northwest Passage, the much-sought-after path from Europe to the Far East through the northern seas. Archeological research and present day expeditions continue to search for the details of the exploration of the passage in the early nineteenth century. Great Britain's Royal Navy and the Hudson's Bay Company both lost many ships and men in the process.

Perhaps the real heroes of the story of the Northwest Passage were the Inuit, who lived along the Arctic Coast for centuries. The natives met and visited with some of the European explorers, serving as guides and interpreters and sometimes traveling with them to Europe and America. Some of the elders today can tell tales handed down over the generations.

A Selection of Tour Operators

Independent travel in Nunavut is possible, but visitors who want to get out into the wilderness should consider hirng a guide. The following is a listing of some of the more established companies; all are quite small.

Adventure Canada. Canadian High Arctic and Greenland on Class A icebreakers equipped with helicopters. ☎ (800) 363-7566, ☎ (905) 271-4000.

Ajagutaq Outfitting. Guided dog team and snowmobile trips in spring along the coast of Baffin Island. ☎ (867) 924-6345.

Alivaktuk Outfitting. Boat and snowmobile trips to Kekerten Island, a nineteenth-century whaling station. ☎ (867) 473-8721.

Arctic Odysseys. Air expeditions to Baffin, Ellesmere Island, and the Arctic Archipeligo. Boat tours to Wager Bay. ☎ (206) 325-1977.

Atlantic Marine Wildlife Tours. Snowmobile and sled trips on North Baffin Island. ☎ (506) 459-7325.

Bathurst Arctic Services. Canoe outfitting and wilderness camping on the Burnside, Mara, Hood, Thelon, and other rivers. ☎ (867) 873-2595.

Calm Air. Scheduled and charter air service. ☎ (204) 778-6471. 🖳 www.calmair.com.

Canadian River Expeditions. Wilderness and natural history expedition to Baffin Island. ☎ (800) 898-7238, ☎ (604) 938-6651. 🖳 www.canriver.com.

Canoe Arctic. Fly-in wilderness canoe trips. ☎ (867) 872-2308.

Central Arctic Tours & Outfitters. Northwest Passage tours. ☎ (867) 983-2024.

Ecosummer Expeditions. Expeditions to Ellesmere Island, Northwest Greenland, and the North Pole. ☎ (800) 465-8884. 🖳 www.ecosummer.com.

Eetuk Outfitting. Boat trips on Frobisher Bay and in the Iqaluit area, and snowmobile and sled expeditions. ☎ (867) 979-1984. 🖳 www.nunanet.com/~eetuk.

Frontiers North. Polar bear viewing, dog sledding, and whale watching expeditions. ☎ (800) 663-9832, ☎ (204) 949-2050.

Huit Huit Tours. Expeditions from Cape Dorset on Baffin Island. ☎ (867) 897-8806. 🖳 www.capedorsettours.com.

Inuit Sea Kayaking Adventures. Trips along the South Baffin coast. ☎ (800) 331-4684, ☎ (867) 979-2055.

Jessco Logistics. Northwest Passage explorations. ☎ (403) 282-2268.

Mayukalik. Boat trips to Crook's Inlet for wildlife viewing. Expeditions to Soper River Falls and Katannilik Park. ☎ (867) 939-2355.

Northwest Passage Expeditions. Boat tours to Coronation Gulf. ☎ (604) 463-2035.

Pikaluyak Outfitting. Dog team trips to eastern Baffin Island, transportation to Auyuittuq National Park, summer boat trips. ☎ (819) 927-8390.

Whitewolf Adventure Expeditions. Burnside and Coppermine Rivers and the Polar Sea. ☎ (800) 661-6659. 🖳 www.nahanni.com.

Wilderness Adventures Co. Hiking in Auyuittuq and Ellesmere National Park and sea kayaking in Greenland and Ellesmere Island. ☎ (705) 746-1372. 🖳 www.blackfeather.com.

Chapter 39
Northwest Territories

Welcome to the rugged Northwest Territories (NWT), the province that nearly became known as Bob.

The huge territory was split into two entities in 1999 with the eastern portion named Nunavut, an Inuit word meaning "our land."

A hard-fought grassroots campaign worked for more than a year to name the western half of the Northwest Territories as "Bob." They almost won.

A government commission in the western half asked citizens to send in suggestions for a new name. A cabal at a neighborhood barbecue came up with the name of "Bob" and began a provincial campaign through T-shirts ("Bob, Canada"); the name garnered second place in the preliminary competition. First place went to the original name, Northwest Territories, and that became the official choice. (Other contenders: Denendeh and Nahendeh, both from the native Dene language.)

The Prehistory of the NWT

The earliest people of the Northwest Territories were the nomadic Dene, who followed the caribou and bison and moved along the rivers with the seasons.

The Inuit hunted whales along the arctic coast, and more recently, the Inuvialuit settled in what is now the Mackenzie Delta.

The first European fur traders and explorers arrived in the early 1700s, including William Stewart in 1715 and more famously, Alexander Mackenzie of the North West Company in 1789.

Prospectors passing through the area on their way to the gold fields of the Klondike in 1896 and 1897 looked around for other minerals; in 1898 they found lead and zinc near the mouth of the Slave River.

Oil was discovered at Norman Wells in 1911, radium at Great Bear Lake in 1930, and gold at Yellowknife in 1934. Vast quantities of gas and oil were found on the shores and in the shallows of the Beaufort Sea in the 1970s, leading to the completion of the Dempster Highway to Inuvik.

Mining continues, with the glimmer of a new diamond mine—the first in North America—near Lac de Gras two hundred miles north of Yellowknife.

NORTHWEST TERRITORIES

The Mackenzie Valley was used for military installations in the 1940s and 1950s, part of the postwar and Cold War defense systems.

Yellowknife

Yellowknife, the capital and Canada's most northerly city, is also the only city in all of the Northwest Territories. Although native settlements go back much further, today's Yellowknife was born as a mining town.

A modern city of about eighteen thousand people, Yellowknife includes a few modestly tall office buildings. Much of the city's frontier mining history is still evident in Old Town on the shore of Great Slave Lake. Mining is still an active industry in the area, with several diamond exploration projects underway and two gold properties located within the city limits.

The city lies at the north end of the Great Slave Lake in the Fort Smith Region. It can be reached by car on NWT Highway 3, which begins about 125 miles north of Alberta on the other side of the Mackenzie River. A ferry crosses the Mackenzie most of the year, with an ice road handling traffic in the winter.

The first stop on the drive lies on the north shore of the Mackenzie at Fort Providence, which was founded in 1861 as a Roman Catholic mission. At this point visitors enter the **Mackenzie Bison Sanctuary**, home to a free-ranging herd of some two thousand pure wood bison.

YELLOWKNIFE

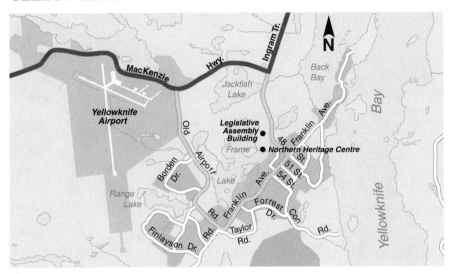

Highway 3 continues north through the Mackenzie Lowlands to Edzo and Fort Rae, two communities on each side of the Great Slave Lake at its northern, narrow end, en route to its terminus at Yellowknife.

Exploring the Northwest Territories

The Mackenzie River forms an off-center spine, heading nearly due north from the Great Slave Lake the length of the territory to empty into the Beaufort Sea, a distance of 1,200 miles; it is the second longest river in North America.

The territory includes some 550,000 square miles of land that is populated by about 30,000 people, one million barren-ground caribou, 50,000 muskoxen, 26,000 moose, 15,000 wolves, 5,000 polar bear, 5,000 grizzly bear, 5,000 black bear, 6,000 Dall's sheep, 2,500 bison, and uncounted small land mammals that include coyotes, beavers, arctic and red fox, lynx, wolverines, weasels, mink, martens, fishers, hares, arctic ground squirrels, marmots, pika, and lemmings.

According to government tourism officials, the entire territory—including the even-more-remote eastern half, now the separate territory of Nunavut—drew about fifty thousand visitors between June and September and fewer than ten thousand the rest of the year. (A popular T-shirt sold to locals and tourists alike may give a clue; the shirt declares the four seasons of the Northwest Territory as June, July, August, and Winter.)

Canada's arctic is one of the few areas in the world where beluga whales can be seen nursing their young in the shallows of river deltas.

Each spring millions of songbirds, shorebirds, waterfowl, and seabirds from six continents converge on Canada's north to breed; about half of Canada's species have been recorded in the NWT, including threatened or endangered species such as the trumpeter swan, American white pelican, whooping crane, peregrine falcon, and Eskimo curlew.

THE NORTHERN ARCTIC

There are four national parks in the NWT, Nahanni and Wood Buffalo in the southern forest, and Tuktut Nogait and Aulavik on the coast and islands.

The Northern Arctic

The northern arctic has been described as a cold desert. The area includes the western third of Victoria Island and all of Banks Island.

The permafrost lies just an inch or two beneath the nearly barren surface in summer. The area has a very dry, cold climate year round with an average of just twenty frost-free days per year. The mean January temperature is about −30 degrees Fahrenheit; in July, the mean is about 45 degrees Fahrenheit.

Plant life is subtle, although there are scattered oases in sheltered areas such as Polar Bear Pass on Bathurst Island where there are relatively lush tundras. Here you'll find Peary caribou, muskoxen, arctichares, collared lemmings, and colonies of birds that nest in the tundra.

Steep cliffs are the hiding places for nests of peregrine falcons and rough-legged hawks. On Victoria Island polar bears migrate across inland areas heading for dinner at the ringed seal pupping areas on Minto Inlet.

The small population is mostly made up of Inuit and Inuvialuit, living in small communities that draw their roots from old fur trading posts.

The Southern Arctic

Early explorers called this region the Barrenlands, but in truth that really isn't fair. The short summer explodes the tundra with wildflowers. The skies are alive in the fall with migrating tundra swans, sandhill cranes, and snow geese. In the winter caribou and muskox paw through the thin cover of snow to expose low-lying grasses and plants.

The southern arctic region spreads north from the treeline to the Arctic Coast, east from the Yukon to Hudson Bay and into Nunavik in the northern reaches of Québec.

The permafrost lies just below the surface, freezing solid in long cold winters. There is relatively little precipitation, with a mean temperature in January of about −34 degrees Fahrenheit; in summer the mean reaches all the way to a balmy 50 degrees Fahrenheit.

The land is shaped by the continental ice sheets that retreated more than six thousand years ago, leaving behind millions of lakes and ponds. Sand and gravel ridges known as eskers snake across the region, reminders of long-gone rivers that flowed from the ice sheets.

The lakes and ponds are home to nesting loons, ducks, geese, swans, and shorebirds that include sandpipers and plovers. The land is also populated by large herds of caribou.

Taiga Cordillera

The Mackenzie Mountains form the continental divide, running through the Northwest Territories and Yukon. Water on the west side flows to the Pacific Ocean or the Beaufort Sea; on the east side water runs to the Mackenzie River.

The Taiga Cordillera is a region where sedimentary bedrock—the remnants of a shallow sea of half a billion years ago—has been lifted and folded into tilted mountain ranges. Cordillera is a geological term for parallel ranges of mountains.

The area's ecology is greatly affected by elevation and orientation. At high altitude, temperatures are cooler and vegetation is sparse; the mountains are home to horned larks and golden eagles above, and pikas, hoary marmots, and Dall's sheep below. Grizzly bears forage for roots, berries, and small mammals.

At lower elevations in the subalpine transition zone, woodland caribou range through thickets of birch and spruce.

Lower down in the montane and lowland zones are dense forests of spruce and stands of Balsam poplar, willow, and alders in the river valleys. This is the habitat of the black bear, lynx, marten, and snowshoe hare. Goldeneye ducks nest in trees, while in the valleys you'll find canvasbacks, mallards, and trumpeter swans nesting in the marshes and muskeg.

Summers are relatively warm in the south, short and cool in the north; winter is long and cold throughout. Mean January temperatures are down around −22 degrees Fahrenheit, reaching to as much as 60 degrees in July.

Visitors to this home of the Mountain Dene and Gwich'in may be there for whitewater thrills on the Natla-Keele River or the Mountain River or for hiking on the Canol Heritage Trail, which climbs up and over the Mackenzie Mountain Barrens.

Taiga Plains

This region includes low-lying plains centered on the Mackenzie River, from northern Alberta and British Columbia to a delta north of the Arctic Circle.

The Mackenzie was created from the outflow of the Laurentide ice sheet. Fossils of clams, ammonites, and other sea life are found along the shore; at numerous places smoke arises from smoldering seams of coal that have been burning for hundreds of years.

This is a place of long, cold winters—down to a mean of −22 degrees Fahrenheit in January—and short, cool summers that reach to about 60 degrees in July. In the south there are about one hundred frost-free days; put another way, that means that in the slightly more temperate portion of the Taiga Plains, the thermometer still dips below 32 degrees Fahrenheit an average of 265 days per year.

In the northern area the sun stays above the horizon for several weeks in summer, just as it disappears for a similar period in the winter.

Moose, wolves, and woodland caribou roam the dense boreal forests, along with smaller mammals that include lynx, red fox, porcupine, ermine, mink, red squirrel, marten, river otter, and wolverine. Here black bear forage as they move in and out of the woods.

Taiga Shield

The southern and southeastern portion of the Northwest Territories is the place where the boreal forest and the Canadian Shield come together. Erosion and glacial carving have scraped all but the hardest rocks, leaving behind low rounded hills. In places permafrost shifts the soil and tips trees at crazy angles, creating sections of "drunken forest."

The open water of the Taiga Shield is home to ducks, geese, loons, sanhill cranes, and grebes. Over the marshes are lesser scaup, mallards, pintails, green-winged teal, and gadwalls.

Black bear hunt for spawning northern pike in the marshes. Other major mammals include moose and caribou.

Much of the population is centered about Yellowknife and Great Slave Lake, with many Dene and Metis working in the mining industry.

Native Cultures in NWT

The Dene and Inuvialuit have inhabited the northernmost regions of Canada for more than a thousand years. Their unique cultures have been shaped by the struggle for survival in harsh arctic and sub-arctic climates.

At the gateway to **Nahanni National Park**, the **Village of Fort Simpson Visitors' Center** offers a glimpse into the traditional Dene way of life, complete with crafts and a reproduction of a Hudson's Bay store.

Visitors can hear the diverse languages of the NWT and experience the aboriginal cultures in many small communities in the western part of the territory. The NWT has eight official languages, although most residents speak English as a first or second language.

The Dene and the Métis originally lived mainly in the forested regions of the Northwest Territory. The homelands of the Inuvialuit and Inuit were along the arctic coast and islands.

In the 1990s Canada began finishing a long, and sometimes contentious, process of settling land claims by natives. As a result, aboriginal nations have become major landowners in the Mackenzie Delta, around Great Bear Lake, and in the Deh Cho region.

Exploring the Wilderness

Boreal forest rivers flow through coniferous forest, their banks lined with spruce trees and populated with moose, beaver, woodland caribou, black bear, lynx, and bald eagles.

Most boreal forest rivers were historic exploration and fur trade routes and are still used as highways between remote northern communities and traditional fishing and hunting camps.

The scenery on rivers such as the Nahanni, the Natla-Keele, the Mountain, and the Slave is spectacular, featuring deep canyons, cataracts, and lesser waterfalls. Virginia Falls on the Nahanni is twice the height of Niagara.

North and east of the boreal forest, the arctic tundra covers about a quarter of the western NWT. Arctic rivers wind through open tundra where most plants are less than a foot tall, offering unlimited views. A short hike out of the river valley offers miles of open land to locate wildlife.

Some arctic rivers such as the Anderson and the Horton flow to the arctic coast through dramatic canyons and sweeping tundra. Other rivers, such as the Thelon, wind through stands of trees and sandy eskers to Hudson Bay. Still other arctic rivers, such as the Thomsen, drain the interiors of the arctic islands.

On tundra rivers visitors can spot indications of ancient Inuit occupation including tent rings, meat caches, and stone game-drive markers known as *inukshuks*.

Many arctic river trips end at small Inuit communities along the arctic coast.

Tour Operators in the Northwest Territories

As in any wilderness area, visitors should consider using the services of tour operators for canoeing, rafting, hunting, and exploration.

Following is a sampling of some operators; a full list is available from NWT Tourism.

Adventure Canada. Mississauga, Ontario. Canyon rafting. ☎ (905) 271-4243 or ☎ (800) 363-7566. 🖳 www.adventurecanada.com.

Arctic Chalet Outfitters. Inuvik, NWT. Outfitting and equipment rentals for self-guided river trips, including air dropoff and pickup. ☎ (867) 777-3535.

Arctic Nature Tours. Inuvik, NWT. Firth River expeditions. ☎ (867) 777-3300.

Arctic Red River Outfitters Ltd. Whitehorse, YT. Hiking and photo safaris in the Mackenzie Mountains. ☎ (867) 633-4934. 🖳 www2.telenet.net/commercial/outfitters.

Arctic Tour Company. Tuktoyaktuk, NT. Camping tours to Banks Island, Herschel Island, Ivvavik (Northern Yukon) National Park. ☎ (867) 977-2230.

Blachford Lake Lodge. Yellowknife, NT. Canoe touring and wilderness camping from Blachford Lake. ☎ (867) 873-3303. 🖳 www.internorth.com/blachford.

Boreal Woods and Waters. Fort Smith, NT. Trips in Slave River basins and Wood Buffalo National Park. ☎ (867) 872-2467

Canadian River Expeditions Ltd. Whistler, BC. Rafting adventures from Ivvavik National Park's mountains to the caribou calving grounds along the shores of the Arctic Ocean. ☎ (800) 898-7238 or ☎ (604) 938-6651

Canoe Arctic Inc. Fort Smith, NT. Fly-in canoe trips on the Thelon river system. ☎ (867) 872-2308. 🖳 www.auroranet.nt.ca/canoe.

Ecosummer Yukon Expeditions. Whitehorse, YT. Raft the Tatshenshini and Firth Rivers, backpack in Kluane and Ivvavik National Park. ☎ (867) 633-8453. 🖳 www.silasojourns.com.

Great Canadian Ecoventures. Yellowknife, NT. Variety of tours to Great Slave Lake and other areas in the Northwest Territories. ☎ (800) 667-9453 or ☎ (867) 920-7110. 🖳 www.thelon.com.

Inukshuk Ventures. Yellowknife, NT. Canoeing and rafting without the whitewater. ☎ (867) 873-4226. 🖳 www.arcticdata.ca/~inukshuk.

Mountain River Outfitters. Norman Wells, NT. Outfitting and canoe rentals for trips to the Mountain and Natla/Keele Rivers. ☎ (867) 587-2285.

Nahanni and Whitewolf River Adventures. Whitehorse, YT. Canoe and raft outfitting for the South Nahanni. ☎ (867) 668-3180 or ☎ (800) 297-6927. 🖳 www.nahanni.com.

Nahanni Mountain Lodge/Simpson Air. Fort Simpson, NT. Sightseeing, photographic trips to Virginia Falls, Ram River Canyons, Nahanni Plateau, Little Doctor Lake. ☎ (867) 695-2505.

Nahanni Wilderness Adventures. Didsbury, AB. Canoe outfitting for the South Nahanni. ☎ (403) 637-3843 or ☎ (888) 897-5223. 🖳 www.nahanniwild.com.

North Nahanni River Tours. Fort Simpson, NT. Power boats on the Mackenzie River and the scenic North Nahanni River. ☎ (867) 695-2116.

Pilot Lake Cabins. Fort Smith, NT. Wilderness camping. ☎ (403) 343-0161.

Ram Head Outfitters. Warburg, AB. Fly-in horseback adventures on the Canol Road, from Norman Wells. ☎ (780) 848-7578.

Red Mountain Adventures. Aklavik, NT. Guided tours by boat or snowmobile to the Richardson Mountains. ☎ (867) 978-2747.

Rendezvous Lake Lodge. Tuktoyaktuk, NT. Outpost camp on the Arctic Coast, in the Anderson River area. ☎ (867) 977-2406.

Subarctic Wildlife Adventures Ltd. Fort Smith, NT. Peace, Slave, and Athabasca rivers through Wood Buffalo National Park in the Taltson and Thelon River basins. ☎ (867) 872-2467.

Taiga Tour Company. Fort Smith, NT. Tours and camping in Wood Buffalo National Park, Peace/Athabasca delta. ☎ (867) 872-2060.

True North Safaris Ltd. (MacKay Lake Lodge). Yellowknife, NT. Guided or unguided tours to Barrenlands north of Yellowknife. ☎ (867) 873-8533.

Tsiigehtchic River Boat Taxi and Tours. Tsiigehtchic, NT. Sightseeing on arctic Red River and the Mackenzie River. ☎ (867) 953-3607 or ☎ (867) 953-3201.

NWT Tourism. For a copy of the Explorers Guide and maps, contact NWT Tourism at:
   NWT Arctic Tourism
   Postal Service 9600
   Yellowknife NT X1A 2R3
   Canada
   Call ☎ (800) 661-0788, or visit 💻 www.nwttravel.nt.ca.

Western Arctic Adventure & Equipment Ltd. Inuvik, NT. Canoe and kayak expeditions on the Horton, Anderson, Mountain, Natla/Keele, Thomson or Kuujjua Rivers. ☎ (867) 777-4542. 💻 www.inuvik.net/~canoenwt.

West to North Tours. Norman Wells, NT. Hiking trips on the Canol Heritage Trail and snowmobile tours. ☎ (867) 587-3043.

Whitney & Smith Legendary Expeditions Inc. Banff, AB. Natural history and wilderness expeditions on the Thomsen River, Banks Island. ☎ (403) 678-3052. 💻 www.legendaryex.com.

Wilderness Adventure Co. Ottawa, ON. South Nahanni and whitewater challenges and hiking on the Mountain and Natla/Keele Rivers. ☎ (705) 746-1372. 💻 www.trailheadCnd.com.

Cruising and Boat Tours

In addition to large cruise ships that call at some arctic communities, a number of operators provide small boat tours and cruises.

Aurora Sport Fishing and Tours. Fort Providence, NT. Cruise and floatplane tours on the Mackenzie from Fort Providence into Mills Lake and Deep Bay. ☎ (867) 699-4321.

Eagle Nest Tours. Hay River, NT. Boat tours on the southeast shore of Great Slave Lake. ☎ (867) 874-6055.

Enodah Wilderness Travel/Trout Rock Lodge. Yellowknife, NT. Boat trips to the North Arm for bird-watching and historical sites. ☎ (867) 873-4334. 💻 www.enodah.com.

Lennie's Guided Tours. Tulita (Fort Norman), NT. Jet boat tours on the Mackenzie and Great Bear rivers. ☎ (867) 588-4815.

North Nahanni River Tours. Fort Simpson, NT. Jet-boat, outboard motor or canoe on North Nahanni, Mackenzie, Ram, Root, and Liard Rivers. ☎ (867) 695-2116.

Norweta (NWT Marine Group). Yellowknife, NT. Luxury cruises on the 103-foot ship, the *Norweta*, from Yellowknife on Great Slave Lake. ☎ (867) 873-2489.

Sail North. Yellowknife, NT. Sail Great Slave Lake. ☎ (867) 873-8019.

True North Safaris Ltd. (MacKay Lake Lodge). Yellowknife, NT. Yellowknife into the North Arm of Great Slave Lake. ☎ (867) 873-8533.

Zegrahm Deep Sea Voyages. Seattle. Submersibles to view the wreck of HMS *Breadalbane*, off Beechey Island. ☎ (206) 285-3743 or ☎ (888) 772-2366.

Getting to the Northwest Territories

There are just a few ways into the Northwest Territory. Major airline service connects Yellowknife to Edmonton and Winnipeg. Small airlines connect to isolated communities from there.

There are three highways leading into the Northwest Territory: the Dempster Highway, which heads east from the Yukon; the Mackenzie Highway (also known as the "Waterfalls Route"), which enters southwestern NWT through Alberta; and the Liard Trail, which provides entry from British Columbia.

The roads are open year-round, weather conditions permitting. The roads are mostly unpaved, hard packed and gravel surfaces, and they're not very crowded. Each road draws only several thousand cars during the course of a season. Vehicles cross most of the historic rivers of the NWT on free government-operated ferries; in winter ice bridges are used.

Services along northern highways are very limited. Most communities on the road have motels, restaurants, and service stations. The distance between communities is considerable, though, and motorists are advised to keep their vehicles well-maintained and full of fuel.

Road reports are broadcast on local radio and available by phone. You can find information on travel at 🖳 www.yukonweb.com/tourism.

Southern NWT highway information. ☎ (800) 661-0750 in Canada or ☎ (867) 874-2208.

Southern NWT ferries. ☎ (800) 661-0751 in Canada.

Dempster Highway and Mackenzie Delta road and ferry information. ☎ (800) 661-0752 in Canada.

Ferry service is free and operated in summers only. In May and November, call ahead to check on operating conditions. In the winter ice bridges are maintained. For information on ferries for Highways 1 and 3, call ☎ (800) 661-0751 in Canada. For Highway 8, call ☎ (800) 661-0752 in Canada or ☎ (867) 777-2678.

The Dempster Highway

The Dempster Highway, a newer and more remote version of the famed Alaska Highway, offers 450 miles of breathtaking vistas across the continental divide en route to the town of Inuvik, about 233 miles north of the Arctic Circle.

Less colorfully known as Highway 8, the road takes its name from Corporal W. J. D. Dempster, a renowned member of the Northwest Mounted Police who mushed the trail in years past. Dempster discovered the bodies of the famed Northwest Mounted Police Lost Patrol, who perished on the trail between Dawson and Mount McPherson in the winter of 1910–1911. Construction on the road began in 1959; but completion didn't come until 1979 after development was spurred by the Beaufort Sea oil boom.

This is a highway in the loosest terms: it is a well-maintained gravel road. Although there are few steeps and switchbacks, vehicles should be in good shape for some rough passages and for great distances between communities.

The Dempster heads due north off the Klondike Highway, east of Dawson City in the Yukon. From the goldfields of the Klondike it passes through the Ogilvie Range, along the ridges and through the black spruce forest of Eagle Plains. It crosses the Arctic Circle and Mackenzie River and through Fort McPherson to end at the town of Inuvik, the gateway to the communities of the Delta and Beaufort Sea.

The Arctic Circle lies about twenty-five miles north of the highway at the highway's halfway point at Eagle Plains, and here summer travelers enter the land of the midnight sun, with twenty-four hours of daylight for fifty-seven days each summer. (Winter travelers endure the arctic night, with the darkness punctuated by the Northern Lights.)

The Dempster leads to the traditional lands of the Gwich'in Dene and Inuavialut. The Gwich'in navigated mountain rivers in huge boats that were covered in moosehide; they also made trading trips by dog team from the Peel to the Yukon rivers.

The Liard Highway

After leaving British Columbia, the Liard Highway (Highway 7) follows the Liard River from Fort Liard to the Fort Simpson junction, with views of the Mackenzie Mountains to the west. Thick spruce forest borders the road, home to moose, black bear, and the rare trumpeter swan.

Fort Liard is a traditional Dene community, renowned for birchbark and porcupine quill baskets. A small hotel serves visitors, and a tiny airport offers flights to Nahanni National Park.

The Mackenzie Highway

The Mackenzie Highway 1 continues north across the Albert/NWT border to Enterprise where it meets Highway 2, which heads north to Hay River and connections to Fort Smith and Fort Resolution. Highway 1 veers west to follow the Mackenzie River to the junction with Highway 3, which heads north to Fort Providence and Yellowknife or continues west to the junction with the Liard Highway or on to Fort Simpson and Wrigley. The small Dene community of Wrigley saw its first summer road travelers in 1994.

Deh Cho Connection

The Mackenzie and Liard highways and a portion of the historic Alaska Highway make up the Deh Cho Connection, a relatively less challenging but nonetheless thrilling loop of 1,100 miles through British Columbia, Alberta, and the southern portion of the Northwest Territories.

To the Dene, the Mackenzie River is the Deh Cho, the "big river." The Mackenzie flows 1,200 miles from the Great Slave Lake north to the Beaufort Sea, collecting the waters from more than one hundred mountain rivers.

From Alberta the trip begins at Mile Zero on the Mackenzie Highway in Grimshaw. The other end lies at Mile Zero on the Alaska Highway in Dawson Creek, British Columbia.

From Grimshaw the road passes through Alberta's Peace River Country and on to High Level, the last full-service town before the Northwest Territories. It's home to a visitors center, as well as an historic northern trading post that has a collection of more than 1,600 food and medicine containers of years past.

At the 60th parallel, visitors are welcomed at a tourism center where they can pick up a "North of 60" certificate to prove their arrival in the arctic.

At this point the road becomes NWT Highway 1, also known as "The Waterfalls Route." Among the high points along the way are the spectacular Alexandra Falls and Louis Falls near the town of Enterprise. The native Dene believed the falls to be a powerful place protected by Grandmother and Grandfather spirits.

The road connects to the Liard Highway at Fort Simpson where there are hotels and services. The gravel road heads south toward the NWT's border with British Columbia, offering views of the Liard River and the Nahanni Mountains and the town of Fort Liard, which also offers a hotel.

Bus Service

Scheduled bus service is available for much of the year from Edmonton, Alberta, to Yellowknife, Hay River, Fort Smith, and other communities in the Northwest Territory. Bus service is suspended each year for a few weeks in the spring and fall because of the break-up and freeze-up on the Mackenzie River, a period when ferries cannot run and ice roads are not reliable.

Frontier Coachlines. 16 102 Street, Hay River. ☎ (867) 874-2566.

Greyhound Lines of Canada. 10324 103rd Street, Edmonton, Alberta. ☎ (780) 413-8747, or ☎ (800) 661-8747. 🖳 www.greyhound.ca.

Air Service

Canadian North, a division of Canadian Airlines, offers service throughout the Northwest Territories. ☎ (800) 426-7000 from the United States, ☎ (800) 661-1505 in Canada.

Within the territory, smaller carriers include:

Alkan Air Ltd. Whitehorse, Yukon Territory. ☎ (867) 668-2107.

First Air. From Ottawa, Montreal, Greenland, Iqaluit, and Yellowknife to points throughout the Northwest Territories. ☎ (800) 267-1247.

NWT Air. Scheduled service throughout the Northwest Territories from Yellowknife and to Edmonton and Winnipeg. ☎ (867) 920-2500.

Chapter 40
Yukon Territory

For a short period at the end of the nineteenth century, the Yukon was one of the most famous and richest places on earth. Today the Yukon is obscure once again, a place that is larger than California but has a population smaller than you'll find on an off-day at Dodger Stadium: thirty-one thousand people are spread over 186,000 square miles.

History of the Yukon

On August 17, 1896, George Carmack, an American, and his friends Skookum Jim and Dawson Charlie of the Tagish First Nations struck it rich on Bonanza Creek. Hardly newcomers, the three men were aware of modest finds in the Yukon by other prospectors.

On a small tributary of the Klondike River, they struck what they thought was a mother lode; they staked their claims the next day and renamed Rabbit Creek as "Bonanza." By today's measures the trio was standing on a billion dollar piece of ground.

Their find started the Klondike Gold Rush, the last and largest of history's great gold stampedes. Some 100,000 fortune-seekers headed for the Klondike, but less than thirty thousand actually made it. Some of those who did became millionaires, and a few among those managed to keep their fortunes intact. The gold rush was the largest mass movement of Americans onto Canadian soil.

The Klondike Gold Rush had a major impact on the growth of Western Canada and the United States. Seattle became a major staging point for fortune hunters headed north. A steady stream of rail cars and visitors by ship doubled Vancouver's size, while Edmonton's population tripled nearly overnight.

In the Yukon the gold rush led to the creation of most of the present-day settlements including Whitehorse, Dawson City, Haines Junction, Watson Lake, and Carmacks.

Dawson City, at the confluence of the Klondike and Yukon rivers, became the most populous place west of Winnipeg and north of San Francisco.

In the past century the Klondike has yielded more than a billion dollars in gold; in recent times miners have taken out more than $54 million per year.

YUKON TERRITORY

Getting to the Yukon

The Yukon is accessible on land by the Alaska and Stewart-Cassiar highways.

The Alaska Highway was a major defense project in the early years of World War II, opening in 1942 as a gravel track. Today it is almost fully paved. It begins at Dawson Creek in British Columbia and travels 1,388 miles to Delta Junction.

Built as a logging road, the Stewart-Cassiar Highway is now an all-weather route through the interior of British Columbia, merging with the Alaska Highway fourteen miles west of Watson Lake in the Yukon. The 470-mile-long road passes through spectacular scenery including the Stikine River Valley and along Dease Lake. Services are limited, though, and motorists need to plan

ahead for lodging and pay attention to fuel
and auto maintenance.

Yukon tourism. www.
yukonweb.com/tourism.

BC Ferries can carry a car from Bellingham, Washington, to Skagway, Alaska. From
there you can drive the Klondike Highway over the White Pass—the route of
the historic Klondike Trail—into Whitehorse. Another route runs from Haines,
Alaska to the Kluane National Park reserve and into Whitehorse.

Buses follow the Alaska Highway from Vancouver, B.C., and Edmonton,
Alberta.

By air, the Yukon can be reached through the capital of Whitehorse, with
service from Vancouver and from Fairbanks and Juneau in Alaska.

Temperatures in Dawson City may occasionally plummet to −58 degrees
Fahrenheit in January, but are just as likely to reach 100 degrees in July; and
in summer there is nearly twenty-four hours of light in the northern sections.

The interior of the Yukon is semi-arid in the winter with relatively little
snow, although winter sports are available. In February the **Yukon Quest Sled
Dog Race** is something of a rival to the famed Iditarod in Alaska. Cross-
country skiing, snowmobiling, and snow shoeing are popular in mountainous
areas, including the Saint Elias Mountains.

Hiking the Chilkoot Trail

In 1898 stampeders in search of gold hauled tons of supplies along the
Chilkoot Trail and over the White Pass. Many of them had to make their way
up and down the pass more than twenty times to hand-carry their loads to the
frozen shores of Lake Bennett. There they would spend the winter construct-
ing rafts to float down the Yukon River to Dawson City.

Today the Chilkoot Trail is a treasure for hikers; it is the largest National
Historic Site in Canada. Summer weather and modern backpacks make passage
easier, but hikers must still be prepared for challenges. Even in the middle of
the summer a hiker needs to be prepared for nearly any kind of weather at the
summit, including snow.

The old prospectors left the route strewn with boots, shovels, picks, wagon
wheels, pot-bellied stoves, and other previous commodities of a time long past.

The Chilkoot begins at sea-level in Dyea, Alaska, about ten miles outside of
Skagway. The Trail passes Crater Lake, Deep Lake, and the Gold Rush towns of
Happy Camp and Lindeman enroute to Bennett, which is the last stop. From
Bennett hikers can continue on to Fraser and ride the White Pass & Yukon
Route train back into Skagway.

The hike takes about three to five days. Hikers should register at the ranger
station at the trailhead in Dyea.

Fishing in the Yukon

The magnificent salmon, after living out their lives in the oceans, return to the
freshwater stream in which they were born to spawn and die. The trip is quite
difficult with watery obstacles, fishing bears, and hunting eagles; only a
fraction of the salmon make it all the way home.

WHITEHORSE

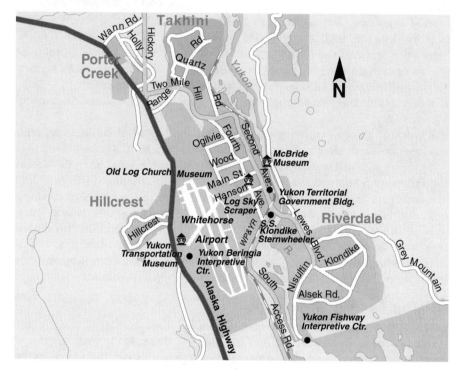

The salmon of the Yukon's Tatshenshini River travel about a hundred miles up from the sea, while others swim up the Yukon River, more than a thousand miles. The best fishing spot is considered to be Dalton Post, but salmon are also common on the Yukon, the Stewart, and other rivers. There are also bountiful numbers of trout, pike, and grayling in streams, rivers, and lakes.

Whitehorse

More than two-thirds of the inhabitants of the Yukon live in and around Whitehorse, population twenty-four thousand.

Whitehorse didn't even exist during the gold rush days, when Dawson reached a population of thirty thousand. The town is named after the rapids on the Yukon River south of the present city that to some resembled flowing manes of a charging white horse. On the "Trail of '98," the rapids and Miles Canyon were considered the greatest peril on the water route to the gold fields; stampeders were forced to go around the water to avoid losing their precious grubstakes by floating on makeshift rafts.

In 1897 entrepreneurs built tramways on both sides of the river at the rapids. For a fee, horse-drawn tram cars on the grandly named Canyon & White Horse Rapids Tramway Company carried goods and small boats on log rails to avoid the rapids. A roadhouse and saloon also sprung up at the tram site.

In 1900 the White Pass & Yukon Route Railway was completed to a point past the rapids, and the town of Whitehorse developed around the terminal.

Most prospectors continued to Dawson by riverboat.

During World War II thousands of American service personnel arrived in Whitehorse to build the Alaska Highway. In the incredibly short period of less than nine months, a highway of 1,534 miles was laid down. The territorial capital was moved to Whitehorse from Dawson in the 1950s.

The construction of a hydroelectric dam in 1958 tamed Miles Canyon and submerged White Horse Rapids within the Schwatka Lake Reservoir.

The **MacBride Museum in Whitehorse** covers the human and natural life of the Yukon from the cultural heritage of the First Nations to the Klondike Days and the present. Among the prizes of the collection is the only remaining tram car from the White Horse Rapids system and Sam McGee's cabin, the Sam McGee immortalized in Robert Service's poem *The Cremation of Sam McGee*. For information, call ☎ (867) 667-2709 or consult 🖳 www.macbridemuseum.com.

You can get a feel for the riverboats that were the region's main form of transport for fifty years by touring the **SS** *Klondike*, one of the last large boats to ply the Yukon's waters. The trip downstream to Dawson, carrying supplies and passengers, took a day and a half; on the five-day upstream trip back to Whitehorse, the vessel was loaded down with gold and silver ore and ingots. The 210-foot-long vessel cruised at a draft of just forty inches.

The ship is now a Parks Canada Historic Site on the Whitehorse waterfront at 300 Main Street. The *Klondike* was launched in 1937 as a rebuilt version of an earlier ship of the same name. For information, call ☎ (867) 667-3910 or consult 🖳 parkscan.harbour.com/khs.

Local entertainment includes *Frantic Follies* at the Westmark Whitehorse, presented nightly from May to mid-September. The vaudeville review somehow manages to combine a version of *The Cremation of Sam McGee* and can-can girls. For information, call ☎ (867) 668-2042.

Planes, trains, ships, and dog sleds are celebrated at the **Yukon Transportation Museum** on the Alaska Highway near the Whitehorse airport. Open daily from mid-May to mid-September. For information, call ☎ (867) 668-4792.

The **White Pass & Yukon Route Railroad**, a narrow-gauge railroad with some spectacular wooden trestles, mountain-hugging roadbeds, rushing torrents, and cascading falls, is open to tourists. Bus service from Whitehorse connects to the rail line and goes onward to Skagway, Alaska. For information on the "railway built of gold," call ☎ (800) 343-7373 or ☎ (867) 668-7245.

Dawson

The Klondike Highway connects Whitehorse to Dawson, which is about a six-hour drive. In some ways Dawson is little changed from the way it was at the height of the gold rush. In between the classic boardwalk sidewalks, the streets are still constructed of hard-packed gravel. This is not just any gravel, though; it comes from gold-bearing creek beds, a highway more or less paved with gold.

Along the levee are shops and souvenir stores of Front Street, including the old Canadian Bank of Commerce Building, the very bank were Robert Service worked and composed some of his later poems. Ironically, it was during his time in Whitehorse—before he'd even set foot in the Klondike—that Service wrote two of his most famous Klondike poems: *The Cremation of Sam McGee* and *The Shooting of Dan McGrew.*

Service's poems are painted on the sides of buildings, and there are regular performances of his works at his old cabin, located next to Jack London's place on Eighth Street. London's tiny sod-roofed cabin was moved into town from the "bush" to create a small literary neighborhood on Dawson's East Side.

The gold mining industry is still alive with some 250 active mines near Dawson. Some of the mines welcome visitors, but it is best to inquire before-hand. Several companies offer tours to the mines from Dawson.

The gold mining method has changed little from the days of the Klondike rush. Miners dig the "pay dirt" (the gold-bearing layer, generally in an ancient stream bed). The pay dirt is shaken down through a rocker box that removes the larger rocks. What's left is run through a sluice, a contraption that mimics stream action by washing the pay dirt down a precisely angled trough.

Gold is a heavier element, nineteen times denser than water; in the sluice, gold flakes sink to be caught in riffles along the bottom. A century after the sourdoughs panned these same streams, the last step still involves shaking down the gold in a rusty steel pan.

Further up Bonanza Creek is the ghost town of Grand Forks, which grew to a population of ten thousand people at a point where the gold-laden Eldorado and Bonanza creeks come together. Today a few shacks on the side of the valley are all that is left of the town. But the rain still brings material down from the valley sides each year, and some of the muck contains gold.

In mid-July the **Dawson Music Festival** draws music lovers from Alaska to Seattle. Held under a large tent in Minto Park, the music usually ranges from folk to danceable rock. Late August brings **Discovery Days**, the celebration of the gold find at Bonanza Creek that put Dawson on the map.

Dredge #4

The earlier prospectors and today's mostly small-scale operators searched the *placers* of the Yukon—the river and streambeds that carried flakes and chunks of gold down from the hills. Prospectors looked for gold in pans and sluices.

In between came the dredges: huge machines that slowly made their way up and down the creek beds, chewing up everything clear down to bedrock and processing it all within before spitting out the rocks behind. The trails of the dredges still spill across the valley floors like giant worm tracks, with mounts of rubble and rounded alluvial rock piled as high as fifty feet.

The dredges are gone, with one exception. Dredge #4, a three-thousand-ton monster, had dredging buckets each weighing two-and-a-half tons, and there were seventy-two of them in a continuous chain that pulled up material from the creek bed and dumped it into the gold sluices. Locals say the noise of the machine in action could be heard eleven miles away, and its vibrations felt nearly as far. Dredge #4 made its way up and down the valley three times until it sunk in 1960. The machine was removed and restored three decades later.

For information on the site, call ☎ (867) 993-5462 or consult 💻 parkscanada. pch.gc.ca/parks/yukon/Dredge_no4.

Appendix

National Historic Sites in Canada

Alexander Graham Bell. Baddeck, Nova Scotia. ☎ (902) 295-2069. 💻 www.parcs canada.gc.ca/parks/nova_scotia/alex_g_bell/Alex_g_bell_e.htm

Banff Park Museum. Banff, Alberta. 💻 www.worldweb.com/ParksCanada-Banff/museum.html

Bar U Ranch. Longview, Alberta. Historic ranch. ☎ (800) 568-4996. 💻 www.parcs canada.gc.ca/parks/alberta/bar_u_ranch

Batoche. Rosthern, Saskatchewan, northeast of Saskatoon. Métis village, site of the 1885 Battle of Batoche. ☎ (306) 423-6227. 💻 www.parcscanada.gc.ca/parks/saskatchewan/batoche

Battle of the Châteauguay. Howick, Quebec, southwest of Montréal. The site of an 1813 battle in defense of Lower Canada. ☎ (450) 829-2003. 💻 www.parcscanada.gc.ca/ parks/quebec/chateauguay

Battle of the Restigouche. Pointe-à-la-Croix, Québec, on the north shore of Chaleur Bay on the Quebec/New Brunswick border. Site of the last naval battle of the Seven Years War. ☎ (418) 788-5676. 💻 www.parcscanada.gc.ca/parks/quebec/ristigouche

Battle of the Windmill. Prescott, Ontario. The site of a failed American invasion in 1838. ☎ (613) 925-2896. 💻 www.parcscanada.gc.ca/parks/ontario/battle_windmill

Beaubears Island. Kouchibouguac National Park, New Brunswick. An Acadian refugee settlement of the mid-eighteenth century. ☎ (506) 876-2443. 💻 www.parcs canada.gc.ca/parks/new_brunswick/beaubears_island

Bellevue House. Kingston, Ontario. Italianate villa, home of Sir John A. Macdonald, Canada's first premier. ☎ (613) 545-8666. 💻 www.parcscanada.gc.ca/parks/ontario/bellevue_house

Bethune Memorial House. Gravenhurst, Ontario. The birthplace of a renowned Canadian doctor, Norman Bethune. ☎ (705) 687-4261. 💻 www.parcscanada.gc.ca/parks/ontario/bethune_memorial_house

Bois Blanc Island Lighthouse. Gravenhurst, Ontario. Round stone light tower of 1837. 💻 www.parcscanada.gc.ca/parks/ontario/bois_blanc_lths/ bois_blanc_lths_e.htm

Butler's Barracks. Niagara-on-the-Lake, Ontario. Home to 150 years of military history. ☎ (905) 468-4257. 💻 www.parcscanada.gc.ca/parks/ontario/butlers_barracks

Cape Spear. West of Saint John's, Newfoundland. The oldest lighthouse in Newfoundland, built in 1836. ☎ (709) 772-5367. 💻 www.parcscanada.gc.ca/parks/newfound land/cape_spear

Carillon Barracks. Carillon, Quebec. Early nineteenth-century stone military building. ☎ (450) 447-4847. 💻 www.parcscanada.gc.ca/parks/quebec/casernecarillon

Carillon Canal. Carillon, Quebec. An operational canal on the same site as two earlier canals. 💻 parkscanada.pch.gc.ca/parks/Quebec/canalcarillon/ index_e.html

Carleton Martello Tower. West Saint John, New Brunswick. Fortification built to defend the city of Saint John during the War of 1812. ☎ (506) 636-4011. 🔳 www.parcscanada.gc.ca/parks/new_brunswick/carleton_ martello_tower

Cartier-Brébeuf. Québec City, Quebec. Wintering place of Jacques Cartier from 1535–36. ☎ (418) 648-4038. 🔳 www.parcscanada.gc.ca/parks/quebec/brebeuf

Castle Hill. Placentia, Newfoundland. Seventeenth- and eighteenth-century French and British fortifications. ☎ (709) 227-2401. 🔳 www.parcscanada.gc.ca/parks/newfoundland/castle_hill

Cave and Basin. Banff, Alberta. Warm thermal springs; the birthplace of the National Parks of Canada system. 🔳 www.worldweb.com/ParksCanada-Banff/cave.html

Chambly Canal. Chambly, Quebec. An operational canal; nine locks and swing bridges. ☎ (800) 463-6769. 🔳 parkscanada.pch.gc.ca/parks/quebec/canalchambly

Chilkoot Trail. Whitehorse, Yukon. The transportation route to the Klondike gold fields. ☎ (800) 661-0486. 🔳 parkscan.harbour.com/ct

Coteau-du-Lac. Coteau-du-Lac, Quebec. Remains of eighteenth-century canal and defense structures. ☎ (450) 763-5631. 🔳 www.parcscanada.gc.ca/parks/quebec/coteau

Dawson Historic Complex. Dawson City, Yukon Territory. Buildings from the Klondike Gold Rush. ☎ (867) 993-7200. 🔳 parkscan.harbour.com/khs

Dredge #4, Dawson City, Yukon Territory. A Bonanza Creek gold dredge built in 1912. ☎ (867) 993-5462. 🔳 www.parcscanada.gc.ca/parks/yukon/Dredge_no4

Fisgard Lighthouse. West of Victoria, Vancouver Island, British Columbia. The first permanent lighthouse on Canada's west coast. ☎ (250) 478-5849. 🔳 parkscan.harbour. com/frh

Forges du Saint-Maurice. Trois-Rivières, Québec. Remains of Canada's first industrial village. ☎ (819) 378-5116. 🔳 www.parcscanada.gc.ca/parks/quebec/forges.

The Forks. Winnipeg, Manitoba. A historic meeting place at the junction of the Red and Assiniboine rivers. ☎ (204) 983-6757 or ☎ (888) 748-2928. 🔳 www.parcs canada.gc.ca/parks/manitoba/the_forks

Fort Anne. Annapolis Royal, Nova Scotia. Fortifications started in 1695; birthplace of the National Historic Sites of Canada system. ☎ (902) 532-2321. 🔳 www.parcs canada.gc.ca/parks/nova_scotia/fort_anne

Fort Battleford. Battleford, Saskatchewan. North West Mounted Police headquarters; 1876. ☎ (306) 937-2621. 🔳 www.parcscanada.gc.ca/parks/saskatchewan/fort_battleford

Fort Beauséjour. Aulac, New Brunswick. Eighteenth-century French and English fortifications. ☎ (506) 536-0720. 🔳 www.parcscanada.gc.ca/parks/new_brunswick/fort_beausejour

Fort Chambly. Chambly, Quebec. A restored 1709 stone fort. ☎ (450) 658-1585. 🔳 www.parcscanada.gc.ca/parks/quebec/fortchambly

Fort Edward. Annapolis Royal, Nova Scotia. The oldest blockhouse in Canada, built in 1750. ☎ (902) 532-2321 or during July and August, ☎ (902) 798-4706. 🔳 www.parcscanada.gc.ca/parks/nova_scotia/fort_edward

Fort George. Niagara-on-the-Lake, Ontario. A reconstructed British fort from the War of 1812. ☎ (905) 468-4257. 🔳 www.parcscanada.gc.ca/parks/ontario/fort_george

Fortifications of Québec. Quebec City, Quebec. A five-kilometer network of walls, gates and squares, dating from the seventeenth century to the twentieth century. ☎ (418) 648-7016 or ☎ (800) 463-6769. 🔳 www.parcscanada.gc.ca/parks/quebec/fortifications

Fort Langley. Fort Langley, British Columbia. An early nineteenth-century Hudson's Bay Company post. ☎ (604) 513-4777. 🔳 parkscan.harbour.com/fl

Fort Lennox. Saint-Paul-de-l'Île-aux-Noix, Quebec. An outstanding example of early nineteenth-century fortifications. ☎ (450) 291-5700. 🔳 www.parcscanada.gc.ca/parks/quebec/fortlennox

Fort Malden. Amherstburg, Ontario. A nineteenth-century border fortification. ☎ (519) 736-5416. 📖 www.parcscanada.gc.ca/parks/ontario/fort_malden

Fort McNab. Halifax, Nova Scotia. A fort built in 1889 to defend Halifax harbor. ☎ (902) 426-5080. 📖 www.parcscanada.gc.ca/parks/nova_scotia/fort_mcnab

Fort Mississauga. Niagara-on-the-Lake, Ontario. A nineteenth-century brick tower within star-shaped earthworks. ☎ (905) 468-4257. 📖 www.parcscanada.gc.ca/parks/ontario/fort_mississauga

Fort No. 1 at Pointe de Lévy. Quebec City, Quebec. A part of the nineteenth-century defenses of the city of Québec. ☎ (418) 835-5182 or ☎ (800) 800-463-6769. 📖 www.parcscanada.gc.ca/parks/quebec/levy

Fort Rodd Hill. Vancouver Island. A late nineteenth-century fort built to defend Victoria-Esquimalt. 📖 parkscan.harbour.com/frh

Fort Saint James. Fort Saint James, British Columbia. A fur trade post founded by Simon Fraser in 1806. ☎ (250) 996-7191. 📖 parkscan.harbour.com/fsj

Fort Saint Joseph. Richards Landing, Ontario, near Sault Ste. Marie. Remains of the most westerly British frontier outpost between 1796 and 1812; active in the War of 1812. Summer: ☎ (705) 246-1796. Winter: ☎ (705) 941-6200. 📖 www.parcscanada.gc.ca/parks/ontario/fort_Saint-joseph

Fort Témiscamingue. Ville-Marie, Quebec. Remains of an important fur trading post operated by English and French companies and by free traders; founded in 1679 and closed in 1901. ☎ (819) 629-3222. 📖 www.parcscanada.gc.ca/parks/quebec/temiscamingue

Fort Walsh. Maple Creek, Saskatchewan. An early North West Mounted Police post. May to October: ☎ (306) 662-3590. 📖 www.parcscanada.gc.ca/parks/saskatchewan/ fort_walsh

Fort Wellington. Prescott, Ontario. Remains of 1813-38 fortifications. ☎ (613) 925-2896. 📖 www.parcscanada.gc.ca/parks/ontario/fort_wellington

Fortress of Louisbourg. Louisbourg, Nova Scotia. A reconstruction of the eighteenth-century French fortress. ☎ (902) 733-2280. 📖 www.parcscanada.gc.ca/parks/nova_scotia/fortress_louisbourg

The Fur Trade at Lachine. Lachine, Quebec. An 1803 stone warehouse used as a depot. ☎ (514) 637-7433 or ☎ (514) 283-6054. 📖 www.parcscanada.gc.ca/parks/quebec/fourrure/en/index.html

Georges Island. Halifax, Nova Scotia harbor fortifications, including Fort Charlotte. ☎ (902) 426-5080. 📖 www.parcscanada.gc.ca/parks/nova_scotia/georges_island

Grande-Grave. Gaspé, Quebec. A former coastal fishing village. ☎ (418) 368-5505. 📖 www.parcscanada.gc.ca/parks/quebec/grande-grave

Grand-Pré. Grand-Pré, Nova Scotia. A commemoration of the history of the Acadians and the Deportation of 1755. ☎ (902) 542-3631. 📖 www.parcscanada.gc.ca/parks/nova_scotia/grand_pre

Grassy Island. Baddeck, Nova Scotia. An eighteenth-century center of the English fishery. ☎ (902) 295-2069. 📖 www.parcscanada.gc.ca/parks/nova_scotia/grassy_island

Grosse Île and the Irish Memorial. Quebec City, Quebec. The quarantine station for immigrants from 1832 to 1937. ☎ (418) 248-8888 or ☎ (800) 463-6769. 📖 www.parcscanada.gc.ca/parks/quebec/grosseile

Gulf of Georgia Cannery. Richmond, British Columbia. An West Coast fish processing complex at historic Steveston Village. ☎ (604) 664-9009. 📖 parkscan.harbour.com/ggc

Halifax Citadel. Halifax, Nova Scotia. A restored British fort from 1828-56. ☎ (902) 426-5080. 📖 www.parcscanada.gc.ca/parks/ nova_scotia/halifax_citadel

Hawthorne Cottage. Saint John's, Newfoundland. Picturesque cottage, home of arctic explorer Captain Bob Bartlett. Summer: ☎ (709) 528-4004. Off-season: ☎ (709) 753-9262. 📖 www.parcscanada.gc.ca/parks/newfoundland/hawthorne_cottage

Inverarden House. Prescott, Ontario. An important 1816 Regency cottage built by North West Company trader John McDonald. ☎ (613) 925-2896. 🖳 www.parcscanada. gc.ca/parks/ontario/inverarden_house

Kejimkujik. An important Mi'kmaq cultural landscape. ☎ (902) 682-2772. 🖳 www.parcscanada.gc.ca/keji

Kingston Martello Towers. Kingston, Ontario. Mid-nineteenth-century British masonry fortifications to protect against American forays. ☎ (613) 545-8666. 🖳 www.parcscanada.gc.ca/parks/ontario/kingston_m_tower

Kitwanga Fort. Between New Hazelton and Terrace, in northern British Columbia. A Tsimshian village. ☎ (250) 559-8818. 🖳 parkscan.harbour.com/kf

Lachine Canal. Montreal, Quebec. A set of former locks with railway and road bridges. ☎ (514) 283-6054. 🖳 www.parcscanada.gc.ca/parks/quebec/canallachine

L'Anse aux Meadows. Saint Lunaire-Griquet, Newfoundland. The only authenticated Viking settlement in North America. ☎ (709) 623-2608. 🖳 www.parcs canada.gc.ca/parks/newfoundland/anse_meadows

Laurier House. Ottawa, Ontario. The 1878 Second Empire home of two prime ministers, Sir Wilfrid Laurier and William Lyon Mackenzie King. ☎ (613) 992-8142. 🖳 www.parcscanada.gc.ca/parks/ontario/laurier_house

Lower Fort Garry. Selkirk, Manitoba. A major center of the nineteenth-century fur trade. ☎ (204) 785-6050. 🖳 www.parcscanada.gc.ca/parks/manitoba/lower_fort_garry

Manoir Papineau. Montebello, Quebec. A nineteenth-century manor, home of Patriot leader Louis-Joseph Papineau. ☎ (819) 423-6965. 🖳 www.parcscanada.gc.ca/ parks/quebec/papineau

Marconi. Glace Bay, Nova Scotia. The site of the first wireless station in Canada. ☎ (902) 295-2069. 🖳 www.parcscanada.gc.ca/parks/nova_scotia/ marconi

Monument Lefebvre. Kouchibouguac National Park, Memramcook, New Brunswick. A landmark of Acadian culture in a nineteenth-century college building. 🖳 www.parcscanada.gc.ca/parks/new_brunswick/monument_lefebvre

Motherwell Homestead. Abernethy, Saskatchewan. The 1912 farmstead of a pioneer farmer and politician. ☎ (306) 333-2116. 🖳 www.parcscanada.gc.ca/parks/ saskatchewan/motherwell_homestead

Navy Island. Niagara-on-the-Lake, Ontario. The site of the first British shipyard serving the upper Great Lakes, it played an important role in the Rebellion of 1837. ☎ (416) 468-4257. 🖳 www.parcscanada.gc.ca/parks/ontario/navy_island

Point Clark Lighthouse. Kitchener, Ontario. An 1859 Imperial Tower and lightkeeper's house on Lake Huron. ☎ (519) 571-5684. 🖳 www.parcscanada.gc.ca/ parks/ontario/ point_clark_lths

Pointe-au-Père Lighthouse. Pointe-au-Père, Quebec. An early reinforced concrete tower at a strategic location on the Saint Lawrence River. ☎ (418) 724-6214. 🖳 www.parcscanada.gc.ca/parks/quebec/phare-pointe-pere

Port au Choix. Saint Lunaire-Griquet, Newfoundland. Prehistoric burial and habitation sites on the west coast of Newfoundland. Summer: ☎ (709) 861-3522. Off-season: ☎ (709) 458-2417. 🖳 www.parcscanada.gc.ca/parks/newfoundland/port_choix

Port-la-Joye-Fort Amherst. Charlottetown, Prince Edward Island. Remains of early British and French fortifications. ☎ (902) 566-7050. 🖳 www.parcscanada.gc.ca/ parks/pei/plj_ftamherst

Port-Royal. Annapolis Royal, Nova Scotia. A reconstruction of the 1605 French settlement. Summer: 902-532-2898. Off-season: ☎ (902) 532-2321. 🖳 www.parcs canada.gc.ca/parks/nova_scotia/port_royal

Prince of Wales Fort. Churchill, Manitoba. An eighteenth-century stone fur trade fort on Hudson Bay. ☎ (888) 748-2928. 🖳 www.parcscanada.gc.ca/parks/manitoba/ Prince_Wales_Fort

Prince of Wales Tower. Halifax, Nova Scotia. A late eighteenth-century stone defense tower. ☎ (902) 426-5080. 🖳 www.parcscanada.gc.ca/parks/nova_scotia/ prince_wales_tower

Province House. Charlottetown, Prince Edward Island. A Neoclassical building, the birthplace of Confederation. ☎ (902) 566-7050. 🖳 www.parcscanada.gc.ca/parks/pei/province_house

Queenston Heights. Niagara-on-the-Lake, Ontario. The site of the 1812 Battle of Queenston Heights; includes Brock's Monument. ☎ (905) 468-4257. 🖳 www.parcs canada.gc.ca/parks/ontario/queenston_heights

Red Bay. Red Bay, Labrador. Sixteenth-century Basque whaling operation. Summer: ☎ (709) 920-2142. Off-season: ☎ (709) 458-2417. 🖳 www.parcscanada.gc.ca/parks/newfoundland/Red_Bay

Rideau Canal. Smiths Falls, Ontario. An operational nineteenth-century canal, 202 kilometers long, with forty-five locks. ☎ (613) 283-5170 or ☎ (800) 230-0016. 🖳 www.parcscanada.gc.ca/parks/ontario/rideau_canal

Riel House. Winnipeg, Manitoba. The family home of Métis leader Louis Riel. ☎ (204) 257-1783 or ☎ (888) 748-2928. 🖳 www.parcscanada.gc.ca/parks/manitoba/riel_house

Rocky Mountain House. Rocky Mountain House, Alberta. Remains of rival Hudson's Bay Company and North West Company posts. ☎ (403) 845-2412. 🖳 www.parcscanada.gc.ca/parks/alberta/Rocky_mountain_house

Ryan Premises. Bonavista, Newfoundland. A complex linked to the fishing industry on the East Coast. ☎ (709) 533-2801. 🖳 www.parcscanada.gc.ca/parks/newfoundland/ryan_premises

SS *Keno*. Dawson City, Yukon Territory. One of last of the Yukon steamboats. ☎ (867) 993-7200 or ☎ (867) 993-7237. 🖳 parkscan.harbour.com/khs/index.htm

SS *Klondike*. Whitehorse, Yukon Territory. The largest and last Yukon commercial steamboat. ☎ (800) 661-0486. 🖳 parkscan.harbour.com/ssk

Sainte-Anne-de-Bellevue Canal. Sainte-Anne, Quebec. An operational canal built on the site of an earlier 1843 canal. ☎ (450) 457-5546. ☎ (800) 463-6769. 🖳 parks canada.pch.gc.ca/parks/quebec/canalsteanne

Saint-Louis Mission. Honey Harbour, Ontario. The site of a Huron village destroyed by the Iroquois in 1649. ☎ (705) 756-2415. 🖳 www.parcscanada.gc.ca/parks/ontario/st-louis_mission

Saint-Ours Canal. Saint-Ours, Quebec. An operational canal; a 1933 lock and remains of the 1849 lock. ☎ (450) 785-2212 or ☎ (800) 463-6769. 🖳 parkscanada.pch.gc.ca/parks/quebec/canalstours

Sault Ste. Marie Canal. Sault Ste. Marie, Ontario. An operational canal that included the world's first electrically powered lock. ☎ (705) 941-6262 or ☎ (705) 941-6205. 🖳 www.parcscanada.gc.ca/parks/ontario/sault_st-marie_canal

Signal Hill. Saint John's, Newfoundland. A commemoration of the defense of Saint John's; includes the Cabot Tower. ☎ (709) 772-5367. 🖳 www.parcscanada.gc.ca/parks/newfoundland/signal_hill

Southwold Earthworks. Leamington, Ontario. The site of an Attiwandaronk village, circa A.D. 1500. ☎ (519) 322-2365. 🖳 www.parcscanada.gc.ca/parks/ontario/southwold_earthworks

Saint Andrews Blockhouse. Alma, New Brunswick. A restored wooden blockhouse from the War of 1812. Summer: ☎ (506) 529-4270. Off-season: ☎ (506) 887-6000. 🖳 www.parcscanada.gc.ca/parks/new_brunswick/ st_andrews_blockhouse

Saint Andrew's Rectory. Selkirk, Manitoba. An example of mid-nineteenth-century Red River architecture. ☎ (204) 785-6050 or ☎ (888) 748-2928. 🖳 www.parcscanada. gc.ca/parks/manitoba/st_andrews_rectory

Saint Peters Canal. Saint Peters, Nova Scotia. An operational canal with structures dating from nineteenth-century. ☎ (902) 733-2280. 🖳 www.parcscanada.gc.ca/parks/nova_scotia/st_peters_canal

Trent-Severn Waterway. Peterborough, Ontario. An operational canal linking lakes Ontario and Huron; 386 kilometers long with forty-five locks. ☎ (800) 663-2628. 🖳 www.parcscanada.gc.ca/parks/ontario/trent-sev-waterway

York Factory. Churchill, Manitoba. The Hudson's Bay Company's principal fur trade depot from 1684 until the 1870s. ☎ (204) 675-8863 or ☎ (888) 748-2928. 💻 www.parcscanada.gc.ca/york

York Redoubt. Halifax, Nova Scotia. Major seaward defenses of Halifax harbor from the American Revolutionary War until the Second World War. ☎ (902) 426-5080. 💻 www.parcscanada.gc.ca/redoubt

Save 10%

Off our regular low rack rate

- FREE Continental breakfast
- FREE 24-hour airport shuttle
- Jacuzzi and family suites
- Guest laundry facilities
- FREE local calls
- Kitchenette rooms
- Exercise room
- Cable TV with free HBO

3 blocks from airport, just minutes from downtown and major mall

Mention VIP Code #0099. Present coupon at check-in. Subject to availability, with advance reservations. Not valid with any other discount or package rate. Not available July 9 through July 13, 2001. Valid through December 31, 2002

CAN02-17

Seattle/Tacoma International Airport
19015 International Blvd. South
Seattle, WA 98188
(206) 244-3600

Save 10%

Off our regular low rack rate. Our NEW hotel offers:

- FREE 24-hour airport shuttle
- FREE Continental breakfast
- Meeting facility
- Guest laundry
- FREE HBO
- In-room coffee
- Pay per view movies
- Exercise room

Only minutes from Seattle/Tacoma International Airport

Present coupon at check-in. Subject to availability, with advance reservations. Not valid with any other discount or package rate. Not available July 9 through July 13, 2001. Valid through December 31, 2002

CAN02-16

SeaTac Airport
20406 International Blvd. South
SeaTac, WA 98188
(206) 878-3600

Save 10%

Off our regular low rack rate

- FREE Continental breakfast
- Kitchenette rooms
- Guest laundry facilities
- FREE local calls
- Jacuzzi rooms
- Cable TV

Minutes from U of W downtown, Edmonds waterfront, and ferry

Mention VIP Code #0099 Present coupon at check-in. Subject to availability, with advance reservations. Not valid with any other discount or package rate. Not available July 9 through July 13, 2001. Valid through December 31, 2002

CAN02-15

North Seattle
19527 Aurora Ave. North
Seattle, WA 98133
(206) 542-6300

$79 Promotional Rate

Included are the following complimentary services:

- FREE Continental breakfast
- FREE 24-hour airport transportation
- FREE Local phone calls
- FREE Parking
- Kids 12 and under eat free

Must mention coupon at time of reservation and present coupon upon check-in. Subject to availability. Not valid July–September.
Expires 12/31/2002

1-800-HOLIDAY

CAN02-18

HOTEL & SUITES

22318 84th Ave. South
Kent, WA 98032
(253) 395-4300

Quick-Find Index to Canada

Academy of Spherical Arts, Toronto (Ont) 175
Acadians 255–256, 272, 280
Acadian Museum (NB). 268
Aero Space Museum of Calgary (Alb) 101
Airlines 29–33
Airports, Alberta 108
Airports, British Columbia. 46
Airports, Edmonton. 127
Airports, Montréal. 209
Airports, Ontario. 157
Airports, Québec City 236
Alberta. 91–136
Alberta festivals and events 95–96
Alexander Galt Museum (Alb) 113
Algonquin Provincial Park (Ont). 193–195
Annapolis Royal (NS). 290
Anne of Green Gables 271–272
Anne's Land (PEI). 271–272
Apex Mountain Resort (BC). 84
Appalachian Mountains. 3, 6
Aquarium des Îles (Que) 248
Arctic 3, 7
Argenteuil Regional Museum (Que) 223
Art Gallery of Greater Victoria (BC) 68–69
Art Gallery of Nova Scotia. 287
Art Gallery of Ontario, Toronto (Ont) 173
Arthur Conan Doyle Collection,
    Toronto (Ont). 175
Artillery Park, Québec City (Que) 239
Athabasca River (Alb) 133
Atikaki Wilderness Park (Man). 154
Atlas Coal Mine (Alb) 110
Baddeck (NS). 294
Baffin Island (Nun) 299–300
Banff National Park (Alb). 129
Bar U Ranch (Alb) 111–112
Barkerville (BC). 87
Basque-American Adventure Park (Que) 245
Bata Shoe Museum, Toronto (Ont) 176
Batoche, Saskatoon (Sask) 147
Battle of the Châteauguay (Que) 232
Bay of Fundy (NB) 280–281
Bay/Adelaide Cloud Forest Conservatory,
    Toronto (Ont). 175
BC Ferries. 47, 48, 49, 317
BC Rail 46
BC Transit 61–62
Bell, Alexander Graham. 294
Bellevue Underground Mine (Alb) 113
Big Nickel (Ont). 196
Big White Ski Resort (BC) 84
Biodôme, Montréal (Que) 217–218
Biosphere, Montréal (Que). 212
Bloedel Floral Conservatory,
    Vancouver (BC). 60
Boldt Castle (Ont) 169
Bombardier Museum (Que) 233
Bonavista Peninsula (Newf) 261–262
Bore Park (NB) 267–268
Botanical Garden, Montréal (Que) 217
Brantford (Ont) 192
Bridal Veil Falls (BC) 44
British Columbia 39–90
British Columbia festivals and events 50–52
British Columbia Forest Museum,
    Vancouver Island (BC) 73

British Columbia Museum of Anthropology,
    Vancouver (BC) 58–59
British Columbia Museum of Mining (BC) . . 81–82
Brittania Beach Mines (BC) 81–82
Bucket shops. See Consolidators
Buffalo Pounds Provincial Park (Sask) 142
Burlington (Ont) 192
Burnaby Heritage Village (BC) 89
Burrard Inlet (BC) 53
Butchart Gardens, Victoria (BC) 70–72
Bytown Museum, Ottawa (Ont) 166
C&E Railway Museum, Edmonton (Alb) 120
Cabane a sucre Lalande (Que) 227
Cabot Trail (NS) 292–293, 294
Calaway Park, Calgary (Alb). 105
Calgary (Alb) 97–114
Calgary Cannons baseball 107
Calgary Flames hockey 107
Calgary performing arts 107–108
Calgary Science Centre (Alb) 101
Calgary Stampede (Alb) 98–99
Calgary Stampeders football 107
Calgary Tower (Alb). 100
Calgary Transit 108
Calgary Zoo (Alb). 100–101
Campobello (NB) 277–278
Canada Olympic Park (Alb) 105
Canada
    Climate. 13–18
    Geological regions 3
    Government 26–28
    History 23–28
    Holidays. 11
    Parliament. 26–27
    Population 2
    Size of provinces. 2
    Time zones 10–11
Canadian Automotive Museum (Ont). 179
Canadian Canoe Museum (Ont). 180
Canadian Museum of Civilization,
    Ottawa (Ont) 165
Canadian Museum of Contemporary
    Photography, Ottawa (Ont) 165
Canadian Museum of Nature, Ottawa (Ont) . . . 165
Canadian National Exhibition,
    Toronto (Ont) 177
Canadian National Historic Windpower
    Centre (Alb) 114
Canadian National Railway 20
Canadian Pacific Railway 20, 94
Canadian Railway Museum (Que) 230
Canadian Shield 3–6
Canadian Warplane Heritage Museum (Ont) . . 180
Canrail Pass 21
Cap Tourmente National Wildlife Area (Que). . 241
Cap-de-Bon-Désir Interpretation and
    Observation Centre (Que) 251
Cape Bonavista Lighthouse (Newf) 262
Cape Breton Highlands National Park (NS). . . . 293
Cape Breton Island (NS) 292–293
Cape Spear (Que) 259–260
Capilano Suspension Bridge and Park,
    Vancouver (BC). 61
Carillon (Que). 223
Carr, Emily 68
Casa Loma, Toronto (Ont) 176

Cathedral Grove (BC) 74
Cave and Basin, Banff (Alb) 129–130
Cavell, Edith 134
Ceilidh Trail (NS) 295
Celsius to Fahrenheit conversion 18
Centrale de la Rivière-des-Prairies (Que) . . 225–226
Centre Catherine de-Saint-Augustin,
   Québec City (Que) 239
Centre d'histoire de Montréal (Que) 215
Centre d'interprétation Archéo Topo (Que) . . . 251
Chapelle des Ursulines,
   Québec City (Que) 237–238
Charlevoix (Que) 249–250
Charlotte's Shore (PEI) 270–271
Charlottetown (PEI) 270–271
Château Frontenac, Québec City (Que) 236
Chateau Lake Louise (Alb) 131
Château Ramezay Museum,
   Montréal (Que) 207, 215
Châteauguay National Historic Site (Que) 232
Chilkoot Trail (Yukon) 317
Chinatown, Montréal (Que) 213
Chinatown, Vancouver (BC) 55
Chinatown, Victoria (BC) 64–65
Chinese Cultural Centre (Alb) 104
Churchill Falls Hydroelectric
   Station (Lab) 265
Cinémathèque Québécoise, Montréal (Que) . . . 215
Citadel, Québec City (Que) 239
City of Gold (Que) 253
Clay Products Interpretive Centre (Alb) 111
Clearwater Provincial Park (Man) 153
CN Imax Theatre (BC) 59–60
CN Tower Toronto (Ont) 172–173
Coastal Islands, Vancouver Island (BC) 76–77
Coastal Mountains (BC) 40, 81–86
Cold Lake Provincial Park (Alb) 127
Columbia Icefield (Alb) 133–134
Commons, House of 26–27
Confederation Bridge (PEI) 268
Confederation Trail (PEI) 269–270
Consolidators, airline ticket 31
Contraception Museum (Ont) 175–176
Cook, Captain James 41
Cosmodôme (Que) 225
Coteau-du-Lac (Que) 232
Cowichan Native Heritage Centre (BC) 72–73
Cowichan Valley Museum (BC) 74
Craigdarroch Castle, Victoria (BC) 66–68
Craigflower Manor, Victoria (BC) 69
Creston Valley Wildlife Management
   Area (BC) 87–88
Credit cards 8
Crystal Gardens, Victoria (BC) 65–66
Currency Museum, Ottawa (Ont) 164
Currency, Canadian 7–8, 10
Cypress Bowl (BC) 84
Cypress Hills Interprovincial Park
   (Sask and Alb) 111, 143
Dawson (Yukon) 319–320
Deh Cho Connection (NWT) 313–314
Della Falls (BC) 44
Dempster Highway (NWT) 312–313
Dinosaur Country (Alb) 109–110
Dinosaur Provincial Park (Alb) 110
Dionne Quints Museum (Ont) 195
Doon Heritage Crossroads (Ont) 122
Dorset Eskimo Soapstone Quarry (Newf) 262
Dredge #4 (Yukon) 320
Dressler Home (Ont) 180
Dressler, Marie 180
Drumheller (Alb) 109–111
Dundurn Castle (Ont) 180
Duplessis (Que) 252
Eastern Townships (Que) 231–233
Eau Claire Market (Alb) 104

Edmonton (Alb) 115–128
Edmonton Art Gallery, Edmonton (Alb) 119
Edmonton Mall, West (Alb) 120–122
Edmonton Oilers football 124
Edmonton Police Museum and
   Archives (Alb) 119
Edmonton rail service (Alb) 127
Edmonton Space and Science Centre (Alb) 119
Edmonton street grid (Alb) 128
Edmonton Transit (Alb) 128
Edmonton Trappers baseball 125
Eel Interpretation Site (Que) 245
Ellesmere Island (Nun) 300
Elgin and Winter Garden Theatre,
   Toronto (Ont) 177
Elizabeth II 27
Elmira Railway Museum (PEI) 273
Emily Carr House, Victoria (BC) 68
Empress Hotel, Victoria (BC) 64
Evangeline region (PEI) 272–273
Exchange rate 7–8
Fahrenheit to Celsius conversion 18
Fairbanks Interpretive Centre (NS) 288
Father Lacombe Chapel (Alb) 127
Fernie Alpine Resort (BC) 84
Ferries
   British Columbia 47–50
   Labrador 263
   Newfoundland 259
   Washington State 49
Festivals and events
   Alberta 95–96
   British Columbia 50–52
   Manitoba 154
   New Brunswick 282
   Newfoundland and Labrador 288
   Nova Scotia 295–296
   Ontario 158–160
   Prince Edward Island 273–274
   Québec 204–206
   Saskatchewan 137–140
Fisgard Lighthouse, Victoria (BC) 69–70
Fisheries Museum of the Atlantic (NS) 289
Fleurieneau-Économusée (Que) 227
Forbidden Plateau ski area,
   Vancouver Island (BC) 75
The Forks (Man) 149
Forillon National Park (Que) 247
Fort Anne (NS) 290
Fort Battleford, Saskatoon (Sask) 147
Fort Beauséjour (NB) 269
Fort Calgary Historic Park, Calgary (Alb) 104
Fort Carlton Provincial Historic Park,
   Saskatoon (Sask) 147–148
Fort Chambly (Que) 232
Fort Edmonton, Edmonton (Alb) 117
Fort George (Ont) 186–187
Fort Henry (Ont) 168
Fort Langley (BC) 90
Fort Lennox (Que) 232
Fort McMurray Oil Sands Interpretive
   Centre (Alb) 126
Fort Museum (Alb) 112
Fort Museum (Que) 236
Fort No. 1 at Pointe de Lévy (Que) 243
Fort Normandeau (Alb) 125
Fort Rodd Hill, Victoria (BC) 69
Fort Saint James (BC) 86–87
Fort Steele Heritage Town (BC) 88
Fort Témiscamingue (Que) 253
Fort Walsh (Sask) 143
Fort Whoop-Up (Alb) 92–93, 113–114
Fort Whyte Centre, Winnipeg (Man) 151
Fort York, Toronto (Ont) 174
Fortress of Louisbourg (NS) 293–294
Frank Slide Interpretive Centre (Alb) 113

Fraser River (BC) 41
Fredericton (NB). 275–276
Fundy Geological Museum (NS). 291
Fundy National Park (NB) 281
Gabriola Island (BC) 76
Galliano Island (BC) 76
Galt, Alexander 113
Garibaldi Provincial Park (BC) 49, 82
Gaspé Peninsula (Que) 247–248
Gastown, Vancouver (BC). 54–55
Glacier National Park (BC). 89
Glenbow Museum, Calgary (Alb) 99–100
Glooscap Trail (NS) 290
Goods and Services Tax 10
Governor General, Canada 26–27, 164
Grain Academy, Calgary (Alb) 101
Grand Canyon des chutes
  Sainte-Anne (Que) 241
Grande-Grave (Que) 247
Grand-Pré (NS). 289–290
Granville Island, Vancouver (BC) 56–57
Grass River Provincial Park (Man) 153
Grasslands National Park (Sask) 143–144
Grassy Island (NS) 292
Great Lakes-Saint Lawrence Lowlands 3, 6
Greyhound Canada 127
Gros Morne National Park (Newf) 262
Grosse Île (Que) 243–244
Grouse Mountain, Vancouver (BC) 57, 61, 85
GST. *See* Goods and Services Tax
Gulf of George Cannery (BC). 90
Guy Lombardo Museum (Ont). 191
Halifax (NS) 284–289
Halifax Citadel (NS). 286
Halifax explosion (NS) 284–285
Hamilton Military Museum (Ont) 180
Harbourfront Centre, Toronto (Ont). 178
Hawthorne Cottage (Newf). 260–261
Head Smashed-In Buffalo Jump (Alb) 112
Hecla Provincial Park (Man) 152
Hell's Gate Airtram (BC) 90
Helmcken Falls (BC) 44
Helmcken House, Victoria (BC) 66
Heritage Park Historical Village,
  Calgary (Alb). 104–105
Historic Atlas Coal Mine (Alb). 110
History of Contraception Museum,
  Toronto (Ont) 175–176
Hockey Hall of Fame, Toronto (Ont) 174
Holidays, Canadian 11
Honey Economuseum (Que) 241
Hongkouver 53
Hopewell Cape (NB) 281
Horseshoe Bay (BC). 48
Hotel rates. 35–36
Hudson's Bay Company 92, 116
Hummingbird Centre for the Performing
  Arts (Ont) 177
Icefields Parkway, Jasper (Alb). 133–134
Île aux Basques (Que) 246
Île d'Orleans (Que) 240
Ile Notre Dame, Montréal (Que). 212
Iles de la Madeleine (Que) 247
Immigration 9
Inglewood Bird Sanctuary, Calgary (Alb). . 101–102
Insectarium, Montréal (Que) 217
Inside Passage (BC) 40, 43
Interior Plains 3, 6–7
International Peace Garden (Man) 154
Iqaluit (Nun) 298–299
Irish Memorial (Que) 243–244
Isle-aux-Coudres (Que) 250
James Bay (Ont). 200
Japanese Garden, Montréal (Que) 217
Japantown, Vancouver (BC) 55–56
Jardin zoologique du Québec 241

Jasper (Alb) 134–136
Jasper House (Alb). 133
Jasper National Park (Alb). 132, 134–135
Jasper Tramway (Alb). 134
Jesuit House (Que). 241
Johnston Canyon (Alb). 130–131
Joliette Museum of Art (Que). 229
Just for Laughs Museum, Montréal (Que). 216
Keewatin (Nun) 300–301
Kerry Wood Nature Centre (Alb) 125
Kejimkujik National Park (NS) 290
Killarney Provincial Park (Ont) 197
Kings Landing (NB). 276
Kingston (Ont). 167–169
Kingston Archaeological Centre (Ont) 168
Kitchener (Ont) 191–192
Kitikmeot region (Nun) 301
Kitwanga Fort (BC) 86
Klondike Days, Edmonton (Alb). 122
Klondike Gold Rush. 26
Kokanee Glacier National Park (BC). 87
Kootenay National Park (BC). 88
Kootenay region (BC) 43
Kouchibouguac (NB) 281
'Ksan Indian Village (BC) 86
La Ronde, Montreal (Que) 213
L'Anse Amour Burial Mound (Lab). 264
L'Anse aux Meadows (Newf). 258, 262
L'estrie (Que) 231–233
Labrador 263–266
Labrador Marine 259
Labrador Straits 264
Lachine (Que) 223
Lachine Canal (Que) 223
Lacombe, Father 127
Lafrance Orchards (Que) 227
Lake Louise (Alb) 131–132
Lake Louise Ski Area (Alb) 131–132
Lanaudière (Que) 229–230
Lake Temiscaminque (Que) 253
Lalande Sugar Cabin (Que) 227
Laurentians (Que). 227–229
Laval (Que) 225–226
Le Centre de la Nature (Que) 226
Les Serres Sylvain Cléroux (Que) 227
Les Vergers Lafrance (Que). 227
Lethbridge (Alb). 113–114
Lethbridge Nature Reserve (Alb) 114
Liard Highway 19, 313
Lion's Gate Bridge, Vancouver (BC) 61
Little India, Toronto (Ont). 178
Little India, Vancouver (BC) 56
Little Tokyo, Vancouver (BC) 55–56
Lombardo, Guy 191
London (Ont). 189–190
Long-distance rail service 46
London Museum of Archaeology (Ont) 190
Lookout! at Harbour Centre, Vancouver (BC). . . 57
Louisbourg Fortress (NS). 293–294
Lower Mainland (BC) 41
Lower Town, Québec City (Que). 235, 240
Mackenzie Highway 19, 313
Magdalen Islands (Que) 247, 248
Magnetic Hill (NB) 280
Magog (Que) 231
Maid of the Mist, Niagara Falls (Ont) 183
Maison Dumulon (Que) 254
Maison Saint-Gabriel, Montréal (Que) 215
Malartic Mines Museum (Que) 253
Maligne Canyon (Alb). 135
Maligne Lake (Alb) 135
Mall, West Edmonton, Edmonton (Alb) . . 120–122
Manicouagan (Que) 251–252
Manitoba Museum of Man and Nature,
  Winnipeg (Man) 149–150
Manitoba 149–154

Manitoba festivals and events 154
Manitoulin Island (Ont) 197
Maps
  Alberta 92
  British Columbia 40
  Calgary 103
  Calgary, Banff, and Edmonton 98
  Calgary, Banff, Jasper, and Edmonton 132
  Canada 4–5, 12
  Charlottetown 270
  Coastal and Interior British Columbia 83
  Edmonton 118
  Fredericton 277
  Halifax 286
  Kingston and the Thousand Islands 168
  Labrador 265
  Laval and the Laurentians 226
  Lower Saint Lawrence 246
  Manitoba 150
  Montréal 208, 211
  Montréal Métro 210
  Montréal downtown 201
  New Brunswick 278
  Newfoundland and Labrador 258
  Newfoundland 261
  Niagara Falls 182
  Niagara-on-the-Lake 187
  North of Winnipeg 153
  Northern Arctic 306
  Northern Ontario 194
  Northwest Territories 304
  Nova Scotia 284
  Nunavut 298
  Ontario 156
  Ottawa and Hull 163
  Prince Edward Island 268
  Québec 202
  Québec City 238
  Queen Charlotte Islands 78
  Regina downtown 142
  Saanich Peninsula 73
  Saskatchewan 138
  Saskatoon 146
  Southwest Ontario 190
  Sudbury 196
  Sydney 293
  Thunder Bay 199
  Toronto 172
  Vancouver downtown 56
  Vancouver and Vancouver Island 55
  Victoria 67
  Western Québec 254
  Whitehorse 318
  Winnipeg 151
  Yellowknife 305
  Yukon Territory 316
Marine Atlantic ferries 266, 293
Marine Drive (NS) 291–292
Marine Mammal Center (Que) 251
Marine Museum of the
  Great Lakes (Ont) 167
Maritime Museum of British Columbia,
  Victoria (BC) 66
Maritime Museum of the Atlantic (NS) 285
Markham Museum (Ont) 179
Marmot Basin (Alb) 135–136
Mary Queen of the World Cathedral,
  Montréal (Que) 220
Mayne Island (BC) 77
McCord Museum of Canadian History,
  Montréal (Que) 214
McGill University, Montréal (Que) 221
McLean Mill National Historic Site (BC) 74
McMillan Space Centre, Vancouver (BC) 57
Medicine Hat (Alb) 111
Merril Collection of Science, Speculation
  and Fantasy, Toronto (Ont) 176

Métro, Montréal (Que) 209
Metropolitan Toronto Zoo (Ont) 177
Miette Hot Springs (Alb) 136
Mingan Archipelago National Park
  Reserve (Que) 252
Minter Gardens (BC) 90
Mission at Lac La Biche (Alb) 126
Molson Centre, Montréal (Que) 218
Moncton (NB) 278–279
Mont Orford (Que) 230
Mont Sainte-Anne (Que) 241
Mont-Tremblant (Que) 229
Mont Saint-Saveur (Que) 229
Mont Sutton (Que) 230
Montérégie, The (Que) 232–233
Montgomery, Lucy Maud 271–272
Montmorency Falls (Que) 240
Montréal (Que) 207–223
Montréal Alouettes football 219
Montréal Canadiens hockey 218
Montréal Casino (Que) 212
Montréal Expos baseball 218
Montréal History Centre (Que) 215
Montréal Museum Pass 216
Montréal Museum of Archaeology (Que) 214
Montréal Tower (Que) 218
Mount Edith Cavell (Alb) 134
Mount Revelstoke National Park (BC) 89
Mount Robson (BC) 87
Mount Robson Provincial Park (Alb) 136
Mount Washington Resort,
  Vancouver Island (BC) 75
Murney Tower Museum (Ont) 168
Musée Armand Bombardier (Que) 233
Musée Armand-Frappier (Que) 226
Musée de Kamouraska (Que) 245
Musée de la Gaspésie (Que) 247
Musée des Ursulines, Québec City (Que) . . 237–238
Musée du fort, Québec City (Que) 236
Museum of Arts and Traditions (Que) 233
Museum of Civilization (Que) 240
Museum of Contemporary Art,
  Montréal (Que) 214
Museum of Fine Arts, Montréal (Que) 213–214
Museum of French America (Que) 237
Museum of Northern British Columbia (BC) . . . 85
Museum of the Augustine Sisters,
  Québec City (Que) 239
Museum of the Regiments, Calgary (Alb) 102
Museum of the Sea (Que) 246
Muttart Conservatory, Edmonton (Alb) 119
Nanaimo (BC) 75
National Aviation Museum,
  Ottawa (Ont) 164–165
National Gallery of Canada, Ottawa (Ont) 164
National historic sites in Canada 321–326
National Museum of Science and Technology,
  Ottawa (Ont) 164
Naval Museum of Alberta Society,
  Calgary (Alb) 102–103
New Brunswick Museum (NB) 277
New Brunswick 275–282
New Brunswick festivals and events 282
Newfoundland 257–263
Newfoundland and Labrador festivals
  and events 266
Niagara Falls (Ont) 181–188
Niagara Falls Botanical Gardens (Ont) 185
Niagara Falls Butterfly Conservatory (Ont) . . . 186
Niagara-on-the-Lake (Ont) 186–187
Niagara Spanish Aero Car (Ont) 184
Nikka Yuko Centennial Gardens (Alb) 114
Nopiming Provincial Park (Man) 154
North America Rail Pass 21
North Coast (Lab) 266
North Pacific Cannery Village
  Museum (BC) 85–86

North Shore (Que) 249–252
Northern Arctic (NWT) 306–307
Northern Lights. 300
Northumberland Strait (NB). 281
Northwest Passage (Nun). 301
Northwest Territories 303–314
Notre-Dame Basilica, Montréal (Que) 208, 219
Notre-Dame-de-Bonsecours (Que). 208, 219
Notre-Dame-de-Québec Basilica-Cathedral,
   Québec City (Que) 237
Nova Scotia 283–296
Nova Scotia festivals and events 295–296
Nova Scotia Museum of Natural History 287
Nunavut. 297–302
Oak Hammock Marsh and Conservation Area
   (Man) 152
Okanagan region (BC) 41–43
Oktoberfest (Ont). 191–192
Old Fort William (Ont). 198–199
Old Port of Montréal 210–211
Old Port of Québec Interpretation Centre,
   Québec City (Que) 240
Old Saint-Sulpice Seminary (Que) 208
Olympic Park Museums, Montréal (Que) 217
Olympic Stadium, Montréal (Que) 218
Omnimax Theatre at the Science Centre,
   Toronto (Ont). 175
Ontario 155–200
Ontario festivals and events 158–160
Ontario Place (Ont) 178
Ontario Science Centre, Toronto (Ont). 173
Orchid Paradise (Que) 227
Ottawa (Ont) 161–169
Pacific Rim National Park Reserve,
   Vancouver Island (BC) 74
Palm House, Toronto (Ont) 175
Panorama Ski Resort (BC) 85
Parc de la Gaspésie (Que). 247
Parc de la riviére des Mille-Îles, Montréal 226
Parc Safari (Que) 233
Parkwood Estate and Gardens (Ont). 179
Parliament buildings, Ottawa (Ont) 162–164
Parliament. 26–27
Passports. 9
Peggy's Cove (NS) 289
Pender Island (BC). 77
Percé Rock (Que). 247
Peterborough Hydraulic Lift Lock (Ont). 180
Petroglyphs Provincial Park, Ottawa (Ont). . . . 179
Place des Arts, Montréal (Que) 218
Plains of Abraham, Québec City
   (Que). 24, 236–237
Planétarium de Montréal (Que) 216
Point Amour Lighthouse (Lab). 264
Point Ellice House, Victoria (BC) 69
Point Pleasant Park (NS). 288
Pointe-à-Callière, Montréal (Que). 207, 214
Pointe-de-l'Est National Wildlife Area (Que). . . 248
Pointe-des-Monts Historical
   Lighthouse (Que). 251–252
Polar Bear Express (Ont) 193
Polar Bear Provincial Park (Ont). 200
Port au Choix (Newf) 262
Port Edward (BC). 85–86
Port of Montréal (Que) 208–209, 210
Postage stamps. 10
Pow-Wows (Ont) 160
Prince Albert National Park, Saskatoon (Sask). . 148
Prince Edward Island 267–274
Prince Edward Island festivals
   and events. 273–274
Prince Rupert (BC). 84–85
Provincial Museum of Alberta,
   Edmonton (Alb) 118
Public Gardens (NS) 287–288
Quaker Whalers' House (NS) 288

Quebéc. 201–254
Québec City (Que) 235–242
Québec festivals and events 204–206
Québec Wax Museum, Québec City (Que) 239
Queen Charlotte Islands (BC) 43–44, 78–79
Quetico Provincial Park (Ont) 199
Radium Hot Springs Pools (BC) 88
Railroad service 20–21, 46
RCMP Centennial Museum,
   Regina (Sask) 141–142
Red Bay (Lab) 264
Red Mountain (BC) 85
Redpath Museum, Montréal (Que) 215, 221
Redpath Sugar Museum, Toronto (Ont). . . 174–175
Regina (Sask) 141–144
Remington-Alberta Carriage Centre (Alb). 112
Resident Alien Cards. 9
Reynolds-Alberta Museum (Alb). 125
Rideau Canal, Ottawa (Ont) 165–166
Rideau Hall, Ottawa (Ont) 164
Riding Mountain National Park (Man) 152
Riel, Louis 25–26, 144
Road system 19
Robson Street, Vancouver (BC) 60
Rocky Mountain House (Alb). 125
Rogers Pass Centre (BC). 89
Roosevelt Campobello International
   Park (NB). 277–278
Roosevelt, Franklin D. 277–278
Ross Farm Museum (NS) 289
Rossland Historic Museum and Gold Mine
   Tour (BC) 87
Royal Botanical Gardens (Ont). 192
Royal British Columbia Museum,
   Victoria (BC) 65
Royal Canadian Mint (Ont) 164
Royal London Wax Museum, Victoria (BC) 70
Royal Ontario Museum, Toronto (Ont). 173
Royal Saskatchewan Museum, Regina (Sask). . . 141
Royal Tyrrell Museum of
   Palaeontology (Alb) 109–110
Ryan Premises (Newf) 261
Sacred Heart Chapel, Montréal (Que). 219
Safari Park (Que) 233
Saguenay-Lac Saint Jean (Que) 250–251
Saint Benoît-du-lac (Que). 231
Saint George's Anglican Church (Que) 220
Saint James United Church (Que). 220
Saint John (NB) 276–277
Saint Joseph's Oratory (Que) 220
Saint Lawrence Islands National Park (Ont) . . . 169
Saint Patrick's Basilica (Que). 219–220
Saint Pierre & Miquelon 257, 260–261
Saint Roch National Historic Site (BC) 58
Saint-Saveur (Que). 229
Salt Spring Island (BC) 76
Sanctuary Sainte-Anne-de-Beaupré (Que) 241
Saskatchewan. 137–148
Saskatchewan festivals and events. 137–148
Saskatchewan Science Center, Regina (Sask) . . . 141
Saskatoon (Sask). 145–148
Saturna Island (BC) 77
Sault Ste. Marie (Ont) 198
Science North (Ont). 196
Science World British Columbia,
   Vancouver (BC). 59
Sechelt Peninsula (BC). 48
Senate 26–27
Separatism, Québec 203–204
Service, Robert. 319–320
Shaw Festival (Ont) 187
Shopping malls, Montréal (Que) 221–222
Signal Hill (Newf) 259
Sir Alexander Galt Museum (Alb). 113
Ski areas
   Alberta. 107

British Columbia. 75, 82
Québec. 230
SkyDome, Toronto (Ont) 178
Skylon Tower (Ont) 186
SkyTrain, Vancouver (BC) 62
Smiths Falls Railway Museum (Ont). 166
Southland Leisure Centre, Calgary (Alb) 106
South Shore (Que) 243–244
Southern Arctic (NWT) 307
Southern Newfoundland Seaman's
   Museum (Newf) 260
Spruce Meadows (Alb) 106
Square Dorchester, Montréal (Que). 211
Saint Boniface Museum, Winnipeg (Man) 150
Stampede, Calgary (Alb). 98–99
Stanley Park, Vancouver (BC). 54
Stephansson House Provincial Historic
   Site (Alb) 125
Stewart Museum at the Fort, Montréal (Que) . . 212
Stratford (Ont). 191
Stratford Festival (Ont) 191
Strathcona, Edmonton (Alb). 119–120
Strathcona Provincial Park (BC) 74–75
Sudbury Basin (Ont). 195–196
Sulphur Mountain Gondola (Alb). 130
Sun Peaks Resort (BC) 85
Sunshine Coast (BC) 48
Sunshine Village (Alb) 130
Sunwapta Falls (Alb). 133–134
Sun-Yat Sen Chinese Garden, Vancouver (BC) . . 60
Supreme Court of Canada 164
Sydney (NS). 293
Taiga Cordillera (NWT) 307–308
Taiga Plains (NWT) 308
Taiga Shield (NWT) 308
Takakkaw Falls (BC). 44
Taxes in Canada. 9–10
Temperature conversion,
   Celsius to Fahrenheit 18
Temperature ranges 13–18
Thetford Mines (Que) 244
Thousand Islands (Ont) 167–169
Thunder Bay (Ont) 198–199
Time zones. 10–11
Timmins Underground Gold Mine
   Tour (Ont) 200
Titanic 284–286
Toronto 171–180
Toronto Blue Jays baseball 178
Toronto Maple Leafs hockey 177
Toronto Raptors basketball. 177
Toronto Transit (Ont) 172
Toronto Zoo (Ont) 177
Transportation
   In Calgary 108
   In Montreal 209
   To British Columbia 46
   To Labrador. 263–264
   To New Brunswick 275
   To Newfoundland and Labrador 259
   To Nova Scotia. 283–284
   To Prince Edward Island 269
   To The Northwest Territories. 312
   To The Yukon 316–317
   To Vancouver Island 47
Travel agencies 34
Trent Severn Waterway (Ont). 179
Trial of Louis Riel (Sask) 144
Tsawwassen (BC). 47
Tweedsmuir Provincial Park (BC). 86
Ukrainian Cultural Heritage
   Village (Alb) 125
Underground City, Montréal (Que) 221
Université de Moncton (NB) 280
Université de Montréal (Que). 221
Université du Québec à Montréal (Que) 221
Upper Town, Québec City (Que). 236–240
Urban Life Interpretation Centre,
   Québec City (Que) 238
Ursuline's Museum (Que). 237
Valley Zoo, Edmonton (Alb). 119
Van Cleeve Coulee (Alb) 113
Vancouver (BC) 53–62
Vancouver Aquarium (BC) 54
Vancouver Art Gallery (BC) 59
Vancouver Island (BC) 63–80
Vancouver Maritime Museum (BC) 58
Vancouver Museum (BC). 57
VIA Rail Canada. 20–21, 127
Victoria (BC) 63–70
Victoria Butterfly Gardens (BC) 72
Visas. 9
Wanuskewin Heritage Park,
   Saskatoon (Sask) 145–146
Wascana Centre, Regina (Sask). 141
Waterfalls in British Columbia. 44
Waterloo (Ont). 191–192
Waterton Lakes National Park (Alb) 112–113
Welland Canal (Ont) 187–188
West Edmonton Mall (Alb) 120–122
Western Canada Aviation Museum (Man) 151
Western Development
   Museum (Sask). 142–143, 145
Western Heritage Centre (Alb) 111
Whale Watching (BC). 79–80
Whirlpool Rapids, Niagara Falls (Ont) 184
Whistler Blackcomb Resort (BC) 40, 82–24
White Pass & Yukon Route
   Railroad (Yukon). 319
Whitehorse (Yukon) 318–319
Whiteshell Provincial Park (Man). 154
Whitewater Rafting (Ont). 166–167
Wickannish Centre (BC) 74
Wildlife resources, BC 44–45
Windsor (Ont). 189
Winnipeg (Man). 149–154
Winnipeg Art Gallery (Man) 151
Witless Bay Ecological Reserve (Newf). . . . 262–263
Wood Buffalo National Park (Alb) 126
Writing-on-Stone Provincial Park (Alb) 114
Yellowhead Highway 127, 136
Yellowknife (NWT) 304
Yukon Territory 315–320
Zoological Garden of Québec (Que) 241